CREATING A PLACE FOR OURSELVES

CREATING A PLACE FOR OURSELVES

Lesbian, Gay, and Bisexual Community Histories

edited by

Brett Beemyn

ROUTLEDGE
New York and London

Published in 1997 by

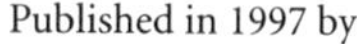

Routledge
29 West 35th Street
New York, NY 10001

Published in Great Britain in 1997 by

Routledge
11 New Fetter Lane
London EC4P 4EE

Printed in the United States of America
Design: Jack Donner

"'Birthplace of the Nation': Imagining Lesbian and Gay Communities in Philadelphia, 1969–1970" from *City of Brotherly and Sisterly Loves: The Making of Lesbian and Gay Communities in Greater Philadelphia* by Marc Stein, forthcoming from University of Chicago Press. Reprinted by permission of the University of Chicago Press.

"The 'Fun Gay Ladies': Lesbians in Cherry Grove, 1936–1960" is an unpublished, earlier, self-contained version of Chapter 8, "The 'Fun Gay Ladies,'" from *Cherry Grove, Fire Island* by Esther Newton, © 1993 by Esther Newton. Reprinted by permission of Beacon Press, Boston.

"The Policed: Gay Men's Strategies of Everyday Resistance in Times Square" © 1991 by George Chauncey. Reprinted by permission of Georges Borchardt, Inc. for the author.

"'I Could Hardly Wait to Get Back to the Bar': Lesbian Bar Culture in Buffalo in the 1930s and 1940s" from *Boots of Leather, Slippers of Gold: The History of a Lesbian Community* by Elizabeth Lapovsky Kennedy and Madeline D. Davis, © 1993 by Routledge.

Library of Congress Cataloging-in-Publication Data

Creating a place for ourselves : lesbian, gay, and bisexual community histories / [edited by] Brett Beemyn.
p. cm.
Includes bibliographical references and index.
ISBN 0-415-91389-6. — ISBN 0-415-9130-X (pbk.)
1. Gay communities—United States—History. 2. Gay men—United States—Social conditions. 3. Lesbian communities—United States—History. 4. Lesbians—United States—Social conditions. 5. Bisexuals—United States—Social conditions. I. Beemyn, Brett. 1966- .
HQ76.3.U5C74 1997 96-46104
305.9'0664--dc20 CIP

Contents

Introduction

Brett Beemyn

Gay history in the United States is not limited to New York and San Francisco. I was reminded of this fact when I moved to Iowa City, Iowa seven years ago to attend graduate school and became involved in an organized lesbian and gay community there that dates back nearly thirty years. While the predominant gay narrative links the process of coming out with migration to New York or San Francisco—on the presumption that these large coastal cities have provided more sexual freedom—lesbians and gay men increasingly chose to remain in this small Midwestern college town and established their own institutions and social networks in the decades prior to Stonewall. One of the first gay student groups in the U.S. was founded at the University of Iowa in 1970, and a group of local lesbians began one of the country's earliest women's centers the following year. Both organizations still exist today, as does a growing bisexual community.

As the case of Iowa City demonstrates, vibrant gay communities have existed for decades in places far from the traditional gay coastal meccas. However, the histories of these communities—particularly those in the South and Midwest—have often been ignored, in part because the popular framework for understanding communities is based on the experiences of lesbians and gay men in large cities with gay-friendly neighborhoods. Since the gay communities that arose in places like Iowa City do not look like the communities in San Francisco or New York, either in size or structure, they are overlooked or seen as less significant. A subtle elitism that views all but a few major metropolises as backward and entirely inhospitable to gays also contributes to this oversight.

But in recent years, more and more historians have begun to examine the richness of gay life in areas not well known today for their lesbian, gay, and bisexual communities, inspired in part by such pioneering works in the field as Elizabeth Lapovsky Kennedy and Madeline D. Davis's *Boots of Leather, Slippers of Gold*, George Chauncey's *Gay New York*, and Esther Newton's *Cherry Grove, Fire Island.* Along with these groundbreaking studies of Buffalo, New York City, and Cherry Grove, this anthology includes provocative new research on relatively small cities (Flint and Birmingham), large cities not often recognized for their longstanding gay communities (Chicago, Philadelphia, Detroit, and Washington), and a "gay mecca" (San Francisco).

The increased focus on individual communities has drawn greater attention to the specificity of gay experience and the importance of place in shaping the lives of lesbians, gay men, and bisexuals. Whereas general histories have often assumed that gays in the U.S. shared many experiences, community studies frequently highlight the distinctions between the lives of gays in different regions, cities, and neighborhoods and the unique circumstances surrounding the development of gay communities across the country. Community studies can uncover, for example, the significance of cars among gay men in Flint, the importance of semiannual costume balls to drag queens in Chicago, and the role of the police in Birmingham. Moreover, by closely examining a specific community, such works seem better positioned to be able to consider the impact of race, gender, and class differences upon the lives of gays—distinctions frequently ignored in texts that take a broader historical approach.

One of the criticisms of the community study method, though, is that by focusing on such differences and the uniqueness of a given location, commonalities across communities are lost and there is a lack of any kind of synthesis. But how accurate are cross-community comparisons, much less syntheses, when so much of the specificity of gay life during the early and mid-twentieth century remains unexplored? Although the amount of research is growing rapidly, the absence of even basic information on the experiences of lesbians, gay men, and bisexuals in many parts of the U.S. makes the writing of a comprehensive gay history difficult at best, and attempts to do so thus far have had to rely heavily upon documentation from only a handful of major cities. This is not to say, though, that a lack of knowledge prevents any effective comparisons between communities. Indeed, one of the purposes of presenting a wide variety of community studies in this volume is to be able to read across these works, to recognize the similarities among and differences between local histories.

Many of the essays included here, for example, point to the significance of bars and cafeterias with a mostly gay clientele in the development of lesbian and gay male communities. Whether in bigger cities like New York and Washington with a relatively large number of gay-dominated establishments or in smaller locales like Flint and Buffalo with only a handful, bars and cafeterias served as important sites for people interested in same-sex sexual relationships to meet and to develop a sense of shared experience. But as these essays also describe, the appeal of such establishments was not universal, and their clienteles were often divided along race, class, and gender lines. In Detroit, for instance, white middle-class lesbians were uncomfortable frequenting bars where harassment from heterosexual men, fighting, and public exposure were strong possibilities. As a result, many establishments relocated and changed their interior and exterior designs in order to attract a more middle-class customer base. Bars and restaurants in the nation's capital were racially segregated by law until the early 1950s and by practice thereafter; they were also often separated by gender and class. Consequently, neither Black working-class gays nor white lesbians and bisexual women patronized predominantly gay bars in large numbers. Instead, both groups pursued other social options, such as frequenting private parties and straight-dominated bars.

Comparisons between the essays in this volume are facilitated by their similar time frames: all address the experiences of gays in the period before or around Stonewall, with most focusing on gay life during the 1940s and '50s. Groundbreaking historical texts such as Lillian Faderman's *Odd Girls and Twilight Lovers: A History of Lesbian Life in Twentieth-Century America* and John D'Emilio's *Sexual Politics, Sexual Communities: The Making of a Homosexual Minority in the United States, 1940–1970* have vividly demonstrated that gay history did not begin with the 1969 riots; the essays included here build upon these pioneering general studies, adding both richness and specificity. But, in limiting the anthology to research before or around the time of Stonewall, I do not mean to suggest that Stonewall was *the* pivotal moment in U.S. gay history. Clearly, the riots served as a potent symbol of resistance and helped galvanize the gay liberation movement, but it is misguided to believe that events at a New York City bar could have a sudden, dramatic impact on gay communities throughout the country. Such a myth fosters the same theoretical narrowness and coastal bias that this anthology seeks to dispel.

The essays in *Creating a Place for Ourselves* are arranged in chronological order. The first two works, by George Chauncey and Elizabeth Lapovsky Kennedy and Madeline D. Davis, demonstrate the tremendous contributions that they have made in uncovering and analyzing gay history. In his work, Chauncey examines Times Square, one of the most important centers of white working-class gay male life in New York City in the 1930s. He shows that men interested in same-sex sexual relationships created a gay culture in the furnished rooming houses, cafeterias, theaters, and streets of the Square which offered them enormous support and the means to resist police harassment. Despite having to engage in constant territorial struggles with agents of the dominant cultural order, gay men were able to transform Times Square into a haven, a space that they could claim as their own.

For white working-class lesbians in Buffalo, the struggle for an affirming public space in the 1930s and '40s centered around bars in which they could socialize openly, making it easier for them to find others like themselves. As Elizabeth Kennedy and Madeline D. Davis demonstrate, the creation of a bar culture enabled lesbians to end their individual isolation and to develop a shared sense of community and group consciousness. Yet their greater visibility also placed these lesbians into conflict with the police and increased the likelihood that their sexuality would be discovered by their families and coworkers. Consequently, the bar communities in Buffalo not only served as spaces where lesbians could socialize and relax in each other's company, but also functioned as sites for lesbian resistance.

San Francisco is known today as a gay mecca, but as Nan Alamilla Boyd makes clear, this reputation is a relatively recent phenomenon. Because of its frontier-town ethics and history of vice, the city developed a permissive culture of sex and gender nonconformity and an image as a wide-open town during the late nineteenth and early twentieth centuries. These factors played an important role in the emergence of a visible gay community in the 1930s and led to San Francisco being perceived as a welcoming environment for lesbian and gay male tourists and migrants in later decades. Ironically, anti-vice campaigns also contributed to the growth of the gay community by publicizing the city's sexual geography in their efforts to eradicate it.

Both David Johnson and Allen Drexel address the experiences of gay men in Chicago but focus on different neighborhoods and, consequently, tell very different stories. Johnson uses a rich and previously untapped resource—interviews with gay men conducted through the University of Chicago sociology department in the 1930s—to demonstrate that the gay culture that developed on the city's Near North Side, an area dubbed "Fairy-town," was highly visible and readily accessible to white men from through-out the city. They did not have to meet in some unlit park or out-of-the-way bar, but could encounter each other on busy neighborhood streets, at a popular local beach, and in a number of disproportionately gay professions. Johnson concludes that the ease with which men could become involved in the gay culture of "Fairytown" belies the popular belief that gay men led tortured, isolated lives prior to World War II.

Allen Drexel considers the experiences of gay men on the opposite end of the city, providing an historical account of drag queens and drag balls on Chicago's South Side. Through his examination of Finnie's Balls, an annual Halloween extravaganza in the 1950s that attracted thousands of spectators, including many Black working-class gays, he shows that race and class played fundamental roles in the development of gay identities and communities. Moreover, given the popularity of the city's drag balls, his work challenges the assumption that the 1950s were a universally bleak and homophobic decade. Although much of white middle-class society was engaged in a concerted campaign against gays, the Black press and Chicago's Black community were frequently much more supportive.

Esther Newton's essay focuses on the small but tenacious group of lesbian residents of Cherry Grove, a predominantly gay summer vacation spot located on Fire Island, a few miles off the coast of New York City. Although gay men dominated the Grove numerically and culturally, white upper-class and upper-middle-class lesbians and bisexual women established a vibrant, close-knit community and an active social life there beginning in the late 1930s and '40s. Whether as homeowners, renters, or weekend visitors, lesbians could be themselves in the Grove, free of the strains of having to conceal their sexuality and away from the unwanted sexual advances of straight men.

Roey Thorpe explores the development of white lesbian life in Detroit by tracing the changing nature and clientele of several of the city's lesbian bars in the mid-twentieth century. In order to accommodate middle-class lesbians, newer establishments sought to provide more physical safety and anonymity by opening in obscure locations and having backdoor entrances to ensure an exclusively lesbian clientele. But these changes meant that the bars increasingly attracted women who were unwilling to support each other in times of trouble or accept other patrons, particularly butches and femmes, on their own terms—qualities that were extremely important to many working-class lesbians. Consequently, by attempting to appeal to more middle-class customers, the bars alienated much of their traditional blue-collar clientele.

General gay histories have typically ignored regional distinctions and their effects on the development of lesbian, gay, and bisexual communities. The works included here, especially the two articles on Southern cities, demonstrate the significance of such regional differences, as well as point to the variations within a particular area. My essay examines lesbian, gay male, and bisexual life in Washington, D.C. during and in the decade following World War II. A growing gay population in these years transformed numerous bars and all-night cafeterias into places where people interested in same-sex sexual relationships could meet others like themselves and socialize together in public. As was the case in New York and other large northern cities, the proliferation of gay-dominated spaces in the capital enabled lesbians, gay men, and bisexuals to forge cultures that helped ensure their survival under oppressive conditions. But since many of the new establishments were restricted by law or practice to white middle-class men, the institutionalization of gay life in a Southern city like Washington contributed to the entrenchment of race, class, and gender segregation.

In Birmingham, the social and physical mobility available to white middle- and upper-middle-class gay men gave them the ability to avoid familial pressure and police persecution—privileges virtually beyond the reach of African Americans, white women, and most working-class men in the mid-twentieth-century South. Focusing on the experiences of a white upper-middle-class man active in Birmingham's gay community, John Howard highlights the importance of place and movement in gay history, challenging the assumption that urbanization was necessary for the development of lesbian and gay cultures and identities in the U.S. As he notes, such a premise denies the agency of many lesbians, gay men, and bisexuals in the South and in rural areas throughout the country.

In Flint, gay and bisexual men established a gay nightlife in the 1950s by using the very product that many helped to manufacture during the day. Tim Retzloff argues that because of the city's relatively small population and geographical dispersal, the car was a necessity for most gays; it provided access to bars and parties in the surrounding area, ensured a level of anonymity, and became an important space itself for same-sex desire. By showing how the automobile made possible the development of a gay community in a less densely populated city like Flint, Retzloff challenges the assumption that an extensive, centralized gay population is a prerequisite for the creation of a gay culture.

Marc Stein's essay on lesbian and gay politics in Philadelphia around the time of the Stonewall riots focuses on the ways that activists in "the birthplace of the nation" have relied on languages of nationalism, patriotism, and citizenship to further their political aims, whether in demonstrating at Independence Hall or participating in the Black Panthers' Revolutionary People's Constitutional Convention. Through his examination of important episodes in gay history, Stein addresses two topics that are directly relevant to the other essays in the anthology and to work in community studies more generally: the place of the Stonewall riots in lesbian and gay histories and the place of national political discourses in local histories.

Finally, in her afterword, Joan Nestle—a pioneer in creating and documenting lesbian, gay, and bisexual histories—reflects on how the study of these histories has emerged and grown in the past twenty years. As she notes, "we have gone from fragments, clues, and bones to sweeping social studies." But as a new wave of historians sets out to challenge previous "truths" and to uncover new ones, she cautions all of us not to lose sight of the contributions of early grassroots researchers and activists "who out of passion and politics showed what was possible when a despised people took history into their own hands."

The inspiration for this anthology arose from InQueery/InTheory/In Deed: the Sixth North American Lesbian, Gay, and Bisexual Studies Conference, which I co-chaired, and where four of these essays were originally presented. For their suggestions, I give my heartfelt thanks to the contributors, particularly John Howard, Tim Retzloff, Marc Stein, and Nan Alamilla Boyd. For their support, I am especially indebted to Martha Patterson, friend and comrade, and William Germano, my editor at Routledge; their faith in me and my abilities throughout this process means very much to me.

1. The Policed

Gay Men's Strategies of Everyday Resistance in Times Square

George Chauncey

"Forty-Second Street was *it* when I was a teenager," recalled Sebastian ("Sy") Risicato, referring to the days in the late 1930s when he still lived with his parents in the Bronx but was beginning to explore New York's gay world. "Forty-Second Street then was our stamping ground," he continued:

> Closet queens, gay queens, black, white, whatever, carrying on in men's rooms, and in theaters. There was a Bickford's [cafeteria] there all night, and a big cafeteria right there on Forty-Second Street, one of those bright cafeterias where johns used to sit looking for the young queens. Lots of queens, everybody was painted and all, but they weren't crazy queens: drugs weren't big then. Forty-Second Street was like heaven—not heaven, [but] it was a joy to go there! And the sailors at the Port Authority, and the soldiers, and the bars. . . . During the war, all the soldiers and sailors used to go to the "crossroads" and you'd pick them up—Forty-Second Street and Times Square—and you'd take them out to the furnished rooms in the neighborhood: furnished rooms, and dumpy little hotels and Eighth Avenue rooms, which you'd rent for the night. There were a lot of gays living in that area, [too,] oh yes, people from out of town, and the boys whose fathers had pushed them out, with the tweezed eyebrows and beards. . . . You'd go down to Forty-Second Street and feel like, *here's where I belong.*[1]

Forty-Second Street was almost heaven in the 1930s for the self-described "painted queens" and "street fairies" like Sy Risicato who were forced to escape the hostility of their own neighborhoods and families in order to forge a community of their own. The world they built in the furnished rooms, cafeterias, theaters, and streets of Times Square offered them enormous support and guidance in their rejection of the particular forms of masculinity and heterosexuality prescribed by the dominant culture. By the 1930s, they had made Times Square one of the most important centers of gay life—particularly white, working-class gay male life—in the city. But the heaven such men created seemed hellish to many of the other people who knew the Square. Risicato's coterie was a notable part of the "undesirable" element regularly implicated in the "decline" of the theater district by more respectable New Yorkers, who mobilized a variety of policing agencies and strategies to eradicate their presence from the Square. They also appalled many other gay men who frequented the theater district, particularly middle-class men more conventional in their behavior, who regarded the "fairies" as undesirable representatives of the homosexual world. These men constructed their own, more carefully hidden gay world in the theater district; but they, too, had to contend with the agencies of moral policing.

Ironically, the world gay men created in the 1920s and '30s has remained even more invisible to historians than it was to contemporaries; most historians who have bothered to consider the matter have assumed that gay men remained isolated from each other and were helplessly subjected to the self-hatred preached by the dominant culture. This essay proposes an alternative view of gay life in these years. It examines the manner in which gay men, like other criminalized and marginalized peoples, constructed spheres of relative cultural autonomy in the interstices of an amusement district governed by hostile powers. It analyzes the stratagems different groups of gay men developed to appropriate certain commercial institutions and public spaces as their own and their complex relationship to the district's commercial entrepreneurs and moral guardians. A battery of laws criminalized gay men's association with each other and their cultural styles as well as their narrowly-defined "sexual" behavior. Their social marginalization gave the police even broader informal authority to harass them and meant that anyone discovered to be homosexual was threatened with a loss of livelihood and social respect. But the culture of the theater district, the weakness of the policers themselves, and the informal bargains struck between the policers and the policed—often with the mediation of certain commercial entrepreneurs, including those of the criminal underworld—enabled gay men to claim much more space for themselves than those obstacles implied.

Thus, while this essay surveys the ways in which the agents of the dominant cultural order sought to police the presence of gay men in the Square, it focuses on the informal strategies gay men developed to resist that policing on an everyday basis in the decades before the emergence of a gay political movement. Analyzing the emergence of a gay world in Times Square illuminates the character of urban gay male culture in the interwar years more generally, since gay men visiting the district were forced to draw on the same panoply of survival strategies they had developed in other settings as well. It also illuminates the history of the Square itself, for the changing fortunes of gay men's efforts in the 1920s and '30s both depended upon and highlighted the changing character of the Square during the transition from the era of jazz and Prohibition to that of Depression and Repeal.

The anonymity of urban amusement districts such as Times Square has often been cited to explain their development as "vice" zones and, indeed, the relative anonymity enjoyed there by gay tourists from the American heartland—and even from the outer boroughs—was one reason they felt freer there than they would have at home to seek out gay locales and behave openly as homosexuals. To focus, however, on the supposed anonymity of Times Square (a quality that is always more situational and relative than its absolutist formulation suggests) is to imply that gay men remained isolated (or "anonymous") from each other. But Times Square was not so much the site of anonymous, furtive encounters between strangers (although there were plenty of those) as the site of an organized, multilayered, and self-conscious subculture or, to use gay men's own term, a "gay world," with its own meeting places, argot, folklore, and norms of behavior. Rather than focusing on the supposed "anonymity" of Times Square, then, it will prove more productive to analyze the ways in which people manipulated the spatial and cultural complexity of the city to constitute the Square as their *neighborhood*, where some of them worked or lived, and where many others joined them to build a community.

Indeed, a gay enclave developed in Times Square in part because so many gay men lived and worked in the area. The theater and the district's other amusement industries attracted large numbers of gay workers, who got jobs as waiters and performers in restaurants and clubs, as busboys in hotels, and as chorus boys, actors, stagehands, costume designers, publicity people, and the like in the theater industry proper.[2] Although gay men hardly enjoyed unalloyed acceptance in such work environments, the theatrical milieu offered them more tolerance than most workplaces. As one man who had been a theatrical writer in the mid-teens observed, "the New York theatrical world [of that era was] . . . a sort of special world . . . with its own standards of fellowship [and] sexual morals."[3] Homosexuality, along with other unconventional sexual behavior, was judged by unusually tolerant standards by people who were themselves often marginalized because of the unconventional lives they led as theater workers. Some men could be openly gay among their coworkers, while many others were at least unlikely to suffer serious retribution if their homosexuality were discovered. The eccentricity attributed to theater people and "artistic types" in general provided a cover to many men who adopted widely recognized gay styles in their dress and demeanor.[4]

Moreover, many men working in the amusement district lived there as well, and they were joined by other gay men who appreciated the advantages of the transient housing the district offered. Times Square and, to the west of Eighth Avenue, Hell's Kitchen together comprised one of the major centers of housing for single adults in the city. In many respects, the area constituted a prototypical furnished-room district, the sort of neighborhood dominated by a nonfamily population in which, as the Chicago sociologists discovered in the 1920s and historians such as Mark Peel and Joanne Meyerowitz have more recently remarked, unconventional sexual behavior was likely to face relatively little community opposition.[5] The district was crowded with rooming houses, theatrical boardinghouses, and small residential and transient hotels serving theater workers, as well as most of the city's elegant bachelor apartments.[6] The housing varied in quality and social status, but most of it shared certain qualities useful to gay men, as well as to transient theater workers. Most of the rooms were cheap, they were minimally supervised, and the fact that they were usually furnished and hired by the week made them easy to leave if an occupant got a job on the road—or needed to disappear because of legal troubles.

Middle-class men tended to live to the north and east of the Square in the West Forties and Fifties, where many of the city's fashionable apartment hotels designed for affluent bachelors were clustered, and where many of the elegant old row houses between Fifth and Sixth Avenues had been converted into rooming houses as the intrusion of commerce resulted in the departure of their original residents. Another, poorer group of men lived to the west of the Square in the tenements of Hell's Kitchen and in the large number of cheap hotels and rooming houses to be found west of Seventh Avenue and Broadway. Many gay men, for instance, lived in the Men's Residence Club, a former YMCA hotel at West Fifty-Sixth Street and Eighth Avenue; a number of the theatrical boardinghouses in the area housed gay men; and, some tenement apartments served as collective homes for the poorest of gay theater workers.[7] Groups of theater and restaurant workers were joined by gay teenagers forced out of their natal homes by hostile parents (as Risicato recalled), gay migrants from small towns and the outer boroughs, hustlers, gay bartenders, and men who had more conventional jobs elsewhere in the city but who valued the privacy, convenience, and tolerance such housing offered. The district also included numerous transient hotels and rooming houses where gay male (or heterosexual) couples who met in a bar or on the street could rent a room for an hour.[8]

The men who lived and worked in the district formed the core of a social world—or several social worlds, really—in which men who both lived and worked elsewhere could participate. Times Square served as the primary social center for many such nonresidents, the place where they met their friends, built their strongest social ties, "let their hair down" (once a camp expression for being openly gay), and constructed public identities quite different from those they maintained at work and elsewhere in the straight world. They built a gay world for themselves on the basis of the ties they developed in the commercial institutions that entrepreneurs had created to serve the needs of the theater workers rooming in the district and the tourists who flocked there.

Gay men mixed unobtrusively with other customers at most of the district's restaurants, but a few places attracted a predominantly gay patronage and developed a muted gay ambiance. Louis' Restaurant on West Forty-Ninth Street, for instance, was well known to gay men and lesbians as a rendezvous in the mid-1920s, and even came to the attention of private anti-vice investigators in 1925 as a "hangout for fairies and lady lovers [lesbians]." But the people who met there were sufficiently guarded in their behavior—at least in the main public dining rooms—that outsiders were unlikely to suspect that they were gay. A sedate 1925 restaurant guide even recommended Louis' to its readers, describing it, clearly without apprehending the full significance of its observation, as "one of the institutions of the neighborhood."[9]

Such restaurants had existed before the 1920s, but, ironically, they proliferated and became more secure during Prohibition. Prohibition had been enacted in part to control public sociability—and in particular to destroy the immigrant, working-class male culture of the saloon, which seemed so threatening to middle-class and rural Americans. But in cities such as New York, Prohibition had resulted instead in the expansion of the sexual underworld and had undermined the ability of the police and anti-vice societies to control it. By depriving the hotel industry of liquor-related profits, for instance, Prohibition led some of the second-class hotels in the West Forties to begin permitting prostitutes and speakeasies to operate out of their premises.[10] More significantly, the popular opposition to enforcement, the proliferation of speakeasies, the systematic use of payoffs, and the development of criminal syndicates to safeguard those speakeasies all served to protect gay as well as straight clubs. It became easier during Prohibition for establishments where gay men gathered, such as Louis', to survive because they stood out less. All speakeasies—not just gay ones—had to bribe the authorities and warn their customers to be prepared to hide what they were doing at a moment's notice.

Prohibition also changed the character of the Square in ways that led to the increased visibility of a group of gay men different from those who patronized Louis'. It drove many of the district's elegant restaurants, cabarets, and roof gardens out of business, to be replaced by cheap cafeterias and restaurants whose profits depended on a high turnover rate rather than on a high liquor-based profit margin. Moreover, by the end of the '20s, the decline of the district's theater industry, due to the collapse of the national theatrical road circuits as well as the rise of the movies, forced growing numbers of theaters to convert into movie houses, often of the cheaper sort. Both factors combined to transform the Square in the 1920s and early 1930s, in the eyes of many contemporaries, from a distinguished theater district to a tawdry amusement district, a development only hastened by the onset of the Depression.[11]

It was in this context that the flamboyant gay men known as fairies began to play a more prominent role in the culture and reputation of the Square. Part of the attraction of amusement districts such as Times Square, after all, was that they constituted liminal spaces in which visitors were encouraged to disregard some of the social injunctions that normally constrained their behavior, allowing them to observe and vicariously experience forms of behavior which in other settings—particularly their own neighborhoods—they might consider objectionable enough to suppress. This appeal was only enhanced by the cultural developments of the Prohibition era, for the popular revolt against the moral policing of Prohibition, the shifting character of the Square, and the culture of the speakeasies themselves encouraged clubgoers to transgress conventional social boundaries and experiment with the norms governing acceptable public sociability.

The Square already had something of a reputation for fairies in the early 1920s (one 1924 account bemoaned the number of "impudent sissies that clutter Times Square"). But as the Square became more of a tawdry amusement park, visiting it became more of a theatrical experience in itself, and fairies increasingly became part of the spectacle of the Square, part of the exotica clubgoers and tourists expected and even hoped to see there. Thus, when *Vanity Fair*'s "intimate guide to New York after dark" noted in 1931 that the tourist could see "anything" on Broadway at night, it included "pansies" among the sights, along with the more predictable "song writers, college boys, . . . big shots, [and] bootleggers." A New York tabloid added: "The latest gag about 2 A.M. is to have your picture taken with one or two pansies on Times Square. The queens hang out there for the novel racket."[12]

If the highly flamboyant, working-class street fairies who gathered at

Bryant Park represented one extreme of gay self-presentation, the highly circumspect middle-class men and women who met at restaurants like Louis' represented another. But the self-described fairies—not the "normal-looking" men at Louis'—constituted the dominant public image of the male homosexual during this period; as a character representing the author in a 1933 gay novel complained, "*we're all*," to the "normal man, . . . like the street corner 'fairy' of Times Square—rouged, lisping, mincing."[13] This distressed many of the more conventional men, who felt that the fairy drew unwanted and unflattering attention to the gay world. Ironically, though, it was the very brilliance of the fairies that diverted attention from those other, more guarded men, and thus helped to keep them safely in the shadows. The presence of the fairies facilitated the process by which such middle-class men constructed their own, more carefully hidden gay world in the theater district.

Different groups of men, then, adopted different strategies for negotiating their presence in the city, and the divisions within the gay world of Times Square became even more complex as the district continued to reel from the impact of Prohibition, the declining fortunes of the theater industry, and the onset of the Depression. The effect of these changes is best seen in the changing organization of the district's street culture. Indeed, the street life of the Square deserves considerable attention, since it was there that much of gay life occurred. Moreover, the shifting spatial and cultural organization of just one aspect of gay street culture—that of male prostitution—highlights the extent to which the bustle and apparent chaos of the most active street scenes masked a highly organized culture whose boundaries and social conventions were well known to the initiated.

The Square, already an important center of female prostitution, became one of the city's most significant centers of male prostitution in the 1920s. Initially, two distinct groups of male prostitutes, whose interactions with customers were construed in entirely different ways, worked the Times Square area. Well-dressed, "mannered," and gay-identified hustlers who served a middle-class, gay-identified clientele generally met their customers as the latter walked home from the theater on the west side of Fifth Avenue from Forty-Second to Fifty-Ninth Streets. Although a regular part of the Times Square scene, neither the hustlers nor their customers attracted much attention, since neither conformed to the era's dominant stereotypes of homosexuals. During the 1920s, though, a second group of prostitutes, much more easily recognized by outsiders, came to dominate Forty-Second Street itself between Fifth and Eighth Avenues: effeminate (but not transvestite) "fairy" prostitutes who sold sexual services to other gay men and to men who identified themselves as "normal," including the Italians and

Greeks living to the west of the Square in Hell's Kitchen, as well as tourists from afar. The self-presentation of the prostitutes operating on the two streets thus differed markedly, as did the self-conception of their customers. Their proximity highlights the degree to which Times Square was the site of multiple sexual systems, each with its own cultural dynamics, semiotic codes, and territories.

The transformation of Forty-Second Street during the late 1920s and early 1930s had enormous repercussions for the street's gay scene, and resulted in a new group of hustlers coming to dominate it. Forty-Second Street was the site of the oldest theaters in the Times Square district, and the city's elite had regarded it as a distinguished address early in the century. By 1931, however, it had effectively become a working-class male domain. The conversion of two prominent theaters into burlesque houses in 1931 had both signified and contributed to the masculinization of the street: not only the strippers inside but the large quasi-pornographic billboards and barkers announcing the shows outside added to the image of the street as a male domain, threatening to women.[14] The masculinization of the street was confirmed by the conversion of the remaining theaters to a "grind" policy of showing male-oriented action films on a continuous basis and the opening of several men's bars and restaurants that catered to the increasing numbers of sailors, servicemen, and unemployed and transient men who frequented the street.

As the gender and class character of Forty-Second Street changed, it became a major locus of a new kind of "rough" hustler and of interactions between straight-identified servicemen and homosexuals.[15] As the Depression deepened, growing numbers of young men—many of them migrants from the economically devastated cities of Pennsylvania, Massachusetts, upstate New York, and the industrial South, and some of them servicemen—began to support themselves or supplement their incomes by hustling. Not gay-identified themselves, many became prostitutes for the same reason some women did: the work was available and supplied a needed income. "In the Depression the Square swarmed with boys," recalled one man who began patronizing them in 1933. "Poverty put them there."[16] The hustlers, aggressively masculine in their self-presentation and usually called "rough trade" by gay men, took over Forty-Second Street between Seventh and Eighth Avenues, forcing the fairy prostitutes to move east of Sixth Avenue, to Bryant Park. Taking note of the shift, the police began conducting periodic "fairy roundups" in the park in the late 1920s and 1930s, arresting any gay men they found loitering there.

The precise locus of the hustlers' and other gay men's activity on Forty-Second Street shifted several times over the course of the 1930s. The details of the shifts are unimportant in themselves, but they reveal something of the social organization of the streets in general, for they resulted largely from the changing geography of the gay bars and other semipublic sites where men met. The hustler street scene followed the bars from Sixth to Eighth Avenue and from the north to the south side of Forty-Second Street, in part because the bars attracted customers and offered shelter from the elements, but also because the streets and bars functioned as extensions of each other. Each site had particular advantages and posed particular dangers in men's constant territorial struggles with policing agents, as the men subject to that policing well knew. On the one hand, the purchase of a beer at a bar legitimized behavior involved in cruising that might have appeared more suspicious on the streets, including a man's simply standing about aimlessly or striking up conversations with strangers. On the other hand, while the police periodically tried to "clean up" the streets by chasing hustlers and other "undesirable" loiterers away, they could not permanently close the streets in the way they could close a bar. Moreover, in a heavily trafficked, nonresidential area such as Forty-Second Street, no one had the same interest in controlling pedestrians' behavior on behalf of the police that a bar owner who was threatened with the loss of his license had in controlling his customers. Thus, while the police might harass men on the street just for standing about with no apparent purpose, bars might evict them simply for touching, and plainclothesmen might arrest them for homosexual solicitation in either locale. The relative dangers of either site varied and depended on the momentary concerns of the police, and much of the talk on the streets was necessarily devoted to their shifting tactics. On more than one occasion in the 1930s and '40s a man noted in his diary that all of the street's hustlers had suddenly disappeared, apparently aware of some danger that their customers did not perceive.

The numerous cheap cafeterias, Automats, and lunchrooms that crowded the Times Square district were perhaps the safest commercial spaces available to poorer gay men. The Automats seem to have become even more secure with the onset of the Depression, when they developed a reputation, due to their low prices and lack of supervision, for being a refuge for the unemployed and luckless. Four Horn and Hardart Automats stood on Forty-Second Street between Madison and Eighth Avenues, and during the winter, according to one 1931 account, the Automat on Forty-Second Street across from Bryant Park became a favorite haunt of the men who gathered in the park during the summer.[17]

Automats were particularly famous for their lack of inhibition, but even the large cafeterias in the Childs chain could become astonishingly open. This was especially true late in the evening, after the dinner hour, when managers tolerated a wide range of customers and behavior in order to generate trade. Indeed, several cafeterias seem to have premised their late-night operations on the assumption that, by allowing homosexuals to gather on their premises, they would be able to attract sightseers wanting to see a late-night "fairy hangout." Gay men seized on the opportunities this portended and quickly spread the word about which restaurants and cafeterias would let them gather without guarding their behavior; moreover, the campy antics of the more flamboyant among them became part of the draw for other customers. One gay man who lived in the city in the late 1920s recalled that the Childs restaurant in the Paramount Building was regularly "taken over" by "hundreds" of gay men after midnight. Even if his recollection exaggerates the situation, it suggests his sense of the extent to which gay men felt comfortable there; in any case, *Vanity Fair*'s 1931 guide to New York informed its readers that the Paramount Childs was particularly interesting because it "features a dash of lavender."[18]

Well-established chains such as Childs usually had sufficient clout to prevent police raids, although some did occasionally occur when either the police or private anti-vice societies thought gay patrons had become too uproarious, or the management feared that the authorities were about to reach that conclusion. In February 1927, for instance, after gay men had been congregating at the Forty-Second Street Liggett's drugstore for some time, the management, perhaps sensing a temporary hardening of police attitudes or simply fearing for its reputation, suddenly called on the police to drive the men from its premises, which led to a raid and the arrest of enough men to fill two police vans.

After the repeal of Prohibition in 1933, gay bars quickly became the most important centers of gay male sociability in the city, but they also became the most sharply contested. The legalization of bars made them more numerous, more accessible, and easier to find—for gay as well as straight men. But it also subjected them to the authority of the newly created State Liquor Authority (SLA), which quickly proved to be a much more effective agent in the enforcement of state regulations than the Prohibition era's Volstead agents had been. From its inception, the SLA threatened to revoke the liquor license of any bar that served homosexuals, whose very presence, it ruled, made a bar "disorderly." In the three decades following Repeal, its agents and the police investigated and closed hundreds of bars in New York that served gay men or lesbians, sometimes through administrative action, sometimes through raids that resulted in the arrest of the staff and, in some cases, even the patrons.

Those bars that profited by serving homosexuals—who would pay higher prices and were in no position to demand better services—were thus forced to devise a variety of extralegal stratagems to protect themselves, such as paying off local patrolmen and negotiating informal limits on the conduct of patrons that were less draconian than those imposed by the law. Most became dependent on the Mafia, the only organization powerful enough to offer them systematic protection. But while police payoffs and Mafia connections served to keep at least some gay bars open, sometimes for years at a time, such arrangements were periodically overwhelmed when enforcement agencies were pressured to close the bars by the press or by politicians seeking publicity for their election campaigns.

During these crackdowns, some straight bars in "suspicious" neighborhoods such as Times Square and Greenwich Village sought to protect themselves by posting signs over the bar reading "If You Are Gay, Please Stay Away" or "It Is Against the Law to Serve Homosexuals—Do Not Ask Us to Break the Law." At other bars, the bartenders were simply instructed to eject anyone who appeared to be gay or, if they had not suspected them initially, to refuse to serve them any more drinks once they did.

Gay bars that continued to serve gay patrons during crackdowns sought to protect themselves by hiring floormen who made sure that men did not touch each other or engage in campy or otherwise "obvious" behavior that might draw the attention of the authorities by marking the bar's patrons as gay. State policies thus had the effect of turning bar managers into agents of SLA policy enforcement. They also exacerbated the class and cultural chasms already dividing the gay world: since the presence of "obvious" homosexuals, or "fairies," in a bar invited the wrath of the SLA and the police, most bars refused to serve them, and other gay men were encouraged in their hostility toward them.

The number of bars serving homosexuals—and particularly those serving *exclusively* homosexuals—proliferated in the 1930s and '40s, but most of them were short-lived, and gay men were forced to move constantly from place to place, dependent on the gay grapevine to inform them of where the new meeting places were. When the SLA launched a campaign against bars serving homosexuals as part of its effort to "clean up the city" in the months before the 1939 World's Fair opened, it quickly discovered just how effective that grapevine could be. After closing several area bars that were patronized by homosexuals, including the Consolidated Bar and Grill on West Forty-First Street, the Alvin on West Forty-Second, and more distant bars that were part of the same circuit, the Authority's investigators discovered that many of the patrons of those bars had simply converged on the Times Square Bar and Grill on West Forty-Second Street and turned it into their new rendezvous. In late October, an SLA investigator, sent to the bar after a police report that "about thirty . . . fairys [sic] and fags" had been seen there, noted that several of the gay men he had previously observed at the other bars were "now congregating" there, along with a large number of soldiers.[19] The owner himself, who sought to cooperate with the police in ridding his bar of homosexuals once he realized that their presence threatened his liquor license, insisted that "we never looked for . . . this kind of business. . . . [The police] close some places; [the fairies] come over here. . . . It was the neighborhood—[the fairies] know what places . . . are [open to them]. The word passes so fast. They knew [when a bar] is [sic] a degenerate place."[20]

Although many men continued to go to gay bars despite the risks, some stopped patronizing them during crackdowns for fear of being caught in a raid, which might result in their being arrested or at least being forced to divulge their names and places of employment, which carried the threat of further penalties if the police contacted their landlords or employers. Nonetheless, they found other places to meet their friends and to continue their participation in gay society. Private parties were especially important at such times, but so, too, were commercial establishments not known for their gay patronage. Not only were the police less likely to raid such places, but a man's homosexuality would not necessarily be revealed if he happened to be seen there by a straight associate.[21] Some men of moderate means joined the fairies in the restaurants and cafeterias in the area which, because they operated without liquor licenses, continued to be relatively safe even after Repeal; men of greater wealth and social status had access to more secure venues, whose very respectability offered them protection against the dangers of being arrested or recognized as homosexual. Several of the elegant nightclubs that opened to the north and east of the Square in the late 1920s and 1930s tolerated or even welcomed such men, so long as they remained discreet.

A somewhat more varied group of men frequented the highly respectable businessmen's bars found in many hotels, such as the Oak Room at the Plaza and the King Cole Room at the St. Regis, whose respectability and political clout offered them protection and where well-dressed men drinking by themselves or with a few male friends would hardly draw attention. The longest-lived and most famous (though not the most elegant) such bar in the Times Square area was the Astor Hotel bar at the corner of Seventh Avenue and Forty-Fifth Street. Although it had served as a gay meeting place since the 1910s, it became particularly well known during the Second World War, when it developed a national reputation among gay servicemen as a place to meet civilians when passing through New York. Gay men's use of the bar was carefully orchestrated—in both its spatial and cultural dimensions—to protect both their identities and its license. Gay men gathered on only one side of the oval bar, where the management allowed them to congregate so long as they did not become too "obvious." As one man who frequented the Astor during the war recalled, "the management would cut us down a little bit when it felt we were getting a little too obvious. . . . If you got a little too buddy, or too cruisy . . . too aggressive, they'd say cut it out, men, why don't you go somewhere else? You had to be more subtle." "Men on the other side of the bar, he added, were allowed to "do anything they wanted; they could put *their* arms around each other, *they* could touch, because it was very obvious that they were butch."[22]

Gay men had to be "subtle" so that the straight men all around them—including the occasional strangers who unwittingly sat down on the gay side of the bar—would not realize that they were surrounded by "queers." Gay men used the same codes they had developed in other contexts to alert each other to their identities: wearing certain clothes fashionable among gay men but not stereotypically associated with them, introducing certain topics of conversation, or casually using code words well known within the gay world but unremarkable to those outside it ("gay" itself was such a word in the 1930s and '40s). Using such codes, men could carry on extensive and highly informative conversations whose real significance would remain unintelligible to the people around them.

Two other examples will illustrate gay men's ability to appropriate public spaces covertly for their own purposes, even in the context of the post-Prohibition clampdown. On a much larger scale than at the Astor, gay men regularly gathered *en masse* at the performances of entertainers who (for reasons beyond the scope of this essay) assumed special significance in gay culture. Whether or not the other members of the audience noticed them, *they* were aware of their numbers in the audience and often shared in the collective excitement of transforming such a public gathering into a "gay space," no matter how covertly. Judy Garland's concerts would take on this character in later years; Beatrice Lillie's concerts were among the most famous such events within the gay world in the early 1930s. "The Palace was just packed with queers, for weeks at a time, when Lillie performed," remembered one man who had been in the audience; one of her signature songs, "There Are Fairies at the Bottom of My Garden," was a camp classic, and twenty years later Lillie noted that she still "always" got requests for it from her audiences.[23]

The Metropolitan Opera, on Broadway at Fortieth Street, was another "standard meeting place," according to the same man, and another man whimsically recalled that "since there were no known instances of police raids on [such distinguished] cultural events, all stops were pulled out as far as costume and grooming. The hairdos and outlandish clothes many gays wore were not to be equaled until the punk rock era."[24] The cultural significance of such events had always been determined as much by the audience as by the stage; but as their role in gay culture suggests, such events were the site of multiple audiences and productive of multiple cultural meanings, many of them obscure to the class that nominally dominated them.

Far from being confined to marginalized locales, then, gay men claimed some of the most conventional of cultural spaces as their own. Such were the politics of public space in much of Times Square. Gay men and straight men often used the same sites in entirely different ways, with the latter not suspecting the presence of the "queers" in their midst, in part because the "queers" did not look or behave like the "fairies" they saw at Bryant Park. Thus the Astor maintained its public reputation as an eminently respectable Times Square rendezvous, while its reputation as a gay meeting place and pickup bar assumed legendary proportions in the gay world; and on certain nights, the Metropolitan Opera became "the biggest bar in town."[25]

Still, gay men's use of the Square was a hard-won and unstable victory which required them to engage in constant territorial struggles with the agents of the dominant cultural order. Different groups of men adopted different strategies of everyday resistance to the dominant order, different strategies for staking out and defining their worlds, and those differences often brought them into conflict. Nonetheless, even those men who chose to remain most hidden from the dominant culture were not hidden from each other. Gay men became part of the spectacle of Times Square, but they also transformed it into a haven.

Notes

1. Sebastian Risicato, interviewed by the author, August 28, 1988. For more extensive documentation, see my book, *Gay New York: Gender, Urban Culture, and the Making of the Gay Male World, 1890–1940* (New York: BasicBooks, 1994), from which this essay is drawn.
2. It is impossible to trace the involvement of gay men in any industry with precision, of course, given the absence of the census records that historians normally use for such purposes, and I offer no estimates of the rate of their participation. My claim is not that gay workers predominated in the theater, hotel, or restaurant industries, but simply that disproportionate numbers of gay men worked in them, and that many of them enjoyed greater tolerance there than they would have elsewhere. This assertion is based primarily on the accounts provided in my interviews with men who worked in the industry or were otherwise familiar with it, including Max Adams, interviewed January 11, 15, and 27, 1988; Harry Hay, interviewed October 6, 1988; and Martin Goodkin, interviewed November 21, 1987; as well as some documentation from the period itself.
3. Harold E. Stearns, *The Street I Know* (New York: Lee Fuerman, 1935), 92.

4. On this point, see my article, "Long-Haired Men and Short-Haired Women: Building a Gay World in the Heart of Village Bohemia," in *The Village of New York*, eds. Leslie Berlowitz and Rick Beard (New Brunswick, NJ: Rutgers University Press, 1992).
5. For general accounts of the culture of lodging and furnished-room houses, and the character of the districts in which they predominated, see Albert Benedict Wolfe, *The Lodging House Problem in Boston* (Boston: Houghton Mifflin, 1906); Harvey Warren Zorbaugh, *The Gold Coast and the Slum: A Sociological Study of Chicago's Near North Side* (Chicago: University of Chicago Press, 1929), 69–86; Mark Peel, "In the Margins: Lodgers and Boarders in Boston, 1860-1900," *Journal of American History* 72 (1986): 813-34; and Joanne J. Meyerowitz, *Women Adrift: Independent Wage Earners in Chicago, 1880–1930* (Chicago: University of Chicago Press, 1988).
6. James Ford, *Slums and Housing: With Special Reference to New York City: History, Conditions, Policy* (Cambridge, MA: Harvard University Press, 1936), 341-44; Robert A. M. Stern, Gregory Gilmartin, and John Montague Massengale, *New York 1900: Metropolitan Architecture and Urbanism, 1890–1915* (New York: Rizzoli, 1983), 275-78; Charles Lockwood, *Bricks and Brownstone: The New York Row House, 1783-1929* (New York: Abbeville, 1972).
7. Daniel O'L., for instance, reported that he and a gay friend took a room in a theatrical boardinghouse when they moved to New York from Boston around 1931, as recorded in George W. Henry, *Sex Variants* (New York: Paul Hoeber, 1941), 431–32. C. A. Tripp, who observed New York's gay scene in the 1930s, has written that "in New York during the depression of the early 1930s, young homosexuals (especially those aspiring to the theater) often lived in groups, saving rent by sharing a single large apartment" (*The Homosexual Matrix* [New York: McGraw-Hill, 1975], 184–85). See also my interview with Donald Vining, January 25, 1986; and the *WPA Guide to New York City* (New York: Random House, 1939), 170, 179.
8. Remarkably little has been written about the theater district as a residential area, but two pieces of evidence generated by police actions indicate its residential significance. The three chorus girls arrested when the police raided a burlesque show at the Gaiety Theater in 1935 all lived in hotels and rooms in the upper Forties between Sixth and Eighth Avenues ("Burlesque Dancers Held," *New York Times*, April 5, 1935). Similarly, all of the men arrested for homosexual solicitation by plainclothes members of the vice squad, who were investigating a Forty-Second Street bar in 1938, lived in the area or made use of its transient hotels. Several of them invited the plainclothesmen home to their apartments or furnished rooms in the West Forties and Fifties between Seventh and Ninth Avenues. Others, whose homes were more distant or unavailable for homosexual trysts, or who had no homes at all, hired rooms in the area for prices ranging from sixty cents to two dollars. These included the Hotel Fulton on West Forty-Sixth Street between Seventh and Eighth Avenues, another hotel on Eighth Avenue and Fortieth Street, and a rooming house on Eighth Avenue at Forty-Fourth Street. See *Times Square Garden and Grill, Inc., v. Bruckman, et al.*, Nathan Kirschenbaum report to the SLA, November 30, 1938, contained in Record on Proceeding to Review, 24–28; Memo, Commanding Officer, 3rd Division [vice squad], to Police Commissioner, "Recommending revokation [sic] of ABC license issued to Times Square

Garden and Grill," December 13, 1938, 31-37; Memo, Commanding Officer, 18th Precinct, to Police Commissioner, "Arrests in premises licensed by the New York State Liquor Authority," December 5, 1938, 38-39.

9. George Chappell, *The Restaurants of New York* (New York: Greenberg, 1925), 127.
10. Herbert Asbury, *The Great Illusion: An Informal History of Prohibition* (Garden City, NY: Doubleday, 1950), 193, 197.
11. On Times Square in the 1920s, see Jack Poggi, *Theater in America: The Impact of Economic Forces, 1870–1967* (Ithaca, NY: Cornell University Press, 1968); Margaret M. Knapp, "A Historical Study of the Legitimate Playhouses on West Forty-Second Street Between Seventh and Eighth Avenues in New York City," unpublished Ph.D. diss., City University of New York, 1982; Irving Drutman, *Good Company: A Memoir, Mostly Theatrical* (Boston: Little, Brown, 1976), 1-74; Asbury, *The Great Illusion*, 192-96; Lewis A. Erenberg, "From New York to Middletown: Repeal and the Legitimization of Nightlife in the Great Depression," *American Quarterly* 38 (1986): 761–78.
12. Charles G. Shaw, *Nightlife:* Vanity Fair's *Intimate Guide to New York After Dark* (New York: John Day, 1931), 22; *Broadway Brevities*, December 14, 1931, 2.
13. Richard Meeker, *Better Angel* (New York: Greenberg, 1933), 259.
14. Knapp, "A Historical Study," 389–90.
15. Tennessee Williams recalled cruising Times Square with Donald Windham in the early 1940s, where he made "very abrupt and candid overtures [to groups of sailors or GIs], phrased so bluntly that it's a wonder they didn't slaughter me on the spot. . . . They would stare at me for a moment in astonishment, burst into laughter, huddle for a brief conference, and, as often as not, would accept the solicitation, going to my partner's Village pad or to my room at the 'Y' " (Tennessee Williams, *Memoirs* [1975; New York: Bantam, 1976], 66, see also 123, 172). Some verification of their activity in Times Square is offered by a letter Williams wrote Windham on October 11, 1940, while he was visiting his family in Missouri: "Have to play jam [i.e., straight] here and I'm getting horny as a jackrabbit, so line up some of that Forty-Second Street trade for me when I get back. Even Blondie would do!" (Donald Windham, ed., *Tennessee Williams' Letters to Donald Windham, 1940–1965* [New York: Holt, Rinehart, and Winston, 1977], 17). See also Donald Windham, *Lost Friendships: A Memoir of Truman Capote, Tennessee Williams, and Others* (New York: William Morrow, 1987), 114.
16. Will Finch, notes on peg-houses, dated April 24, 1962, Kinsey Institute Library.
17. Frank Thompson, interviewed June 1 and 2, 1988, reported that this was still the case in the 1940s.
18. Dorr Legg, interviewed October 4, 1988; Shaw, *Nightlife*, 66.
19. Nathan Kirschenbaum report, SLA, November 30, 1938, included in *Times Square Record on Review*, 28. Kirschenbaum also reported that a gay man at the bar had told a plainclothes policeman on October 15 that the "'Queers' [who] frequented the premises . . . were the same crowd that hung out in the Consolidated . . . and at Ryans" (25).
20. Testimony of Morris Horowitz, *Times Square Record on Review* (1939), 245.
21. As one man who frequented the Astor in the Thirties and Forties recalled, it was his favorite bar "because it wasn't a gay bar. People didn't know you were gay. It was never raided" (Martin Leonard, interviewed July 16, 1988).
22. Nat Fowler, interviewed August 13, 1986. Other accounts of the Astor were

provided by Robert Mason, interviewed November 20 and December 4, 1985; Wayne Hendricks, interviewed August 19, 1986; Frank McCarthy, interviewed September 5, 1986; and Willy W., interviewed September 2 and 5, 1986. The Astor was so famous in the gay world that upon the demolition of the hotel in 1966, a gay magazine published in Philadelphia ran a tribute to it: Paul Forbes, "Mrs. Astor's Bar," *Drum*, no. 20 (n.d. [ca. 1966]): 11-12. See also Allan Bérubé's account of the Astor in *Coming Out Under Fire: The History of Gay Men and Women in World War Two* (New York: Free Press, 1990), which appeared after this essay was written.

23. Dorr Legg interview; "An Evening with Beatrice Lillie," reviewed by John Mason Brown, *Saturday Review* (n.d. [1952?]); article on Lillie by T. B. F., *Town and Country* (December 1952): "And, inevitably, the fairies at the bottom of her garden are once more revisited. 'They are,' she admits, '. . . growing elderly but people simply adore them. They always ask for them.'" Both in Lillie clipping file, Billy Rose Theatre Collection, New York Public Library, Lincoln Center. On the audiences at Judy Garland's concerts, see Richard Dyer, "Judy Garland and Gay Men," in his *Heavenly Bodies: Film Stars and Society* (New York: St. Martin's Press, 1986), 141-94.
24. Donald Vining, *How Can You Come Out If You've Never Been In?* (Trumansburg, NY: Crossing Press, 1986), 57.
25. Dorr Legg interview.

2. "I Could Hardly Wait to Get Back to that Bar"

Lesbian Bar Culture in Buffalo in the 1930s and 1940s

Elizabeth Lapovsky Kennedy and Madeline D. Davis

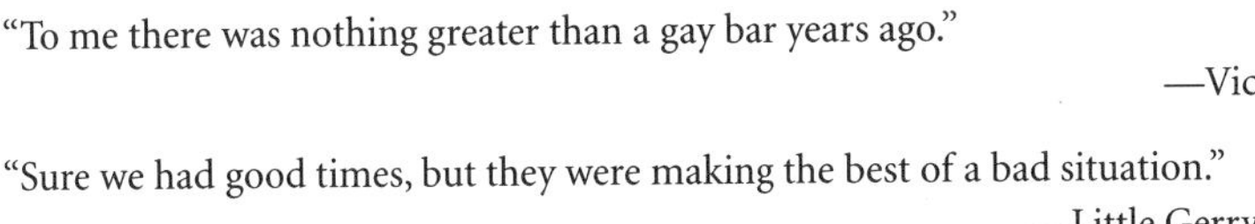

"To me there was nothing greater than a gay bar years ago."

—Vic

"Sure we had good times, but they were making the best of a bad situation."

—Little Gerry

In the '30s, '40s, and '50s, lesbians socialized in bars for relaxation and fun, just like many other Americans.[1] But at the same time, bars (or, during Prohibition, speakeasies) and public house parties were central to twentieth-century lesbian resistance. By finding ways to socialize together, individuals ended the crushing isolation of lesbian oppression and created the possibility of group consciousness and activity. In addition, by forming community in a public setting outside of the protected and restricted boundaries of their own living rooms, lesbians also began the struggle for public recognition and acceptance. The time lesbians and gays spent relaxing in bars was perhaps sweeter than for other Americans, because they were truly the only places that lesbians had to socialize; but it was also more dangerous, bringing lesbians into conflict with a hostile society—the law, family, and work. Thus, bar communities were not only the center of sociability and relaxation in the gay world, they were also a crucible for politics.

A small, though significant body of writing exists on the complex nature of lesbian and gay bar life, but little if any considers changing forms of lesbian resistance. Due to the popularity of Radclyffe Hall's *The Well of*

Loneliness, its depressing image of bars as seedy places where lesbians went to find solace for their individual afflictions has become embedded in the Western imagination.[2] Lesbian pulp novels, as well as journalistic fiction of the 1950s and '60s, were the first to convey the centrality of bars to lesbian life, portraying both their allure and their depressing limitations.[3] In the 1960s, pioneering research in the social sciences established that bars were the central institution for creating lesbian and gay culture, and for teaching gays about their identity. Nancy Achilles shows that bars provide a place of socialization, a means of maintaining social cohesion, a context for each individual to confirm gay identity, and a setting for the formation of alliances against the police.[4] Ethel Sawyer documents how Black lesbian behavior is shaped by the norms and values of the bar subculture.[5] Although this research has been invaluable for subsequent scholarship, it is limited by an aura of timelessness and the lack of a framework for understanding resistance.

The new social history of lesbians and gays, despite its emphasis on changing forms of gay politics, has tended to extend these earlier approaches and treat bar communities as an unchanging part of the gay landscape. When we began researching how the bar culture of the mid-twentieth century contributed to the formation of gay liberation, we also held a static model of bar culture. Our discoveries led us to tell a significantly different story: in the context of the changing social conditions of the twentieth century, lesbians acted to shape the possibilities for their future.

The turn of the century was a time of transition for leisure-time activities. The nineteenth-century community and family-based forms of entertainment and relaxation were replaced by commercialized leisure. At the same time, the homosocial forms of socializing, such as quilting parties, were supplanted by heterosocial forms, which brought young men and women together in movie houses, dance halls, and amusement parks.[6] Kathy Peiss argues that this new leisure culture, while offering women some autonomy in the pursuit of pleasure and romance outside of the strictures of their families, also institutionalized a restrictive heterosocial culture.[7] Thus, while working-class lesbian culture of the 1930s could draw on a tradition of working-class women's independent pursuit of fun and pleasure, it also by definition had to counter the powerful forces creating an exclusively heterosocial environment.

For lesbians to establish a public social life was a challenge; each opportunity had to be created and persistently pursued. Bars were the only possible place for working-class lesbians to congregate outside of private homes. They were generally unwelcome in most social settings. Open spaces like parks or beaches, commonly used by gay men, were too exposed for women to express interest in other women without constant male surveillance and harassment. This was a time when it was still dangerous for unescorted women to be out on the street. In addition, many working-class lesbians could not even use their own homes for gatherings. If they were young they often lived with their parents, and once mature and living alone, most could not afford large apartments. Those who had apartments of an adequate size ran the risk of harassment from neighbors and/or the law should they entertain a large gathering.

Even the use of bars by lesbians was dubious. Bars have been profoundly men's dominion throughout U.S. history, to the extent that the active social life of single working-class girls at the turn of the century did not include bars. The temperance movement, the most significant women's campaign in relation to bars, fought not to allow women in, but to get men out. In New York City before the First World War, working women increasingly entered saloons particularly to avail themselves of the reasonably priced good food available to men, but their presence was still controversial. Often saloon owners would not allow women, single or escorted, at the bar, but would serve them in a room in the back.[8] The fragile relation of women to bars continued through World War II, when several cities, including Chicago, passed laws prohibiting women's entrance into bars in an attempt to limit the spread of venereal disease.[9] (Buffalo seriously considered such a move but did not undertake it.)[10] In this situation, most bars which catered to lesbians were usually located in areas known for moral permissiveness and the availability of women for male pleasure. Such areas were therefore extremely dangerous for unescorted women.

That lesbians were able to come together and build community in bars is a testimony to their tenacity, their drive to find others like themselves, and their desire for erotic relations with other women. In the 1930s, gay and lesbian bars were already well established in New York City—in Harlem and Greenwich Village—but not throughout the country in smaller cities. John D'Emilio and Allan Bérubé identify the 1940s as the turning point when gay and lesbian social life became firmly established in bars in most cities of the U.S.[11] In part, this change has to do with the general trend in U.S. capitalism toward the increasing commercialization and sexualization of leisure culture and the concomitant increased acceptance of sexual expression. But the immediate catalyst for these 1940s changes was World War II. "By uprooting an entire generation, the war helped to channel urban gay life into a particular path of growth—away from stable private networks and toward public commercial establishments serving the needs of a displaced, transient, and young clientele."[12]

D'Emilio and Bérubé argue that the bringing together of sixteen million men in the armed forces radically transformed gay male social life in the United States. Even though the armed services officially excluded homosexuals, most gays and lesbians who applied were already expert at hiding their gayness, and were not detected. The discussion of the military's exclusionary policy in newspapers, books, and pamphlets and the routine questions about homosexual interest in the physical examination combined with an intensely same-sex environment to heighten young men's awareness of their homosexual potential. Soldiers explored these new interests on leave in major cities, where the fervor of the war made many people anxious to support and help servicemen, and their numbers were too large to be controlled by the military police. As a result, male gay life became firmly lodged in commercial establishments. This same analysis cannot apply directly to women since they did not join the armed forces in significant numbers—in 1943, the number of women in the armed services was less than 300,000—and therefore enlisted women never had a powerful presence in civilian life.[13]

The story of the impact of the war on lesbian social life still needs to be told and is the subject of this essay. Moving from the fragmented lesbian culture of the 1930s to the well-established bar culture of white lesbians in the 1940s, we explore the kinds of culture and consciousness that lesbians created in bar communities, paying particular attention to the strategies they developed when their new culture increased the risk of public visibility. We reflect on the reasons for the changes in lesbian social life, delineating the role of lesbians in shaping their own history.

Searching for Lesbians in the 1930s

Narrators identify the 1930s as qualitatively more difficult than any subsequent period. They consider World War II the turning point in lesbian life and judge it impossible for anyone who did not live through the 1930s to imagine what they were like. Arden and Leslie, two white butches who are well known from their many years in the bars, console themselves about the difficulty of having had to live through such hard times by reflecting on how much harder it must have been for those who came out before them.

> Can you imagine what it was like in the 1900s when all the women had to wear those long skirts? How could you show it? How could women live together? I guess only a few could do it, who had an independent income. But even so, how could they leave their families? It was hard to leave when I was young.

At this point in the interview, we share a bit of women's history and describe the intense friendships between married women in the nineteenth century.

But this does not strike the narrators as part of their lesbian heritage. They are unquestionably modern lesbians, who identify themselves as different from other women because they desire to build a specifically sexual life with women outside of marriage. Leslie responds, "There must have been some who didn't marry." Arden then worries, "Those who didn't marry would be stuck at home." But her faith in the indomitable spirit of the modern lesbian wins out: "Some must have run away. But if they ran away who could work? . . . There must have been a lot of masturbation and repression in those days."

Despite the severe oppression, narrators took for granted their ability to create independent lives as lesbians during the 1930s based on opportunities for work and housing. For them, the painful difficulty of the 1930s was the intense isolation. "When I finished high school, I knew who I was and that I was attracted to girls, but I didn't know another person on earth like myself. That would not happen today" (Leslie). Arden had two gay friends, a man and a woman, while growing up in her neighborhood, but this did not significantly lessen her feelings of being alone. Lesbians knew that society did not approve of or accept who they were, and that they should hide it. "I can't imagine how we knew it, but we certainly knew it," Leslie states emphatically, and gives the following example:

> I was very rough on my shoes and they had to be replaced every two weeks. My father worked at the railroad, and was tired of buying me shoes so frequently. So he took me to where he bought his shoes, and told the man, "Put a pair of shoes on her that she can't wear out in two weeks." The man felt sorry for me and would bring out the daintiest shoes and my father said "no." He thought he was punishing me. I couldn't let my father know that I liked them. Inside I was elated, absolutely elated. But I knew I couldn't let my father know because he thought he was punishing me. I lived in those shoes. My mother did not like them. She would say, "Why the hell do you always have them on?"

Debra, a respected Black butch who grew up in the South, expresses her intuition of the need for secrecy about the sexual affair she had in Virginia in 1934 .

> I [was] thirteen. And I [was] going to school, and it was a very beautiful young lady in school, but she was about three years older than me. And I used to ask her to let me take her books home, carry her books for her. And I was very much interested in that girl. So finally when I was fourteen we went out. And after we went out, I knew then that was what I wanted. I really wanted her. And finally I got her and we stayed together for about three years. We weren't living

> together now, we were seeing each other, and it was kept from my family and also kept from hers. Because at that time, well we felt that . . . we actually felt ourselves that it wasn't a natural thing to do. . . . We had heard it somewhere, as kids, you know how you hear people talking. And we felt that it was something wrong with us.

When asked if she and her girlfriend were scared, she replies, "No, I don't think so. But I often think what would have happened if they had a caught us. Because she was white and I was Black. And at that time, boy! It would have been *very* bad."

Some narrators were less fortunate and were caught for expressing their sexual feelings as adolescents during the 1930s and were chastised and punished. Leslie recalls:

> My mother and I had a room in a rooming house. I was doing my homework with the girl downstairs, and people in the neighborhood had clued this girl's mother in to the fact that I was "kind of funny" and they were watching me. I leaned over and kissed the girl, and the mother was looking in the window. She came in and made a fuss. My mother came and kept calling me "a dirty rotten thing," and whacked me around, and told me to get upstairs. That kind of thing cooled me down.

The isolation, punishment, and ignorance did not deter narrators from acknowledging in their teens their preference for women.[14] Arden remembers how people talked about her in her neighborhood, but it didn't change her. "I did not conform and had no intention of it." Debra took a little more time to fully accept who she was: "And I guess I was about eighteen before I found out it wasn't anything wrong with me. It was my preference. If I wanted a girl that was my business. And I carried it like that throughout life. I didn't go around broadcasting it, but I didn't try to hide it either."

The process of knowing oneself, admitting one's difference, generated the desire to find others like oneself. This was difficult because Buffalo's few gay bars were both hidden and short-lived. Also, cultural references to lesbianism were extremely limited. The only literary source on lesbianism known to our narrators was Radclyffe Hall's *The Well of Loneliness*, which was published in the U.S. in 1929 and read by several narrators during adolescence in the 1930s. Therefore, the search for other lesbians required initiative and persistence, not to mention courage. For white narrators, this meant primarily finding gay and lesbian bars; for Black narrators, it meant finding a community that socialized together at parties.

Arden, the narrator with the longest experience in the gay community, went to her first gay bar, Galante's, in 1932 when she was eighteen. Galante's was a speakeasy in the downtown area behind City Hall on Wilkeson Street, a rough area that was dark and forbidding even then. This was right before the end of Prohibition, and Galante's served wine and home brew. The clientele was mixed—gay men and women, with a few straights straggling in. Her gay male friend from childhood had told her she would find lesbians there. When she first went, she felt some animosity directed at her.

> You know how it is when a new lesbian comes in. The boys were sitting downstairs. The women were upstairs. There was a big round table. If you were in, you sat at the round table, otherwise you were an outsider. Then someone came over to me and said, "You look like a nice kid," and helped me to join. One woman was the leader of this group. She would say things like, "Get these kids out of here. There are too many kids." The leader insulted me several times and I would answer back, and then we became friends.

Arden went back every Saturday night, became a part of the group, and learned "appropriate" butch behavior. For instance, on the first trip to Galante's she wore a skirt and sweater and no hat, but afterwards she "learned how to dress." The starched shirt was an essential part of a butch's attire. They didn't starch the blouses they wore to work, but "starched shirts were for Saturday night." She socialized with this crowd long after Galante's closed; many of them remained friends until separated by relocation or death.

A lesbian bar by definition was a place where patrons felt relatively safe, otherwise they would not go. Arden remembers that her crowd stopped going to Galante's before it closed shortly after Prohibition. "It lost its glamour." There were a lot of raids, and people no longer felt comfortable there.[15] Being caught in a raid could be very dangerous. She, however, was never caught in one at Galante's, although she knew people who were:

> It was the first Saturday night I missed. I was sick with the flu. Otherwise I went out every Saturday. People's names were in the paper. [The mother and father] of a gay friend of mine saw it in the paper. It was serious. God help you if you worked in a small factory, it would go around and you would lose your job.

Leslie remembers hearing a story about this raid. Even a straight couple was treated brutally by the police:

> I know there were some straight stragglers at [Galante's] because one Saturday night there was a raid. A friend of mine was in it. The cops were roughing

> people up, and she knew this one cop. He asked her what she was doing there. She said that she had just come for spaghetti and she didn't know anything about the place. He let her go. But there was a straight couple there who really didn't know anything about the place. They were sitting there eating spaghetti and the cops came over and the man said he was just there for spaghetti and that he didn't know anything about the place; then he introduced his wife, and the cops knocked him in the mouth with their clubs, breaking all his teeth. He sued the police and eventually won, but they drove him out of town. Wherever he parked his car he was bothered.

Narrators are not sure why Galante's became the target of frequent raids but guess that the owner was not making an adequate payoff to the police.

Leslie, who came out in Buffalo in the 1930s, had no gay acquaintances while growing up and took longer to find a lesbian bar. After years of isolation, she was introduced in the late 1930s to the Hillside, a bar on Seneca Street far from the center of town, beyond the streetcar line. A woman who "got around" told her about this bar, which was in a farmhouse. After a few unsuccessful tries, the two of them finally bought gas for the car and kept going until they found it.

> When we went in, there was a straight couple dancing and we didn't really see anything else. We bought some drinks and then the straight couple left and some boys went up to the juke box and started dancing. Two men together dancing. I had never seen this before. I couldn't stop looking. My friend had to tell me to close my mouth, I was standing there with my mouth wide open, like a hick, I was so excited. I met several women there.

The Hillside lasted about a year, and Leslie did not become part of a stable social group there. But, by the late 1930s, other gay bars began to open, all of which lasted well into the 1940s. It was in one of these that she established friendships that would continue for years.

Dee, a reserved white narrator who participated erratically in the public lesbian community, had less trouble finding a bar. She didn't think of herself as different or interested in women until she was twenty and fell in love with a woman at work. Her lover was slightly older and had some lesbian friends she had met through work, who invited them to Eddie's.

> We used to go down to a little tavern on Sycamore and Johnson, where Eddie was very kind to gay women. Our whole crowd would gather there on a Saturday night and we'd take up the whole back room, and could dance when women dancing was rather frowned upon. We used to spend thirty-five cents for a half

> of fried chicken with french fries and ten cents for a glass of beer and for under a dollar had a great time.... [It was called] Eddie's Tavern. [Eddie] would not let any of the bar men, straight men, come back and annoy us. And we used to do a lot of things, our crowd, which I might add, I am friends with some of these gals even today.

We know from other sources that Eddie's was a gathering place for women involved in amateur and professional sports teams, which were very popular at the time.[16] However, if these women were lesbians, they did not openly acknowledge it.[17]

Black lesbian life in the 1930s seems to have been somewhat different.[18] Debra, who came to Buffalo in 1938, met her first lesbian friends through her church group, which was racially mixed. They socialized at parties:

> We didn't go to bars, we usually went to someone's house, if we wanted to do any drinking at all. She [her first partner in Buffalo] knew quite a few gay people, but at the time, they didn't go out and broadcast it. There would be quite a few of them like maybe [on] a Friday night or a Saturday night like that.

The parties were fairly large, with usually more than 20 people. "It was almost the same as the bar life, but ... going out to the bars, they couldn't do the things that they wanted to do like dance and stuff like that, so they would meet at someone's house where they could let their hair down." White lesbians also socialized at parties during the 1930s, particularly during the middle of the decade, when for several years there were no gay bars in Buffalo. The leader of Galante's social group, a well-paid private secretary, used to have parties, a tradition that lasted into the 1940s.

Narrators remember that the bars—and we imagine the same would be true of parties—made a tremendous difference in their social lives. Before locating the bars, they ran around with one special friend and went back and forth to each others' houses because they didn't know other people. Once they went out to the bars, Leslie and Arden reminisce that they met other people and "things started to happen.... There was quite a bit of exchange. The bars were important for meeting people. How could you approach someone in a straight bar? You couldn't."

Debra concurs on the difficulty of meeting people at this time.

> Well, yes, it's different from now, because now you go out there and you meet one of them, and you like her and you figure that she likes you, you're going to let her know that. Well, at that time, you wouldn't because you didn't know exactly how she felt. You didn't know whether she was the type that was going to

> broadcast it and other people would find out. Do you understand what I mean? So you would be a little leery. At that time, it was always best to let them hit on you first, then you know where you stood.... But it was plenty of gay people at that time, but as I said, they kept it in the closet and they were more careful about exposing [themselves].

Going to the bars also made a difference in lesbian consciousness. Butches who regularly frequented the bars understood the value of proclaiming themselves and had definite opinions about those who did not.[19] Arden captures this distinction in her reminiscing about women she knew in her bowling leagues during the 1950s. "I never saw such a bunch of gay girls who would not admit it."

Lesbians of the period were highly motivated to go out. They were pushing beyond the limitations of socializing in their own houses with close friends. In addition to frequenting parties and gay bars, when they were available, they went to the entertainment bars—the Little Harlem, the Club Moonglo, the Vendome, Pearl's, and the Lucky Clover—in the Black section of Buffalo. They were all located close to one another on or near "the Avenue," as Michigan from Broadway south was called. Many famous Black entertainers of the time, such as Billy Eckstine and Lena Horne, performed at these bars. Since it was expensive to get into the back room, lesbians would sit in the front and try to hear the music. These were not gay bars, but they were hospitable to lesbians. They had a mixed Black and white clientele that included gamblers, call girls, and lesbians, as well as people who went primarily to enjoy the show. Arden, who frequented these bars in the 1930s, explains why lesbians were welcome: "Because it was free and open and there was no pretense. Remember, there was not too much money around. They were only too glad to have you buy drinks." The easy acceptance of lesbians suggests that the cosmopolitan culture of the Harlem Renaissance had extended to the entertainment clubs in Buffalo's Black section.

This neighborhood and these bars remained important for lesbians' good times, at least through the 1940s. Debra, who used to do most of her socializing there during the 1940s, characterizes them in much the same way as Arden. She remembers that they had a mixed Black and white clientele and were popular with gays. "I knew it wasn't [a gay bar] but you did meet a lot of gay people there. Remember, entertainers and stuff coming in at all times.... Naturally if you didn't know anything about gay people you wouldn't know if they were gay or not.... That's how I met a lot of gay people."

Lesbians have warm memories of "the Avenue," and unquestionably felt at home there. In the 1940s, Arden used to go up and down "the Avenue" at night, and on weekends she would even go in the daytime. She remembers the owner of the Little Harlem, Ann Montgomery, tossing mail out the window, and asking her to take it to the post box. Ann Montgomery would then say, "Go into the bar and ask George [the bartender] to give you what you want." Arden, a gallant butch who was more than willing to please a distinguished lady, would always say "it wasn't necessary." Ann Montgomery was a dynamic woman with a colorful reputation. One night she even referred publicly to Arden as a lesbian, indicating that she was fully aware of who patronized her bar. Arden still remembers this event vividly with pride and embarrassment forty-five years later.

> There was a whole slew of people at the bar and Ann came in and told the bartender to give everyone a drink. They were all Black at the bar. I was the only white. The bartender hesitated when he got to me and Ann said, "Yes, give that lesbian a drink too." I nearly died. There I was with all those Black racketeers. They never bothered you though.

The special place of the Little Harlem and the other entertainment bars in lesbian life in the 1930s and 40s can be seen in the way narrators distinguished these bars from straight bars. When asked if a bar we had seen advertised in a 1940s newspaper was gay, Arden and Leslie concur: "It was not gay. It was mostly men, straight men, and not a place for us, not for homos. You'd be better off in the Little Harlem" (Leslie). Although the entertainment bars were not gay space in the sense that gays and lesbians could not be open about who they were, they did provide a space where lesbians were comfortable and could have a good time without having to fear being ridiculed or harassed.

The Flowering of Lesbian Bar Culture in the 1940s

Narrators remember World War II as having a tremendous impact on lesbian life, offering lesbians more opportunities for socializing and meeting others. Before doing this research, we had assumed that the war's major influence was to allow more lesbians to be self-supporting by opening up more and higher paying jobs for women. But according to narrators, jobs for lesbians were not a result of the war. They and their friends had been working since their teens in offices, shops, and factories, and had never doubted that they could find work. In their minds, the important effect of the war was to give more independence to all women, thereby making lesbians more like other women and harder to identify.[20] Women working in defense industries were out on the street going to work, alone or in groups, at all hours of the day and night. In addition, it was no longer unusual for women to have money to spend nor for women to go out to bars or restaurants alone. Many women even went out to gay bars for an evening of fun; some became regulars at the bars and entered lesbian relationships until their husbands returned. Leslie remembers wisecracking, "Here come the war brides," when groups of straight women would come into Ralph Martin's, a popular bar of the period.

Finally, and in narrators' minds, most importantly, the dress code for women changed, allowing lesbians to more openly express their erotic interest in women through their clothing. Since all women were now able to wear pants to work and to purchase them in stores off the rack, butches who only wore pants in the privacy of their homes in the 1930s could now wear them on the street. Arden recalls how, when she used to work the afternoon shift during the war, she would go in to Ralph Martin's after work. "A woman used to come in who worked on the railroads. She would come in her work clothes, with her lantern, her overalls, and cap. She would look real cute. Some of the girls would go out of their way to come into the bars with their work clothes on."

Joining the armed forces was not a priority for narrators or their friends. One woman thought about it but didn't want to join alone. She couldn't get any of her friends to go with her. "They said, 'We can't leave our girlfriends.'" Others never seriously considered the armed forces. "I didn't want to go. I was making a lot of money; having a lot of fun. I didn't want to go into something I didn't know anything about" (Arden). For most Buffalo lesbians, the armed forces had little to offer. Since Buffalo was a thriving industrial center, made even more so by the presence of war industries, lesbians had ample opportunities for high-paying jobs.[21] They had active social lives in the bars, and with men away in the war, they had more opportunity to be with women in the public world. They were no longer easily identified when they went out together dressed in trousers without male escorts.

The changes in the 1940s manifested themselves in the proliferation of bars and the extensive social life that developed around them. The bars tended to be in or adjacent to the downtown section, although a few were in residential neighborhoods, and a few on the outskirts of the city. "You know how gay bars were in [not nice] parts of town; they were looked down on so they never opened in halfway decent neighborhoods." Two bars spanned the entire decade and were central to the growth of lesbian community: Ralph Martin's, a large mixed gay and lesbian bar, and Winters, a small lesbian bar. In addition, Down's, which catered to a discreet men's crowd, opened in the late 1930s and continued into the mid-1940s. Polish John's and the Shamrock were rougher men's bars that catered to laborers and sailors. All of these men's bars were sometimes frequented by women. Eddie Ryan's Niagara Hotel, in the heart of downtown, had primarily well-dressed and discreet lesbian patrons in the evening and was a hangout for showgirls who performed at the nearby Palace Burlesque.[22] The Tudor Arms, an elegant downtown mixed bar, and the 670, a neighborhood bar, both started in the late 1940s and lasted into the 1950s. Although neighborhood bars were not too common because of local residents' hostility toward gays, the 670 stands out in narrators' memories. "It was the only neighborhood bar like that where the neighborhood people were nice to you. The men treated you well. If a man bought me a drink, then I would buy him the next drink. It worked well" (Arden).

In addition, there were many short-lived bars. The Roseland, in an Italian neighborhood, discouraged lesbian patrons after the neighbors complained. And the Del-Main sponsored a women's softball team and hosted an after-game lesbian clientele; it closed when the "girls" stopped playing softball. Finally, there were bars that were not primarily gay but which gay people frequented. In addition to the entertainment bars on "the Avenue," Grogan's was popular because it had gay entertainment. Hahn's also stands out in narrators' memories because it had a girls' band—all butches. Some narrators met and had drinks with the members of the band; they also danced to the live music. "It was a lot of fun with the orchestra. . . . The foxtrot was very popular, and you did a lot of dipping. If you were any kind of butch in those days, you had to do a lot of dipping" (Leslie).

In the 1940s, gay bars were opened primarily as business enterprises, rather than from sympathy or concern for the gay clientele. Some started as gay while others became gay, often with some negotiating on the part of lesbians. Narrators think but are not certain that Ralph Martin's opened as a gay bar, and that Eddie Ryan opened the Niagara Hotel shortly after, when he saw how much money Ralph Martin's was making. "He probably said, 'listen, jump on the bandwagon,' you know, and Ralph was making a lot of money at the time" (Joanna). Other bars became gay more gradually, however. When business was bad, a couple of lesbians would go in, and if they were accepted, a few more would, until eventually enough people would be going that it would become gay.[23] For instance, Arden speculates that the woman who was the leader of the group in Galante's discovered Winters as early as 1938. "She was a groundbreaker and had a big following," and found many bars. Although they themselves did not take leadership in this process, they do recall bars that gradually became gay and bars that rejected gays. They remember running around "the Avenue" when a group of people started going into a bar and the bartender realized there was quite a bit of revenue there, so decided to "let it go." They also recalled once going to a place on Niagara Street on the West Side and meeting a lot of hostility, so no one went back. Seeking new bars meant taking chances. Leslie recalls, "It was kind of like being out and stepping in [somewhere] and not really knowing, but guessing."

In some cases, the negotiations were more direct, although this did not necessarily mean greater success. Arden remembers that a woman who was dissatisfied with Ralph Martin's went out looking for another bar.

> She went into neighborhood bars on the West Side and talked to the owners. The Roseland agreed to it, but it didn't last long. It was where it is now, and the owners began getting flack from the neighborhood, all those Italian men. She wasn't nasty about it; she rather politely told us she could do without our business. She was an old lady, and explained that she didn't want us girls getting hurt.

Lesbian and gay bars had an ambiguous relationship to the law in the 1930s, '40s, and '50s. The section of the state law that was most relevant to the existence of gay bars read: "No person licensed to sell alcoholic beverages shall suffer or permit any gambling on the licensed premises, or suffer or permit such premises to become disorderly."[24] In the 1940s, the mere presence of homosexuals was interpreted by the State Liquor Authority as constituting disorderly conduct.[25] Gay bars, therefore, had to constantly walk a fine line between allowing gays to express themselves enough to be comfortable and want to spend time at the bar, and not allowing so much obvious gay behavior that it would attract special attention from the public and the police. They struck a successful balance during the 1940s in which there were very few raids or police closings.

Narrators are unanimous that the Mafia did not protect these 1940s bars.[26] The prevailing wisdom is that the owners paid off the local police when necessary.[27] Ralph Martin's was the only bar narrators remember being raided, and this happened rarely. In fact, we have unanimity about only one raid that occurred at the end of the decade, shortly before Ralph Martin's closed.[28] Some feel he must not have made his payoff, while others feel the police had to do such things to keep their credibility, particularly around election time, since Ralph's was a notorious club. Its reputation came from the presence of flamboyant gay men, and the raid narrators remember was on the night of a drag show. "The boys were doing a drag show and someone tipped the police off. It had to be a tip-off because the boys didn't come in drag" (Arden). This raid did not adversely affect all the clientele. D.J., an amiable white butch who has been a regular bar patron since she found Ralph Martin's, remembers the evening as a high point.

> The best time I can remember, and Pepe and I still talk about it. They had a drag show in there one night for his birthday, when they raided the joint. In fact, the cops were all on the outside, you know, the detectives or whatever you want to call them. They let the show go on all the way right up to the end, you know, with the girls ... in their drag and everything. And then they waltzed in, so everyone started diving under the tables. There was only one that got out of it.... He dove under our table; so we all pulled the thing down and got our legs close together and got 'em under there [so they] didn't see 'em. But the rest of them they all took down.... [They] just [took] the drag queens, the ones that were putting on the show.... At that time, you weren't supposed to have drag shows and all this without a license or permission or some dumb thing. So they all got hauled in. But it was a beautiful night though. They used to make their own costumes, and they were gorgeous.

Raids were more common in the after-hours clubs, but, again, lesbians were not the main target. When asked if she had ever been in jail, Arden responds, "No, I don't know how I missed it. I certainly was in enough after-hours clubs. But usually when they came in they were not after the people, only the owners. That would take too much writing up for them to get them all."[29]

Even though the owners made some kind of peace with the law, the threat of police intervention was always present. The law, therefore, loomed in the background, shaping the boundaries of what was permitted and standing guard against "going too far." It even affected plans for renovation and decoration of bars. Reggie, a white butch who was underage when she entered the bars and developed close relationships with the older butches and Ralph Martin, remembers his discussing the frustrations of owning a bar: "So we [Ralph and I] used to sit and talk quite a bit. He used to look around and he'd say, 'You know, I wanna do this and this and this with this place, but the cops won't let you.' I never asked him really what he meant by that, but he did pay a good buck."

The clientele of these gay bars was primarily white, with a few Indians and even fewer blacks.[30] Some Indians were regulars at the bars. In fact, a leader of the core group at Ralph Martin's was of Indian descent. Narrators cannot remember any Blacks who were regulars in the bars. Debra is sure that there were not any Black gay bars in the 1940s. After prodding, she recalls that she had been to a few white gay bars—Ralph Martin's, Eddie Ryan's Niagara Hotel, and the Tudor Arms—more than once. On the one hand, this indicates that she could and did go to these bars. On the other hand, it suggests that they were not central to her life. Although this was only one woman's experience, it does coincide with some white narrators' views that there were few, if any, Black lesbians in the lesbian and gay bars of the 1940s. Black lesbians continued to socialize primarily at parties throughout the decade.[31] They also frequently visited the entertainment bars and Black straight bars, and occasionally went to white gay and lesbian bars.

The absence of Black lesbians in the bars is particularly striking, since one of the popular lesbian bars, Winters, was in the Black section of the city, on "the Avenue," and was owned by two Black women.[32] Several factors seem relevant in explaining the Black lesbian community's preference for house parties over bars in the 1940s. First, the Black community was not yet large enough to provide anonymity for a Black lesbian social life. Although the Black community in Buffalo dates from before the turn of the century, it was relatively small. It began to increase dramatically during the 1920s due to migration from the South. During the 1940s, the Black population of Buffalo more than doubled.[33] Debra, who socialized in Buffalo during the 1930s and '40s, recalls the need for discretion to prevent the Black community from knowing she was a lesbian. This would make it unlikely that Black lesbians would want a bar in their own neighborhood. Leslie, when queried about Black lesbian bars, doubted if they existed in the Black section. She describes it as the "old ethnic problem . . . that you can't be funny in your own neighborhood." For this reason, the majority of gay and lesbian bars were downtown. Second, at this point in the history of race relations in the U.S. in general, and in Buffalo in particular, well before the Civil Rights Movement, there was little possibility of a Black lesbian bar, or a fully integrated bar, in the downtown area of the city.[34] A primarily Black gay and lesbian bar would have been too vulnerable to racist attack. And the process of integration of gay bars did not occur in Buffalo until the 1950s, and still caused tension well into the 1960s.[35] Third, Black urban culture has a strong history of house parties; rent parties and buffet flats are noted in most Black community histories of the first half of the twentieth century.[36] Thus, in having regular parties, Black lesbians were adapting their ethnic culture to their own specific needs.

The lesbians who patronized bars in Buffalo were not only white but also working-class.[37] They came primarily from working-class families, and they themselves worked hard to earn a living as beauticians, sales clerks, secretaries, or factory and hospital workers. Some sacrificed a lot to pursue an education and became skilled workers or technicians. A few with luck and effort were able to go into business for themselves.

The homogeneity of the lesbian bar population makes a striking contrast with gay male culture, which has a long tradition of explicitly erotic cross-class socializing.[38] In general, middle-class women did not go to the bars because they were afraid of being exposed and losing their jobs. Charlie, a chic and competent white fem, remembers how rarely a gym teacher friend would go to the bars: "Once in a while she would go. She was very nervous about her job. And I can understand it now because that many years ago, and sometimes even now, people want to make problems. They feel that somebody might attack their children." However, upper-class lesbians in Buffalo were more public about their behavior. Working-class lesbians knew about them through gossip—for instance, from a gay man who worked for them, or a friend who sometimes went to their parties—or through newspaper stories, particularly about an older group that had been quite prominent in the social life of the city in the 1920s and '30s. But the upper-class lesbians did not socialize with working-class lesbians in the bars or any other settings. Joanna, a popular and worldly white fem who socialized in several groups, remembers:

> The people [they'd] hang around with were all like professionals, and [their] families were influential, very affluent, and I don't think that [they] would have considered even hanging around with us, say at the bars.... Maybe they did go slumming once in a while, but they sure never came to the bars when I was there. And I used to always think, gee, where do they go? Then I found out ... to the Westbrook and the Park Lane ... Can you imagine? And Beatrice was very butchy looking. Wish I had a picture of her, 'cause you would have died when you [saw] her. Very, very masculine woman, and I mean really masculine looking.... They could get in anywhere, are you kidding. They wouldn't have turned her away. Probably spent a fortune in these places.

In addition to not going to working-class bars, the upper-class women did not welcome working-class women into their parties. Arden remembers going with a friend to one of the parties, and the hostess asked, "Who the hell are you and how did you get in here?" Arden took the question in stride and had a pleasant evening, but did not go back frequently. All narrators are adamant that these upper-class women had little impact on their lives, and the fact that they were known lesbians did not make it easier for working-class lesbians. They think the difference was greater in the old days between those with money and those without. They were more concerned with making ends meet—working every day, setting up an apartment—while the upper-class women had the money they needed and could concern themselves more with leisure activities.

Several factors seem to account for this lack of contact between different classes of lesbians. First, the location of bars in rough sections of the city made it too risky for upper-class women to patronize them. Their money bought them space to be lesbians in much safer environments, but did not provide them protection in less reputable sections of the city. In addition, we can deduce that lesbian culture did not eroticize power differences; there was not an erotic force bridging the gap between the classes.

Those going to gay bars for the first time in the 1940s did not have to search for them in the same way as during the 1930s. Gay and lesbian bars were relatively visible, with reputations that extended far beyond their regular clientele. Ralph Martin's, in particular, was known by many people in the city. "Ralph's was notorious. It was one of the hugest, biggest. Anyone came from out of town right away knew where Ralph's [was]" (Reggie). In fact, today straight, white, working-class women who have had no contact with the lesbian community over the years remember going to Ralph Martin's in the 1940s as part of an evening out with friends.

Two narrators went to Ralph Martin's without consciously looking for a lesbian bar. Reggie, who knew she had liked girls from the time she was six but never suspected that there were others like her, had started dating men in her teens. She went to Ralph Martin's with a man—who almost became her fiancé—and his brother, at their suggestion, and then came to realize that there was a category of person like herself, a homosexual.

> His brother came home on furlough.... [He says,] "I've got to make the best of my days that I'm in town," so he mentioned some queer place to me. And, of course, inside I was very excited, I wanted to go, but I couldn't afford to let them know how excited I was. And Jimmy [my boyfriend] would give me my way, anything I wanted, and I said, "Let's go to Ralph Martin's." It used to be one of the biggest places here, and he said, "O.K., why not." And, of course, all the girls I met were my future [friends].... And this one gay boy, Bobby LaRue, floated by ... and [Jimmy's] brother makes a crack, "That no good queer, look at him." And I got red and I got mad and I says, "You're in their territory, why don't you leave them alone, why did you come?" So he turned to Jimmy and he says, "What, are you going to get married to a queer lover?" Jimmy said, "Shut up, she's right." So when they wanted to leave, I wouldn't leave with his brother, I wouldn't get in the car.... Of course, I didn't have a license or a permit, you know, big shot, fifteen, right. So Jimmy left me the keys, he said, "Do you need any money?" And, of course, I needed a couple of dollars, I wasn't working, I was only fifteen, and they left.... So this little Italian girl [came over] ... and she went in a circle with her finger, "Do you want to dance?"

This experience transformed her life. "I wasn't concentrating on my school work, 'cause I was so enthused and so happy, I don't know, it's like you're in a cocoon." And in time she broke off with her boyfriend because she felt she couldn't accept the engagement ring after she had started going to Ralph Martin's regularly.

Joanna, who went to Ralph Martin's completely unaware that it was a gay and lesbian bar, was also enthusiastic about her experience, and couldn't wait to return. She was brought by a female high school friend who had been once before, but didn't tell Joanna until they were inside.

> Like I said, we were supposed to go out bowling, right, so we wound up at this bar. Now previous to this I had never been to a gay bar. I didn't even know they existed. It was a Friday night and that was the big night you know, bigger than Saturday. And we walked in and I thought, my God, this is really something. I couldn't believe it.... [I] don't think there were any straight people in the bar that night.... There were an awful lot of lesbians.
>
> So we ... sat down. We had a drink. Oh maybe about twenty to twenty-five minutes we were sitting there. We were talking and watching, you're really in awe of all this.... And she and a friend wandered over, same thing, another lesbian. Asked if they could buy us a drink and I said, "Sure," didn't have that much money anyway. Actually, if anybody asked us, we would have had the drink because at that time money was scarce. I guess some people were making good money at the defense plants. We were too young to work in the defense plants. They sat down and started asking what our names were, you know, the first time we were there, blah blah blah. Well I could hardly wait to get back to that bar! We left in about an hour.... But I think it was only like a couple of days later we went back. Now, it was a dull night so there were only a few people in the bar, a couple of gay boys and a couple of girls.... But, on Friday, we went back again. And there were the same two people, and they were so happy to see us, it was really funny.

Leslie, one of the women she met on this first night, became her partner for the next eight years.

D.J. found Ralph Martin's by herself, having heard about it from friends in Syracuse. She already had had lesbian relationships in a girls' reform school. When she went to Ralph Martin's for the first time in 1945 at the age of nineteen, it was a refuge, offering her a safe place where she could be herself.

> And then when I really got down and out and I said, ah, the heck with that, just traveling.... So I ended up right on the corner where Ralph Martin's was, when

> the Decos were going full blast.[39] Well I went in there one night and I was tired and I was sleeping in the booth. And I had gone in the place a couple of times during the day, just to feel it out. This one night I was sleeping in the booth and Pepe, he's a Black boy, but he worked there nights as a porter, and strictly gay, and he asked me if I would like a bed to sleep in, and I've never forgotten him since. So he took me up to his place and he lived almost right above Ralph Martin's. Oh I hit that bed and I was out like a light. So he says, "Don't worry about nothing, nobody will bother you." 'Cause he's down portering, cleaning, and everything. Then I started getting to know a few people, and then I started getting a few jobs, oddball jobs, dishwasher and that kind of stuff, you could find it then. Now that was a fabulous bar; there'll never be another one like it.

No matter how or why butches and fems found the bars, once inside they embarked on an exciting and fulfilling social life. Part of the exhilaration came from the dramatic contrast between the acceptance and warmth found in these gathering places and the isolation and hostility lesbians experienced in their daily lives. They met and socialized in relative safety in the bars and felt as if they belonged. On weekends, butches and fems regularly went out with lovers and/or friends, and enjoyed themselves flirting with women who often became affairs or serious partners; they also established new friendships, many of which lasted for life. They would usually frequent several bars in one night, always ending up at their favorite. Sometimes butches might first go to a bar that served cheap beer, "get a bun on and go out and pick up their girls for the evening" (Leslie). Narrators remember starting Saturday afternoon and staying out all night. Fems also looked for a good time in several bars, as Charlie reminisces: "I can't imagine that I missed many of them. . . . I would sit with other women that I knew that were feminine friends." Some bars rented rooms for those who were living at home, or were visiting from out of town, to stay the night. "I think we were kind of wild then. We would go out to the bars, have a good time, and after they closed, go on to the after-hours clubs." All the narrators—those who first came to the bars in the 1930s, and those who became regulars during the 1940s—still remember these times vividly and with affection. "They were good years. They were great; they really were" (Charlie).

Of the many lesbians who participated in bar life, some came erratically, due to temperament or fear of exposure, while others came regularly. Even for those whose attendance was irregular, the bars meant a lot. Dee remembers, "I guess it was the novelty of having a place of your own to go to that was strictly gay." Those women who came to the bars frequently usually had one bar where they spent most of their time and developed a close circle of friends. Winters and Ralph Martin's both had core groups whose consistent presence made them instrumental in building a bar community. The culture of each group was slightly different due to the patrons and the atmospheres of the bars.

Winters was small and intimate, and felt like home to its steady clientele. However, like most bars of this period, it was not particularly well kept. Arden, who liked Winters better than Ralph's, is quick to mention that it was not because it was cleaner.

> It had a long narrow bar with a room on the side with booths, and then in the back was another room with a big table and couch. There was a bathroom off of it, and in the back was a kitchen. What a terrible kitchen, with rats running around up on the stove. Things can't be as bad as that today. They have to be more glamorous, though you still do see some dirty johns.

The bar also had rooms upstairs where people—most usually "gay girls and showgirls"—could spend the night.

The core crowd at Winters was the group of women who had been together since Galante's in the 1930s. Leslie remembers that the women at Winters were two or three years ahead of her. "Probably if I had stuck it out I would have been accepted. The [people at Ralph Martin's] were much more friendly." In addition, the Winters clientele had the reputation of being "a way-out group." "They did things that gay people didn't do at the time" (Leslie). They were older than the Ralph Martin's crowd, with some married women in the group. They had lively parties and talked about and experimented with sex. Leslie, who was familiar with the conversation and activities of the group at Winters, reminisces, "It was ahead of its time. Gay life by itself was outrageous enough. When you think of it between parents and religion, by the time you wake up in the morning you think you have already done ten wrong things."

Winters was the closest thing to woman-defined space that could be imagined for a public bar of the 1940s. Sometimes a few of the Black "racketeers" would come in, but they got along quite well with the lesbians. Leslie even recalls a friend leaving her fem in their care for a few hours. It wasn't that gay men weren't allowed or weren't wanted, they just did not come in any numbers. "They didn't like it too well. They wanted to cruise and Winters was predominantly women" (Arden). Thus, in the 1940s, lesbians and gay men, consciously or unconsciously, created some separate space from one another. This is curious, particularly given narrators' unanimous and emphatic statements that in the past, unlike today, gay men and lesbians always mixed easily. The difference they perceive might be that in the past there was no ideological commitment to separatism, and no overt hostility between the two groups. The separation might have been due as much to economic factors as social preference. Perhaps Winters was not a large enough or high-class enough bar for men to want to frequent. Perhaps the owners discouraged men, given that, at this point in history, they were viewed as more troublesome, more likely to get into fights, or to attract the attention of the law.

It is important to clarify that although Winters was primarily a woman's bar, it was not refined or discreet. Arden remembers, "There were quite a few rough butchy girls . . . they were older than me. . . . They swaggered around. They used foul language." Leslie confirms this, remembering how she used to be uncomfortable when many of the butches at Winters would make passes at her young girlfriend.

Ralph Martin's was also loved by its regulars, who often refer to it as "the club" and recall it with reverence.[40] "There'll never be another like it, fabulous bar." It was larger than Winters, "the biggest gay bar in the city of Buffalo," with two big rooms, "a nice big back room, a nice front bar and two entrances." During the week, the atmosphere was "dull, but weekends were hopping." With a capacity for about two hundred people, it was usually "packed to the gills" on weekend nights. There was dancing—Jimmy Dorsey on the jukebox and people dancing the Big Apple—and entertainment such as drag shows. The atmosphere was very congenial. Typically, patrons remember, "I made half a million friends there." The clientele consisted of both gay men and women. Narrators emphasize, "Everyone got along beautiful. . . . We were never segregated like they are now. There was never any question about a gay guy's bar. There was no such thing. Really! We always went to the same bars, this is how we got to know so many gay boys" (Joanna). In addition to gay men and women, since Ralph Martin's was such a well-known bar, it always had some straight spectators.

Ralph Martin's was unquestionably the most open gay bar of the 1940s. At Ralph's, gay men and lesbians could be themselves and develop their own ways of living. Reggie captures the distinctiveness of Ralph's when she explains why she preferred it, and always finished her evening there, even though she considered "the action was still at Ryan's," where she waitressed and tended bar. At Ralph's, "you could do more, you could dance. Your friends were there." Women could be openly affectionate, and slow dance together. Most other bars required more discretion. Ryan's, for instance, did not have dancing. It was part of a hotel, right off the lobby. During the day it served lunch and had a primarily straight business crowd. At night its patrons were primarily well-dressed women, including showgirls and strippers, who gave the bar its distinctive reputation for action.

Fems remember Ralph Martin's particularly because they loved to dance there:

> They did so many different [dances] that I can't really remember all the names. However, I'll try. They did a double-time step which is similar to the Lindy. . . . [What] the heck are the other things? I guess they called them the Big Apple or crazy names . . . and the Shag. . . . That's what I think really got to me was watching the dances. They're cute. . . . [A] lot of different little steps that [they'd] improvise, variations of the boogie type things. (Joanna)

Although gay men and women danced together both for enjoyment and as a kind of protection for the image of the bar, men also danced with men and women with women. Since women dancing together sometimes alarmed straight spectators and endangered the bar's liquor license, Ralph Martin relegated all dancing to the back room.

Ralph Martin himself had a colorful and controversial reputation. Some narrators, including those who were regulars at his bar, are absolutely adamant that he was not gay, "I knew his girlfriend." Others, again including regulars, claim that he was. Everyone agrees that he "looked" gay. He was always beautifully dressed, had a "characteristic" walk, dyed his hair, and wore makeup. Regulars such as Reggie have fond memories of him.

> Ralph, oh God, I used to choose his suits for him. I used to like to pick out his ties and shirts, it became a habit. Sportscoats. What to wear, you know, for the weekend. He was an older man, Ralph, and wore an awful lot of makeup. He was a good businessman. Very kind, when you needed anything he was always there, helping you out. You know he'd help the fellows out, and the girls. He just loved his job, he loved his business, and he was happy to see that his dream came true.

Ralph Martin definitely extended himself for his patrons and tried to be supportive. Reggie continues:

> And he knew how old I was and he kind of took me under his wing. He called me one afternoon and he says, "You don't have to answer this if you don't want to, [but how old are you?"] He was very direct, he didn't like liars. He always said, "I'd rather have a thief, they steal then leave, but a liar and you don't know whether to believe them or not." As long as you never lied to Ralph, well I didn't know this at the time. And, of course, right away I had to stop and think, he owns this place, should I tell him the truth, I won't be allowed in here. Because

> he could lose his license, even though I didn't drink. So I debated and I said, "Yes, I'm only fifteen." He said, "Well, I knew that, but I wanted to hear what you were going to say." He said, "If you had lied to me, I wouldn't have let you come back in."

Ralph Martin also helped his clients who became entangled with the law. Leslie recalls that he facilitated her release from jail when she was picked up by the police before going into an after-hours club.

> They put me straight into the clink. Oh what a feeling that was when they closed the door behind me. There was a woman on the floor who kept asking for a cigarette. They had taken everything, my wallet and all. Meanwhile [my lady friend] called [somebody] who called Ralph who came down and got me out. They were nice to Ralph. I got my wallet back. I was never charged, nothing happened, what did I do? . . . I sure was glad to see Ralph Martin that night.

In addition, Ralph Martin protected his clientele; if anyone started trouble, they were put out. Joanna distinguishes Ralph's from bars existing concurrently in Greenwich Village on exactly this point:

> I was very uncomfortable even in Greenwich Village because there were an awful lot of degenerate type people that I thought were nutsy acting. It just seemed there were an awful lot of straight people in these bars. . . . Tourists used to come in. . . . Like let's watch the freaks, you know. . . . No, I never found that in Buffalo. Well, don't forget, in Buffalo, as I said, Ralph . . . protected people. If anybody came in, they didn't stay too long. Because he didn't encourage it. In fact, he discouraged it. . . . New York was a little too fast at that time. There was an awful lot of servicemen getting out and . . . we were deluged. One particular night we were in a gay bar. And we had a whole bunch of, I don't know if they were coast guards or sailors. . . . [A] couple of the guys had come over to us and said something and . . . you know you don't want to be bothered. . . . "Just leave us alone." They were waiting for us when we got outside. . . . We were really frightened. . . . They were asking us all kinds of things. Oh it was awful. Really . . . horrible . . . not so much hassle in Buffalo. A little, but not that much. As I said, most of the bars, they really protected the kids. . . . A lot more than they do now.

Ralph Martin did not keep order himself, but had bartenders who carried weapons.

Not everyone had such positive experiences at Ralph Martin's. Narrators remember Ralph Martin's being picketed in 1945, the first gay picket we have found in Buffalo. A fem had a run-in with Ralph Martin and she was banned. Arden remembers clearly, "She was six feet tall, rather an imposing figure." People weren't sure what caused the banning.

> [She was] a mouthy woman and could have said anything. It might have been as simple as her saying, "Why do you wear all that powder?" And he was the major-domo there and didn't like anybody talking fresh to him and that was that. She hadn't been out long. It was all new to her. She was quite a woman and could get to be quite a leader. (Arden)

Narrators remember this fem's boldness with affection. Rumor has it that she later fell in love with a masculine-looking woman from a small town of about fifty people in the Midwest, left Buffalo to live with her, and was subsequently appointed sheriff by her girlfriend, who had been elected mayor.

The picket is a testimony to the developing sense of solidarity among lesbians. Even though it was not successful and could not attract a significant number of women over an extended period of time, it was certainly a significant first step. This woman organized the picket with a group of friends. The picketers carried placards, front and back saying, "Gay people, do not frequent this bar" (Leslie). The picket was small. Many people didn't join because they were afraid of being banned themselves, or as Arden, who was not a fan of Ralph Martin's, says, "I was not about to be walking in front of the place and have one of those hoodlums [bartenders] hit me on the head." Narrators remember going into the bar while the picket was occurring, and the organizer saying:

> "Don't go in there, don't go in there, I'm picketing." The picket didn't last long. It fell flat. It went for about a week. It started with twelve women and then got smaller. Her group diminished as people became afraid that it would hit the paper or that Ralph would call the police. (Arden)

Some lesbians who were not involved in the picket also disliked Ralph Martin's. Arden does not remember Ralph Martin with affection. Although she went to his bar, she disliked it. She considered it a depressing gay bar, and filthy. She feels he was a fake, "a South Irish dummy who knew money." What the regulars viewed as protection, she views as brutality. She remembers that he did terrible things to people. "He threw a woman out and she hit her head on the pavement. Brutal. His bartenders were Italian hoodlums and carried clubs. Ralph Martin would not do these things himself. He would just raise his hand and they would go into action." She is also of the opinion that Ralph was involved in a prostitution syndicate. "If a young girl would come into his bar and was pretty and didn't have any money, he would coax her into thinking about prostitution and would send her to work in [other nearby states]."[41] Arden thinks that Ralph did these ugly things on weeknights so that the regulars would not see them. This must have been the case because some of the patrons claim to be ignorant of such goings-on.

However, others confirm that there was a lot of prostitution and violence connected with Ralph's. The regulars at the bar did not consider Ralph primarily responsible for them.

> Like Ralph [was surrounded by] young guys . . . and the one was a nut. His name was Danny. And when I'd walk in, he'd say, "I'm gonna get you." And, of course, my two great big butch "friends," Lee and Barb, if I wanted to go next [door] to Deco and get a hamburger or something, I'd walk between them. And another time he showed his thing in the window. I saw him rape his girlfriend he was supposed to be engaged to. He had two guys hold her down in the car. And many a time he was reported to Ralph . . . and Ralph, well, he just couldn't believe it, until he found out, then you never saw Danny again. But I used to be afraid of him [Danny] to a certain extent, that I would never walk out of there alone. (Reggie)

This level of violence against women was not surprising for bars that sheltered illegal activities in the 1940s. They often assumed and encouraged male control of women's sexuality.

The disparate views about whether Ralph Martin established a protective or brutal environment grow from the contradictions of the bar environment. Protection did not mean a completely safe environment that respected women and was fully accepted by the law. It was often gained by the use of force and other illegal means, and also linked lesbian and gay life with other sexually stigmatized groups in society. Thus, each perception is probably correct, and whether one approved of Ralph's or not is related to what one expected was possible in a gay bar. Those who felt most at home in Ralph's appreciated what he could do given the bar's popularity and inevitable notoriety, even if they knew of the brutality involved; whereas Arden, who was a regular at Winters, appreciated that bar's less blatant use of force to establish a protected environment, an approach allowed perhaps by the absence of men and its relatively limited reputation.

Just as in Winters, some of the regulars at Ralph's formed close-knit groups or cliques that socialized together outside of the bar, and continued to see one another for years. One group in particular stands out as central to the social life at Ralph's. Reggie remembers this group with affection:

"Leslie, Terry, Denny, Barb, the whole group was there, much older than me, naturally. . . . And like I say, they were a different bunch, they didn't have to act tough, they could if they wanted to when the circumstances arose, but they weren't, they were very good girls. . . ." This group had strong ties to one another.

> I'm talking about a [tight-]knit little group you know. Where you went to each other's homes and that sort of thing. . . . They did a lot of home entertainment then too. Especially during the bad weather. . . . These were close people. These were not just people that you saw in the bar. . . . I'm saying twenty-five to thirty people, not couples. (Joanna)

Friends in this group helped one another solve the daily problems they faced as lesbians. For Joanna, this meant that gay people were concerned about each other and wanted life to be as easy as possible given the circumstances.

> It was a good life when they discussed things openly with people that they were good friends with, I don't mean acquaintances. . . . They talked about their ups and downs and how, when they first started working, how tough it was. . . . Because I remember listening to these discussions. . . . Like what they looked like [on their job] and how they went in, and they felt funny.

The butch who was more or less the leader of this group was particularly known for her supportiveness.

> She was unique. . . . I've never known anybody who encouraged people more. Especially for education. Or even if they didn't want to go to school, she'd make sure they read good things and were aware of like everyone that was appearing, like a lecturer. And it was really interesting. As I said, there were a lot of things that I said, "Oh I don't want to go to that," she'd say, "You'll enjoy it," and I did. (Joanna)

The core group at Ralph Martin's was cohesive enough to develop some of its own distinctive customs. "I mean they had a thing called Butch Night Out, where they went out like the boys go out. That was Friday night. . . . That was the busy night. But . . . [you] very seldom ever saw a lesbian there with her girlfriend on Friday night. Isn't that odd?" (Joanna). Every Friday night at least ten butches of the Ralph Martin's core group went to the bar to meet single women and begin a flirtation or something more serious; if they were in a couple, they went without their girlfriends. D.J., who claims to have always been monogamous, conveys the romance and sexual interest of these evenings when trying to explain that only twenty percent of butches were monogamous like her: "'Cause when the butches went out, any girl at the bar, you know." A lady's equivalent to this practice did not exist. Butch Night Out was not part of the social life at Winters. Although the Winters regulars followed butch-fem roles and would sometimes join Butch Night Out at Ralph Martin's, they would finish the evening at Winters, and never initiated the practice there.

A lively social life in the bars, be it Winters or Ralph Martin's, did not substitute for other types of leisure activity, but rather seems to have encouraged lesbians to do things together in various settings. When we asked Arden, who had described herself and a friend as having been active during the 1940s and '50s, what she meant by active, she answers, "To be out barring, having fun, going to parties in homes." Large parties are not prominent in narrators' memories, but they did occur. The woman who stands out for her initiative and gumption in picketing Ralph Martin's was also known for her parties, and was the only white woman to have given pay parties:

> [She] had a big house and her parties were wild. . . . She was quite an aggressive woman, nothing fazed her at all. She was a very forceful person. She used to have parties on Saturday night. They were pay parties; you would pay two dollars for the whole evening, and could have all the beer you wanted. One time I asked her, "What does your family think of all these people traipsing in?" She said, "It doesn't matter, I'll get rid of them." She would send her daughter out to her aunt's. (Arden)

These were open parties for lesbians and gay men. The Winters crowd went regularly, whereas the Ralph Martin's crowd did not. Perhaps the Winters crowd attended because they had been together a longer time—since Galante's—and had gone to these kinds of parties during the period in the 1930s after Galante's closed and for several years there were no gay and lesbian bars. This suggests that the younger Ralph Martin's crowd had already adapted to the social life of the 1940s, and made commercial establishments the central place for public socializing among lesbians.

Narrators all went to private parties, which were smaller and limited to a close circle of friends. They also played cards together. In addition, they went with their friends for outings to the country and parks. "Drives were big in those days." Their photos show them relaxing out-of-doors and included such activities as sleigh rides and summer picnics.[42]

> Oh we had a lot of picnics together in the summer. We used to, in fact, I wonder if she still has any of those pictures. They were really good. You know we had a lot of fun and everybody would bring their own food and bring extra stuff and we, we'd go to like Letchworth Park or Chestnut Ridge. The ones that were really close. Or else we'd go to Detroit, Chicago, Cleveland. Like sometimes the softball games were on in different places, and [we] went to see [them]. (Joanna)

In the late 1940s, going to summer resorts became popular. Arden began to spend her summers at Sherkston, a recreation area in Canada less than an hour from Buffalo. She recalls, "I first went there because I liked the area, it was near the Quarry and the Lake." At the time, she and a couple of friends were the only gay people in the colony. The others were couples and families. She would rent for the whole summer, and continued to go every summer for twenty years. She was not the first lesbian to spend her summers at Sherkston. She remembers how even before this, in the 1930s, an older woman "who was gay but kind of closety" had one of the first cottages. "Her lady friends would come over and have a good time, telling stories. They would have too many beers and do funny things, like one time they dumped the outhouse over.... You would go over there and they would be giggling." These women were twenty years older than this narrator. Over the years, Sherkston became more and more of a gay resort, so that by the 1960s, when Leslie began to rent, the area was predominantly gay, with a lively social life centering around parties.

Handling the Increased Risks of Exposure

Hostility and social disapproval from the straight world defined the context for all lesbian social life. Narrators assumed danger as the setting for good times. This is vividly reflected in narrators' attitudes to introducing newcomers to the gay life. Despite the good times people had in the 1940s and the friendship groups they developed, narrators were notably reserved about introducing people to gay life. They were hesitant to do it, either in sleeping with a newcomer or in taking newcomers—men or women—to their first bars. They felt that it was something people had to come to by themselves, "since at times it is not the happiest life" (Arden). They don't recall being role models for anyone, or anyone being role models for them. Arden remembers a younger butch who would keep asking her questions, and she would always tell her, "I will not tell you anything, anything you find out will be on your own. Do what you have to do."

The nature of lesbian oppression was such that as lesbians and gays came together to end their isolation and build a public community, they also increased their visibility and therefore the risks of exposure. Lesbians had two basic strategies for handling this situation: separation of their lesbian social life from other aspects of their life and avoidance of conflict when confronted about being a lesbian. And although these might not be the approaches that lesbians would choose ten years later, or for that matter today, they were effective strategies of resistance for the time.

Women were concerned about losing their jobs should they be identified at work as lesbians. They were also worried about the effect of exposure on their families, either because of what the family might do to them, or what having a lesbian relative might do to the family. In addition, they had to be prepared to meet harassment on the street from strangers who suspected their sexuality. Finally, they had to deal with harassment by the law, the worst effect of which was not so much going to jail or having a police record, but suffering increased visibility due to being named in the newspaper, dealing with the courts, or having to ask someone, often family, for help in getting out of jail. The primacy of the concern for family and work, and also the willingness to fight the unfair and unrestrained arm of the law, are expressed concisely in Leslie's recollections of her dealings with the police when they picked her up on the way to an after-hours club: "I told him, 'I have nothing to lose, I don't have my family here, if I lose my job over this, I will make this all public, going to the papers, because then I'll have nothing more to lose.'"

Work was considered essential by 1940s lesbians; it was a necessary complement to having a good time because their social lives required money. As Arden aptly responded when asked whether she ever had fears that she wouldn't be able to find work, "I always thought I had to work. I wanted a social life, and I needed money." Social life was organized around work schedules and relegated to weekends. "During the week, we would go to work, come home, do the food shopping and such. We went out strictly on weekends" (Arden).

In order to remain employed, lesbians had to keep their sexual identities hidden. They handled the greater visibility they gained as a result of participating in bar culture and community by creating as clear a separation between work life and social life as possible. All narrators for the 1940s emphasize how discreet they were at work. Leslie was hired in the late 1930s by a large Buffalo factory, where she worked for five years, until she moved on to a more skilled job during the war. She never had any trouble, but she was very cautious. "I would dress alright and be quiet and polite, and there was no trouble. There were two other gay women that I knew, and then I recognized [another one], and got to know her. We would sometimes eat together and talk together, but we wouldn't carry on conversations that would single us out." She didn't have to learn to be this careful, she just knew it was essential. "We were smarter than we thought. How did we know that people were going to scorn us if we weren't careful? I wonder how we knew these things." Arden, who started working at a large Buffalo factory in 1936 and held the job for thirty years until retiring, emphasizes a different aspect of the discretion required at work, restraint on flirting. "In high school, I was more free to make passes; that was before we went out to the working world. Then I knew I needed money and I had to tone things down to keep a job."

Continuous contact with people at work sometimes made it very difficult to keep work life separate from social life. Leslie remembers a very uncomfortable situation with her boss.

> He and these two women were my riders to work and back every day. He would sit in front and gradually told me his story and dropped hints about what he was interested in. The girls sat in the back. He said there was this widow who owned a grocery store in his neighborhood and she used to lure him to the store and they had oral sex. He liked it lots, but would never think of taking his new interest in sex home because he was afraid his wife would divorce him and take his kid. He thought I might know girls who would like someone to have oral sex with them. I don't know why he was looking for other partners . . . if he was getting tired of it with the woman in the deli or not. One night, I was convinced to lead them all to Ralph Martin's for an evening of a few drinks. I was very uncomfortable about this, but I didn't know what to say to him. He was my boss. Once we were there, it was very difficult. They were just sitting there and not even a floozy walked in that I could introduce him to. After we had drunk a bit, I and this guy were dancing with the two girls, who were having a great time. The guy took me aside and said, "Both of these girls like you." I didn't want either of them. That was the last time I went out with them. I didn't like mixing work with play.

In general, the strategy of careful separation of work life and social life, and discretion about identity, was effective. Only one narrator, Debra, lost her job because she was gay; in fact, she lost two jobs. Based on our knowledge of the history of discrimination in the Buffalo workforce, we suspect that lesbian oppression was worse for Black women.[43]

> I lost a job one time when they just got suspicious and thought I was gay. They didn't actually know, and I got fired. In fact, I got fired off [of] two jobs for the same reason. . . . One was an elevator operator and the other one was . . . right

> after the war, and I was working in a plant. Those were the only two jobs I lost because of that, because after then, whenever I would get a job, I would never let anyone on the job know. I didn't trust them that well because I had trusted someone before and they had carried it back in the plant and gave it to the personnel manager, you know. And so for that reason I kept my mouth shut. I just kept it in the closet as it was.

Her strategy of greater vigilance on future jobs was her only option at the time, but had its limitations. The separation of work and social life was ultimately not entirely within narrators' control, a fact that kept some people from ever socializing in the bars. Going out inevitably entailed the risk of meeting people from work. Arden remembers meeting a man at Ralph Martin's with whom she worked. "He never said anything, but always had that smirk, . . . 'Remember where I saw you,' . . . when I used to see him at work." In her case, she was lucky; there were no further repercussions. Straight people were not the only ones who could cause trouble at work. Another lesbian could be indiscreet. Arden also recalls, "When one of the gay girls I knew came to work, I was nervous because this woman was mouthy and talked a lot and said she knew me. But she only lasted there a week and a half."

As in work life, discretion was the rule for family life. However, the goal of keeping employers and fellow workers completely ignorant of one's lesbian identity, and the strategy of absolute separation between work life and social life, were not directly applicable to family life. By definition, family takes an active interest in its members' social life, and expects its members to participate in the same activities. For a lesbian to separate her social life and family life inevitably raised suspicion at the same time that it offered protection. This was particularly true in the 1930s and '40s, when unmarried working-class women were expected to live at home with their families rather than developing independent lives. Joanna thinks this is the reason her family couldn't accept that she moved with a friend to New York City: "In the short time, couple of years, I was gone, my family was still kind of angry because I left my mother. Because, you know, being Italian and all that you don't leave the house until you get married." While leaving home aroused consternation, and focused family attention on narrators' friends and the partner with whom they were living, staying at home was no better; it drew family attention to where and with whom a daughter went out every weekend.

As a result of the contradictory demands of family life and of lesbian community, all of the narrators' families suspected that they were gay. They experienced varying degrees of disapproval, ranging from avoidance of the topic to violent beatings. However, none were completely rejected by their immediate families, nor were any warmly accepted. Within several years of coming out, each established a truce, so-to-speak, with their families and maintained contact. The goal of discretion in family life, therefore, was not so much to keep members of the immediate family ignorant of one's lesbianism, but rather to avoid further disruption of family relationships and to protect one's immediate family from general social disgrace and from ridicule by fellow workers, neighbors, or relatives. Another distinct aspect of discretion in family relationships was its reciprocal nature. For extended family relationships to be maintained over time, members of a lesbian's immediate family had to be cautious about pursuing the topic of sexuality and causing repeated confrontations.

The families of more than half of these narrators did not explicitly know that they were lesbians. So the fear of being discovered was always present. Leslie and Arden both lived with their immediate families for a long time after they became involved in bar life. Arden lived with her aunt who had raised her, and Leslie lived with her mother [the father had left when Leslie was a young adolescent]. Each one's strategy for dealing with family was to be as discreet as possible without eliminating participation in lesbian community. And, in both cases, it is fair to say that not only were they discreet, but so were their families, for they never pushed a confrontation. For example, Arden was always respectful of her aunt's values but never gave up her own social life. She reminisces, "In those days, the only real suits they had for women were really tailored white-linen suits. My aunt used to work ironing them for hours, then they would be such a mess when I came home covered with stains." But she would not go too far. "I stayed away from fights. I didn't like fisticuffs. If I got a marred face, how could I explain it when I got home?" Her lesbianism was never mentioned; "it was kind of an undercurrent thing." She has been able to maintain this kind of close but discreet relationship with her family until this day. Although this type of relationship avoids any direct confrontation, it nevertheless takes a toll on both parties. Leslie, who had the same relationship of mutual discretion with her mother, felt awkward about that relationship. "My mother never mentioned it, but it was the kind of thing that was held over my head, so that I would feel that I owed my mother something."

Some mothers were a little more direct in questioning their daughters. But even they did not push too far. Dee remembers vividly a difficult moment with her mother:

> I was working at the war effort and everybody wore pants, as she [my mother] called them.... We were driving down River Road.... And she said, "You have

> some strange friends these days." And I said, "Oh, I work with them." And she said, "Yes, but everybody's gonna think you're one of them." And I was very tempted to say, "I am," and my common sense came to the fore and I said, "Well, all I know is they're my friends." So we never discussed it . . . from that day on.

This mother came to accept her daughter's friends; some even stayed for periods at her house.

D.J. managed to keep her family's awareness of her identity at the level of suspicion by participating in lesbian life in a different city. Family pressure was so great that several narrators left home for several years shortly after coming out. D.J., however, was the only one to leave home permanently. She was from Syracuse, a smaller city, with a smaller lesbian community. For ten years, she moved back and forth between Buffalo and Syracuse, but relegated most of her lesbian social life to Buffalo. Finally, in 1953, she decided to move permanently. Her explanation of this decision emphasizes the desire to protect her family and also conveys the mutual discretion that family members followed during this time period.

> I myself, being gay and all this, I have a very high standard of morals, depending on how people look at it but I do. I have my sisters, their children, I have great nieces right now. I came right out and told my sister last year, first time she ever heard . . . the reason I really left, I would never have thrown it to my family that you got a queer for an aunt. Now this is hard for any kid to swallow, I don't care whose kid it is. And I just come out and told her, 'cause she always figured why I was never around. 'Cause I used to come up on holidays or whatever, and I even used to bring a few of the women that I lived with. And there was never any conversation, you know, "honey," and all this garbage over the table. She would sit there, I would sit there. My nieces and that would come around, especially Christmas-time, 'cause I'd always give them two Christmases. And my sister always accepted my friends and I have never thrown it up in their faces. . . . So I figure, well, they live their lives, I live my life; we still are together as far as sisters are concerned, but that's one of the reasons I left.

A few narrators' families knew explicitly that they were lesbians. They had not told their families themselves; rather, their relatives had heard or deduced it as a consequence of narrators' activities in a public community. In a manner characteristic of the courage of lesbians who participated in the public lesbian community of this period, they made no attempt, when confronted, to deny that they were gay. For two women, Reggie and Joanna, the consequences were severe, highlighting the risks that everybody faced when joining a lesbian community at the time. In Reggie's case, she was beaten by her father and eventually was sent to reform school. Her mother had died when she was young, and she was raised by her father and siblings. Somehow, her father learned that she was a lesbian, and he came after her. She had only been going to Ralph Martin's for a couple of months.

> And he followed me, and he kicked me, literally kicked and punched my fanny all up Main Street on the way home. He said, "No daughter of mine's gonna be queer." And he'd never argue this one point; like I said, he was very strict. He'd hit first, ask questions later. You were lucky if he asked a question later. . . . It [Ralph Martin's] was a huge place, big back room and bar, had another door on Seneca Street, and if he came in one door, they'd warn me and I'd either run in the john or go outside.

People in the bars protected her, so her father did not catch her often. However, one day, due to a misunderstanding, she did not come home at night when her father expected her. Her brother, while on furlough, had rented a cabin. He was recalled suddenly and offered Reggie and her friends the cabin for the remainder of the weekend.

> So I told my brother, "Don't forget to tell Dad where I am, that I'll be home Sunday." Well, in the rustle and bustle of my brother packing and being shipped out so fast, he forgot to tell my father. Meanwhile, like I said, my father is strict and strong-headed, he swore out a warrant. I came home, I had to go to court Monday. . . . The lady [who] worked on the courts for years, she begged my father, she said, "You don't know what you're doing 'cause she's not bad; she didn't run away. . . ." But he was very defiant. She said, "Well why don't you put her maybe six months in Good Shepherd," which was on Best Street. "No, I want her out of town, I want her away." So again you're grouped, he's gonna bring me out of town, shove me away, because he feels that I'm getting in with the wrong people, but yet, where he can shove you, there's all kinds of people. . . . So you're thrown in jail like a common criminal, you have to go before a psychiatrist, which is court-ordered.[44]

Reggie spent her sixteenth birthday in jail and then the next two years in the New York State Reformatory. When she came out, she lived with her father only a short time before getting an apartment with a girlfriend. Her father did not continue to harass her.

Joanna was beaten by her brothers and then kept by her family as a sort of prisoner at home; she was never allowed to go out by herself. She, along with her butch, devised an elaborate and successful plan of escape and went to New York for a few years. Her family did not pursue her, perhaps because she was already eighteen years old. She did not take any chances, however, and changed her name while she was away.

The family was alerted to the fact of her lesbianism by an anonymous call to her widowed mother. It could have been anyone, because part of going out involved making oneself vulnerable to many people. "I wished I did [know who did it]. . . . I mean, I'm glad they told her because it saved me from telling her . . . but . . . I didn't want her to find out that way, but I never found out who told her. She said it was a woman. Nice, huh?"

The mother then told Joanna's brothers, who waited for her outside of the bar one night.

> They caught me outside. I was coming out of the bar. . . . They didn't do anything to [my friend], thank God. . . . I said, "Just go. Right away." Well I wasn't living with her then. I was living at home. Don't forget, if I had been a little older, I'd have been smarter. Maybe I should have had them arrested for assault and battery.

In later years, Joanna discussed this with her brothers, and they explained that it was the ridicule they received from others that bothered them. Thus her problems stemmed from much more than one phone call to her mother. Unfortunately, her participation in the lesbian community had become known throughout her brothers' circle of friends.

> Oh they die when I talk about it. Never even want to hear about it. My one brother said that "the only reason why I did it, when I came out of the service, I went to this bar, first thing I heard, this guy told me your sister's a lesbian. Your sister's queer." I think this is what riled him. So he talked to my other brother, and they knew where I was hanging around by then. So they waited outside the bar till I came out. They didn't come in the bar. They had a long wait too. I think that was even what made them madder.

Going to New York didn't immediately resolve Joanna's conflicts with her family. But over the years they came to accept her.

> I called my mother many times from New York and she'd always cry, and wanted to know, "Why did you do this to me, blah, blah, blah." You know, I felt horrible. But, when I came back, I didn't go to see her right away. I think maybe a couple of months passed and I finally said, "Well I've got to go see her." And I went to see her. She was all right. She was not as bad as I thought it would be, and I went there for dinner and sat around and talked with her and, of course, I had to leave. That didn't set too well. She wasn't really too happy about that, but

> she kind of came around, accepted [my friend].... Yeah, she came to my house for dinner. She had to accept her. She got to know her, she liked her. My family still likes her. It's amazing.

Of all the narrators, Debra's family treated her the most positively after learning about her lesbianism.[45] She went to New York City for several years to get away from a marriage that did not turn out well. Soon after she returned, in the late 1940s, her sister asked directly if she was gay.

> So after I went to New York and came back my sister said to me one day, I guess I had been back about three months, something like that, she says, "You know, I well understand now why you married him, [and it] didn't last but one day." I said, "Why?" She said, "You're not interested in men at all, you seem to be more interested in women than in men." I said, "So well you know, so let's forget it, hear...." I told her, "No more conversation concerning women or me or my private life. I live my life to suit myself, you live yours to suit you."

The sister did accept her life to the extent that they never talked about it further, although they continued to see one another. From her one-day marriage, Debra had a child whom a cousin raised for ten years. Her concern was always to protect her family from any trouble that her being a lesbian might cause them. She did this by maintaining a clear separation between socializing in the gay community and socializing in straight society. This was not an impossible feat, since she was not so much hiding from her family as presenting a proper image to those who knew her family. A most effective way of carrying this off, and one often used by lesbians in this era, was to use gay men as a cover. She and a gay man would go to social functions as a heterosexual couple.

> I know when I was out there in the life that I had gay men friends. Not the swishy kind, no, I couldn't afford to do that because I had a [child] and I didn't want it to get back.... I mean the guys that knew how to act. See, I have a family, and as I said, most of my family is in government or state or county, working. And I didn't want all that to go back, so the fellows I went out with was gay, but you['d] never know they were gay, not unless you were gay yourself. Then they would let you know. But out among straight people or like that, they weren't known as gay guys.

This concern to protect the family was unanimous among the narrators. It is as if their own suffering from social rejection and ridicule made them more sensitive and they did not wish to create more suffering for others.

Perhaps they had to insure this kind of protection to earn minimum acceptance by their families and continue contact.

The danger of increased visibility for lesbians, brought about by creating a social life and culture with its own dress codes, extended beyond the loss of jobs and difficult family and work relations. Lesbians were generally stigmatized by straight society and rarely if ever accepted as "normal," valuable human beings. Narrators remember vividly the harassment and insults from strangers on the street who suspected them of being lesbians, particularly because of the appearance of butch-fem couples. "There was a great difference in looks between a [butch] lesbian and her girl. You had to take a street car, very few people had cars, and people would stare and such" (Leslie).[46]

Harassment on the streets and in one's neighborhood was more severe than in gay and lesbian bars, which were by definition somewhat safe. However, most bars, particularly one as well known as Ralph Martin's, had straight observers. Lesbians used humor to deal with the inevitable objectification and were successful at deflecting the tension.

> In other words, back then you had an awful lot of your soldiers, sailors, straights come in, it was like going to the zoo and seeing the monkeys dance. So we'd put on a show for them.... And half of the women that used to walk out with their boyfriends would come back. But you know they're eyeing, it's a gay spot in town, "Oh boy, look at that, look at that." So we'd put on a show.... Oh I'd probably grab my girlfriend, ... and the gay boys would flit around more so, gab, and carry on. But basically when they came back in again they were very nice. (Reggie)

Relationships with the straight women were sometimes difficult to handle, as evidenced by a humorous incident Leslie recalls. She was in the bathroom.

> There was no door in the john so [people] would go in together and block the view for one another. If there were gay kids coming in, they would all come around, but sometimes straight girls would come in. This night they were in there tee heeing at this and that. Suddenly there was banging on the door. It was their boyfriends shouting that we should let their girlfriends out. Even the girls assured their boyfriends that we had done nothing.

Although usually in the bars and on the streets men did the harassing, sometimes "women, too, could cause trouble; they might feel that you would follow them into the bathroom and attack them" (Leslie).

The general strategy of creative passive resistance was used outside of the bars as well. During the 1940s, these lesbians did not respond to harassment with physical violence, even when provoked:

> It was always trouble if you went out for breakfast. There would be guys standing in front waiting, and you would be scared to leave. . . . One time, a guy came over to me and said, "Don't worry, I'm watching you." He was trying to be helpful. The guys would invariably say something. There was no point in fighting them. What can you do against hoodlums? (Arden)

However, their strategy of passive resistance should not be confused with passivity in relation to the straight world. As we have indicated, the act of going out increased visibility and involved risk. The ways lesbians found new bars typifies the initiative required for participating in bar community life.

The fights narrators do recall during this decade were between lesbians, and even these were not that frequent. Leslie, the sole narrator who fought during this period, can recall only two instances of physical confrontation. She felt that her reputation far exceeded her performance.

> One was in the middle of Michigan Avenue. It began at Winters. [My friend] was young and used to be bothered at Winters. Normally she wouldn't go there because women wouldn't leave her alone. She used to ask me to go to the bathroom with her because people would pester her. This night [Denny] yanked her up on the floor, and I took [her] home and told [Denny] I would come [back]. When I came back, they [Denny and her sidekick, Jamie] followed me out, they thought it would be two on one, I suppose. And there we fought on Michigan Avenue. Soon some gay guys came by and they took us off two by two, two took me and two took Jamie. We got into their cars. It was a good thing because we would have run into trouble. Pretty soon we could hear the sirens coming, the police.

Unquestionably, these women could fight, but did not do so as a regular part of socializing and going out, except for the occasional conflict among themselves.

Public socializing as part of the process of community building inevitably increased chances for exposure to and confrontation with some aspect of the legal system. Despite the fact that raids were infrequent and very few lesbians were involved, everybody was always aware that they were a possibility, and that they were unpredictable; even private large parties were occasionally raided. Only Leslie, of all the narrators, was actually picked up by the police and jailed because she was participating in lesbian social life. Her memories of the arrest convey the unpredictability of police action.

> It [the after-hours club] was a lively place, wide open, all the lights were on, but I never got inside. [My friends] went in, but while I was parking my car, a cop came over to me and said, "Park your car and go home.... Who's with you?" I said, "Nobody," because my friends had already gone in. He said, "If I come back and find you in there you'll go to the clink." So after he left, I said to [my partner], "I think we had better not go in there" and I drove off. As I pulled around Broadway, there was the same cop. Two cops came over to me and one pulled me out, and the other guy who had harassed me to begin with got in the car and drove it off with [my friend] to the police station. I said to the cop I was with, "What is the matter with him? Would you leave your car here? What the hell is the charge?". . . The cop suggested that the other had a problem and took me to the police station. I got there, and I had no [chance] to say [anything]. They put me straight into the clink. [My friend later] said that while she was in the car with the wild guy, she figured he wanted a payoff. But she didn't have the money.

The random nature of police harassment served the purpose of controlling lesbian activity. The consequences could be severe, due to the exposure that inevitably followed. Leslie sympathetically remembers the problems of a friend who was busted: "He was at an attic party and it got raided. His parents had to go and get him out of jail. They didn't let him forget it for a while." Joanna comments on having avoided the raid at Ralph Martin's: "I was thinking.... Thank God that you weren't there, because I guess it had been embarrassing. They dragged a lot of people downtown and took photographs of them, and just made it kind of rough for them." The power of the law was not likely to be underestimated or idealized by this group of women, since some of them had spent time in reform schools before turning eighteen.

Conclusion

Lesbian history provides a new perspective on women in the 1930s and '40s. It highlights that World War II not only provided jobs for women, but created a social atmosphere which encouraged women's independence. More women could socialize together outside of the home without endangering their reputations. They also could decide how they would spend their money, using it for leisure as well as necessities. In addition, the absence of sixteen million men actually made work and neighborhoods safer and more congenial for women. These changes were instrumental in the movement of white lesbian social life from private networks to bars in the 1940s.

In a middle-sized, industrial, northern city like Buffalo, the Black lesbian community did not make the shift into bars until later, and then never completely. However, the meaning of the categories "lesbian," "homosexual," or "gay" crossed racial boundaries. Individual Black lesbians occasionally went to predominantly white lesbian and gay bars in Buffalo. But the power of racism and of their own ethnic traditions interacted to keep their social life more based in private networks. For the development of a public lesbian community, a city has to be large enough to provide some form of anonymity to lesbians when they are out socializing. Until the surge in growth of Buffalo's Black population in the 1940s, the city could not offer anonymity to Black lesbians. Because of this, many Black lesbians spent time in New York City, where they went to bars in Harlem and Greenwich Village. Though Black lesbians in Buffalo during the 1940s, like white lesbians, were not unaware of nor unaffected by the changes occurring nationally in bar life, Buffalo was not yet safe enough for taking the risks to either patronize white bars or have their own.

The white lesbian community in the 1940s already had many of the characteristics we associate today with lesbian social life. Distinct from gay male social life, it was located primarily in bars and did not make extensive use of public parks and beaches for meeting others and making sexual contacts. In our view, the concentration of lesbian social life in bars derives from the danger lesbians faced as women in a patriarchal culture based on the sexual availability of women for men.[47] Lesbians required a protected environment to pursue sexual relations with women, otherwise they would be assumed to be prostitutes looking for men, or would risk being raped by men for stepping out of line. The need for protection is a central theme in lesbian history and emerged repeatedly throughout our research.

In addition, lesbian bar life was notably homogeneous, giving little encouragement to cross-class sexual or social interaction. The lack of eroticization of class difference is particularly striking given that lesbian sexual culture was based on the eroticization of the difference between masculine and feminine. It is perhaps lesbians' interest in relationships as well as sex that makes the eroticization of class difference less compelling.

During the 1940s, lesbians began to develop a common culture, community, and consciousness, as evidenced by their working together to find new bars or to picket Ralph Martin's, and by their formation of strong friendship groups that lasted a lifetime. These groups explored what it meant to be lesbian, talked about the difficulties they faced as well as the fun, and supported one another to develop plans and strategies for working and maintaining relationships with families while still socializing as lesbians. Lesbians whose social life was based completely on private networks did not have to consider these issues.

By coming together in public places, lesbians began to challenge the sexist and homophobic structures of U.S. society. They expanded the possibilities for women to live independent lives away from their families and without men. They made it easier for lesbians to find others like themselves and to develop a sense of camaraderie and support. They also increased public awareness of the existence of lesbians, as more people became familiar with gay bars. This movement for acceptance was nevertheless limited. The strategy of complete separation of work and family life from social life did not challenge the attitudes and behaviors of employers, and only gave families a minimal awareness of lesbians' existence. As working-class women who had grown up in the Depression, they were painfully aware of the ravages of unemployment and felt the need for family support. Their strategies pushed to the maximum what was possible at the time while still maintaining the means to earn a living and the connections to their families. Although they did not dramatically change sexism and homophobia, they did begin to mitigate the disastrous effects of individual isolation and feelings of worthlessness. In doing this, they set the stage for increasing solidarity and consciousness that could lead to a political movement in the future.

Acknowledgments

"'I Could Hardly Wait to Get Back to that Bar': Lesbian Bar Culture in Buffalo in the 1930s and 1940s" is chapter 2 of Elizabeth Lapovsky Kennedy and Madeline D. Davis's *Boots of Leather, Slippers of Gold: The History of a Lesbian Community* (New York: Routledge, 1993). The book documents the development of lesbian communities in Buffalo, New York from 1930 through 1960 and explores the connection between these communities and the emergence of the gay liberation movement. We would like to thank Brett Beemyn for valuing our work and insisting that it be included in *Creating a Place for Ourselves.*

Notes

1. Useful studies of straight bar life include Sherri Cavan, *Liquor License: An Ethnography of Bar Behavior* (Chicago: Aldine, 1966) and Julian B. Roebuck and Wolfgang Frese, *The Rendezvous: A Case Study of an After-Hours Club* (New York: The Free Press, 1976).
2. Radclyffe Hall, *The Well of Loneliness* (1928; London: Transworld Publishers, Corgi Books, 1974), 439–53. It is possible that, at the time Hall was writing, bars

were not centers of resistance. It is also possible that class factors shaped Hall's portrayal of bars. It might have been difficult for an upper-class woman to be part of a working-class culture of resistance.

3. See, for instance, Ann Bannon, *Odd Girl Out* (New York: Fawcett, 1957), *I Am a Woman* (New York: Fawcett, 1959), *Women in the Shadows* (New York: Fawcett, 1959), *Journey to a Woman* (New York: Fawcett, 1960), and *Beebo Brinker* (New York: Fawcett, 1962); Ann Aldrich, *We Walk Alone* (New York: Fawcett, 1955), and *We Too Must Love* (New York: Fawcett, 1958).
4. Nancy B. Achilles, *The Homosexual Bar*, M.A. Thesis, University of Chicago, 1964.
5. Ethel Sawyer, *A Study of a Public Lesbian Community*, M.A. Thesis, Sociology-Anthropology Honors Essay Series, Washington University, St. Louis, 1965.
6. Kathy Peiss uses the concept of heterosocial to parallel the concept of homosocial. The latter means a social life organized around one sex, the former a social life organized around the interactions of men and women. Kathy Peiss, *Cheap Amusements: Working Women and Leisure in Turn-of-the-Century New York* (Philadelphia: Temple University Press, 1986), 183–84. Her use of the term "heterosocial" is helpful because it highlights just how gender and class interacted to create heterosexual culture as we know it today, and thus contributes to an understanding that heterosexuality, as well as homosexuality, is created. For further discussion of this topic, see Jonathan Ned Katz, "The Invention of Heterosexuality," *Socialist Review* 20.1 (February 1990): 7–34.
7. Peiss, *Cheap Amusements*, 114.
8. Ibid., 28–29.
9. Allan Bérubé, *Coming Out Under Fire: The History of Gay Men and Women in World War Two* (New York: The Free Press, 1990), 113.
10. "Women Drinking at Bars Declared Cause of Vice," *Buffalo Courier-Express*, February 27, 1944, sect. 5, 1, and "City Will Ask Legislation Banning Girls from Bars," *Buffalo Courier-Express*, February 29, 1944, 1.
11. John D'Emilio, "Gay Politics and Community in San Francisco Since World War II," in *Hidden From History: Reclaiming the Gay and Lesbian Past*, eds. Martin Bauml Duberman, Martha Vicinus, and George Chauncey, Jr. (New York: New American Library, 1989), 458–59; John D'Emilio, *Sexual Politics, Sexual Communities: The Making of a Homosexual Minority in the United States, 1940–1970* (Chicago: University of Chicago Press, 1983), 22–39; and Bérubé, *Coming Out Under Fire*, 98–127.
12. Bérubé, *Coming Out Under Fire*, 126.
13. For figures on the size of the women's branches of the service in 1943, see Bérubé, *Coming Out Under Fire*, 28; and D'Emilio, *Sexual Politics, Sexual Communities*, 29.
14. The process of identity formation is quite complex and is dealt with in detail in chapter 9 of our book, *Boots of Leather, Slippers of Gold: The History of a Lesbian Community*.
15. After hours of microfilm research, we were not able to find any mention of these raids in the newspaper.
16. Susan Ware writes: "During the 1930s, women's softball and basketball teams flourished." Susan Ware, *Holding Their Own: American Women in the 1930s* (Boston: Twayne, 1988), 174.
17. The daughter of a well-known local sports figure shared with us her mother's photo collection that included pictures of Eddie's. The daughter suspects that her

mother was a lesbian but she lived a heterosexual life. She also has good reason to suspect that many of her mother's friends were lesbians.

18. The reasons for the difference will be discussed later in the essay.
19. Butch consciousness and fem consciousness were somewhat different, as is discussed throughout *Boots of Leather, Slippers of Gold.*
20. Our analysis is consistent with and furthers that of D'Emilio, *Sexual Politics, Sexual Communities*, 29; for another discussion of lesbians and World War II, see Lillian Faderman, *Odd Girls and Twilight Lovers: A History of Lesbian Life in Twentieth-Century America* (New York: Columbia University Press, 1991), 118–38.
21. According to Allan Bérubé in a phone conversation, February 1989, the WACS paid less than jobs in defense industries, about $20 per month plus room and board.
22. Allan Bérubé mentions the discreet male bars at posh hotels in the downtown section of major metropolitan centers like "the Astor Bar in New York's Times Square, the Top of the Mark at the Mark Hopkins in San Francisco, and the Biltmore men's bar just off Pershing Square in Los Angeles" (*Coming Out Under Fire*, 114). This is an example of a discreet women's bar in a downtown hotel. Although Eddie Ryan's Niagara Hotel was not as elegant as the Mark Hopkins, it was respectable.
23. This fact contradicts the findings of Nancy Achilles in her early study of the homosexual bar in San Francisco. She says that "[h]omosexuals rarely infiltrate an already established bar and make it their own, a gay bar is gay from the beginning" (*The Homosexual Bar*, 65). It could be that San Francisco was different from Buffalo. It is also possible that she was using a framework that did not encourage her to assign full agency to gays and lesbians, and therefore hid homosexuals' activity on their own behalf.
24. The relevant law is Subdivision 6, Section 106 of the New York State Alcoholic Beverage Control Laws. From *New York Consolidated Laws Service, Annotated Statutes with Forms*, vol. 1, 1976, c. 1950. We are grateful to George Chauncey for clarifying our understanding of the law (telephone conversation, January 1989).
25. We had difficulty in finding information on the activities of the State Liquor Authority in Buffalo during this period. Our information comes from a telephone conversation with George Chauncey, January 23, 1989. According to his research on gays in New York City, the State Liquor Authority was very punitive. In the 1940s and '50s, the legal strategy of most bar owners was to deny the presence of homosexuals. They did not fight the policies of the State Liquor Authority until the 1960s. Chauncey's findings have been published in *Gay New York: Gender, Urban Culture, and the Making of the Gay Male World, 1890–1940* (New York: Basic Books, 1994).
26. According to George Chauncey, most of the gay and lesbian bars in New York City had some relationship to the Mafia (telephone conversation, January 1989). The reason for this difference awaits further research.
27. This view is backed up by evidence of some conflict between the State Liquor Authority and the Buffalo Police in 1944. See "State Cancels Liquor Permit of Night Spot," *Buffalo Courier-Express*, April 7, 1944, 11.
28. After hours of microfilm research, we were unable to find a reference to this raid in newspapers.
29. In the 1940s, the mayor ordered all taverns and bowling alleys to close at 11 p.m. due to fuel shortages. This must have increased the popularity of after-hours clubs. *Buffalo Courier-Express*, February 2, 1945, 1.

30. In this essay, we use the terms Black, white, and Indian, rather than African-American, European-American, and Native American to indicate the significant racial/ethnic groups in Buffalo. The latter terms are more appropriate analytically and reflect the thinking of the past twenty years on the subject. But the former terms are the ones used by our narrators; since this work draws so heavily on oral history narratives, we have decided to use the language of the narrators.
31. These parties were not necessarily all Black. Debra had a racially mixed group of friends and often went to mixed parties. A white woman's desire for discretion could have led her to socialize primarily at small parties, rather than at bars.
32. These two women were friends and were not gay, but "were making money on the gay girls" (Arden).
33. The population of Buffalo Blacks was 4,511 in 1920; 13,563 in 1930; 17,694 in 1940; 36,745 in 1950; and 70,904 in 1960. Henry L. Taylor, Jr., ed., *African Americans and the Rise of Buffalo's Post-Industrial City, 1940 to the Present*, vol. 2 (Buffalo: Urban League, 1990), 23.
34. For a discussion of race relations in Buffalo, see Lillian Serece Williams, *The Development of a Black Community: Buffalo, New York, 1900–1940*, Ph.D. diss., SUNY/Buffalo, 1978; Lillian Serece Williams, "To Elevate the Race: The Michigan Avenue YMCA and the Advancement of Blacks in Buffalo, New York, 1922–40," in *New Perspectives on Black Educational History*, eds. Vincent P. Franklin and James D. Anderson (Boston: G. K. Hall, 1978), 129–48; Ralph Richard Watkins, *Black Buffalo, 1920–1927*, Ph.D. diss., SUNY/Buffalo, 1978; and Niles Carpenter, "Nationality, Color and Economic Opportunity in the City of Buffalo," *The University of Buffalo Studies* 5 (1926–27): 95–194.
35. Reggie, who spent several years in New York City during the 1940s, remembers that bars in Greenwich Village were racially mixed. Bérubé, *Coming Out Under Fire*, 116–17, reports racially mixed bars in New York and Chicago, which suggests that desegregation of the gay community occurred earlier in large metropolitan centers.
36. St. Clair Drake and Horace R. Cayton, *Black Metropolis: A Study of Negro Life in a Northern City* (1945; New York: Harper and Row, 1962), 608–09; and David Lewis, *When Harlem Was in Vogue* (New York: Vintage, 1982), 107, mention rent parties that were open to the public and attended by lesbians.
37. Half of the narrators for this period finished high school and half did not. "Working-class" is probably not the term narrators would use to designate themselves today, because it now has derogatory connotations, and in general they feel proud of who they are.
38. See Esther Newton, "Sex and Sensibility, Social Science and the Idea of Lesbian Community," unpublished paper, for a provocative discussion of homogeneity in the lesbian community today. She relates the diversity in the gay male community to its sexual institutions—fuck bars, baths, tearooms, cruising areas, and all-male porn movie houses—and suggests that the eroticization of power differences might undermine as well as uphold power structures.
39. The Deco Restaurants were popular coffee shops in the Buffalo area that advertised "Buffalo's best cup of coffee." They served low-priced meals and were "hangouts" for students, neighborhood residents, and workers.
40. The term "the club" was used in the 1950s and, we suspect, also in the 1940s to denote gay and lesbian bars without having to specifically name them. This method was employed prior to the advent of gay liberation and may still be used by some today.

41. According to narrators who had some knowledge of prostitution, it was common for women who became involved in a prostitution ring to work a circuit that included Pennsylvania, Ohio, Washington, D.C., and West Virginia. They would work in a different house each week and would be off the week they were menstruating.
42. Our narrators think that the famous Erie, Pennsylvania annual gay summer picnic might have started as early as the mid-1940s.
43. See, for instance, Williams, *The Development of a Black Community*; Carpenter, "Nationality, Color, and Economic Opportunity in the City of Buffalo"; Chester W. Gregory, *Women in Defense Work during World War II* (New York: Exposition Press, 1974); U.S. Department of Labor, "Women Workers in Ten War Production Areas and Their Postwar Employment Plans," *Women's Bureau Bulletin* 209, 1946; and U.S. Department of Labor, "Negro Women War Workers," *Women's Bureau Bulletin* 205, 1945.
44. Sending a daughter to jail was relatively uncommon in the community during the 1940s, and putting a daughter into a mental institution was unheard of. Not one narrator knew anyone who had been hospitalized. In part, this had to do with the working-class suspicion of psychiatrists, but also the working class did not trust state institutions with their children.
45. This raises the possibility that Black families, even if they disapprove of a member's gayness, continue to value, or at least be loyal to, that member despite his or her choice of lifestyle. Thomas B. Romney, "Homophobia in the Black Community," *Blacklight* 1 (1980): 4, argues exactly this point. He states that homophobia is strong in the Black community, yet individual Black families "tend to be very accepting of family members who identify themselves as sexual minorities." In contrast, most Black lesbian intellectuals write about the severity of the oppression of lesbians in the Black community. See, for instance, S. Diane Bogus, "The Black Lesbian," *Blacklight* 1 (September/October 1980): 8; Evelyn C. White, "Comprehensive Oppression, Lesbians and Race in the Work of Ann Allen Shockley," *Backbone* 3 (1981): 38–40; Ann Allen Shockley, "The Black Lesbian in American Literature: An Overview," *Conditions* 5 (1979): 132–42; Anita Cornwall, *The Black Lesbian in White America* (Tallahassee: Naiad Press, 1983), 5–34; Audre Lorde, "Scratching the Surface: Some Barriers to Women and Loving," in *Sister Outsider: Essays and Speeches by Audre Lorde* (Trumansburg, NY: Crossing Press, 1984), 45–52; and Cheryl Clarke, "The Failure to Transform: Homophobia in the Black Community," in *Home Girls: A Black Feminist Anthology*, ed. Barbara Smith (New York: Kitchen Table: Women of Color Press, 1983), 197–208. The Black narrators of the 1950s hold divergent opinions on whether the Black community is more accepting of homosexuality than the white. Some are adamant that it is, while some think it is even more oppressive than the white community. Perhaps the approach of separating the community view from the actions of individual families helps to explain these differing points of view. Perhaps different churches also foster different views.
46. For this narrator, a "lesbian" is a "butch." Her conceptual system is explored more fully in chapter 9 of *Boots of Leather, Slippers of Gold.*
47. We are indebted to Judy Grahn's *Another Mother Tongue: Gay Words, Gay Worlds* (Boston: Beacon Press, 1984), 207–11, for pointing out vividly how much lesbian social life is affected by the male objectification of women.

3. "Homos Invade S.F.!"

San Francisco's History as a Wide-Open Town

Nan Alamilla Boyd

> Why, you might wonder, does San Francisco in particular have such a dense population (relatively speaking) of those "social outcasts"—transvestites, transsexuals and homosexuals? San Francisco, after all, has deservedly been called the gay capital of the United States.
>
> —*Sun West* (1968)

> You've got to remember that San Francisco, dating back to its Gold Rush days, has always been known for its tolerance. That's what drew all these people here—its liberalism and its acceptance of everything. Everything and everyone.
>
> —Reba Hudson

"HOMOS INVADE S.F." blares the July 11, 1949 headline of *The Truth*, a short-lived sensationalist San Francisco newspaper. The article claims that "San Francisco is rapidly becoming a central gathering-point for lesbians and homo-sexuals [sic] in California" and insists that San Francisco lawmakers withdraw the welcome mat reading, "HOMO-SEXUALS AND LESBIANS WELCOME TO SAN FRANCISCO—HALF-A-DOZEN CENTERS AVAILABLE FOR YOUR USE—YOU MAY FREQUENT WITHOUT MOLESTATION COUNTLESS THEATERS AND PARKS—WE CATER TO YOUR NEEDS." In a lurid style popular with anti-vice news journals, the front-page article describes San Francisco's thriving homosexual underworld, identifying theaters, show-houses, and parks that have become "a sexual cess-pool" where old men "prey largely not on their own kind but on the very young and the very innocent." The article asks, "City Fathers, are you going to do something about it?" and challenges the city's police department to shut down San Francisco's homosexual "liquor-joints," clean up the parks, and build "psychiatric centers to rehabilitate, where possible, and institutionalize, where not, the homo-sexuals and lesbians who clutter up our streets."[1]

In a field with few written sources, scandal sheets like this are often an historian's best guide to San Francisco's queer urban history because they frequently listed the bars, taverns, parks, and theaters that catered to "sex deviates" and "homo-sexuals."[2] But scandal sheets, yellow journalism, and political broadsides functioned at cross-purposes, decrying the decadence of an incumbent administration, for instance, and rallying anti-vice/anti-homosexual coalitions, while advertising and, in many ways, producing knowledge about the city's queer social geography. In other words, anti-vice scandal sheets publicized San Francisco's reputation for vice while they worked to undercut it. And although these sources remain speculative, they reveal a tension between reputation and reality, openness and repression that raises a number of questions about San Francisco's queer urban history. Were homosexuals really "invading" San Francisco in the post-World War II era? Did San Francisco, as the above article suggests, welcome sex and gender "deviates" to its shores? Was San Francisco different from other U.S. cities or unique in its function as a destination point or "mecca" for gay men, lesbians, bisexuals, and the transgendered? When and why did San Francisco become an important city in lesbian and gay history?

Recent scholarship positions World War II as a watershed in U.S. lesbian and gay history. San Francisco stands out as emblematic of this shift in that, as John D'Emilio and Allan Bérubé explain, it served as a port of demobilization for GIs who served in the war's Pacific Theater. This meant that servicemen and women who had homosexual experiences during the war and did not want to return home might more often choose San Francisco for their new residence. Also, a larger proportion of ex-military homosexuals may have remained in San Francisco because homosexual purges in the armed forces (which increased towards the end of the war) often deposited large numbers of dishonorably discharged servicemen and women, "sometimes hundreds at a time," in the city, where many stayed "to carve out a new gay life."[3] While these facts remain integral to understanding the development of San Francisco's gay and lesbian communities and mark the impact of World War II on the city's growth, this essay seeks to broaden the scope of San Francisco's gay and lesbian history by looking beyond World War II for information about how and why San Francisco became a target for national and, later, international queer migrations. What, specifically, was it about San Francisco that earned the city its reputation as a gay capital? When did this reputation begin?

This essay argues that San Francisco's function as a gay capital is a relatively recent and culturally specific phenomenon. Through the twentieth century, San Francisco shifted from being a "haven for sex deviates" to a gay mecca and later, a gay capital.[4] In this essay, I use the phrase "gay mecca" to imply both a place and a process whereby San Francisco's North Beach, Polk Street, and Castro Street neighborhoods (along with New Orleans's French Quarter and New York City's Greenwich Village) evolved through the first half of the twentieth century as targets in a specifically gay and lesbian geography that attracted gay and lesbian tourists and migrants.[5] I distinguish "mecca" from "capital" in that while other cities continued to function as gay meccas, San Francisco grew to be a distinct and unique center for lesbian and gay culture and political organizing in the United States through the late 1960s and '70s. This essay traces the shift from "haven" to "mecca" and "capital" by aligning "haven" with San Francisco's nineteenth-century queer history of sex and gender nonconformity and "mecca/capital" with the emergence of San Francisco's mid-twentieth-century lesbian and gay communities. Certainly, these histories overlap rather than replace or supersede each other; nevertheless, through the mid-twentieth century, as an effect of postwar demographics, the city's reputation as a gay mecca and, later, a gay capital sharpened around a successful minority-based discourse of civil rights and sexual identity.

Traces of this shift appear in the popular press's iconographic use of queer vernacular terms. In 1955, for example, *Men* magazine ran an article on San Francisco entitled "Don't Call Us Queer City," which described the city's anti-homosexual police details, underscoring its reputation as a haven for homosexuals and "sex deviates." This publication reached a wider audience than local broadsides, illustrating San Francisco's growing national reputation as, indeed, a "queer city."[6] A decade later, Guy Strait, the publisher of several local gay newspapers, playfully dubbed San Francisco "Queen City of the West,"[7] and in 1967, *Confidential* magazine, with a circulation of over 300,000, ran an article on San Francisco's National Homophile Planning Conference, noting that this "Queen City" had attracted an estimated 10,000 gay visitors to the event.[8] In these instances, the descriptive terms remained within the vernacular, associating San Francisco with a culture of gender and sexual transgression ("queer," "queen") rather than medical pathology ("invert," "deviate," "homosexual," "lesbian") or civil rights or liberation movements ("homophile," "gay").

Through the 1970s, however, the idea of San Francisco as a gay mecca—a place where lesbians and gay men migrated to be with other lesbians and gay men—had taken hold. In April 1970, for example, *San Francisco* magazine published a sympathetic and informative article appropriately entitled "The Gay Mecca."[9] Here, a semantic shift balances "homosexual," the official, non-vernacular term, against "gay," the vernacular term of sexual liberation. The article stated that while "San Francisco is still no utopia for homosexuals," homophile activism, gay liberation, and negotiated police relations advertised San Francisco as a relatively gay-friendly environment and, thus, a popular destination point for gay migrants. "Homosexuals come here from all over the country," explained Tom Maurer, who in 1970 surveyed over 1,000 gay and lesbian San Franciscans for the Institute for Sexual Research.[10] Moreover, as another 1970 publication noted, "[c]andidates for the city's Board of Supervisors make their pitch for the homosexual vote, estimated by some at 90,000," illustrating San Francisco's critical mass of lesbian and gay migrants as well as their imminent political power.[11]

The politicization of San Francisco's gay and lesbian communities in the 1960s and '70s raises questions about the impact of queer mobility and migration on the city's self-definition. How did gay and lesbian migration transform San Francisco? How did migration transform migrants? Did mobility and the construction of a city of migrants have an impact on the emergence of visible, self-actualized, and political gay and lesbian communities? More broadly, how did San Francisco's history of sex tourism and queer migration shape its patterns of accommodation and repression, its incorporation (or not) of lesbians and gay men into the body politic? This essay argues that queer migration and the politicization of San Francisco's lesbian and gay communities emerge from the city's reputation for vice and its history as a "wide-open town." The city's nineteenth-century boom-town entertainments and its turn-of-the-century tourist economies constructed a popular image of San Francisco as a haven or refuge for sex- and gender-nonconformists. In order to document the relationship between reputation, tourism, and migration, I focus on the post-Prohibition emergence of queer public space in the city's North Beach district. As a bohemian enclave, North Beach sat at the juncture of nineteenth-century influences and, through the 1930s, promoted a tourist economy that brought gender-transgressive and "homosexualized" entertainments into the public sphere. North Beach, as a result, linked San Francisco's nineteenth-century reputation as a wide-open town to its twentieth-century queer cultures and nascent political communities.

The Construction of a Reputation: Gold Rush Migrations and the Barbary Coast

Through the nineteenth century, San Francisco emerged as a vibrant, opulent, cosmopolitan city with a reputation for licentious entertainment and tourist trade, and its North Beach district sat at the center of these images and effects. In fact, at the start of the Gold Rush in 1849, a colony of Mexican and South American prostitutes settled on the southeastern slopes of Telegraph Hill (the centerpiece of San Francisco's North Beach neighborhoods), forming the nucleus of what was to become the Barbary Coast.[12] And while the Gold Rush made San Francisco a destination for transnational and transcontinental migrants, its nineteenth-century history of persistent lawlessness, boss politics, and administrative graft solidified its reputation as a wide-open town. Through the second half of the nineteenth century, however, periods of extraordinary economic growth stimulated anti-vice campaigns which played out the tension between San Francisco's reputation for vice and the reality of periodic purges. Most famous are the Vigilance Committees of 1851 and 1856, which followed on the heels of Gold Rush prosperity, price inflation, and exponential population growth.[13] Arguing that city police could not protect citizens' "security to life and property" and promising that "no thief, burglar, incendiary or assassin, shall escape punishment," the Vigilance Committee of 1851 executed three men during its ten-day tenure.[14] It also demanded heightened regulation of the in-migration of "undesirables," linking law and order with border control.

The revival of the Vigilantes in 1856 stemmed more directly from the association of sex and lawlessness. The 1856 Committee was organized initially to ensure the speedy trial and execution of two men accused of killing James King (of William), the owner of an anti-vice daily, *The Evening Bulletin.* Before his death, King had crusaded against police corruption in his daily editorials, but he aimed his most caustic attacks against gambling and its associated evil, prostitution, which he saw as the city's foundational weaknesses. While Vigilante action diminished after the 1850s, San Francisco's history repeats a pattern of anti-vice crusades, particularly during election years, that called for the protection of property through the regulation of borders and the control of sexual capital through the regulation of brothels and "bawdy houses." Ironically, periods of anti-vice activism—the 1850s, 1870s, 1910s, and 1950s—produced a wealth of print material that advertised and drew international attention to San Francisco's vice districts, particularly North Beach and its infamous Barbary Coast.

The Barbary Coast was the entertainment district for San Francisco's gold digging migrants. Through the second half of the nineteenth century, the economic boom from gold and even more lucrative silver mining attracted a steady stream of single men to the California foothills and Sierras, and the vast immigration of miners, speculators, and merchants to San Francisco created a city of bachelors.[15] This, compounded by the fact that San Francisco functioned as a port city—its economy trafficked through the Golden Gate—meant that the city sustained large transient populations who were less likely to conform to social rules and regulations.[16] San Francisco's architecture and city planning, particularly its streets lined with boarding houses and one-room flats, also reflected a bachelor existence and lodging-house culture.[17] In fact, the Montgomery Block Building, an immense North Beach rooming house (which, upon completion in 1853, was the largest building west of the Mississippi River), would figure importantly in San Francisco's post-World War II bohemian revival for many of the same reasons it was built: to provide housing for the city's migrant, tourist, and pleasure-seeking populations.[18] All this meant that a permissive quality of life evolved around bachelor entertainments, and the Barbary Coast, "that section of San Francisco where the unattached men were concentrated," filled with licentious distractions, enhancing San Francisco's reputation as "the gayest, lightest-hearted, most pleasure-loving city on the Western continent."[19]

The Barbary Coast emerged in the 1860s around the dilapidated storefronts on what was San Francisco's most important commercial thoroughfare during the initial years of the Gold Rush. This was Pacific Street, between the waterfront and Kearney, or "Terrific Street," as it was called in the 1890s. The Barbary Coast came to be known as San Francisco's roughest vice district, "the haunt of the low and the vile of every kind," an indignant historian reported in 1876. "The petty thief, the house burglar, the tramp, the whoremonger, lewd women, cut-throats, murderers, all are found here."[20] Contributing to its reputation, the Barbary Coast hosted a battery of cheap amusements: groggeries with sawdust-covered floors, wine and beer dens (also known as "deadfalls"), melodeons (liquor dens with mechanical music boxes), dance halls, and concert saloons.

Barbary Coast entertainments catered to single men who had money to spend, and although an early 1870s city ordinance forbade the employment of women in dance halls and saloons, most Barbary Coast establishments hired women to sell liquor and dances to men, to prostitute themselves, and, more generally, to separate patrons from their money.[21] While the smallest grog houses and deadfalls hired only a handful of women, larger dance halls and concert saloons employed up to fifty women. These enterprising women, called "pretty waiter girls," earned a weekly wage of fifteen to twenty-five dollars, a commission on the liquor and dances they sold, and often half the proceeds of their own prostitution, netting up to fifty dollars a week.[22] The Barbary Coast also housed a number of up-scale brothels where "Madams," who enjoyed a relatively high status in San Francisco's social circles, ran the business end of things, and employees earned considerably more—up to $200 a week.[23] In fact, prostitution was so central to Barbary Coast amusements that when Progressive Era legislation shut down its brothels in 1917, the Barbary Coast collapsed.

The rise and fall of the Barbary Coast foretold the story of post-Prohibition entertainments and the emergence of queer public space in that the tension between vice and regulation, highlighted in the press, advertised San Francisco's nighttime entertainments even while it worked to curb and control them. For instance, after the earthquake and fire of 1906 burned the Barbary Coast to the ground, it resurfaced anew—and bigger—at the same time that a renewed sense of civic pride pressured police to quell violence on the waterfront and clean up the city's vice districts. As a result, the Barbary Coast became something of a tourist strip, a slummer's paradise, with cleaned-up entertainments and variety shows designed to shock rather than repulse. Through the early 1900s, the Barbary Coast thus gained a wider appeal and its large dance halls drew tremendous crowds. It was here, Herbert Asbury claims, that the most popular dances of this era—the turkey trot, the bunny hug, the chicken glide, and the pony prance—originated. And proprietors, "in direct violation of the ancient code of the Barbary Coast," did their best to protect slumming tourists from theft and harassment.[24]

By 1913, however, Progressive Era anti-vice campaigns found their way to San Francisco. William Randolph Hearst's *Examiner* ran a series of full-page anti-vice editorials calling Barbary Coast corruption a product of police graft and civic inefficiency—at once announcing vice districts and ostensibly condemning them. Smarting from Hearst's attacks and pressured by a new anti-vice mayor, the Police Commission responded with a series of city ordinances aimed at shutting down the Barbary Coast.[25] They prohibited dancing where liquor was sold and forbade women patrons and employees in the areas bordered by Clay and Stockton Streets, effectively siphoning liquor revenue from the North Beach districts. The end of the Barbary Coast came in 1917, after the California Supreme Court upheld the State Legislature's 1914 Red-Light Abatement Act and San Francisco police blockaded the Barbary Coast, ordering prostitutes to vacate the area. Finally, on February 14th, "the red-light district was deserted; eighty-three brothels had been closed and 1,073 women had been driven from their quarters."[26] Still, many of San Francisco's brothels persisted through the 1920s, as did gambling houses and speakeasies, and the repeal of Prohibition in 1933 revived the city's well-known reputation for vice and sex tourism.

Bohemian North Beach and Queer Public Space

In the post-Prohibition era, San Francisco regained its reputation as a wide-open town because, as the city's economy and population diversified, its much-touted tolerance for cultural difference or "the exotic" became its calling card. Through the first half of the twentieth century, tourists flocked to San Francisco to enjoy its temperate climate and spectacular scenery, but the most popular attractions were the exotic cultural experiences and lascivious entertainments a daring tourist might enjoy.[27] Most famous, of course, was Chinatown. Only a few blocks up from Market Street, Chinatown became one of the first stops in excursions through the city, and in the 1940s, regular sightseeing tours rambled through several Chinatown nightspots such as "The Ricksha" and Charlie Low's "Forbidden City."[28]

Adjacent to Chinatown was the equally vibrant Italian section. One guidebook called Grant Avenue, the main artery that ran between Chinatown and Little Italy, "perhaps the most interesting street in the United States."[29] It was here, on the border of two densely populated and culturally distinct neighborhoods, that a thriving "bohemian" nightlife developed. Intermingled with Italians, especially in the low-rent Telegraph Hill area, were a number of unconventional artist households where a certain measure of youthful exuberance and sexual freedom mocked the ambitions of middle-class San Franciscans. "You don't think all those people who live in neat little houses with daisy bushes in the front—all those thousands and thousands of hard-working San Franciscans—are like the people on Telegraph Hill, do you?" asks the protagonist of a breathy travel novel. "Don't you know," she continues, "that a Californian (my kind, I mean) never talks about his soul, or a purpose in life, or any of those things? It makes him uneasy."[30] It was in this context, in San Francisco's North Beach neighborhoods, that the city's first publicly visible queer communities began to develop.

Bohemian attitudes and lifestyles thus stretched back through the nineteenth-century and emerged from a unique blend of "sinful" mining camp traditions and unconventional artistic expression, and in the Post-Prohibition Era, San Francisco's bohemian traditions forged a foundation for the emergence of the city's queer subcultures. According to Lucius Beebe, a popular travel writer and food critic for *Holiday Magazine* and *The New Yorker*, not since the city's "preconflagration grandeur has San Francisco's night life achieved the fever pitch it now boasts." He claimed that the old Barbary Coast, "long mourned as a wistful souvenir of vanished and happier times, is having a revival which would bug the eyes of Manhattanites." Marking a contrast between New York's post-Prohibition nightlife and San Francisco's, Beebe chronicled North Beach's flamboyant entertainments and described a number of restaurants and night clubs "frequented by dinner-jacketed slummers."[31] Of particular note, in his opinion, were two nightclubs: Mona's barrel house and Finocchio's, where "nothing—but utterly nothing—is barred."[32] Not unknown to Beebe and, perhaps, his most discerning readers was the fact that both Mona's and Finocchio's were places where local bohemians and voyeuristic tourists could catch cross-gender drag shows. Mona's, in particular, was one of the most popular bohemian clubs in North Beach, and by the late 1930s, it had become infamously known as the first lesbian nightclub in San Francisco.[33]

In many ways Mona's owner, Mona Hood, personified the intersection between San Francisco's bohemian cultures and its nascent queer communities. "We [bohemians] are not offended at how the other fellow lives, that's why I was a true bohemian," Mona proudly recalls.[34] In 1929, she was nineteen years old and living in the "Monkey Block," the aforementioned block-long residential building on Montgomery Street between Washington and Jackson. Because it was cheap and in North Beach's bohemian section, the Monkey Block attracted a number of writers, painters, and local artists. For a few dollars a month, one could rent a small room with a hot plate, bring in a bed, and set up a small studio. The building became a central meeting place for local bohemians, and those who lived elsewhere often kept a studio there "for their fun place."[35] As Mona remembers, "when anybody had a birthday or anything important we locked the front door. We had our own crowd in there—there was musicians also. We moved the piano out and danced up and around the hall."[36] Despite the stock market crash and subsequent Depression years, the building's residents enjoyed semi-communal living through the 1930s, and as Mona recalls, "nobody felt bad about having little money because everybody shared."[37]

Mona was young, charming, and very popular, so in 1933 with the end of Prohibition, a friend offered Mona a loan to establish her own club:

> I opened it up right away. A man [who] knew [my then-husband] Jim and me knew that I knew from living in the Monkey Block all kinds of kids and artists and writers mostly that were struggling there. He said, "Well, Mona knows everybody . . ." You know it only took about five hundred dollars, which was like five thousand now. But the man said, "I'll loan you the money that you need." I said, "Well, I don't know," . . . [but] the guy said, "No, I've got the money. I'll start you out." I don't even remember the man's name, but I knew he died a few years later. He was always just a nice person. He just thought, he had money and it would be a cute thing since things were legal. He liked me, he thought I was a, well he called me "the kid." Everybody was older than me. I was about 23 but going on 18 or something.[38]

On December 3, 1933, "Mona's" opened at the foot of Telegraph Hill. Originally intended as a hangout for her artist friends, Mona's gained a reputation for its unconventionality, and it soon became one of San Francisco's hot spots. "Bohemia! How that fascinating word has been abused, until now it hardly stands for anything more than the Pseudo artistic," one reviewer exclaimed. "But once in a blue moon we run across something that fits the word so aptly that we just must use it in all sincerity. Such is Mona's at 451 Union street."[39]

In 1935, Mona's relocated to 140 Columbus Avenue in the basement of what would later become the Purple Onion. Locally known as "Mona's barrel house," it was in this location that Mona's became a nightclub—her lesbian waitresses started singing show tunes, and campy male impersonation shows soon followed. By 1939, Mona's had moved again, to 440 Broadway, where it gained even more notoriety as an overt lesbian nightclub, and in Mona's words, "girls came in!"[40] Mona's club ran (at various locations) from 1933 to 1957, and it became one of the first public spaces where butch and fem lesbians could find each other outside of a tightly regulated network of formal introductions. Both butches and fems dressed in men's clothing and performed, singing campy show songs to each other and, often, to crowds of tourists. As Jack Lord and Jenn Shaw's *Where to Sin in San Francisco*, a Beatnik guidebook, noted in its 1939 edition, cross-dressed entertainers performed from 4 P.M. to 2 A.M.[41] A group of favorite performers such as Kay Scott, Beverly Shaw, and Gladys Bentley became well known in San Francisco, and these women set the stage for the evolution of lesbian bar culture and public life in the city through the postwar period.[42]

Like the Barbary Coast, as Mona's became more popular, it drew the attention of San Francisco's tourist industry. Mona's was listed in hotel magazines such as *San Francisco Life*, and Herb Caen, a leading columnist for the *Examiner*, often favored her in his columns.[43] *Where to Sin in San Francisco* characterized Mona's as a "Boy-Girl" bar where "The little girl waitresses look like boys . . . and many of the little girl customers look like boys." The accompanying cartoon graphic, featuring a pair of cigar-smoking, cross-dressing women with the caption "the little girl customers," highlighted the fact that its clientele was, perhaps, just as interesting as its entertainers.[44] Despite the tourism, or perhaps because of it, Mona's became a site on Broadway where lesbians were publicly visible, both as performers and customers.

> [Tourists] were always there . . . They'd see the name and somebody'd say, "Oh, there are all the nutty bohemians in there." Then they [tourists] just say, "Gee, look at that." It just built up from there.[45]

The popularity of Mona's illustrates the complex relationship between San Francisco's nineteenth-century reputation for vice, its turn-of-the-century sex tourism, and the early twentieth-century emergence of queer pubic space in the city's North Beach district. As mainstream advertising drew tourists to North Beach, it simultaneously generated a queer reputation, and lesbian clubs emerged around Broadway's tourist strip. In fact, after Mona's 440 closed in 1948, lesbians could find each other at a number of other lesbian nightspots in North Beach, including Mona's Candlelight (1948–57) at 472 Broadway; the Chi Chi Club (1949–56) at 467 Broadway; Ann's 440 Club (1952–62) at 440 Broadway; Tommy's Place (1952–55) at 529 Broadway; 12 Adler Place (1954–56); Miss Smith's Tea Room (1954–60) at 1353 Grant Avenue; and the Anxious Asp (1958–67) at 528 Green Street.[46] Thus, from the 1940s through the 1960s, lesbian nightlife remained a fixture in San Francisco's North Beach district.

Finocchio's, a San Francisco nightclub where young men still perform as female impersonators, has advertised itself from the time of Prohibition (when it operated as a speakeasy) as the place "where boys will be girls."[47] Unlike Mona's, however, Finocchio's has never been a public space where local homosexuals gather. José Sarria, San Francisco's famous drag queen performer and the first openly gay man to run for public office in the city, remembers:

> Number one, Finocchio's was not a gay bar ... It was a show place where men dressed as women and performed. You sang, you told stories. That was the thing ... It was a place that tourists would go, would go into just like they would go to Chinatown ... People went there to see this phenomena of men dressing like women, looking like women, and putting on a very, very interesting show.[48]

Finocchio's floor show was self-consciously constructed to appeal to heterosexual tourists, and performers retell stories of couples who wandered in "unaware of the show policy and thinking a customary, all-girl revue was going through its paces."[49] Geared to naive out-of-towners, the show culminated in a surprise ending where male entertainers doffed the wigs and bared their chests to reveal their "true" sex. In fact, the listing for Finocchio's in *Where to Sin in San Francisco* included a graphic of a man and a woman, presumably heterosexual, drunk, and leering across their table at the stage. The accompanying text described the club as a place where "guys and their gals in the know sit at least three tables from ringside and let themselves be sucked in by insidious illusion."[50] The reference to "insidious illusion" highlights a heterosexual point of view and identifies an assumed heterosexual clientele.

"Wigged, gowned, rouged, lipsticked, and mascara-ed," performers at Finocchio's delighted in their ability to fool the unknowing, but they maintained that their show was more about masquerade than homosexuality:

"... because I dress as a woman ... doesn't mean I'm homosexual—nor does it necessarily mean I'm a transvestite ... Ours is a fine art that has been practiced since the beginning of time."[51] Finocchio's developed a reputation as a "bastion of a bizarre art"—a part of San Francisco's long history of sex and gender nonconformity—rather than as a public space where homosexuals gathered. "I've got a standard in my show," Joe Finocchio asserts, "[and] I've never had a scandal—never!"[52] Finocchio's was thus a place where tourists could safely view the exotic (and illegal) without fear of police harassment or persecution.[53]

Although neither Mona's nor Finocchio's were "gay-owned" establishments, both nightclubs were immensely popular and made a name for themselves by marketing cross-gender performances to tourists.[54] And although Mona's evolved into an explicitly queer public space while Finocchio's did not, their position on Broadway queered San Francisco's North Beach district and helped create a "homosexualized" bohemian subculture. Mona's and Finocchio's became popular and prosperous because they were able to tap into aspects of the city's history of and market for gender nonconformity and sexual license; as a result, cross-gender behavior and homosexuality became an increasingly visible part of bohemia's sexual iconography through the 1930s, '40s, and '50s. Furthermore, Finocchio's and Mona's high visibility advertised San Francisco's North Beach district as a queer neighborhood. This made it possible for lesbians and gay men to find each other, which was important to the emergence of queer communities in San Francisco.

Queer in the Public Sphere: Gay and Lesbian Bar Life

San Francisco's post-Prohibition nightlife emerged as flamboyantly gender-transgressive, and through the 1930s, a publicly visible queer culture flourished in the city's tourist districts. Homosexuals continued to socialize publicly alongside adventurous heterosexuals and voyeuristic tourists in central locations such as Mona's and, to a lesser degree, Finocchio's, where cross-gender performances drew crowds. At the same time, the 1930s and '40s saw the emergence of bars that catered specifically to gay and lesbian populations, typically off Broadway, although many continued to exist at the center of San Francisco's tourist districts. In contrast, New York City saw the separation of gay life from the heterosocial and bohemian aspects of the city's nightlife. There, the post-Prohibition transfer of authority over the sale and consumption of liquor from local and Progressive Era agencies to the newly formed State Liquor Authority resulted in the criminalization and increased marginalization of gay social spaces. SLA officials, as George Chauncey, Jr. argues, exercised a pervasive presence in New York City through the employment of plainclothed, undercover agents who revoked the liquor license of any establishment catering to a gender-transgressive or homosexual clientele.[55] San Francisco's queer cultures remained central to its Broadway nighttime amusements, however, because the city's tourist industry depended on perpetuating its reputation for sexual license, particularly since Progressive Era politicking had shut down the Barbary Coast, forfeiting the liquor and tourist revenue that this area once provided.[56]

Moreover, until the early 1950s, California was one of ten states to control the post-Prohibition distribution of liquor licenses through a fiscal agency, the State Board of Equalization, rather than through a specially appointed state liquor agency. "Liquor control as a state function, as far as these states are concerned, amounts to liquor tax collection," a 1936 publication reported.[57] California's Board of Equalization also refused to share the administration of liquor licenses and the control of licensed establishments with municipal agencies; it would not initially cooperate with city police, nor would it administer liquor licenses on a local level.[58] Perhaps overzealous in protecting liquor traffic from potential police payoffs, and more concerned with tax revenue than homosexuals, California's State Board of Equalization was less effective than New York's State Liquor Authority in regulating queer public spaces.[59] Finally, while police payoffs, both civilian and military, were frequently noted in San Francisco newspapers, crime syndicates never gained a foothold in San Francisco as they did in other large U.S. cities like New York.[60] As a result, the 1930s saw a proliferation of nightclubs and drinking establishments in San Francisco, many of which had a mixed bohemian, homosexual, and tourist clientele.[61] And, although gay and gender-transgressive bars and taverns emerged in San Francisco's post-Prohibition era as vulnerable and highly contested public spaces, they continued to function visibly as part of an urban economy of highly trafficked sex tourism.

Tourism remained central to the emergence of San Francisco's queer and gender-transgressive nightlife, but gay and lesbian bars, unlike bohemian bars with cross-gender entertainment, existed at the margins of respectability, often beyond tourist industry protections, and were consequently subject to state regulation and harassment. In order to serve a homosexual clientele, bar owners (as well as patrons) fought ongoing battles with the state liquor authority, military police, and city and county police. However, these battles remain hidden from history, except when newspapers recorded large-scale police attacks or bar owners waged lengthy and expensive legal battles. The accounts of bar raids and shutdowns that do exist document San Francisco's transformation from a wide-open town where iconoclastic sexual subcultures flourished to a city frequently hostile to its emergent gay and lesbian communities.

The persecution of gay bars and the control of gender-transgressive public spaces began in earnest in the 1940s under the purview of the Armed Forces Disciplinary Control Board (AFDCB). In 1942, the first summer after the U.S. declaration of war, military officials initiated anti-vice crackdowns in many U.S. cities, particularly ports, in an effort to regulate the vast influx of servicemen and women. In San Francisco, between 1942 and 1943, these efforts resulted in the citation or suspension of almost one hundred bars and nightclubs, many of which served a gay clientele.[62] In July 1942, for example, military police were stationed outside three taverns—the Silver Dollar, the Pirate's Cave, and the Silver Rail—to warn away military personnel.[63] Located in San Francisco's Tenderloin district, each of these taverns catered to homosexuals and were popular with servicemen.[64] Although the armed forces did not have the authority to shut down or revoke the licenses of gay bars and taverns, placing them off-limits to servicemen and women and stationing military police outside their doors was, no doubt, bad for business.[65]

AFDCB actions, like previous efforts to clean up vice in San Francisco, had the complementary effect of publicizing not just the existence but the locations of gay bars and taverns. The Disciplinary Control Board's practice was to send warning letters to "trouble spots," inviting the establishments' owners to meet with the Board and describe how they had "cleaned up conditions."[66] Bars and taverns that did not stop serving homosexuals (or prostitutes) became off-limits to military personnel, and the establishments' names and addresses were listed in local newspapers. Gay bars at once harassed and highlighted by the Disciplinary Control Board's actions through the late 1940s and '50s included Club Inferno, the 150 Club, the Crystal Bowl, Lena's Burger Basket, and the Rocket Club.[67] By the mid-1950s, the city police joined forces with the Armed Forces Disciplinary Control Board. "It is our intention," Police Chief Gaffey stated in 1954, "to continue this drive indefinitely to rid the city of the unwholesome and offensive situation resulting from the recent influx of undesirables to San Francisco." In order to aid AFDCB efforts, Gaffey organized a special detail of plainclothed police who began to make "periodic visits to known gathering places for sex deviates."[68]

Through the mid-1950s, AFDCB and police efforts also drew the newly reorganized state liquor authority, the Alcoholic Beverage Control Department (ABC), into the business of harassing homosexual bars, and the ABC's power to suspend and revoke liquor licenses soon became as big a threat to gay bars as police harassment. The February 20, 1956 raid on a gay bar in South San Francisco illustrates this point. Although the local sheriff's office had been quietly watching Hazel's Inn for two months and could have handled the raid by itself, it brought extra deputies, ABC agents, Army military police, and Highway Patrol agents (35 law enforcement officials in total) along to help with the raid and arrests. "Prior to the entry of uniformed officers," the next day's news reported, "five undercover agents—including Harry Kunst, San Francisco District enforcement supervisor for the liquor control unit—mingled with 'Hazel's' predominantly male clientele" before they started making arrests. Shortly after midnight, this coterie of law enforcement personnel rounded up the almost 300 patrons, picked out 90 "regulars" (77 men, 10 women, 3 minors), and booked them on vagrancy charges.[69] Police also arrested Hazel Nickola, the owner, for "operating a dance without a permit" and three bartenders for "serving drinks to a minor."[70] Calling the action "headline hunting" and illegal, the ACLU took up the case, arguing that it denied due process and ignored the statutory requirement of a speedy trial. More importantly, ACLU lawyers challenged the constitutionality of vagrancy law. "Vagrancy," the group's appeal brief read, "is a crime of condition, of status; one in which character is involved."[71] Given the strength of the ACLU's legal arguments, the police had a hard time prosecuting the arrestees, even though ABC agents collaborated with local police throughout the lengthy court proceedings. A separate ABC investigation, however, was much more effective and resulted in a quickly issued state order to revoke Hazel's liquor license.[72]

San Francisco's history of gay and lesbian bar raids reveals the boundaries of tolerance in a city that not only prided itself on its nonconformity but also depended on a tourist economy that mixed good weather and spectacular views with a vibrant sex trade. As queers moved away from touristy bohemian taverns and nightclubs and gathered in bars outside of North Beach, police harassment and bar raids forced them to assert a publicly visible presence as homosexuals. Ironically, as the increased public visibility of gay and lesbian bars drew fire from local police, the AFDCB, and ABC agents, newspaper coverage of bar raids and disciplinary measures worked to advertise San Francisco's bustling gay nightlife to the nation, articulating anew its reputation as a haven or refuge for sex- and gender-nonconformists. In fact, because newspapers listed the bars and taverns suspected of being "havens for sex deviates," they unwittingly served as a directory of gay life for migrants and newcomers to the city. San Francisco's authoritarian response to the emergence of gay and lesbian public space—its history of bar raids and court battles—thus contributed to the emergence of a tenacious and visible queer community. The dynamic tensions between reputation and reality, openness and repression, as they unfolded over the first several decades of the twentieth century, led directly to the politicization of San Francisco's gay and lesbian communities in the 1950s and '60s.

Conclusion: Postwar Demographics

As John D'Emilio and Allan Bérubé persuasively argue, World War II and postwar social and economic change directly influenced the consolidation and politicization of San Francisco's lesbian and gay communities through the 1950s and '60s.[73] The emergence of politicized lesbian and gay communities has a much longer history, however, and cannot be separated from San Francisco's nineteenth-century reputation as a wide-open town, its turn-of-the-century sex tourism, or its post-Prohibition gender-transgressive amusements. In fact, San Francisco's reputation as a flamboyant and international tourist town sustained its postwar demographic growth. Reba Hudson, for example, moved to San Francisco from Phoenix, Arizona in 1943 with the intention of getting a high-paying war job. She and a carload of girlfriends, all in their early twenties, made a stop in Los Angeles—another wartime boom town—but decided to push on to San Francisco. "L.A. was not at all like a big city, but . . . San Francisco was just the height of cosmopolitan—it was very like Europe at that time, very European." Hudson settled in San Francisco after renting a room on Bush Street with a group of lesbian friends and got a military job as a truck driver.[74] Because San Francisco was a focal point of wartime industrial production, especially ship building, migrants like Hudson moved to the city for high-paying war jobs, but San Francisco's reputation for pleasure both preceded and sustained its wartime migrations.

Post-World War II demographic change also reshaped San Francisco's neighborhoods. While large numbers of military personnel pushed through San Francisco, inflating the city's wartime population by almost 60,000, its overall population jumped from 635,000 to 825,000 between 1940 and 1945, reflecting new labor opportunities, particularly for people of color.[75] For example, jobs in wartime industries opened up to Black workers during these years (as a direct result of President Roosevelt's 1941 Executive Order 8802), and the city's African American population jumped 800 percent (4,846 to 43,460) between 1940 and 1950.[76] Postwar prosperity also impacted the reorganization of San Francisco's neighborhoods.[77] While African Americans moved from Hunter's Point into Ocean View and Lake Merced Heights as these neighborhoods "became sort of upward-scale areas for the minorities in the city who heretofore had not had a lot of options of buying," gay and lesbian households consolidated within San Francisco's North Beach and Tenderloin districts.[78] New populations, industries, and ideologies meant greater potential for economic mobility, social change, and community building.

Therefore, while wartime mobility drew individuals and families eager to secure a better life to San Francisco, the city's reputation as a wide-open town continued to attract adventurous pleasure-seekers to its bohemian and queer neighborhoods. As a result, San Francisco's early twentieth-century reputation as a refuge or haven for sex- and gender-nonconformists expanded in the 1950s and '60s to that of a gay mecca. By the mid-1970s, San Francisco had also become a gay capital, a unique center for queer culture and gay political organizing, and lesbians and gay men flocked to the city to carve out new lives. A late 1960s underground tourist pamphlet even cautioned gay readers that "if you're going to San Francisco to live, and you don't know anybody you might do well to take a few weeks to decide on an apartment... swingers are moving into the Bay City every day, and you'll very likely find one you'd want for a roommate."[79] San Francisco's reputation as a gay capital proves to be so persistent that it clouds memories of a less welcoming time when homosexuals had to seek each other out while guarding against constant harassment and persecution—or times when San Francisco was not a center of gay life in the United States, but one of a number of cities that housed queer subcultural communities.[80]

San Francisco remains unique, however, in that its frontier-town ethics, its tourist economies, and its sexually adventurous nightlife allowed the city's queer populations to stabilize and publicly emerge through the 1930s. These populations provided a large enough pool of lesbians and gay men to support both a proliferation of subcultural queer communities through the 1940s and the emergence of explicitly political gay and lesbian organizations through the 1950s and '60s. Thus the wartime migration of lesbians and gays and their postwar visibility was part of a much larger process of urban development that has everything to do with San Francisco's boom-town gold rush era, its history of vice, its anti-vice campaigns, and its coincident location as a strategic western seaport. Through these overlapping conditions, San Francisco (along with a number of other cities) slowly gained a reputation as a gay town and became a focus for gay tourism, as well as a point of gay migration. San Francisco was wide open to the emergence of homosexual communities not by serendipitous demographics or political design but because its founding social and urban structures provided a refuge for social outcasts and an outlet for sexual adventure. Finally, because San Francisco's tourist industries exploited and advertised these qualities, what was an in-house secret became a world-class phenomenon.

Acknowledgments

My thanks to the Center for Lesbian and Gay Studies for the Rockefeller Fellowship that allowed me to work on this essay; the Gay and Lesbian Historical Society of Northern California for its incredible wealth of publicly accessible materials; Allan Bérubé for his insight; and Polly Thistlethwaite for her resourcefulness.

Notes

1. "Homos Invade S.F.," *The Truth* 1:2 (July 11, 1949).
2. "Homosexual" was a common self-referential term through mid-twentieth-century San Francisco. It was also the most common term, along with "lesbian," used by the local press through the 1930s, '40s, and '50s to describe men and women who practiced same-sex sexuality. "Sex deviates" was also a common term used in the press, though it functioned more derisively, connoting sexological pathology. The term "gay" in this sense begins to appear in the *San Francisco Chronicle* and *San Francisco Examiner* in the 1940s.

   In this essay, I use the term "queer" in its broadest sense to signify non-normative sex/gender configurations and identities (such as dyke, homosexual, transsexual, etc.). However, I use the phrase "queer history" more actively and in the same spirit as Jennifer Terry's "new archivist of deviance" and Michael Warner's "queer" activist/scholar. "Queer history" thus becomes a disruptive process, critical of the minoritizing logic of toleration, and inclusive of transgender and bisexual histories (or any queer sex/gender practice that confronts heteronormalcy). Finally, I use the phrase "lesbian and gay history" to signify a specific historical field that, on the whole, has concerned itself with "gay men" or "homosexuals" and, to a lesser degree, "lesbians." See Jennifer Terry, "Theorizing Deviant Historiography," *differences* 3:2 (Summer 1991): 57; and Michael Warner, "Introduction," *Fear of a Queer Planet: Queer Politics and Social Theory* (Minneapolis: University of Minnesota Press, 1993), xxxvi.
3. John D'Emilio, "Gay Politics and Community in San Francisco Since World War II," in *Hidden from History: Reclaiming the Gay and Lesbian Past*, eds. Martin Bauml Duberman, Martha Vicinus, and George Chauncey, Jr. (New York: New American Library, 1989), 459. See also Allan Bérubé, *Coming Out Under Fire: The History of Gay Men and Women in World War Two* (New York: The Free Press, 1990) and the documentary film based on his book, produced and directed by Arthur Dong, "Coming Out Under Fire" (Deepfocus Productions, 1994).
4. The phase "haven for sex deviates" was common to scandal sheets through the mid-twentieth century. However, because of San Francisco's history of police repression, it was hardly a haven. San Francisco might be better characterized as a refuge. My thanks to Bill Walker of the Gay and Lesbian Historical Society of Northern California for making this distinction.
5. The Random House Dictionary (2nd edition) defines "mecca" as "any place that many people visit or hope to visit." For information on New York City's gay geographies, see George Chauncey, Jr.'s *Gay New York: Gender, Urban Culture, and the Making of the Gay Male World, 1890–1940* (New York: Basic Books, 1994).
6. *San Francisco Mattachine Review* 22 (March 15, 1955).
7. He also called San Francisco "Sodom," reserving "Gamorrah" [sic] for Los Angeles. Guy Strait, *Cruise News* 1:1 (July 1965); 1:2 (August 1965); 2:9 (September 1966).
8. The article also estimated San Francisco's "stationary population" of homosexuals to be near 90,000, ". . . what may be the highest per capita concentration of gayfolk since Zeus presided over the now-famed fun and games on Greece's Mount Olympus." *Cruise News* 3:2 (January 1967): 10.
9. John Burks and Geoffrey Link, "The Gay Mecca," *San Francisco* (April 1970): 30–45.
10. Quoted in ibid., 30. See also Alan P. Bell and Martin S. Weinberg, *Homosexualities:*

A Study of Diversity Among Men and Women (New York: Simon and Schuster, 1978).

11. Howard S. Becker and Irving Louis Horowitz, "The Culture of Civility," *Transaction: Social Science and Modern Society* 7:6 (April 1970): 12.
12. Herbert Asbury, *The Barbary Coast* (New York: Capricorn Books, 1933), 32–38; Stephen Longstreet, *The Wilder Shore: A History of the Gala Days in San Francisco* (Garden City, NJ: Doubleday and Co., 1968), 258.

    San Francisco's early colonial history is rich with cross-class and cross-race sexual traffic due, in part, to the Spanish colonial uses of mestizo labor. In 1776, for example, when Spanish settlers constructed a mission and precidio (the twin pillars of Spanish-American colonization) near the territories of the Coast Miwoks, Winturns, Tokuts, and Costanoans, they did so with Indian labor, luring Indian settlers into a colonial township at the northern edge of a tenaciously expanding Spanish empire. With Mexican independence from Spain in 1821, however, San Francisco village (then called Yerba Buena) became part of Mexico's northern territory and barely governable as the port secularized and became increasingly active for ships seeking commerce with traders and trappers. By the mid-1840s, as Mexico braced for war with the United States, Yerba Buena's population grew as foreign-born (Anglo/Yankee) merchants moved into town and married the daughters of Mexican landowners and civic leaders, using sexual/familial connections to create wealth, social standing, and political alliances. Thus, in 1846, when the United States annexed California and Yerba Buena was renamed San Francisco, the city's international population of merchant settlers and their children reflected not just San Francisco's history of shifting colonial rule but a pattern of transnational migration and cross-class, cross-race sex. See Oscar Lewis, *San Francisco: Mission to Metropolis* (San Diego: Howell-North Books, 1980), 12–16; Antonia I. Castenada, "Sexual Violence in the Politics and Policies of Conquest," in *Building with Our Hands: New Directions in Chicana Studies*, eds. Adela de la Torre and Beatríz Pezquera (Berkeley: University of California Press, 1993), 15–33; Tomás Almaguer, *Racial Faultlines: The Historical Origins of White Supremacy in California* (Berkeley: University of California Press, 1994).
13. San Francisco's population boomed from 469 in 1847 (excluding the military and residents of Mission Dolores) to approximately 35,000 in 1850. Lewis, *San Francisco*, 46–48. For information on San Francisco's mid-nineteenth-century vigilante history, see Robert Senkewicz, *Vigilantes in Gold Rush San Francisco* (Stanford: Stanford University Press, 1985); Lewis, *San Francisco*, 58–78. See also David Beesley, "Communists and Vigilantes in the Northern Mines," *California Historical Quarterly* 64:2 (Spring 1985): 143. For fictionalized accounts of San Francisco's vigilante period, see Richard Summers, *Vigilante* (New York: Duell, Sloan, and Pearce, 1949) and Stanton A. Coblentz, *Villains and Vigilantes* (1936; New York: A.S. Barnes and Co., 1957).
14. Article 1 of the Vigilance Committee of 1851, cited in Lewis, *San Francisco*, 61.
15. Howard M. Bahr, ed., *Disaffiliated Man: Essays and Bibliography on Skid Row, Vagrancy, and Outsiders* (Toronto: University of Toronto Press, 1970), 15, 20–21.
16. For a detailed analysis of a predominantly single men's quarter, see Alvin Averbach, "San Francisco's South of Market District, 1885–1950: The Emergence of a Skid Row," *California Historical Quarterly* 52:3 (1973): 197–223.

17. Lewis, *San Francisco*, 144–46.
18. Ibid., 70.
19. Will Irwin, quoted by William Hogan, "Fabulous Frisco," *Saturday Review* 39 (May 1956): 17; Hamilton Basso, "San Francisco," *Holiday* 14:3 (September 1953): 32. See also Asbury, *The Barbary Coast*; Douglas Henry Daniels, *Pioneer Urbanites: A Social and Cultural History of Black San Francisco* (Philadelphia: Temple University Press, 1980), 144–60.
20. Asbury, *The Barbary Coast*, 101; Lance S. Davidson, "Shanghaied! The Systematic Kidnapping of Sailors in Early San Francisco," *California Historical Quarterly* 64:1 (Winter 1985): 11.
21. Same-sex prostitution and sexuality undoubtedly existed alongside other Barbary Coast entertainments, although few sources document these activities. Stephen Longstreet, however, mentions a "small huddle of homosexuals who worked out of a certain Turkish bath . . ." in the 1890s. See Longstreet, *The Wilder Shore*, 262–63.
22. Asbury, *The Barbary Coast*, 98–124.
23. Ibid., 232–77; Longstreet, *The Wilder Shore*, 253–65; Lucius Beebe and Charles Clegg, *San Francisco's Golden Era* (Berkeley: Howell-North, 1960), 126–27. See also Curt Gentry, *The Madams of San Francisco* (Garden City, NJ: Doubleday, 1964); Sally Stanford, *The Lady of the House* (New York: G.P. Putnam's Sons, 1966).
24. Asbury, *The Barbary Coast*, 291–93.
25. Mayor James Rolph, Jr. took office in 1912 promising to clean up vice, graft, and payoffs. Asbury, *The Barbary Coast*, 299; Longstreet, *The Wilder Shore*, 264–65; Lewis, *San Francisco*, 207–14.
26. Asbury, *The Barbary Coast*, 299–314. See also Ernest Lenn, "New Decorating Center to End Barbary Coast," *Examiner*, June 5, 1957.
27. Lucius Beebe, "Where to Eat in San Francisco," *Holiday* 11 (February 1952): 62–68; Beebe, "Spendthrift Tour of San Francisco," *Holiday* 24 (September 1958): 62–65.
28. On "The Ricksha," see Margaret Parton's *Laughter on the Hill* (New York: McGraw-Hill, 1945), 67; on "The Forbidden City," the best source is Arthur Dong's movie of the same title.
29. Basso, "San Francisco," 38.
30. Parton, *Laughter on the Hill*, 155.
31. See Chauncey, *Gay New York*, for a description of New York's post-Prohibition era and its effect on queer nightlife.
32. Lucius Beebe, "This New York," circa 1935, Mona Hood's personal papers.
33. A popular tourist guide lists Mona's in 1936 (at 451 Union) as one of a handful of preferred "Bohemian" nightclubs in San Francisco; *San Francisco Life* 4:3 (February 1936): 46. In 1939, the same magazine lists Mona's 440 (at 440 Broadway) as one of six Bohemian nightspots and describes the bar as having "Drinks served by 'women waiters' . . . definitely different entertainment . . . now and then a celebrity"; "Rambles in San Francisco's Bohemia," *San Francisco Life* 7:17 (November 1939): 4.
34. Oral history interview with Mona Hood, Rikki Streicher, and Reba Hudson, July 25, 1992. All interviews cited in this essay were conducted by the author.
35. Ibid.

36. Ibid.
37. Ibid.
38. Ibid.
39. Virginia Fields, "Bright Lights," circa 1933, Mona Hood's personal papers.
40. Interview with Hood, Streicher, and Hudson.
41. Jack Lord and Jenn Shaw, *Where to Sin in San Francisco* (San Francisco: The Book Cellar, first edition, 1939), 57.
42. For more information on Gladys Bentley, see Eric Garber, "Gladys Bentley: The Bulldagger Who Sang the Blues," *OUT/LOOK* 1 (Spring 1988): 52–61; Hazel V. Carby, "'It Jus Be's Dat Way Sometime': The Sexual Politics of Women's Blues," *Radical America* 20 (1986): 9–22.
43. *San Francisco Life* 4:3 (February 1936): 46. See also Herb Caen, "Baghdad-by-the-Bay," December, 7 1955, and "San Franciscaena," January 13, 1964, in the *Examiner.*
44. Lord and Shaw, *Where to Sin in San Francisco,* 1939; 1940; 1943; 1945. Each of these editions ran the same description of Mona's with slight changes (such as hours). The 1948 edition of *Where to Sin* included the Mona's graphic alongside a description of "The Paper Doll," a popular North Beach gay bar, with the caption "very confusing."
45. Interview with Hood, Streicher, and Hudson.
46. Eric Garber, "A Historical Directory of Lesbian and Gay Establishments in the San Francisco Bay Area," Gay and Lesbian Historical Society of Northern California. See also Elizabeth Lapovsky Kennedy and Madeline D. Davis, *Boots of Leather, Slippers of Gold: The History of a Lesbian Community* (New York: Routledge, 1993) for a much more engaged discussion of how lesbians have used public space.
47. John Stanley, "Finocchio's: A Reputable Bastion of a Bizarre Art," *San Francisco Chronicle,* January 8, 1967, pink section; oral history interview with Mona Hood, July 25, 1992. Also interesting is Harry Hay's remembrances of Finocchio's in Stuart Timmons, *The Trouble with Harry Hay* (Boston: Alyson, 1990), 19, 46.
48. Oral history interview with José Sarria, May 20, 1992.
49. Stanley, "Finocchio's."
50. Lord and Shaw, *Where to Sin in San Francisco* (1945), 93.
51. Ibid., 93; Stanley, "Finocchio's." George Chauncey notes in *Gay New York* that the Italian word "finocchio" was used in New York City as a vernacular term for "fairy," arguing that its literal translation, "fennel," refers to "licorice," an Italian-American term for cocksucker.
52. Stanley, "Finocchio's." Finocchio's remained off-limits to servicemen and women between August 1950 and June 1955, however, by order of the Armed Forces Disciplinary Control Board, even though the San Francisco Police Inspector's office maintained that there had been no complaints to the police during that time. "29 Area Bars Reported to U.S. Military," *Examiner,* June 30, 1955.
53. Prior to 1961, cross-dressers could be prosecuted under City Ordinance Section 440, which prohibited "wearing of the dress, clothing and apparel not ordinarily worn by persons of the same sex with the intent to deceive."
54. In San Francisco, the success of a gay bar was more dependant on having gay bartenders than gay or lesbian ownership. Guy Strait, "What Is a 'Gay Bar,'" *Citizen's News* 4:5 (December 1964): 7.
55. Chauncey, *Gay New York,* 331–54.
56. In 1890, with 3,117 liquor licenses distributed in San Francisco (a ratio of 1 for

every 96 residents) and over 2000 "blind pigs" or speakeasies, city authorities estimated San Francisco's annual liquor revenue at almost $10 million. During Prohibition, liquor revenue was driven underground, and two years after Repeal, in 1935, the revenue for the entire state of California was just over $10 million, the same as it had been in just the city of San Francisco prior to Progressive Era legislation and the post-Prohibition reorganization of liquor sales and authority. See Asbury, *The Barbary Coast*, 123–24; Leonard Harrison and Elizabeth Laine, *After Repeal* (New York: Harper and Brothers, 1936), 144.

57. Harrison and Laine, *After Repeal*, 48, 54–56, 84–87.
58. California was one of four states that held exclusive state-administrated authority over the distribution of liquor licenses rather than allowing local municipalities to participate in the licensing process. The others were Connecticut, Delaware, and South Carolina. Harrison and Laine, *After Repeal*, 48.
59. My thanks to Molly McGarry for her insight into San Francisco and New York's comparative histories.
60. "2 Officers Accused," *Examiner*, December 23, 1954; "Jury Will Hear Shakedown Charge," *Chronicle*, June 15, 1957; "'Bar Bribe' Trips Agent," *Chronicle*, May 3, 1960. See also Humbert S. Nelli, "American Syndicate Crime: A Legacy of Prohibition," in *Law, Alcohol, and Order: Perspectives on National Prohibition*, ed. David E. Kyvig (Westport, CT: Greenwood Press, 1985), 123–37. In New York, on the other hand, the organized crime syndicates who established control over liquor traffic during Prohibition became "the only entities powerful enough to offer bars systemic protection," and they "took over the gay bar business." Chauncey, *Gay New York*, 347.
61. By 1935, California had issued a larger number of liquor licenses, 73,189, than any other state. New York's total in that year was 59,296 (even though San Francisco's liquor revenue, at $10,780,046, was far below New York's, at $37,121,318). Harrison and Laine, *After Repeal*, 58.
62. Bérubé, *Coming Out Under Fire*, 123–27.
63. "Taverns Put 'Off Limits,'" *Examiner*, July 5, 1942.
64. Garber, "A Historical Directory of Lesbian and Gay Establishments in the San Francisco Bay Area."
65. Military police did have the authority to arrest servicemen and women who frequented off-limits establishments, however.
66. "New Military Unit Ordered to Clamp Down on S.F. Bars," *Examiner*, July 28, 1954.
67. Club Inferno was located at 340 Mason; the 150 Club at 150 Mason; the Crystal Bowl at 1032 Market; Lena's Burger Basket at 1747 Post; and the Rocket Club at 236 Leavenworth.
68. "Military Aids S.F. Drive on Sex Deviates," *Examiner*, July 1, 1954.
69. Vagrancy was a catchall offense which, in this case, included citations for "being lewd and dissolute persons and committing acts outraging public decency." Ernest Besig, "Alleged Homosexuals Victims of Lawless Mass Arrests," *ACLU News*, reprinted in *Mattachine Review* 2:2 (March 1956): 5–6; Ernest Besig, excerpted in "American Civil Liberties Union Acts to Appeal California's Lewd Vagrancy Law After Convictions Resulting from Mass Raids and Arrests," *Mattachine Review* 2:3 (June 1956): 3–4.
70. "Peninsula Raiders Net 90 at Alleged Sex Deviate Hangout," *Chronicle*, February 20, 1956; "Sex Deviate Case—30 Forfeit Bail," *Examiner*, March 2, 1956.

71. "Sharp Park Police Case on Appeal," *ACLU News* (December 1956), Gay and Lesbian Historical Society of Northern California Archives.
72. "Bar Appeals License Loss in 'Perversion,'" *Examiner*, February 15, 1957.
73. John D'Emilio, *Sexual Politics, Sexual Communities: The Making of a Homosexual Minority in the United States, 1940–1970* (Chicago: University of Chicago Press, 1983); Bérubé, *Coming Out Under Fire*. See also Manuel Castells, *The City and the Grassroots* (Berkeley: University of California Press, 1983) and Stephen O. Murray, "Components of Gay Community in San Francisco," in *Gay Culture in America: Essays from the Field*, ed. Gilbert Herdt (Boston: Beacon Press, 1992), 107–46.
74. Oral history interview with Reba Hudson, May 29, 1992. For more information on San Francisco's sophisticated self-perception, see Mrs. Fremont Older, *San Francisco: Magic City* (New York: Longmans, Green, and Co., 1961) and Gertrude Atherton, *My San Francisco* (New York: Bobbs-Merrill, 1946). Both of these books tell the history of San Francisco from the perspective of the wife of one of the city's social elites. See also "City of Sophistication," *San Francisco Life* 4:3 (February 1936): 27.
75. Between 1940 and 1945, the number of people of color in San Francisco (denoted as "non-white" or "Negro," "Chinese," "Japanese," "Filipino," and "Mexican") increased from 31,835 to 55,046. "Special Census of San Francisco, California, Population by Age, Color, and Sex, for Census Tracts: August 1, 1945," Department of Commerce, Bureau of the Census, Washington, D.C.
76. Many Black workers were also recruited from Arkansas and Louisiana by industrialist Henry Kaiser for wartime industry jobs. Daniels, *Pioneer Urbanites*, 165–67; Albert Broussard, *Black San Francisco: The Struggle for Racial Equality in the West, 1900–1954* (Lawrence: University of Kansas Press, 1993), 143–65.
77. While the highest concentrations of "non-white" residents in San Francisco in 1945 lived in Chinatown, the Western Addition, and the Hunter's Point areas, the populations of people of color in Chinatown and the Western Addition remained relatively static between 1940 and 1945, and the number of "non-white" residents in the Bay View/Hunter's Point districts jumped from 143 in 1940 to 9,547 in 1945. "Special Census of San Francisco, California, Population by Age, Color, and Sex, for Census Tracts."
78. Oral history interview with "Jim," January 11, 1992. Castells, *The City and the Grassroots*, 138–64; Daniels, *Pioneer Urbanites*; Broussard, *Black San Francisco*. On intra-city gay mobility and the gentrification of African American neighborhoods in the late 1970s, see "Gays Who Invested in the Black Areas" and "Black Leaders Call Housing the Real Issue," *San Francisco Chronicle*, September 1, 1979; and "Spotlight: Lower Fillmore," *San Francisco Chronicle*, March 12, 1982.
79. "San Francisco's Tenderloin Square," *Sun West* (1968), Gay and Lesbian Historical Society of Northern California Archives.
80. Self-proclaimed lesbians and gay men did not begin moving en masse to San Francisco until the late 1960s, when national attention focused on the sexual irreverence of the city's hippie generation. See Murray, "Components of Gay Community in San Francisco," 125–31, and Becker and Horowitz, "The Culture of Civility."

4. The Kids of Fairytown

Gay Male Culture on Chicago's Near North Side in the 1930s

David K. Johnson

On a Saturday night in April 1934, Harold, the sixteen-year-old son of a Polish immigrant family, was making his way from his working-class Chicago neighborhood to the bright lights of North Michigan Avenue. As a high school student, Harold enjoyed an active social life with a bohemian crowd that favored "smoking, nightclubs and beer flats." Although sexually involved with the same woman for over a year, "there was no love affair," he confessed. Despite these social and erotic involvements, Harold felt "listless" and was searching for something "different." He had recently read the novel *Twilight Men* and was intrigued by the life of the main character, a self-identified "queer" who lived in New York's Greenwich Village. In quick succession, he read *Strange Brother*, *Better Angel*, *Goldie*, *Scorpion*, and *The Well of Loneliness*, all recently published novels with gay or lesbian themes. Then he heard a friend remark that "a whole bunch of fairies" hung around the Michigan Avenue Bridge. As he later recalled, "so the first possible chance that I had I went out on Michigan Ave, Saturday night, April 1934, intending to meet some of these so-called fairies."

When Harold arrived at the bridge, a downpour caused him to seek shelter in the doorway of the nearby Wrigley Building. There he drifted into conversation with a boy who "happened to be queer," although Harold confessed that he "had never met any of his kind, and [would] like to meet more of his kind and learn more about it." The boy, whom Harold found to be "refined" and "rather nice looking," obliged by introducing him to a large group of his friends that night. Intrigued by this new crowd, he "came out every night on the boulevard" for the next several weeks. As Harold recalled, "I was like a child with a new toy trying to find out about it." Convinced that he could support himself "because a few friends of mine were making money hustling," Harold left home and moved to Chicago's Near North Side. Harold had entered what he and his new friends called "queer life."[1]

Harold was one of a large number of gay men interviewed during the 1930s by students and faculty associated with the University of Chicago department of sociology. Professors Robert Park and Ernest Burgess, pioneers in the technique of conducting research in "urban ecology," encouraged their students to use the rapidly growing and culturally diverse city of Chicago as their prime laboratory. As a result, many undergraduate and graduate research projects throughout the 1920s and '30s incorporated gay men into their analyses of urban life. Student papers describe frequent, casual encounters with gay men, and less often lesbians, throughout the city—at cabarets, dance halls, and street corners. As one student observed, "The college student studies the subject in his social psychology or social pathology text and becomes acquainted with the habitat, places of congregation and characteristics of the homosexual." By 1938, an examination in Burgess's sociology course included this true/false question: "In large cities, homosexual individuals tend to congregate rather than remain separate from each other." The correct answer was "true." By the 1930s, gay men had become a fixture of Chicago urban life and a legitimate subject for sociological research.[2]

Although gay men were the focus, in whole or in part, of a variety of student work at the University of Chicago, the most extensive and systematic study was conducted by Earle Bruce. A graduate student in the late 1930s, Bruce interviewed almost forty gay men, and administered personality tests to over fifty, for a masters thesis on the personality traits of homosexuals. Following a standard practice within the sociology department, Bruce relied on personal recommendations within the gay community to locate subjects for his study. Such referrals were used not because of the difficulty in locating gay men, but rather to elicit trust and cooperation during the interview process. As Bruce acknowledged, this methodology meant that his study focused on a core group of gay men who tended to know one another and fit a similar profile. They were almost all white, openly effeminate, and actively involved in the gay world. The majority of his subjects were under twenty-five years old, and almost all were under thirty. "Masculine" as well as older gay men, he suggested, were underrepresented. His study focused on what were variously known as fairies, belles, or "the kids," the gay men who formed the center of the gay male subculture in Chicago, both in the eyes of the larger community and the subculture itself.[3]

These first-person "life history" narratives provide a rare window on the pre-World War II gay male consciousness in Chicago.[4] Although certainly not representative of all homosexually active men during this period, these documents capture something of the lives of the most visible segment of the gay subculture. In conjunction with student term papers, personal correspondence, memoirs, newspapers, and contemporary fiction, they reveal the existence of a gay social world which was not only easily accessible to young, working-class men, but which was instrumental to many men in the adoption of a gay identity. Same-sex sexual behavior may have preceded or followed their discovery of the gay subculture, but it was their relationship to the gay world more than their sexual behavior which led to a transformation in these men's self-identities. Moreover, despite the wide dissemination of the psychiatric discourse on homosexuality by the 1930s, it seems to have played little or no part in the self-concepts of the gay men most closely associated with the subculture. The gay male subculture in 1930s Chicago supports the growing argument in the history of sexuality that youth-oriented, working-class urban culture, rather than intellectual discourse, played a crucial role in establishing modern sexual identities. In this time and place, the activities, rituals, and language of the gay community—"queer life" and "queer words"—provided the discourse through which gay men interpreted their experiences.[5]

Bright Lights, Big City

Like many young men in the 1930s, Harold had no trouble finding the gay world. Even before he encountered it directly on Michigan Avenue, he read about it in novels and heard about it on the street. After picking up a copy of *Twilight Men*, Harold "wanted to find out more about the life that was in the book." He then read six other recently published works with gay or lesbian themes, all available in his working-class Chicago neighborhood. According to an extensive field study conducted by a University of Chicago sociology student (probably Bruce), commercial, rental libraries all over the city—not just in bohemian neighborhoods—were carrying one or more of the half dozen gay-themed novels available in the early 1930s. Andre Tellier's *Twilight Men* and Blair Niles's *Strange Brother* were among the most popular. Although the books' titles only hinted at their contents, commercial libraries provided descriptions to guide their customers' selections. One private rental library with a city-wide delivery service advertised *Strange Brother* as dealing with "problems of the unfortunately sexed" and promoted Robert Scully's *A Scarlet Pansy* by suggesting that "what the 'Well' did for the man-woman this does for the woman-man," referring to the British lesbian novel *The Well of Loneliness*, which received widespread publicity during an obscenity trial. These novels may have actually been more available to working-class readers than to their middle-class counterparts. The survey indicated that such upscale retailers as Carson's, Brentano's, and Kroch's refused to carry them because of their suggestive titles.[6]

Easily available and readily identifiable at local rental libraries, these gay-themed novels reached a large reading population. *Twilight Men* went through four printings in the first few months after its release in 1931 and reportedly sold nearly one hundred thousand copies. But in an era prior to the rise of the paperback, commercial rental libraries allowed hardcover books to circulate much more widely than their sales figures indicate. The proprietor of one rental library on Drexel Boulevard reported that all six copies of *Strange Brother* had been rented over one hundred times and were worn out. Marshall Field's had sold only fifty copies but had rented another six copies fifty times each. "Queer people asked for *Twilight Men*," according to the sales clerk, but "the type that asked for *Strange Brother* was not so obvious." One library proprietor on East 75th Street said he did not approve of "this kind of literature" but, after receiving several calls, decided to stock them and subsequently had to establish a waiting list.[7]

Although dismissed by a post-Stonewall generation of scholars as "a few tragic novels" because they end with the obligatory death or suicide of the gay protagonist, these texts often articulate defiant and self-affirming sentiments along the way.[8] In the 1930s, readers generally interpreted them as romanticizing homosexuality. Medical authorities denounced them as pro-gay propaganda. Writing in *The Modern Psychologist* in 1932, Dr. W. Beran Wolfe, for example, lamented that the effort to eradicate homosexuality was being undermined by the way "many of the more cultivated homosexuals make a virtue of their weakness, and openly make propaganda for their inversion by writing novels and plays about inversion, in which the phenomena of homosexuality are depicted in their ultimate drawing-room niceties." For the general public, these novels served as educational tools, providing many with their first view inside the gay world. One Northwest Side librarian commented, "I thought of these people as pansies, low down. After I read the books I realized that they were human, a person [sic]." For gay men, they were a source of inspiration. Jimmy, who worked at a Chicago hotel, corresponded with gay men in several other cities and exchanged information about "temperamental books that are very beautiful." Most tellingly, Harold's encounter with these representations of the gay world piqued his interest and encouraged further exploration.[9]

Harold's experience with queer life quickly moved beyond the printed page when "somebody made a crack one day" about a group of fairies who hung around the Michigan Avenue Bridge. Although a chance remark, such observations about Chicago's fairies were not unusual, since their haunts were common knowledge to a wide segment of the city. For example, a number of naturalist writers in what became known as the Chicago Renaissance had used fairies in their literary depictions of American life. Sherwood Anderson's "Hands," the story of a male schoolteacher run out of town for allegedly fondling a male student, was inspired by Anderson's observations of fairies on the streets of Chicago. Some juvenile delinquents who frequented the West Madison Street rooming-house district were not only aware of the existence gay men but made a living by "jack-rolling" or robbing them. It was fairly easy to find potential targets, one thief observed, because "there'd always be some man to stop me and coax me into having sex relations with him." Moral reform groups such as the Juvenile Protective Association also took notice and warned in their reports that "in one neighborhood where a colony of sex perverts live, no child is really safe." Some non-gay-identified men shared information about where to locate fairies in order to use them sexually. John, a sixteen-year-old working as a copy boy at the *Chicago Examiner*, heard of guys "being made" at Oak Street Beach. As one writer commented in 1933, "today there is scarcely a school boy who doesn't know what a 'pansy' is. On nearly every vaudeville stage and in every sophisticated review we hear broad references to 'fairies.'" As historian George Chauncey, Jr. argues about New York, gays were in many ways more integrated into the life of the city during the first decades of the twentieth century than they were in later decades.[10]

Perhaps the best evidence of this integration is the location of Harold's first encounter with the gay subculture. Although he had to travel downtown, his pursuit required little sleuthing. Harold discovered the fairies he was intent on meeting not in some dark alley or obscure tavern but in the doorway of the Wrigley Building—one of the most central, well-lit, public locations in all of Chicago. According to one architectural historian, the headquarters of the Wrigley chewing gum corporation at Michigan Avenue and the Chicago River enjoyed "a strategic, conspicuous location with no equal in the city." Moreover, since its construction in 1921, the skyscraper's terra-cotta facade was brilliantly floodlit at night. One 1930s guide to Chicago called the adjacent Michigan Avenue Bridge, opened in 1920 to connect the Loop business district with the upper-class residential neighborhood of the Gold Coast, "the world's busiest bridge." Even allowing for some hyperbole, that this was a known gathering place for Chicago's fairies suggests a remarkable degree of openness and visibility.[11]

Fairytown: "That's Where All the Boys Go Down"

Civic boosters often referred to Michigan Avenue as "Boul Mich," an invocation of the nickname for the main thoroughfare in Paris's Latin Quarter—the Boulevard St. Michel. Others simply dubbed it "the boulevard." As nicknames for the central commercial artery in Chicago's bohemian district, both terms were apt. Extending south to the Chicago River and north to Division Street, this neighborhood featured rooming houses that attracted a wide variety of single men and women who sought to live outside traditional societal conventions, including many of the city's aspiring artists and writers. One study in the 1920s suggested that the Near North Side contained over 20,000 people living in furnished rooms, approximately half of whom were single men. Catering to this large population of unmarried men and women were a variety of cafeterias, coffee shops, and theaters. Its "quaint restaurants, interesting art shops and book stalls, tearooms, stables, and garrets with flower boxes" also made the neighborhood a popular tourist destination.[12]

Among the "bizarre and eccentric divergences of behavior" that made the neighborhood titillating to some and dangerous to others was homosexuality. As one voyeuristic writer commented, "a number of times I have followed a cab through the 'village,' the lights of my car revealing its occupants, two men or two girls, fondling each other." A 1930 issue of *Variety* suggested that thirty-five gay tearooms or "pansy parlors," with waiters in female attire and young men sipping tea, were operating on the Near North Side. Run by "boys who won't throw open the doors until at least two hours have been spent adjusting the drapes just so," they were said to be patronized by Chicago's more famous mobsters. Chicago "is going pansy," *Variety* proclaimed. By 1933, with Chicago gearing up for visitors to the World's Fair, a nationally circulated tabloid warned civic leaders that their plans to publicize Chicago's bohemian neighborhood, where "the queers of the third sex seek refuge," might lead some tourists to discover a "Fairy's Paradise." Though more commonly known as "Towertown," in reference to the landmark Chicago Water Tower at the heart of the neighborhood, one popular gay party song dubbed it "Fairytown."[13]

Earle Bruce's study confirmed the importance of Towertown to the gay subculture. Of the fifty-three gay men he contacted, thirty-four lived in this Near North Side neighborhood. Several of them, including Harold, moved from other neighborhoods within Chicago because of the freedom from familial scrutiny available there. Although this world was partly defined geographically, one did not have to live on the Near North Side to be a part of it. According to Bruce, his entire sample, regardless of place of residence, frequented the "social world of the homosexuals, where they have their particular status, participate in common activities, ... [and] can express themselves in their particular fashion." Bruce even speculated that "the 'whirl' of 'gay' life with all its excitement, sexual interest, disappointments, and disillusionments" was so all-consuming as to impede gay men from attending night school and furthering their education. One gay man identified only as Mr. F seemed to corroborate this impression: "When I first came out in homosexual life I thought I had lost so much, and I wanted to do everything in a day. I wanted to know everything about queer life . . . I wanted to go every place, meet all the kids. . . ."[14]

If the Michigan Avenue Bridge was a point of initiation into the gay world for some men, Oak Street Beach at the northern end of the avenue was another. Many Chicago men recalled that their first contact with gay life occurred along the lake front at Oak Street. When Rodney first came to Chicago for the 1933 World's Fair, he met "loads of belles" at Oak Street Beach. Because they "threw their arms around one another and carried on," Rodney observed, "you would think they were in a Turkish Harem." In 1929, at age sixteen, George decided to visit Oak Street Beach after hearing rumors about its denizens. He met a man there who invited him to go to his residential hotel. "I got awfully drunk and he showed me dirty pictures," George remembered, "and you know what happened then." Another gay man, Harvey, compared the scene at the beach to "the Easter Parade." Commenting on both the expansive, open walkway along the shoreline of Lake Michigan and the secluded areas of the adjacent park, Harvey declared that "all the way up to North Avenue . . . that was *the* place to be and nobody ever bothered you."[15]

With gathering spots at its northern and southern extremities, much of North Michigan Avenue served as a gay cruising area. At the center of this activity, at the northwest corner of Michigan Avenue and Ohio Street, was the most popular commercial rendezvous spot for young gay men, a branch of the Thompson's cafeteria chain. As with branches of Childs cafeteria in New York, Thompson's proximity to cruising areas, combined with its cheap prices and late hours, helped establish it as a gay hangout. A typical outing, whether with friends or alone looking for a sexual encounter, involved a visit to Oak Street Beach, a stroll down the west side of Michigan Avenue, and coffee or a bite to eat at Thompson's. It was on just such an outing that Harold met Max, his lover of two years at the time that both were interviewed by Bruce. Although a resident of suburban Elgin and an employee of a watch factory there, Max made frequent forays into fairytown. He describes a typical outing when he was twenty-five years old:

> I was cruising the [Oak Street] beach one night and I met a few of the kids, just by cruising there and being introduced to this one and that. And we started to go to Thompson's and get something to eat and got on the corner of Michigan and Oak and I was introduced to Harold, and we talked a few minutes and we all went down to Thompson's.

Oak Street Beach, Michigan Avenue, and Thompson's cafeteria were anchors in what Bruce termed the Near North Side's "homosexual world."[16]

At night, a number of area cabarets enjoyed both a gay and lesbian clientele. At the Bally Hoo Cafe at Halstead and Armitage, a sociology student in 1933 observed twenty-five "queer gals," many of whom wore drag and "mostly kept to their own sex," and seventy-five "queer fellows." For a twenty-five cent cover charge, one could see Mack and Marge emcee a drag competition in which the winner received a bottle of gin.[17] None of these commercial establishments, though, were exclusively gay or lesbian. It seems that, as in New York, only with the repeal of Prohibition in 1933 did bars catering exclusively to gay men appear in Chicago. The most popular of these, Waldman's, featured two grand pianos in its plate glass windows overlooking Michigan Avenue near Randolph Street. Bruce Scott remembers visiting Waldman's for the first time in 1936 and seeing a table of male students from the University of Chicago, from which he had recently graduated. His subsequent Saturday night outings involved visits to Waldman's and nearby Symond's on Rush Street, both of which catered to a middle-class gay male clientele. Charles B. recalls Waldman's in the late 1930s as "a very, very big . . . [and] busy place, strictly gay" where, as a teenager, he would wear a suit and tie to try to look more mature.[18]

Although the commercial establishments, streets, and parks of the Near North Side were important social sites, much gay socializing also took place at private parties. Because they occurred behind closed doors, parties are easily dismissed as examples of the furtiveness of gay life. But the many fictional and nonfictional accounts of gay parties from the 1920s and '30s reveal that they served as an integral part of a larger gay world, a sort of semipublic environment. They were of particular importance to men too young to enter nightclubs or cabarets. Meeting someone at Oak Street Beach could lead to a party invitation and thereby serve as an introduction to a whole social network. Many men attributed their adoption of a queer identity not to their first homosexual experience but to their first entry into a gay social environment, often a party. As one man said, "I came out about eight months ago when I began to go to parties and made myself known amongst the groups. That is to say I got next to the ways of the other temperamental people."[19]

Unlike nightclubs and cafes prior to the repeal of Prohibition, private parties were likely to be exclusively gay environments. They provided men a space in which to "let their hair down," act campy, and even dress in drag. By allowing same-sex dancing, kissing, and other forms of physical intimacy, they encouraged the expression of homosexual desire. Jazz musical recordings—with sexual and often homosexual themes—underscored the emphasis on sexual self-expression. Because such parties often attracted a diverse crowd, games were played to facilitate interaction. As depicted in James Farrell's short story "Just Boys," a favorite gay party activity was the game "Truth," in which participants were required to answer revealing questions after swearing honesty on a Bible. Thus gay parties were more than occasions for a few friends to get together in private; they were events orchestrated to affirm and express gay sexuality in a group setting and served as important entry points into the gay world.[20]

The social networks engendered by gay private parties, commercial institutions, and cruising areas facilitated both easy sexual encounters and long-lasting relationships. Many of the men Bruce interviewed spoke of romantic relationships that lasted months or years, with some gay male couples going through a marriage ceremony at a "bull daggers ball." The complex social networks of the gay male world, however, did more than provide social and emotional support; they were also a source of economic assistance. This was the height of the Depression, and couples like Harold and Max not only supported one another financially when one was unemployed, but had a group of friends to whom they could turn for monetary help. When both Harold and Max were without work, for example, a mutual friend loaned them money to keep them afloat. With many gay men cut off from their families, they turned to one another in times of trouble. Moreover, such financial interdependence could engender a kind of group solidarity, as when a minister suggested to Max that he was going to hell because of his association with "a notorious bitch." Max responded, "there are a lot of people going with me."[21]

"Why, All the Fellows Are Sissy Around Here"

Clearly the gay social networks, parties, commercial establishments, residential neighborhoods, and cruising areas in Chicago constituted important elements in what sociologist Earle Bruce labeled "the differentiated social world" of the homosexual. All of these have been documented in other large U.S. cities during this same period, most notably in New York. What has received less attention is the way in which a gay subculture formed in some work environments. Chicago's fairies tended to congregate in certain fields—notably prostitution, entertainment, retail sales, and office work. By choosing such professions, they extended the gay subculture into their work and underscored the importance that it had in the way they structured their lives.

The profession most directly associated with the gay subculture was male prostitution. The University of Chicago interviews suggest that some form of prostitution was commonplace among fairies at this time. For example, hustling was Harold's first job after he entered queer life, and the key factor in his decision to move to the Near North Side. As he recalled, "a few friends of mine were making money hustling, *so* I left home at the age of seventeen." Prostitution provided him with an economic incentive to join the gay subculture and to assume the role of a fairy. Netting him twenty to thirty-five dollars a week, it was also a relatively lucrative occupation. Other young men who would not consider themselves hustlers engaged in occasional prostitution when other jobs were unavailable, a common occurrence during the Depression. Resorting to some form of prostitution to supplement one's income was, according to historian Joanne Meyerowitz, an "economic strategy" shared by single, independent women in the same neighborhood. Both young women and gay men in the furnished-room district exchanged sexual favors for dinners, nights on the town, and sometimes cash to alleviate their poverty while preserving their independence from their families. Many young men found in prostitution the means, and sometimes the incentive, to sustain an openly gay lifestyle.[22]

But hustling was not the only type of employment open to those in the gay subculture—that is, the only type of "gay work." The entertainment and retail industries offered particularly favorable environments for gay men. Harold exemplified both of these trends, since after hustling, he went on to work as a female impersonator and a sales clerk in a department store. As early as 1911 the Chicago Vice Commission noted that a large number of gay men worked as department store clerks or "counter jumpers." One commissioner stated that they found "rooming houses that were occupied by young men, mostly of the counter jumper variety (dry goods people, sales people), and that after work half of the considerable number of inmates of this house would don women's clothes for the night." The portion of State Street in front of Marshall Field's Department store was a notorious gay cruising area, and one list of gay venues collected by a University of Chicago sociologist contained reference to the "floor walkers" on the fourth and fifth floors of Marshall Field's. In the 1930s, a gay clerk explained that "at work practically all the people are gay or wise [sympathetic to gays]. I prefer the department store or entertainment business because you find gay people there."[23]

Perhaps the most common occupation of Chicago's fairies—and the one least studied—is clerical or office work. In Bruce's study, close to half the interviewees were listed together under the category "office clerks, stenographers, billing clerks, music clerks, and stock clerks." Graeme Davis, who moved from South Dakota to Chicago in the 1920s, lived with three other gay men in "two rooms which are better not described." Only one of the four was employed—a seventeen-year-old chorus boy who aspired to enter vaudeville as a female impersonator—but Davis had a temporary job "typewriting" and another roommate had recently lost his job as a stenographer. To support one another on their meager incomes, Davis noted that "everything is common property from pennies to powder (all make up madly)."[24] Another seventeen-year-old, who moved to Chicago during the 1933 World's Fair, explained how a man he met at the Chicago Theater paid for "a secretarial course" for him. "I couldn't hustle, because I could not make any money," he offered by way of explanation. In his mind, secretarial work represented one of the few alternatives to prostitution. But it was one of Earle Bruce's interviewees who best illustrated how prevalent gays could be in clerical work. "I knew that I would not be lonesome when I came to Chicago," he confided. "Where I am staying I have many homosexual friends. When I got myself a job today, I looked around the office and said to the manager, 'Why, all the fellows are sissy around here.' The boss put his hand on my knee and said that he liked me." He even claimed, with a bit of bravado, that when inquiring about clerical positions, he told prospective employers that he was "homosexual."[25]

What marginalized these men and steered them into distinct professional tracks was not so much their sexual orientation as their effeminacy. They were, as the office worker remarked, "sissies," otherwise known as fairies, pansies, or belles—effeminate gay men who announced their homosexual identity through gender inversion. In describing his entrance into gay life, Harold highlighted his adoption of effeminate mannerisms and clothing styles: "I did every possible thing to imitate the effeminacy of the queers that I had come in contact with. I began to wear flashy and obvious clothes, and use cosmetics to a greater extent." These changes, more than his moving to the Near North Side or first having sex with a man, signalled his adoption of a gay identity. But this transformation was not the expression of some suppressed, natural self—the liberation of a female soul trapped in a male body. Rather, he "did this just to get in the swing of the thing," later saying that, despite appearances, he thought of himself as essentially "masculine." Clearly, for men like Harold, effeminacy was what George Chauncey, Jr. has called "a deliberate cultural strategy ... a way to declare a gay identity publicly." But such a strategy was a public avowal of one's sexuality that only some could negotiate—mostly younger, working-class men—hence the term "kids" that many of these men used to describe other gay men. Thus while kids or fairies represented only a portion of the subculture, they were its most prominent members and, according to Chauncey, served as the dominant icon of gay culture in the larger society during the first half of the twentieth century.[26]

Many men adopted the fairy role for a time, but then abandoned it as they grew older, advanced professionally, or were otherwise unwilling to run the risk of being openly gay. One man interviewed by Bruce said that in his first few months in the gay world, "I travelled from one end of the city to the other, and I wore makeup and screamed and carried on just like the other kids." However, when he was arrested for being in a "homosexual tavern" and his parents discovered his activities, he decided to abandon the fairy role. He acquired "a man's job" that he believed he could not have kept if he were "feminine like the other fellows." Nevertheless, he did not abandon his homosexual identity. He made frequent forays into gay social circles, negotiating the norms of two separate worlds by being what he characterized as a "man by day and a woman by night." Similarly, when Robert began his professional life as a stenographer he "used make up and was quite a sissy," but ten years later, at the age of thirty-three, he had become a chief clerk and office manager and had "outgrown" his effeminacy. He was accepted by his business partners, whom he assumed knew nothing of his homosexuality. Interestingly, his professional advancement meant that he had four male stenographers who worked for him—all of them gay.[27]

Adopting the role of the fairy for these men was what George Chauncey has called "a transitional phase in the project of self-reconstruction." An integral part of that effort, a way of sustaining it economically, was retail and clerical work. Historians have begun to study the expanding role of department store clerks and secretaries in early twentieth-century cities, but most of this work focuses on changing patterns of female employment. Lisa Fine demonstrates how, by 1930, the majority of clerical workers in Chicago were female, although clerical work was still an entry-level position for many men in business. More importantly, within stenography, a subfield favored by many of the gay men mentioned here, women held ninety-seven percent of the positions. Beyond mere numbers, "clerical work became women's work," Fine argues, "not only because a majority of those engaging in it were female, but also because clerical work became intimately associated with so-called feminine qualities and was not considered a threat to women's domestic role." Susan Porter Benson has done a similar study of female department store clerks. What has not been investigated is what happened to the minority of men who continued to do clerical and retail work as these occupations became feminized. These interviews suggest that such jobs became havens for gay men.[28]

Although the fields of retail sales and office work seem to have offered comfortable environments for young, effeminate gay men, they were not completely safe. Perhaps the complexity of the situation is best illustrated by the case of Tummo, who lost his job as a stenographer "because he was too effeminate in manner and appearance." Despite the large number of gay men working in clerical jobs, a fairy who obtained such a position was clearly not secure. But rather than being merely an indication of repression, the dismissal suggests that Tummo understood that generally such work would not require him to alter his appearance. He was fired not because his secret had suddenly been discovered, but because he was already acting "*too* effeminate." His firing thus highlights both the limits and the possibilities of open effeminacy in certain clerical positions. It also suggests that his appearance—an integral part of his gay identity—was more important to him than a job. His roommate Graeme Davis, for instance, emphasized that Tummo wore his hair long and "won't cut it." Living an economically marginal existence in order to retain his fairy image held more appeal, at least at this stage of his life, than conforming to a middle-class masculine norm.[29]

By the late 1930s and early '40s, the idea that gay men were often department store clerks or office workers had become a stereotype exploited by the mass media. Jack Benny's popular radio comedy program used recurring "sissy" characters who were often department store clerks. As one joked, "Of course I'm the floorwalker, Lily Pad. Do you think I'd be in this madhouse if I wasn't getting eighteen dollars a week and my lingerie wholesale?" Another character, an effeminate male secretary, hinted at his unabashed homosexuality by comparing himself to a female coworker: "Oh, she's his private secretary. *I'm* right out in the open." By World War II, the notion of "homosexual work" became institutionalized in the military's job classification process. According to historian Allan Bérubé, a wartime military study of homosexual men concluded that they had "considerable talent in stenographic, musical, clerical and special service [entertainment] activities." Given the tremendous need for clerical workers, military officers often followed such stereotypes when assigning jobs to recruits whom they perceived as gay. Moreover, gay servicemen frequently sought such duties, since they were less dangerous and allowed for more open contact with other gay men than more conventional assignments. The fact that gay men congregated in these fields thus generally had less to do with innate ability or even negative stereotyping than with their resourcefulness in finding and establishing environments where they could be most at home.[30]

"People Who Live Their Own Lives"

Men who moved to Chicago in the 1920s and '30s had ready access to a gay subculture. They could live with other gay men in a rooming house on the Near North Side, cruise Oak Street Beach, meet friends at Thompson's cafeteria, attend gay parties, and find work where many of their colleagues would be gay. Undoubtedly this highly developed subculture was limited to Chicago, New York, and perhaps a handful of other large cities. But given the general rise of mass media in this period, the trends established in these cities began to affect gay men throughout the U.S. Jimmy, who worked at Chicago's Plymouth Hotel, put a personal advertisement in a nationally circulated periodical in 1934 and got responses from gay men in Saginaw, Michigan; South Bend, Indiana; and Baltimore, Maryland. Although the original advertisement has not survived, it probably used the word "gay," a code word for queer or homosexual that was largely unintelligible to the dominant society as late as the 1950s. Paul, who responded from Saginaw, knew of Chicago's "gay parks and beaches." He hung around with "fellows who wore make-up and plucked eye brows" and went to Detroit on weekends to visit "gay places." They exchanged information about gay life, swapped photos of one another, and made arrangements to meet at the World's Fair being held in Chicago.[31]

Historians of gay and non-gay communities traditionally rely on the existence of formal, political organizations to document group identity. For instance, gay community-based historians are fond of noting that a small group of men in Chicago led by Henry Gerber founded the Society for Human Rights, the first gay rights organization in the United States. Although an interesting anecdote, documented with an official 1924 charter from the state of Illinois, the group's short life and restricted membership limited its impact. In contrast, the University of Chicago interviews suggest that the social networks, cruising areas, commercial establishments, professions, and novels shared by hundreds if not thousands of gay men contributed much more to a sense of a common gay community. Although lacking any formal recognition, these ties were no less real. Henry Gerber himself understood the importance of the gay subculture to the well being of those he tried to organize politically. For example, he argued that the tragedy of Stephen Gordon, the lesbian protagonist in *The Well of Loneliness*, was her involvement with a heterosexual woman and her attempt to conform to a society which ridiculed her. "Had she joined her own circle, which is large in every metropolitan city," Gerber contended, "there would have been no morbid story." Gerber's analysis suggests how participation in a gay subculture was an empowering form of resistance to the norms and expectations of the larger society. As one singer in a nightclub suggested, "Gay people are generally people who live their own lives, speak their own thoughts, and are in love with their own sex." Their collective refusal to conform provided a strong sense of community.[32]

The communal nature of the gay subculture is underscored by the absence from the University of Chicago interviews of any notion of the closet. Although Harold and his contemporaries did use the term "to come out," they did not "come out of the closet"; they do not describe a period of isolation in which they privately came to terms with their sexuality. Rather, they came out into a new social world. This is in keeping with the term's origin, since use of the phrase "to come out" began with debutante balls, where a woman comes out or makes her debut into "proper" society. Although it has since come to be associated with coming out of "the closet," in the 1930s the expression had a more social, less somber, connotation. It was less a declaration of one's sexuality after a period of isolation than a marker of one's entrance into a new social context.[33]

Another striking absence from the narratives of these young gay men is any internalization of the notion that homosexuality is a sickness. When Max's stepbrother found out that Max was gay, he insisted it was a "mental sickness" and threatened to send him to a state hospital to have him "cured." Max, however, was defiant, declaring that if people could not accept him as he was, "the hell with them." Although he talked at length about mental illness and how he underwent a mental breakdown, Max never associated these problems with his sexuality. Instead, he attributed his nervousness to financial worries brought on by the Depression, his parents' divorce, and the prospect of losing his factory job if his employer found out that he was gay. Despite its currency amongst his non-gay contemporaries, Max seems not to have adopted the notion that homosexuality was a sign of mental illness. The sense of gay community provided an alternative to the medical discourse of deviance and psychopathology that was increasingly prevalent in the 1930s.[34]

Although most Chicagoans had never read a medical text on homosexuality, Harold's list of the books that introduced him to gay life did include one work by a medical expert. La Forest Potter's *Strange Loves: A Study in Sexual Abnormalities* was an attempt to bring medical expertise on the nature, causes, and curability of homosexuality to a general audience to help eradicate "the problem." But by outlining the prevalence of homosexuality—how America had "Gone Pansy," as he titled one of his chapters—he inadvertently suggested that it was normal. Potter asserted that "homosexuality . . . is diffused not only through all the anthropological forms of mankind—savage and civilized life—but also throughout every strata of society, and among every class of population." Like many of the novels that Harold read, Potter's text alluded to the homosexuality of famous writers and artists, including Shakespeare, Marlowe, Michelangelo, Tschaikovsky, and Whitman. To Harold and undoubtedly many others, Potter's line of argumentation intrigued more than it dissuaded. Only one other interviewee, an African-American teenager who had attended a Catholic boarding school in Milwaukee, mentioned reading "doctors books" about masculine women and effeminate men. At first alarmed by the medical analysis, he dismissed it after a boarding school friend who worked as a theater usher introduced him to "the groups in Chicago." As he explained, "among the faggots I could talk as I choose and not act under a strain and could be my real self." The medical attributes of unnaturalness and deviance were much less compelling than the reality of gay sociability at parties and cafes. If some were ignorant of the medical discourse, others found in it an unintended message of acceptance, and still others rejected it altogether.[35]

The criminal justice system also had little impact on the consciousness of these men. Despite the visibility of a gay male subculture in Chicago in the 1930s and the potential for its suppression through laws banning sodomy, solicitation, cross-dressing, loitering, and disorderly conduct, gay men revealed a remarkable lack of concern for the police. When law enforcement officials were mentioned at all, they appeared within the context of criminal activity unrelated to sexuality. For example, one man, who commented on how fairies carried on at Oak Street Beach like it was a "Turkish Harem," noted that the police only chased them away for smoking marijuana. Moreover, semiannual drag balls were actually held with police protection. Although an examination of court records might tell a slightly different story, fear of the police was not a preoccupation of these gay men. This is in striking contrast to the situation in New York, where, according to contemporary gay novels and the recent work of historians, fear of arrest was an integral part of gay life at this time.[36]

In the later half of the 1930s, however, accounts of police harassment and arrest in Chicago markedly increased. Harold, who was arrested on more than one occasion for soliciting and loitering in Washington or "Bughouse" Square, remarked that "the law got hot" after 1935. An undergraduate paper two years later on "The Case of Sex Morons (so-called): Crime Waves and Publicity" described a recent police crackdown, during which plainclothes police officers arrested men in theaters for fondling other men, and judges, under pressure from a frightened populace, gave maximum $200 fines for the crime. The increased police activity was part of a nationwide sex crime panic that, according to Estelle Freedman, was precipitated by a series of highly publicized brutal child murders, but reflected a more generalized anxiety about the prevalence of unemployed men during the Depression. Many municipalities and states, including Illinois, established sexual offense offices to more effectively regulate public morality. This increasing criminalization and politicization of homosexuality posed particular risks to the more overt fairies, many of whom became more circumspect in their behavior and demeanor. For example, after Harold was arrested several times in the late 1930s for prostitution, he moved to Elgin with his lover Max, who encouraged him to act more masculine so that he could keep a "respectable" job in a local factory. Harold's trajectory from an open gay life on Michigan

Avenue to a discreet existence in the suburbs calls into question the conventional view of U.S. history—particularly U.S. gay history—that society is progressively becoming more liberal and tolerant. It supports the more nuanced periodization proposed by Chauncey, who argues that "the state built a closet in the 1930s and forced gay people to hide in it."[37] It now seems clear that the very visibility that this culture enjoyed in the early part of the century contributed to its subsequent suppression.

"We Are at a Premium Here"

Floyd Dell's 1921 novel *The Briary-Bush* chronicles the arrival in Chicago of Felix, a young man from the rural Midwest who hopes to make his fortune in the city, a narrative which had autobiographical overtones for Dell and many other members of the growing literary movement in Chicago. On one of his first nights in the city, Felix encounters a theater set designer at a party, "an affected-looking young man" with a mincing, "prissy" accent the out-of-towner immediately disliked. Apologizing for the set designer's strange airs, his female host explains: "We're all a little like that—I mean queer. I'm sure I seem quite as queer as that to my family down in Springfield." When the young man inquires as to how such freaks are accepted by Chicago society, she responds, "Chicago is beginning to realize that it needs us. Chicago wants to be a metropolis. And all the stockyards in the world won't make a metropolis. . . . Just now we are at a premium here."[38]

If gay life in the 1930s remains hidden to historians today, it was less so to contemporary observers. Because of the presence of young fairies, gay life in the 1930s was highly visible, both on the streets of Chicago's Near North Side and in the fiction of the Chicago literary movement. Writers and graduate students mined the gay subculture so frequently that some gay men complained about the number of local investigators imposing on them for information.[39] With queers at a premium, and social science investigation in its heyday, a remarkable amount of material on Chicago's gay subculture was collected. Both the richness of the culture and the wealth of materials documenting it suggest promising possibilities for further study.

This preliminary analysis suggests that both the leisure and work environments where gay men congregated provided crucial supports for the establishment of a gay identity. The books they read, the streets they cruised, the cafeterias they frequented, the neighborhood they inhabited, and the jobs they chose all functioned to open up spaces in which they could enjoy a gay identity and express homosexual desires. The ease with which gay men entered Chicago's "queer life" in the 1930s—while walking down North Michigan Avenue, visiting Oak Street Beach, shopping at Marshall Field's, or attending a party—belies the notion that, prior to World

War II, gay men led tortured, isolated lives. In telling their stories, the gay men Bruce interviewed did not speak of an individual, private realization that they were homosexual, but rather highlighted their discovery of "queer life," which led to a new identity and often a new place of residence, wardrobe, circle of friends, and job. Prior to this discovery, they may or may not have been engaging in same-sex sexual activity, but they rarely understood themselves as different. Indeed, for many men, contact with the gay world and adoption of a gay identity were concurrent events. Bruce's mentor, Ernest Burgess, came to a similar conclusion, arguing that the homosexual's "awakening" did not occur "until introduction into the world of the homosexual at adolescence or youth."[40]

The early age at which many men discovered the gay world and the way in which "kids" formed a central part of the subculture may seem strange to us today. But since at least World War I, a peer-oriented, youth subculture has played a central role in shifting the center of social life from the home to the streets, theaters, and dance halls of urban America. Given the importance by 1930 of a youth culture organized around heterosexual dating, petting parties, and commercialized amusements—that is, around heterosexual desire unassociated with family or reproduction—the existence of a parallel world of homosexual desire seems almost unremarkable. Recall that when Harold discovered the gay world in the doorway of the Wrigley building, he was seventeen and already part of an active heterosocial life centered around a public high school. With his bohemian friends, he frequented nightclubs, smoked cigarettes, drank beer, and had sex with women. This context helps explain Harold's rather effortless transformation into one of the kids of fairytown. On a rainy night in 1934, he simply moved from one youth subculture to another.[41]

Acknowledgments

This essay began as a research paper in the graduate program of Northwestern University's Department of History, where it won the department's George T. Romani Prize. I wish to thank Micheal Sherry, Harold Perkin, Mitchell Stevens, Christino Arocho, Lane Fenrich, George Chauncey, Chad Heap, and Steven Anderson for their assistance at various stages of this project.

Notes

1. Transcript of interview with "Harold," (1937?), Folder 8, Box 127, Ernest W. Burgess Collection, Special Collections, Joseph Regenstein Library, University of Chicago. For clarity, I have edited typographical errors in the hurriedly transcribed text.

2. Pauline Redmond, "Term Paper for Social Pathology," n.d., Folder 7, Box 148, Burgess Collection; "Sociology 270 Exam," February 1938, Folder 10, Box 145, Burgess Collection. On Parks and Burgess's methodology, see T.V. Smith and Leonard D. White, eds., *Chicago: An Experiment in Social Science Research* (New York: Greenwood Press, 1968) and Robert E.L. Faris, *Chicago Sociology, 1920–1932* (San Francisco: Chandler Publishing, 1967).
3. Earle W. Bruce, "Comparison of Traits of the Homosexual from Tests and from Life History Materials," M.A. thesis, University of Chicago, 1942, 11–15. Bruce conducted the interviews in the 1930s, but being a part-time student, he did not complete his thesis until 1942. Author's interview with Beverly Bruce, February 1993.
4. Fragments of the life history narratives are scattered throughout the Ernest W. Burgess Collection. Many have no title, date, nor even a name to identify them. Gregory Sprague, who had been researching this collection before he died of AIDS, left his papers to the Chicago Historical Society. See Gregory Sprague, "Chicago's Past: A Rich Gay History," *Advocate*, August 18, 1983. The only scholarly publication to draw on the material on homosexuality in this collection is Kevin White's *The First Sexual Revolution: The Emergence of Male Heterosexuality in Modern America* (New York: New York University Press, 1993), 95f.
5. Lewis Erenberg, *Steppin' Out: New York Nightlife and the Transformation of American Culture, 1890–1930* (Westport, CT: Greenwood Press, 1981); Joanne Meyerowitz, *Women Adrift: Independent Wage Earners in Chicago, 1880–1930* (Chicago: University of Chicago Press, 1988).
6. "Survey of Rental and Retail Book Outlets," n.d., Folder 11, Box 98, Burgess Collection; Andre Tellier, *Twilight Men* (New York: Greenberg, 1931); Blair Niles, *Strange Brother* (New York: Liveright, 1931). On *The Well of Loneliness*, see Felice Flanery Lewis, *Literature, Obscenity and the Law* (Carbondale, IL: Southern Illinois University Press, 1976), 108–11.
7. "Survey of Rental and Retail Book Outlets."
8. Allan Bérubé, *Coming Out Under Fire: The History of Gay Men and Women in World War Two* (New York: Plume, 1990), 6.
9. "Survey of Rental and Retail Book Outlets"; Letters to Jimmy, May/June 1934, Folder 11, Box 98, Burgess Collection; La Forest Potter, *Strange Loves: A Study in Sexual Abnormalities* (New York: National Library Press, 1933), 64. For an introduction to the novels, see Roger Austen, *Playing the Game: The Homosexual Novel in America* (Indianapolis: Bobbs-Merrill, 1977). On "temperamental" as a code word for gay, see Jonathan Ned Katz, *Gay/Lesbian Almanac* (New York: Harper and Row, 1983), 439.
10. Sherwood Anderson, *Sherwood Anderson's Memoirs: A Critical Edition* (Chapel Hill: University of North Carolina Press, 1969), 339–40, 415–17; Clifford R. Shaw, *The Jack-Roller: A Delinquent Boy's Own Story* (Chicago: University of Chicago Press, 1930; reprint ed., 1966), 85, 97; The Juvenile Protective Association, "1926 Annual Report," 7; "John" interviewed by Larry Lesparance, Gregory Sprague Collection, Chicago Historical Society; Potter, *Strange Loves*, 4–5; George Chauncey, *Gay New York: Gender, Urban Culture, and the Making of the Gay Male World, 1890–1940* (New York: Basic Books, 1994), 9.
11. Sally Chappell, "As if the Lights Were Always Shining," in *Chicago Architecture 1812–1922: Birth of a Metropolis*, ed. John Zukowsky (Munich: Prestel-Verlag,

1987), 290–301; John Ashenhurst and Ruth L. Ashenhurst, *All About Chicago* (New York: Houghton Mifflin, 1933), 1.

12. Harvey Warren Zorbaugh, *The Gold Coast and the Slum: A Sociological Study of Chicago's Near North Side* (Chicago: University of Chicago Press, 1929), 69–104; Ashenhurst and Ashenhurst, *All About Chicago*, 133; Meyerowitz, *Women Adrift*, 108–16.
13. Zorbaugh, *The Gold Coast and the Slum*, 100; "Song of Frankie and Johnnie," Folder 2, Box 98, Burgess Collection; "Pansy Parlors: Tough Chicago Has Epidemic of Male Butterflies," *Variety*, December 10, 1930, 1; Shwanda Schweik, "Chicago World's Fairies," *Brevities*, December 7, 1931, 1. I thank Chad Heap for bringing the *Variety* article to my attention and Jon-Henri Damski for sharing the *Brevities* article with me.
14. Bruce, "Comparison of Traits of the Homosexual," 11, 14; "Case History of Mr. F," Folder 8, Box 127, Burgess Collection.
15. "Regarding Love Affair of Jim and Rodney" and "Sept. 30, 1932," Folder 4, Box 98, Burgess Collection; Interview with "Harvey," Gregory Sprague Collection.
16. Folder 11, Box 98, and Folder 8, Box 127, Burgess Collection; John Drury, *Dining in Chicago* (New York: John Day Company, 1931), 133; Chauncey, *Gay New York*, 163–68. Another branch of the Thompson's chain—at Randolph and State Streets—had a gay following because of its proximity to another cruising area by the Marshall Field's department store.
17. Lillian Faderman, *Odd Girls and Twilight Lovers: A History of Lesbian Life in Twentieth-Century America* (New York: Penguin Books, 1991), 80; Folders 2–3, Box 98, Burgess Collection. Unfortunately, this is one of only a handful of references to lesbians in the Burgess Collection. They appear only peripherally, in descriptions of cabarets and drag balls.
18. Interview with Bruce Scott, 1978, and Interview with Charles B., 1980, Gregory Sprague Collection. Waldman's Restaurant at 164 North Michigan Avenue first appears in the August 1935 edition of the Chicago Classified Telephone Directory (Reuben H. Donnelly Corp.). Although Chauncey suggests that several bathhouses in New York were the first exclusively gay commercial institutions in the city, it is unclear if Chicago bathhouses frequented by gay men, such as Jack's Turkish Baths at 829 N. Dearborn Street, were exclusively gay. Bathhouses were not a regular part of these working-class fairies' social lives. See Chauncey, *Gay New York*, 207–25.
19. "4/18/33," Folder 4, Box 98, Burgess Collection. On parties in New York, see Chauncey, *Gay New York*, 278–80.
20. Earle Bruce, "Observations of a Homosexual Party," Folder 4, Box 127, Burgess Collection; Ralph Berton, *Remembering Bix: A Memoir of the Jazz Age* (New York: Harper and Row, 1974), 216–17; Zorbaugh, *The Gold Coast and the Slum*, 100; Paul Oliver, *Blues Fell This Morning* (New York: Cambridge University Press, 1990), 98–103; James T. Farrell, "Just Boys," in *Calico Shoes and Other Stories* (New York: Vanguard Press, 1934), 81–98.
21. Folder 8, Box 127, and Folder 11, Box 98, Burgess Collection.
22. Folder 8, Box 127, Burgess Collection; Myles Vollmer, "Boy Hustler—Chicago," 1933, Folder 8, Box 144, Burgess Collection; Meyerowitz, *Women Adrift*, xxiii. On the historical relationship between male prostitution and the gay subculture, see Jeffrey Weeks, "Inverts, Perverts, and Mary-Annes: Male Prostitution and the

Regulation of Homosexuality in England in the Nineteenth and Early Twentieth Centuries," in *Hidden From History: Reclaiming the Gay and Lesbian Past*, eds. Martin Bauml Duberman, Martha Vicinus, and George Chauncey, Jr. (New York: New American Library, 1989), 195–211.

23. Folder 11, Box 98, Burgess Collection; Vice Commission of Chicago, *The Social Evil in Chicago: A Study of Existing Conditions* (Chicago: Gunthrop-Warren, 1911), 295–98; Interview with William Healy, January 1960, John C. Burnham Collection, Chicago Historical Society.
24. Letter of Graeme Davis to Sappho, September 13, 1920, Elsa Gidlow Papers, Gay and Lesbian Historical Society of Northern California Archives. I thank Ross Higgins for sharing this letter with me. See also Elsa Gidlow, *Elsa, I Come with My Songs* (San Francisco: Bootlegger Press, 1986).
25. "Billy?," and "Case J," Folder 8, Box 127, Burgess Collection.
26. Folder 8, Box 127, Burgess Collection; Chauncey, *Gay New York*, 56.
27. Bruce, "Comparison of Traits of the Homosexual from Tests and from Life History Materials," 35; Folder 8, Box 127, Burgess Collection.
28. Lisa M. Fine, *The Souls of the Skyscraper: Female Clerical Workers in Chicago, 1870–1930* (Philadelphia: Temple University Press, 1990), 16, 46; Susan Porter Benson, *Counter Cultures: Saleswomen, Managers, and Customers in American Department Stores, 1890–1940* (Urbana: University of Illinois Press, 1986).
29. Letter of Graeme Davis to Sappho.
30. Margaret T. McFadden, "'America's Boy Friend Who Can't Get Date': Gender, Race, and the Cultural Work of the Jack Benny Program, 1932–1946," *Journal of American History* 80 (June 1993): 128–29; Bérubé, *Coming Out Under Fire*, 57–66.
31. Letters to Jimmy. On the use of "gay," see Donald Webster Cory [Edward Sagarin], *The Homosexual in America: A Subjective Approach* (New York: Greenberg, 1951), 108–09.
32. Marie Kuda, "Chicago's Gay and Lesbian History from Prairie Settlement to World War II," *Outlines* [Chicago] (June 1994): 25–32. Henry Gerber (1934), quoted in Jonathan Ned Katz, *Gay American History: Lesbians and Gay Men in the U.S.A.* (New York: Harper and Row, 1976), 405; Folder 11, Box 98, Burgess Collection. On pre-political forms of resistance, see Lawrence Levine, *Black Culture and Black Consciousness: Afro-American Folk Thought from Slavery to Freedom* (New York: Oxford University Press, 1977), 54.
33. Chauncey, *Gay New York*, 6–8.
34. Folder 8, Box 127, Burgess Collection. For a history of psychiatric views of homosexuality, see Kenneth Lewes, *Psychoanalytic Theory of Male Homosexuality* (New York: Quartet Books, 1988).
35. Potter, *Strange Loves*, 42–48; "Leo, Age 18, Colored," Folder 11, Box 98, Burgess Collection.
36. "Regarding Love Affair of Jim and Rodney"; Chauncey, *Gay New York*, 141, 153, 198–206; Niles, *Strange Brother*, 63f.
37. Ruth Padnos, "The Case of Sex Morons (so-called): Crime Waves and Publicity," Winter 1937, Folder 7, Box 145; Folder 8, Box 127, Burgess Collection; Estelle B. Freedman, "'Uncontrolled Desires': The Response to the Sexual Psychopath, 1920–1960," in *Passion and Power: Sexuality in History*, eds. Kathy Peiss and Christina Simmons (Philadelphia: Temple University Press, 1989), 199–216; Chauncey, *Gay New York*, 9.

38. Floyd Dell, *The Briary-Bush* (New York: Macaulay Corp., 1921), 31–34. Kevin White discusses Dell's use of gay characters in *The First Sexual Revolution*, 65.
39. Folder 4, Box 98, Burgess Collection.
40. Ernest W. Burgess, "Sociological Aspects of the Sex Life of the Unmarried Adult," in *The Sex Life of the Unmarried Adult*, ed. Ira S. Wile (New York: Garden City, 1940), 148.
41. On heterosexual youth culture, see John D'Emilio and Estelle B. Freedman, *Intimate Matters: A History of Sexuality in America* (New York: Harper and Row, 1988), 256–65; Paula Fass, *The Beautiful and the Damned: American Youth in the 1920s* (New York: Oxford University Press, 1977); Frederick Lewis Allen, *Only Yesterday: An Informal History of the Nineteen-Twenties* (New York: Harper and Row, 1931), 73–101; Lizabeth Cohen, *Making A New Deal: Industrial Workers in Chicago, 1919–1939* (New York: Cambridge University Press, 1990), 144–47.

5. Before Paris Burned

Race, Class, and Male Homosexuality on the Chicago South Side, 1935–1960

Allen Drexel

Introduction

> Twice a year, with the knowledge and protection of Chicago's officialdom, do the homosexuals of the city gather in great numbers for their semi-annual costume ball, at which conventions and repressions are flung to the winds. New Year's Eve, and Halloween, mark the occasions for the celebrations of the "shadow world."[1]

So observed Myles Vollmer, who attended the University of Chicago as a divinity school student during the first years of the Great Depression. The remarkable document from which the above commentary comes, "The New Year's Eve Drag," raises some of the central questions and themes of the present essay, an historical account of drag queens and drag balls on Chicago's South Side from the 1930s through the 1950s.[2] Despite its critical importance in gay male cultural and political history, as well as its current prominence in feminist and lesbian/gay/bisexual theoretical debates concerning the production of gender and sexual identities, the history of drag and drag balls has been relatively underdocumented.[3]

The history of gay male drag in the United States merits scholarly scrutiny, not only because of its relevance to the recent work of cultural critics whose interest in drag has been sparked in part by Jennie Livingston's film documentary *Paris Is Burning* and the popularity of the drag queen disco diva RuPaul, but also because, as these two examples suggest, the history of drag is at many points closely interwoven with the currently undocumented histories of working-class and black gay male identities, cultures, and politics.[4] This essay, in the course of surveying the drag world of Chicago's South Side, sets out to achieve two principal goals:

first, to problematize commonplace assumptions of virulent, transhistorical homophobia within "the black community"; and second, to critique and build upon aspects of John D'Emilio's groundbreaking account of the political origins of the gay liberation movement, *Sexual Politics, Sexual Communities: The Making of a Homosexual Minority in the United States, 1940–1970*, by asserting the fundamental roles of race and class in organizing gay identities, experiences, and communities.[5] Though my work is indebted to D'Emilio's study in important respects, this essay suggests alternate ways of conceptualizing the multiple, complex origins—as well as the varying significance—of gay liberation to the different groups which made it possible.

In *Sexual Politics, Sexual Communities*, D'Emilio points to the rapid emergence and growth of a highly visible gay liberation movement following the 1969 Stonewall riots in New York City—generally regarded as the inaugural moment of gay liberation—and asks an important question: How could tens of thousands of lesbians and gay men, who had for decades clung to secrecy and silence as means of self-preservation in an intensely homophobic society, have been so rapidly and publicly mobilized in support of their own political cause? He asserts, "Isolated men and women do not create, almost overnight, a mass movement premised upon a shared group identity."[6] D'Emilio acknowledges the significance of several historical factors that helped make this swift, forceful mobilization possible in the early seventies, including the proliferation of gay bars in U.S. cities that began during and immediately following World War II. "Of all the changes set in motion by the war," he writes, "the spread of the gay bar contained the greatest potential for reshaping the consciousness of homosexuals and lesbians."[7] Ultimately, however, D'Emilio largely credits the energetic launch of the gay liberation movement to the collective efforts of activists working in the Mattachine Society and the Daughters of Bilitis—small, overwhelmingly white, middle-class reform organizations that had been operating, often secretly, in major U.S. cities during the previous two decades. Energized by the Stonewall riots, "a small, thinly spread reform effort suddenly grew into a large, grassroots movement for liberation. The quality of gay life in the U.S. was permanently altered as a furtive subculture moved aggressively into the open."[8]

Sexual Politics, Sexual Communities powerfully chronicles the ferocious antihomosexual and anticommunist terror campaign that swept the nation during the 1950s, leaving in its wake thousands of alleged homosexuals who were expelled from military, civil service, faculty, and other professional positions, and countless others who were arrested in bar raids or subjected to unprecedented levels of police harassment and brutality.[9] As D'Emilio writes, communism and homosexuality were often conflated in the paranoid logic of McCarthyism:

> Communists taught children to betray their parents; mannish women mocked the ideals of marriage and motherhood. Lacking toughness, the effete, overly educated male representatives of the Eastern establishment had lost China and Eastern Europe to the enemy. Weak-willed, pleasure-seeking homosexuals—"half-men"—feminized everything they touched and sapped the masculine vigor that had tamed a continent. The congruence of the stereotypical communist and homosexual made scapegoating gay men and women a simple matter.[10]

Ironically, however, it was during precisely this period that Halloween drag balls on Chicago's South Side, called "Finnie's Balls" after their founder Alfred Finnie, probably attained their highest levels of visibility and popularity. Throughout the 1950s, these annual extravaganzas, which originated and always took place in predominantly black, working-class, and poor areas of the city, drew thousands of spectators of remarkably diverse ethnic, racial, class, and sexual identities. The balls also attracted extensive coverage in the black press: *The Chicago Defender* as well as *Jet*, and for a few years, *Ebony* magazines, ran captioned photos and news stories documenting the events. The simultaneity of the height of Cold War antihomosexual hysteria and the peak popularity of Chicago's Finnie's Balls calls into question the bleak, and at times monochromatic, picture of the 1950s given to us by D'Emilio and other social historians of the Cold War era.[11] Moreover, it challenges this depiction in ways that have meaningful consequences for our understanding of the interactions between race, class, and homosexuality in the construction of urban gay cultures, and of the relationship of these cultures, in turn, to the gay liberation movement that exploded in the early seventies.

A more comprehensive understanding of the sources of the radical impulse evident in the Stonewall riots and their aftermath (riots which were instigated by a butch lesbian and a group of black and Puerto Rican drag queens) requires a look beyond the legacy of the bourgeois homophile organizations that are the principal subject of *Sexual Politics, Sexual Communities* to the long tradition of informal homosexual resistance represented by drag queens and balls in U.S. cities. In keeping with the work of cultural theorists Dick Hebdige, Kobena Mercer, and Judith Butler, and historian Robin D.G. Kelley, I take styles and public performances—drag style and performance in the case of gay culture—to be signifiers of identity and status that are produced, circulated, and variously understood within specific historical-ideological frameworks.[12] As Hebdige writes:

> Style in subculture is ... pregnant with significance. Its transformations go "against nature," interrupting the process of "normalization." As such, they are gestures, movements towards a speech which offends the "silent majority," which challenges the principle of unity and cohesion, which contradicts the myth of consensus.[13]

During the 1940s and '50s, drag queens—or "female impersonators," as non-gay audiences more frequently referred to them—publicly performed a version of male homosexuality, very often at considerable physical risk to themselves. As the most visible figures in male homosexual culture, they were persistent, flamboyant, public transgressors of an otherwise apparently "natural" and uniform heterosexual regime.

I do not wish to overstate or oversimplify the political meanings and significance of drag as a style: to argue, for example, that in its characteristic defiance of hegemonic gender norms, drag represented an uncomplicated, unqualified form of political resistance or self-emancipation deployed by gay men. As Esther Newton has observed in her classic ethnographic study of drag culture, the meanings of drag are not nearly so straightforward. Indeed, while drag may challenge the "naturalness" of gender and sexual roles on the one hand, it can also have quite the opposite effect, reinscribing these very roles and, by doing so, reinforcing the stigma of male homosexuality. As she suggests,

> Drag in the homosexual subculture symbolizes two somewhat conflicting statements concerning the sex-role system. The first statement symbolized by drag is that the sex-role system really is natural: therefore homosexuals are unnatural (typical responses [of drag queens]: "I am physically abnormal"; "I can't help it, I was born with the wrong hormone balance"; "I am really a woman who was born with the wrong equipment"; "I am psychologically sick").
>
> The second symbolic statement of drag questions the "naturalness" of the sex-role system *in toto*; if sex-role behavior can be achieved by the "wrong" sex, it logically follows that it is in reality also achieved, not inherited, by the "right" sex ... The gay world, via drag, says that sex-role behavior is an appearance; it is "outside." It can be manipulated at will.[14]

Despite the ambivalence and contradiction that drag queens certainly embodied, their persistent presence, and the historical association of this presence with male homosexuality, did constitute a significant kind of early, informal resistance to the antihomosexualism of the pre-gay liberation period. Particularly when considered against a backdrop of widespread Cold War antigay witch hunts, this resistance was striking and exceptional.

In their study of working-class lesbian bar communities in Buffalo, New York, *Boots of Leather, Slippers of Gold: The History of a Lesbian Community*, Elizabeth Lapovsky Kennedy and Madeline D. Davis provide a useful framework for conceptualizing the role of social class in relation to the formation of homosexual identities and communities.[15] While specifically pertaining to Buffalo's lesbian communities, their characterization of the ways in which women of different classes related to lesbian social life and culture from the 1930s through the '50s is applicable in significant respects to gay male communities and culture in Chicago during the same period. Kennedy and Davis assert that middle-class lesbians, who depended for financial security and social status on their reputations as "morally upstanding women," were generally unable to initiate "the early effort to make lesbianism a visible and viable opportunity for women," whereas working-class lesbians, whose jobs presumably did not require the same image of respectability, were better situated to effect social change that would benefit lesbians. Kennedy and Davis emphasize especially the role of the working-class butch lesbian—one half of the butch-fem relational dyad then dominant in working-class lesbian culture. Butches, according to the authors, "defied convention by usurping male privilege in appearance and sexuality, and with their fems, outraged society by creating a romantic and sexual unit within which women were not under male control."[16]

It would be quite wrong to equate the political meanings and significance of gay male drag and the role of the butch lesbian from the 1930s through the '50s; after all, gender-crossing performances of "the feminine" and "the masculine" by gay men and lesbians have distinct histories and meanings, and have tended to evoke very different public responses over time.[17] As Kennedy and Davis document, butches were widely regarded—indeed, they regarded themselves—as usurpers of male privilege, and many faced vicious attacks by men as a consequence. Drag queens, on the other hand, were often perceived as men who had "degraded" themselves by relinquishing their claims to male status and privilege. Still, the styles of the butch and the drag queen were similar in that both were predominantly working-class styles involving explicit stylistic/performative transgressions of gender and sexual norms. Like the butch lesbians whose lives Kennedy and Davis document, and unlike most of their middle-class white male counterparts, drag queens in Chicago were highly visible participants in an evolving tradition of gay, often black gay, stylistic/performative transgressions of heterosexual standards. The history of public transgression by these mostly working-class men, and the resistant impulse it in part reflected, were crucial elements in the evolution over time of the sense of shared identity and experience among lesbians and gays that underlay and energized the launch of the lesbian/gay liberation movement of the 1970s. It was ironic, given the central importance of drag queens and drag balls in lesbian/gay/bisexual history, that this movement largely excluded them from its vision.

The "Shadow World": 1935–1950

"Nancy Kelly," a retired clerical worker, vividly remembers his first encounter with a drag queen. Born Lorenzo Banyard on August 17, 1917, in New Orleans, Kelly (his drag name) migrated with his grandmother and sister to Chicago in 1924. He grew up in the city's Black Belt in a brothel owned and operated by his aunt. Roughly fourteen years after arriving in Chicago, Kelly saw "Joanne" for the first time. He recalls the sense of identification with and awe for Joanne that he felt then:

> The first drag queen I saw was Joanne, and I saw Joanne at the corner of 31st and State Street. And the guys was laughin', you know, so I laughed too, until I saw her. She was standing on the corner with her hand on her hip, her hair drawn to the back into the ponytail like, you know. But they wasn't botherin' her or nothin' . . . She worked at the Cabin Inn, you know. They'd do her, you know. I was fascinated . . . I knew I was gay since I was twelve years old. But I just watched her. That makeup was scintillating. And I thought, "I'm gonna do that."[18]

This anecdote illustrates the considerable attention queens could draw within this working-class milieu. As public deviators from dominant gender and sexuality norms, drag queens were commonly subjected to ridicule, harassment, and even violent attack. However, their status was more complex, and certainly less unambiguously abject, than this observation alone would indicate. Queens were derided, as the laughter of "the guys" suggests. But they were also seen to be, and often in fact were, as Kelly asserts here, potential sex partners of "normal" men who desired sex with other men. In his pathbreaking study, *Gay New York: Gender, Urban Culture, and the Making of the Gay Male World, 1890–1940*, George Chauncey persuasively argues that adherence to normative gender roles in sex acts and physical appearance, more than the choice of "actual" female sexual partners, was the key practice from which working men derived their sense of masculine integrity during this period. Referring to the "fairies" and "pansies" who populated the streets of New York's working-class and amusement districts in the first decades of the century, Chauncey writes:

> The determinative criterion in the identification of men as fairies was not the extent of their same-sex desire or activity (their "sexuality"), but rather the gender persona and status they assumed. It was only the men who assumed the

> sexual and other cultural roles ascribed to women who identified themselves—and were identified by others—as fairies. . . . The fundamental division of male sexual actors . . ., then, was not between "heterosexual" and "homosexual" *men*, but between conventionally masculine males, who were regarded as men, and effeminate males, known as fairies or pansies, who were regarded as virtual women, or, more precisely, as members of a "third sex" that combined elements of the male and female.[19]

Like the fairies and pansies of New York, drag queens in Chicago during the first decades of the twentieth century represented themselves, and were widely understood by others, as figures who combined conventionally feminine and masculine traits. The effeminacy of the drag queen meant that "normal" men, so long as they performed conventionally masculine roles (e.g., were insertive rather than receptive in intercourse and carried themselves as "men" in other social contexts), could engage in sex with drag queens without jeopardizing their status *as men.*

By the 1930s, this conceptual distinction between the practice of having sex with a "fairy" and the identity of *being gay* was becoming blurred. Although not yet dominant in working-class milieus, the modern practice of classifying individuals primarily according to sexual identity (hetero/homo) rather than gender style (masculine/feminine) was growing increasingly influential. The story of one man, who gave an interview to a University of Chicago sociology student in 1933, suggests the ambiguous symbolic meaning that could be ascribed to having sex with a drag queen.[20] After providing an extensive account of a blow job given to him by "Co.Co.," this unidentified man hastened to add that, "To myself I know in my own heart that I am not a real bitch, because a woman thrills me. A man will do when there is nothing else in the world, *preferably a she man, because he is more womanly or closer to a woman.*" Although the speaker asserts that he is not "a real bitch," insisting on his general sense of comfort with his role in the encounter (along with a misogynistic disdain for his male sex partner, whom he perceives as a virtual woman), there is an element of uncertainty and anxiety in his words: he seems in part to be reassuring himself that his masculinity has *not* in fact been compromised by his involvement with this "she man." The same anxiety is discernible in his insistence that his positive "reaction" to Co.Co., whom he had met at "one of my first parties of the queer world," was "purely from an educational standpoint. I wanted to find what the real thing was all about," and in his reiteration that, "It felt good because he was impersonating a woman so it was something like having a woman do me."[21]

By the turn of the twentieth century, and perhaps earlier, a number of public dance halls, saloons, and clubs in Chicago had become well known as gathering places for gay men. Gays who frequented these public sites could often be identified by their "feminine" style, whether they appeared in full drag or merely wore makeup or particular items of jewelry. Indeed, so visible was the city's emergent gay male culture that as early as 1911 the city's vice commission felt compelled to draw attention to "the great increase of sex perversion in Chicago" in their book-length report, *The Social Evil in Chicago: A Study of Existing Conditions, With Recommendations.*[22] In a section devoted exclusively to "sex perverts," one of the commission's investigators, who claimed to have come into contact with "whole groups and colonies of these men," emphasized the prevalence of "femininity" among them:

> In this community there is a large number of men who are thoroughly gregarious in habit; who mostly affect [sic] the carriage, mannerisms, and speech of women; who are fond of many articles ordinarily dear to the feminine heart; who are often people of a good deal of talent; who lean to the fantastic in dress and other modes of expression, and who have a definite cult with regard to sexual life.... Many of them speak of themselves or each other with the adoption of feminine terms, and go by girls' names or fantastic application of women's titles. They have a vocabulary and signs of recognition of their own, which serve as an introduction into their own society.[23]

Drag queens were the most readily identifiable members of this "society." As the vice investigator wrote, "Two of these 'female impersonators' were recently seen in one of the most notorious saloons on (X1262c) street. These 'supposed' women solicited for drinks, and afterwards invited the men to rooms over the saloon for pervert practices."[24]

Blues and jazz clubs on the city's South Side were especially popular congregating sites for homosexuals, male and female, black and white, from the 1920s through the '40s. Musicologist Sandra Lieb has written that "songs of unconventional sexuality were not unusual in the blues and in live black entertainment.... and 'freak shows' and drag shows—evenings set aside for homosexuals, lesbians, and transvestites—were common in many ... Chicago nightclubs."[25] For example, the legendary Cabin Inn at 35th and South State Street, where Joanne worked, featured a transvestite chorus line and allowed same-sex and interracial dancing.[26] Nancy Kelly, too, danced during the 1940s as the sole cross-dressing member of an "all-female" chorus line at Joe's Deluxe, another popular South Side show club.

Significantly, however, socializing among drag queens was not confined to the interiors of nightclubs and private homes, but also took place in full view of their fellow Chicagoans. The presence of these queens, who often walked boisterously together in small groups through the streets of the South Side, defied University of Chicago divinity school student Myles Vollmer's sweeping characterization of the city's gay community as a "shadow world." Kelly, for example, remembers on several occasions watching Valda "swishing" with some of his/her friends in the early 1940s:

> They'd be comin' down the street corner swishin' all over Michigan Avenue to catch the bus to go to the club, you know. And *I'd* be standing on the corner of Forty Third Street, 'cause I *admired* them, you know, they had this long hair . . . and the makeup and everything. . . . Plus they was making *money*, too, for dancing.[27]

These flamboyant public displays by drag queens were risky for several reasons, including the fact that they violated a local ordinance, frequently if capriciously enforced by vice squads, which prohibited the wearing in public of "a dress not belonging to his or her sex."[28] Black gay drag queens' open violation of this law and myriad social conventions, and their apparent willingness to suffer the punishment and opprobrium that resulted from such violations, constituted a form of everyday political resistance. The presence of drag queens in the streets, and on buses and streetcars, signified a refusal on the part of these black gay men, though vilified and often physically vulnerable, to mask their differences or simply go away.

It also reflected to some extent the ambivalent status of drag queens, and gay men more generally, within black families and communities from the 1930s through the 1950s. Interestingly, the history of drag queens and drag balls in Chicago seems to suggest, in some respects at least, that black gay men were in fact more fully accepted within the city's black working-class and poor communities prior to the 1960s than they have been in more recent decades. Before exploring at some length the complex social status of black gay men in these communities during the pre-gay liberation period, it will be useful for comparison to consider briefly the work of two contemporary black writers which addresses the trenchant problem of homophobia among black intellectuals and in black communities today. In his moving essay "Don't Turn Your Back on Me," Stephan Lee Dais has asserted:

> I want to serve my community as a man, a gay man, and a member of the black community. I also want my human rights respected as a man, a gay man, and [a] member of the black community. I don't want to be labeled faggot anymore than I want to be called nigger. I have been forced by society to pay a price for being black. I don't want to pay yet another price when I come home.[29]

Joseph Beam placed a similar stress upon the importance of "home" in his important essay, "Brother to Brother: Words from the Heart":

> When I speak of home, I mean not only the familial constellation from which I grew, but the entire Black community: the Black press, the Black church, Black academicians, the Black literati, and the Black left. Where is my reflection? I am most often rendered invisible, perceived as a threat to the family, or I am tolerated if I am silent and inconspicuous. I cannot go home as who I am and that hurts me deeply.[30]

Like Dais and Beam, black gay Chicagoans who came of age during the thirties and forties, including Nancy Kelly and his friends, were frequently discriminated against in the communities where they lived and worked: being targeted on the streets as "sissies" or "queers" was hardly an unusual occurrence for them. But for complex reasons related to the poverty and racism impacting upon these communities, they were often able to create niches for themselves within individual families and even in the public life of black communities. The contradictory treatment of Nancy Kelly by his relatives and the residents of the South Side community where he grew up illustrates the ambivalent status of gay men in black working-class communities during this period. On the one hand, Kelly was frequently taunted by family members for his perceived failure to achieve a prescribed masculine norm. On the other hand, these same family members also consistently and energetically protected him from threats and attacks made by people outside the family. As Kelly recalls:

> I was so thin and skinny and I used to swish all the time, and [my uncle] told my mother, "That boy got gal in him!" And Mama said, "Leave him alone! Leave him alone!" But you know my mother never, until the day she left me, she never said nothin' to me. Women would tell her, you know, church women would tell her about me . . . like when I started out on the drag scene, "Well, you know, your son is a sissy—he wear women's clothes." She'd say, "I ain't got nothin' to do with that! You ain't got nothin' to do with it . . . leave it alone! . . ." When them women would get on me, you know, I didn't pay them no attention, 'cause I'd swish on down the street with my drags on, I'd be goin' to the clubs . . . I was goin' to make *money*, you know. My sister, she would look out the window and see me, [and she'd say,] "You tryin' to be like me, you ain't nothin' but a sissy. . . ." My sister was a funny kind of a person. Now, she called me all kind of sissies, but now *you* better not do that. She'd go to war. My uncle was the same way, 'cause the boys was gonna beat me up one day—they's so hard on the queens—and they told my uncle, "He's a sissy" and he says, "Well, he's *my* sissy!" and he had

the biggest fight on 45th Street. My uncle whipped all those little punks up there. And later on in years they became trade. Yeah. They used to come down to the 430 [a popular gay tavern located in the 400 block of 43rd Street].[31]

In the economically depressed decade preceding World War II, professional drag entertainers like Kelly and his friends Valda, Joanne, and Jeanne Lerue distinguished themselves not only by their sartorial style and transgressive sexual practices, but also, as the above comments imply, by the significant fact that they often had relatively well-paying, if unstable, jobs. Kelly could earn up to forty dollars a night as a club dancer, in stark contrast to the twelve dollars a week he brought home from his job as a dishwasher at the main branch of the YMCA. The money Kelly earned as a female impersonator enabled him to fulfill a normatively masculine role as his family's principal financial provider, ironically enough. This more than justified the physical risks that doing such work entailed. The following anecdote suggests the influence of economic factors in the decision of drag queens like Kelly to perform professionally. It also evokes the sense of collective identity shared by many drag queens, demonstrates the high visibility achieved by these queens and the multiplicity of responses (sometimes surprisingly affirmative) to them, and suggests the bold, resistant impulse that some of them possessed:

There was a place on West Roosevelt Road called 1410 West Roosevelt Road. A Jewish fellow owned it. And he was payin' the girls ten dollars a night to do a show, to build up his crowd, you know. And there was another queen was workin' in there: Jeanne Lerue. Jeanne Lerue asked me did I want to go. And everybody avoided that place like the plague. They'd say, "Oooh, no! 1410. Uh-huh, no amount of money!" The boys was so hostile. They'd tear your drags off, tear your wigs off. . . . They would make nasty remarks, call you all kind of "Sissy motherfuckers" and everything like that. . . . But we needed some money, 'cause the war hadn't started. And I borrowed a drag from one of the queens and she said, "Sister, where in the world do you think you're going?" And I'd put my makeup on and get on the streetcar and *shock* the people! We wore greasepaint, you know. . . . It was Max Factor greasepaint. Number 8. And I told my best friend, she said, "Where do you think you're going?"—I had just turned at 43rd Street and South Park—and I said, "Well I'm going to 1410 West Roosevelt Road." And she said, "Oh, sister, don't do that. They could *kill* you over there." And I said "Well, I'm goin' anyhow because the man is paying ten dollars a show" and I knew I could do three shows. I could hit that floor three times, you know. And so I went.

I got on . . . this streetcar and this little lady was sittin' right across from me,

> you know, and here I got all this makeup on and eyelashes, you know, and jewelry, and lipstick and . . . Cuban-heeled shoes. . . . So anyway, this little ole lady was sittin' right across from me, and there comes this big drunk dude, you know, and [he said,] "Hey, Baby! You sure do look good!" I say, "Jesus." 'Cause now I'm gonna have to rustle with him until I get to Roosevelt Road, you know. He sit down and plump his ass down next to me, you know, and I said, "What's your problem, man?" He said, "Oohh" [moaning noise]. The little lady say, "Come here honey. Come here. Come here honey, sit over here. Sit over here." She say, "We women are not even safe anymore. That old . . . I would like to curse him but I'm a Christian, you know." Everybody that was on the streetcar was lookin' at me. I didn't say nothin', I just sit there and crossed my legs, you know. And when we got to Roosevelt Road, I got off, and I could see everybody lookin' out the window, you know, to see where this man is going with all this makeup on her! And when I got to 1400, I'll never forget it. . . . I saw all these little punks out there in the front. My heart fell. I say, "Oh, lord." 'Cause I ain't nothin' much of a fighter. But I was gonna fight them with my makeup kit. The little boy said, "Oh, here she comes. Here she comes. We're gonna beat your mother-fuckin' ass when you come outa there, you know." And Jeanne Lerue, she was peepin' through the venetian blinds.[32]

Professional drag shows at South and West Side taverns and clubs like the 1410 West Roosevelt Road, the Cabin Inn, and Joe's Deluxe took place before predominantly non-gay male audiences. These performances were delivered by drag queens and included a great deal of explicitly gay content—much of the humor of the shows came in the form of ironic references to the reputed gender inversion and sexual practices of gay men. They did not, however, typically occur in spaces coded as gay.

Drag balls, in contrast, brought together hundreds, sometimes thousands, of gays in large, elaborate public rituals that at once reflected and reinforced a growing sense of shared cultural identity among these men. The nation's first drag balls probably took place during the last decades of the nineteenth century and, importantly, from their inception their appeal seems to have transcended racial lines. Two of the earliest documented balls reportedly took place in Washington, D. C. and New York City, and were, according to one account, attended exclusively by black gay transvestites.[33] In 1893, Dr. Charles H. Hughes of St. Louis described the Washington "drag dance" as it had apparently been related to him by another doctor. Hughes's remarks were laden equally with racist stereotyping and antihomosexual hysteria:

> In this sable performance of sexual perversion all of these men are lasciviously dressed in womanly attire, short sleeves, low-necked dresses and the usual ball-

> room decorations and ornaments of women, feathered and ribboned head-dresses, garters, frills, flowers, ruffles, etc., and deport themselves as women. Standing or seated on a pedestal, but accessible to all the rest, is the naked queen (a male), whose phallic member, decorated with a ribbon, is subject to the gaze and osculations in turn, of all the members of this lecherous gang of sexual perverts and phallic fornicators.[34]

It is unclear precisely when the first drag balls took place in Chicago or who sponsored them. But like those in New York and other major cities, the balls in Chicago by 1930 had begun attracting considerable public attention and crowds of several hundred attendees. Remarks made by some observers in the early 1930s that New York's drag balls had surpassed those in Chicago and New Orleans in size and opulence suggest that Chicago's balls had by that time been occurring for at least several years.[35] As in New York, city officials in Chicago not only sanctioned the semiannual balls (despite the fact that the events violated the local ordinance prohibiting public cross-dressing), but they actually dispatched uniformed and plainclothed police officers to guard the affairs. Myles Vollmer described the drag balls as "the one occasion when official Chicago put its approval on the public appearance of its intermediate sex."[36] In reality, this official "approval" was made possible by the fact that the events regularly took place on Halloween and New Year's Eve, and thus for official purposes were able to pass as conventional masquerade balls.

The first Chicago balls, like those in subsequent years, were racially integrated, a fact frequently remarked upon by those who attended or wrote about them. Vollmer, for example, observed:

> Physically, all types are there. Homosexuals thin and wasted, others slender and with womanish curves; others overfed and lustfully fat. Most of the younger homosexuals have pallid complexions with rather thin hair, due, perhaps, to overindulgence. There is a preponderance of Jews and the Latin nationalities, although homosexuality is no respecter of races. Many of the men are of Polish blood. Negros mingle freely with whites. There seemingly is no race distinction between them.[37]

"All types" may have attended the balls, but the great majority who went did so in full drag. As Vollmer further commented,

> The picture is repeated over and over—colorful evening gowns, satin slippers, French heels, silken hose, gracefully displayed, tiaras, feathered fans, flashing jewelry,—all gliding about the Hall. Gliding is the only name for it; no woman

> could be more graceful. Trains are carefully held up by curled and manicured fingers.... The "girls" (men homosexuals in female costume) move about swaying their shoulders, rolling their hips, and the only clue to their masculinity is their heavier skeletal frames, or occasionally a more masculine featured face.[38]

In regard to New York's balls, George Chauncey has asserted that "The theater of the drag balls enhanced the solidarity of the gay world and symbolized the continuing centrality of gender inversion to gay culture."[39] The same could be said of Chicago's balls, where men who were otherwise at pains to appear "normal" would turn up each year in full feminine attire. One man interviewed in 1933 told a University of Chicago student that "I do not like to be seen with Swishy bells [sic] on public street [sic], because people will think I am the same way and quite a few people are wise to cock suckers and they will class me with the. [sic]" The student who interviewed this man, however, reported later seeing "the above person at the Coliseum dressed in drag."[40]

Perhaps more easily than in New York, though, it was possible, and not uncommon, for gay men dressed *as* men to dance with each other at Chicago's balls. Chauncey has written of the New York balls that "The drag organizers could allow men to dance together ... so long as one (or both) of them wore a dress, but if both of them were wearing pants the police might force the organizers to stop them."[41] Myles Vollmer and Nancy Kelly both describe a somewhat more relaxed atmosphere at the Chicago events during the thirties and forties. Vollmer, for instance, wrote of seeing "two young men in street clothes dancing together, cheek to cheek, holding one another in close embrace, as any girl and boy would at any dance, save, perhaps, that the two youths were much more intense in their forbidden roles." He saw additional "men in street clothes, lacking courage to come in Drag, who [were] dancing with other men, occasionally embracing and kissing them in moments of abandon."[42]

The relative informality of Chicago's balls reflected in part the fact that they rarely took place in venues as "respectable" as those in which many of New York's events occurred.[43] In contrast to the New York affairs, which were often staged at the most glamorous halls in midtown Manhattan and Harlem, Chicago's balls during the thirties and forties generally took place in rented rooms or halls adjoining taverns or clubs on the city's predominantly black, poor South Side, or at the Coliseum Annex, a large convention hall located in a commercial district on the Near South Side.

Though it is unknown exactly when and by whom Chicago's first drag ball was organized, the origins of the Finnie's Ball, the city's most prominent such event from the 1940s through the '70s, are somewhat more clear. The first Finnie's Ball, staged in 1935 by a black gay street hustler and gambler named Alfred Finnie, was held in the basement of a tavern on the corner of 38th Street and Michigan Avenue. Guests of the ball paid twenty-five cents to attend. Nancy Kelly, who went to his first Finnie's Ball in 1938, recalls that the event in its first years was relatively small, drawing an almost exclusively gay and mostly black crowd of about one or two hundred drag queens and their friends. (Non-gays did not, to his recollection, start attending Finnie's Balls in significant numbers until the late forties.) Until 1943—the year that Finnie was killed in a gambling brawl—the ball was held up to five times annually at a number of different venues.[44] As Kelly remembers, "They'd just pick out a random little shack, you know. Decorate it, put up some balloons ... and stuff like that. It was more homey than it is now."[45] In contrast to the extravagant, commodified spectacles they would later become, the balls during the thirties and forties had the feel of relatively intimate social gatherings for gays and lesbians. As Kelly recalls:

> There'd be music. There'd be food.... They would have a big band, maybe a seven or eight piece band, you know, and everybody'd be dancin' with one another; they'd be drinkin'. They had tables, like a cabaret ... and you'd dance with a friend, you'd dance with somebody else's friend. And the lesbians would be there. Not too many of them.... They would dance with the queens.... The first lesbian I ever danced with I thought was a man ... her name is Billy. I thought sure Billy was a man, you know, until she told me, "No, baby, it ain't like that."[46]

From 1935 through the 1940s, Finnie's drag balls provided rare opportunities for working-class, mostly black gay men and lesbians in Chicago to socialize publicly in spaces that they could claim, if only temporarily, as their own. The events, advertised by word-of-mouth and even by placards festooned around South Side neighborhoods, at once created, symbolized, and celebrated a growing sense of solidarity among homosexual men and women.

Attendance at the balls was not risk-free, however. Recalling the Finnie's Balls of the thirties and forties, Kelly said of the straight gawkers who would form crowds outside the buildings where the events were held, "They'd see you coming in ... and they'd jeer at you, you know, call you all kind of names. It was horrible."[47]

Christmas in October: Finnie's Balls, 1950–1960

> Two of the gayest, most frenetic masquerade balls in the country are held annually by female impersonators in New York and Chicago. This year in each city more than 3,000 contestants and spectators gathered to watch the men who like to dress in women's clothing parade before judges in the world's most unusual fashion shows. Clothed in clinging silks and satins, male doctors, lawyers, undertakers, truck drivers and dishwashers minced across the stage to compete for cash prizes in New York and huge cups and statuettes in the Windy City.[48]
>
> —*Ebony*, March 1953

It was during the 1950s, at the very height of antihomosexual and anticommunist Cold War crusading, that Chicago's Finnie's Balls achieved their greatest levels of visibility and popularity. Significantly, the balls were promoted and reported extensively, and almost exclusively, in the black press, even though they drew roughly equal numbers of black and white spectators and performers throughout the decade. In the early fifties, *The Chicago Defender*, *Jet*, and *Ebony* (until 1953) became the first newspaper and serials respectively to carry extensive photo and news coverage of the drag balls.[49] But this often celebratory coverage hardly amounted to a tacit endorsement of homosexuality. Indeed, the tone of the articles and photo captions in general suggested a deep ambivalence on the part of the black press and its readership toward gay men and lesbians. It did, however, point to an exceptional openness toward and even an open fascination with representations of homosexuality and drag within black communities which were rarely, if ever, evident in the mainstream white press during the 1950s.

The mass circulation of gay and transvestite images and news stories by the black press, and the great popularity of Finnie's Balls themselves, call for a reevaluation of prominent accounts of the fifties, which by focusing primarily on the experiences of white, middle-class Americans, have tended to portray the fifties in fairly stark, sweeping terms as a dreary decade dominated by Cold War ideology and domestic revivalism. For example, Elaine Tyler May's influential book, *Homeward Bound: American Families in the Cold War Era*, finds that "the domestic ideology encouraged private solutions to social problems and further weakened the potential for challenges to the Cold War consensus. Personal adaptation, rather than political resistance, characterized the era."[50] In a similar vein, John D'Emilio's *Sexual Politics, Sexual Communities*, while acknowledging the important presence of "an urban [gay] subculture," stresses the view that, during the 1950s:

> ... the harsh reality of oppression shaped the contours of gay identity and *the gay world*. The condemnations that did occur burdened homosexuals and

> lesbians with a corrosive self-image. The dominant view of them—as perverts, psychopaths, deviates, and the like—seeped into their consciousness. Shunted to the margins of American society, harassed because of their sexuality, many gay men and women internalized the negative descriptions and came to embody the stereotypes.[51]

May's and D'Emilio's claims about "the domestic ideology" and "the gay world," while useful as generalizations, elide crucial class and racial distinctions and hierarchies within the formations they seek to describe. They also overlook the significance of everyday forms of resistance during the fifties, such as drag performance and drag balls. At a time when gay and lesbian workers were under intense fire from federal, state, and local governments, as well as from private employers, and when written and printed materials relating to homosexuality were being targeted for suppression by censorship groups, these drag performances and the coverage of them by the black press, provided rare, bold representations of male homosexuality.[52] At least as important as the everyday collective experience of participating in the burgeoning, but constantly policed, bar culture that D'Emilio documents, these representations were central to the construction of that sense of shared cultural identity which would ultimately fuel the lesbian and gay liberation movement.

The extreme homophobia and anticommunism that seized much of middle-class white America during the 1950s—which to a significant degree came to define middle-class white America—did not seem to so forcefully grip the segregated poor and working-class black communities in which the Finnie's Balls were staged each year on Chicago's South Side. In these communities, racial oppression and pervasive poverty perhaps remained more significant concerns than the presence of homosexuality and homosexuals. Regularly denied access to housing, employment, and equal justice under the law, working-class blacks might understandably have been less preoccupied with the threatened encroachment of communism upon the "free" world, and by the putative connections between communists and homosexuals, than were their counterparts in middle-class white society. The comparative lack of antihomosexual fervor within black communities and the black press during the 1950s made possible the continued production, promotion, and media coverage of Finnie's Balls throughout the decade, at a time when nonhomophobic representations of gays and lesbians were largely absent in white middle-class communities and in the mainstream press.[53]

In fact, far from being suppressed within black communities and the black press, Finnie's Balls were among the most popularly attended and highly publicized social events held on the South Side each year. The balls, which during the 1950s drew at least as many straight as gay spectators, were seen by many to be fashionable, glamorous affairs at a time when, according to sociologist E. Franklin Frazier, fashion and glamour were particularly prized signifiers of status among the burgeoning black middle class. In his 1957 classic, *Black Bourgeoisie*, Frazier discussed Negro "society," whose activities, he argued, "serve[d] to differentiate the black bourgeoisie from the masses of poorer Negroes and at the same time compensate[d] for the exclusion of the black bourgeoisie from the larger white community."[54] In Frazier's account:

> For that section of the black bourgeoisie which devotes itself to "society," life has become a succession of carnivals. In cities all over the country, Negro "society" has inaugurated Debutante Balls or Cotillions which provide an opportunity every year for the so-called rich Negroes to indulge in lavish expenditures and create a world of fantasy to satisfy their longing for recognition. . . . The weekly accounts in the Negro press of the activities of Negro "society" are invariably stories of unbridled extravagance. These stories include a catalogue of the jewelry, the gowns, and mink coats worn by the women, often accompanied by an estimate of the value of the clothes and jewelry, and the cost of the parties which they attend. One constantly reads of "chauffeured" Cadillac cars in which they ride to parties and of the cost of the homes in which they live.[55]

Consistent with Frazier's observation, news accounts of Finnie's Balls typically drew attention to the most "extravagant" aspects of the events. *Ebony*'s story on the 1953 ball, for example, reported that "More than 1,500 spectators milled around outside Chicago's Pershing Ballroom to get a glimpse of the bejeweled impersonators who arrived in limousines, taxis, Fords, and even by streetcar."[56] A photo caption accompanying the story reiterated that "At both [the Chicago and New York] affairs there were contestants who arrived in chauffeur-driven Cadillacs," while acknowledging that "there were also many who used public transportation." The same magazine's coverage of the 1952 Finnie's Ball had made the connection between drag balls and "society" more explicit. In a description typical in its mixture of mockery and adulation, *Ebony* observed:

> The men who don silks, satins and laces for the yearly masquerades are as style-conscious as the women of a social club planning an annual charity affair or a society dowager selecting a debutante gown for her favorite daughter. Many of the men, some of whom are dress designers by profession, spend months and

> hundreds of dollars readying wardrobes for the one-night appearance before the public.[57]

The attendance of well-known public figures at Finnie's Balls underscored the prominence of the events in South Side culture during the 1950s. In *The Chicago Defender*'s extensive coverage of the 1955 ball, for example, John Earl Lewis, the honorary "Mayor of Bronzeville," was depicted on stage flanked by "the finery bedecked winners" of that year's extravaganza.[58]

The Finnie's Balls meant different things and appealed in different ways to the thousands of people who went to them. For most gay men, whether or not they actually attended in drag—and many did not—the balls were rare, critical opportunities to meet and socialize openly with one another, and in doing so, to reaffirm and celebrate a shared sense of cultural identity. For Jacques Cristion, a black gay dancer and dressmaker who attended his first ball in the late fifties, the event was the highlight of each year: "It was *the thing* to go to. You lived for that, really. I mean, just like a child lives for Christmas. The same way." Jacques was introduced to the world of drag balls by a beautician friend of his, Donald Caraway, who attended the balls every year as Olivia de Haviland. As Jacques recalls:

> He was telling me how fabulous the ball was, and how, you know, you really hadn't lived until you went to the ball. And he said you'd see the lights, and the . . . speaker, oh, the loudspeaker outside and it was really fabulous with the limousines, people getting out of the limousines and what not, and just, it was beautiful—and it sounded so interesting, and I just began to go right after that.[59]

Recalling a Finnie's Ball of the late fifties, Jim Darby, a retired white schoolteacher who currently heads the Chicago chapter of a lesbian and gay veterans' association, describes a similarly spectacular scene outside the event:

> It was a big, big deal. Actually, it was like a Hollywood première, because I can remember, you know, people would usually . . . rent limos or come up by cab or whatever and they actually had the police horses—you know, the yellow wooden horses to hold the crowd back as you came in—and all the screaming and applauding and everything else. All the local folk in the neighborhood would stand around and watch all these strange birds get out of these cars in their costumes and go in, and I don't even know if people knew if they were men or women or what.[60]

The action at Finnie's Balls during the 1950s centered around elaborate fashion shows replete with runway competitions and—the climactic moment of each year—the "parade of beauties," during which all the contestants would file down through the middle of the ballroom before being judged. The winner of the fashion competition each year would then be named "Queen of the Ball" or, in 1953 and 1957, when the ball was patterned after Hollywood's Oscar ceremony, "Academy Award winners."[61] Participants in the fashion competition frequently impersonated screen actresses, singers, and other celebrities, the most popular among whom seem to have been Barbara Stanwyck, Josephine Baker, Lana Turner, Joan Crawford, Bessie Smith, and even, one year, a pregnant Eva Marie Saint.[62] These impersonations, generally infused with generous portions of camp wit, simultaneously celebrated and parodied the various stars whose personas were being enacted. Camp humor surfaced in the announcement by one drag queen at the 1952 ball that "'Gloria Swanson' isn't here yet. You know some of these big shots like to wait until the last minute so they can make a grand entrance," and in the assertion by another that, "'Alexis Smith' won't be here tonight. She's been drafted into the army."[63]

Interracial couples were a common sight at Finnie's Balls, a fact often emphasized in reporting of the events by the black press. The presence of these couples reflected the relatively high levels of interracial socializing within gay male social networks in Chicago during this period. John Fiers, a white hairdresser who attended his first ball in the late 1950s, recalls:

> At the time integration hadn't come into existence yet [sic], but the gay world was integrated long before . . . Well, the gay world was *always* integrated. Not one hundred percent, certainly. Some white gays didn't like blacks. Some black gays didn't like whites. But gay people could go into black areas and black nightclubs and feel perfectly safe because blacks knew that white gays were quite liberal.[64]

The common experience of being gay did encourage many black and white gay men to transgress a racial line not as frequently or as openly crossed in heterosexual society. However, the common reference by white gay men to other white gays who were known to prefer black sexual partners as "dinge queens," and the characterization by some white gays of socializing with blacks as "chic" and "interesting," demonstrated the limits of white "liberalism." No matter how often the racial line might have been crossed, it was rarely if ever forgotten, and in fact structured black-white relations within the relatively "integrated" gay world in a fundamental way.[65]

The extensive coverage of Finnie's Balls in *Jet*, *Ebony*, and *The Chicago Defender* throughout the 1950s reflected a deep ambivalence toward homosexuality on the part of the black press and, presumably, much of its straight readership as well. On the one hand, the coverage betrayed an obvious fascination with, and even admiration for, the gender and sexuality transgressions featured at the balls. A caption accompanying *The Defender*'s prominent front-page photo coverage of the 1951 event reflected this fascination. It began, "Female impersonators take the stage at Finnie's club's 13th annual Halloween masquerade ball. The 'bolder' of the male species dared to cross the sex line for 'one mad night' and thrilled, shocked and amused over 5,000 spectators who jammed the Pershing ballroom on Chicago's Southside Halloween night."[66] On the other hand, the relatively positive coverage accorded the drag balls was frequently offset by articles which promoted a decidedly less sanguine view of homosexuality. Examples of these included, "Sex in the Church," a blistering condemnation by the Harlem minister Adam Clayton Powell, Jr. of alleged "sexual depravity" among black preachers; "Can Science Eliminate the Third Sex?," which promoted "surgery and other treatments" for homosexuals and hermaphrodites; and "I am a Woman Again," in which the renowned lesbian entertainer Gladys Bentley recanted her lifelong participation in "the sex underworld."[67]

But perhaps the most startling and, from the perspective of lesbian and gay history, most significant feature of the black press's coverage of Finnie's Balls and other lesbian and gay themes during the fifties was the fact that this coverage existed at all. At a time when much of white middle-class society was mobilized against homosexuals and the public representation of them, the black press, and black communities in general, demonstrated considerably greater openness.

Still, the 1950s were dangerous years for gay men, as Jim Darby and Nancy Kelly knew. Darby was arrested several times in bar raids. Kelly, too, was arrested—for "appearing in public in clothes of the opposite sex."[68] He was sentenced, without benefit of a trial, to ninety days in a Chicago jail and lost his job as a result. Kelly's story, moving in its own right, powerfully illustrates the double bind many gay men faced during this period:

> So [I] did them ninety days.... When I went back out to Kraft, [the boss] asked me where had I been for ninety days. Now what could I tell that man? "I been in jail." That's what I told him: "I been in jail." *And I didn't tell him what I'd been in there for*, but I said, "I been in jail." And I was such a good worker, you know, the man said, "Well, you know, you've been gone so long." He said, "The union can't even help you." So they cut me loose. Gave me the rest of my money.[69]

Drag queens in Chicago's South Side from the 1930s through the '50s took major risks by identifying themselves as gay in public. Yet long before the birth of gay liberation, these queens, most of whom were working-class black gay men, regularly did so. A story included in *Ebony*'s coverage of the 1953 Finnie's Ball captured vividly both the grave danger drag queens routinely faced and the fierce resistant impulse many of them possessed:

> On the street following [the] end of the Finnie's Ball, a crowd of about a hundred teen-age youths chased one husky impersonator down the street and the gown-wearing man defended himself by throwing bottles, one of which crashed through the window of a real estate office.[70]

In the Stonewall riots sixteen years later, the same resistant spirit was in ample evidence as a small contingent of drunken drag queens helped launch the lesbian and gay liberation movement.[71]

Epilogue

In his book *Stonewall*, Martin Duberman has compellingly described the central roles played by drag queens in the riots, which he suggests began when a drag queen named "Tammy" took a swing at a police officer.[72] More humorous, but perhaps no less important, was another kind of resistance deployed by the queens. Duberman writes that in the midst of the riots,

> When the police whirled around to reverse direction at one point, they found themselves face to face with their worst nightmare: a chorus line of mocking queens, their arms clasped around each other, kicking their heels in the air Rockettes-style and singing at the tops of their sardonic voices:
>
> "*We are the Stonewall girls*
> *We wear our hair in curls*
> *We wear no underwear*
> *We show our pubic hair . . .*
> *We wear our dungarees*
> *Above our nelly knees!*"[73]

It is ironic, considering drag queens' long tradition of public, performative resistance, that the political movement they helped instigate has never included them in its vision. Indeed, the modern lesbian and gay liberation movement has often been defined in opposition to the stigmatized figure of the drag queen, or at least to the gender inversion model of homosexuality that she/he is seen as representing.[74] Much gay male historiography, too, with its focus upon white, middle-class experience, has often overlooked the critical contributions made by drag queens, most of whom, in Chicago at least, were working-class, and many if not most of whom were black. As historians develop a more comprehensive understanding of the origins of the lesbian and gay liberation movement, it is essential that they pay careful attention to the vexed relationship between that movement and the histories of communities of color and working-class lesbians and gays. This pursuit will necessarily entail continued study of dissident cultural identities and practices not conventionally seen by historians in "political" terms, including drag queens and drag performance.

Acknowledgments

This essay was first presented in 1994, in somewhat different form, at the Sixth North American Lesbian, Gay, and Bisexual Studies Conference held at the University of Iowa. It is dedicated with much love to the memory of Robert Ford (1961–1994), founding publisher/co-editor of *Thing* magazine, without whose inspiration, guidance, and good-humored encouragement the research involved in this project would simply not have been possible. Thanks as well to George Chauncey, Annelise Orleck, Tom Holt, Liz Kennedy, and John Shovlin for their excellent support and advice along the way.

Notes

1. Myles Vollmer, "The New Year's Eve Drag" (unpublished paper), 1, undated, Ernest Burgess Collection, Box 139, Folder 2. Special Collections, Joseph Regenstein Library, University of Chicago. Vollmer's enrollment as a divinity student between 1929 and 1933 was confirmed by the office of the Registrar at The University of Chicago.
2. Of multiple possible definitions, "drag," for purposes of this article, will denote the phenomenon of female impersonation. Any exceptions will be noted in the text.
3. For important contributions to this discussion, see, for example, Judith Butler, "Imitation and Gender Insubordination," *Inside/Out: Lesbian Theories, Gay Theories*, ed. Diana Fuss (New York: Routledge, 1991), 13–31; Eve Kosofsky Sedgwick, "Queer Performativity: Henry James's *The Art of the Novel*," *GLQ: A Journal of Lesbian and Gay Studies*, vol. 1, no. 1 (1993): 1–16; David Bergman, ed., *Camp Grounds: Style and Homosexuality* (New York: Routledge, 1993); Marjorie Garber, *Vested Interests: Cross-Dressing and Cultural Anxiety* (New York: Routledge, 1992); and Esther Newton, *Mother Camp: Female Impersonators in America* (Chicago: University of Chicago Press, 1972).
4. On this debate, see Judith Butler, *Bodies that Matter: On the Discursive Limits of "Sex"* (New York: Routledge, 1993), 121–40; and bell hooks, *Talking Back: Thinking Feminist, Thinking Black* (Boston: South End Press, 1984), 120–26.

5. John D'Emilio, *Sexual Politics, Sexual Communities: The Making of a Homosexual Minority in the United States, 1940–1970* (Chicago: University of Chicago Press, 1983).
6. Ibid., 2.
7. Ibid., 32.
8. Ibid., 239.
9. Ibid., Ch. 5
10. Ibid., 49.
11. Other important accounts of gender and sexuality conventions—and the enforcement and transgression of them—during the Cold War era include Lynne Segal's *Slow Motion: Changing Masculinities, Changing Men* (New Brunswick: Rutgers University Press, 1990), especially chapter 5; Allan Bérubé's *Coming Out Under Fire: The History of Gay Men and Women in World War Two* (New York: Plume, 1990); and Elaine Tyler May's *Homeward Bound: American Families in the Cold War Era* (New York: Basic Books, 1988).
12. Important works by these writers include: Dick Hebdige, *Subculture: The Meaning of Style* (New York: Methuen and Co., 1979); Kobena Mercer, "Black Hair/Style Politics," *New Formations*, vol. 3 (Winter 1987): 49; and Robin D. G. Kelley, "'We Are Not What We Seem': Rethinking Black Working-Class Opposition in the Jim Crow South," *The Journal of American History*, vol. 80, no. 1 (June 1993): 75–112.
13. Hebdige, *Subculture*, 18.
14. Newton, *Mother Camp*, 103.
15. Elizabeth Lapovsky Kennedy and Madeline D. Davis, *Boots of Leather, Slippers of Gold: The History of a Lesbian Community* (New York: Routledge, 1993).
16. Ibid., 6.
17. A useful, though in some instances a surprisingly homophobic, discussion of drag in relation to gay men and lesbians appears in Sarah E. Murray's "Dragon Ladies, Draggin' Men: Some Reflections on Gender, Drag and Homosexual Communities," *Public Culture*, vol. 6, no. 2 (1994): 343–63.
18. Lorenzo Banyard, Interview by author, February 27, 1994, Chicago, tape recording in author's possession.
19. George Chauncey, Jr., *Gay New York: Gender, Urban Culture, and the Making of the Gay Male World, 1890–1940* (New York: Basic Books, 1994), 47–48.
20. Interview by University of Chicago Sociology student, "Christmas Time," 1933. Transcript, Special Collections, Joseph Regenstein Library, University of Chicago.
21. Ibid.
22. The Vice Commission of Chicago, *The Social Evil in Chicago: A Study of Existing Conditions, With Recommendations* (Chicago: Gunthorp-Warren Printing Company, 1911), 296.
23. Ibid., 297.
24. Ibid., 297.
25. Sandra Lieb, *Mother of the Blues: A Study of Ma Rainey* (Amherst: University of Massachusetts Press, 1981), 123.
26. Frank Driggs and Harris Lewine, *Black Beauty, White Heart: A Pictorial History of Classic Jazz, 1920–1950* (New York: William Morrow and Company, 1982), 83. I thank Chad Heap for bringing this book to my attention.
27. Banyard interview.
28. Francis X. Busch, ed., *Revised Chicago Code of 1931, Containing The General Ordi-*

nances of the City of Chicago in Force May 27, 1931, and Repealing All Former General Ordinances With Certain Exceptions Therein Noted, 1514.

29. Stephan Lee Dais, "Don't Turn Your Back on Me," *In the Life: A Black Gay Anthology*, ed. Joseph Beam (Boston: Alyson, 1986), 61–62.
30. Beam quoted in Essex Hemphill, ed., *Brother to Brother: New Writings by Black Gay Men* (Boston: Alyson, 1991), xvii.
31. "Trade" here refers to non-gay-identifying men who had sex with gays. bell hooks has documented similar contradictions in the treatment of lesbians and gays in contemporary black communities. In her essay "Homophobia in Black Communities," she observes:

> Black communities may be perceived as more homophobic than other communities because there is a tendency for individuals in black communities to verbally express in an outspoken way anti-gay sentiments. I talked with a straight black male in a California community who acknowledged that though he has often made jokes poking fun at gays or expressing contempt, as a means of bonding in group settings, in his private life he was a central support person for a gay sister. Such contradictory behavior seems pervasive in black communities. It speaks to ambivalence about sexuality in general, about sex as a subject of conversation, and to ambivalent feelings and attitudes toward homosexuality. Various structures of emotional and economic dependence create gaps between attitudes and actions.

hooks, "Homophobia in Black Communities," in *Talking Back*, 122.

32. Banyard interview.
33. Charles H. Hughes, "An Organization of Colored Erotopaths," quoted in Jonathan Ned Katz, *Gay American History: Lesbians and Gay Men in the U.S.A.* (New York: Meridian, 1992), 42–43.
34. Ibid., 42–43.
35. Chauncey, *Gay New York*, 251.
36. Vollmer, "The New Year's Eve Drag," 1.
37. Ibid., 4.
38. Ibid., 2.
39. Chauncey, *Gay New York*, 254.
40. Paul, Interview by University of Chicago Sociology student, 29 June 1931, Transcript, Special Collections, Joseph Regenstein Library, University of Chicago.
41. Chauncey, *Gay New York*, 252.
42. Vollmer, "The New Year's Eve Drag," 1–2.
43. Chauncey, *Gay New York*, 251.
44. Banyard interview.
45. Ibid.
46. Ibid.
47. Ibid.
48. "Female Impersonators," *Ebony*, March 1953: 64.
49. I am grateful to Gregory Conerly at Cleveland State University for permitting me to view his "Index of *Ebony/Jet* articles on Homosexuality: 1950–1959."
50. May, *Homeward Bound*, 208.
51. D'Emilio, *Sexual Politics, Sexual Communities*, 52–53, *emphasis added*.
52. Ibid., 131–33.

53. Significantly in this regard, my review of *The Chicago Daily News, The Chicago Tribune*, and *The Chicago Sun-Times* unearthed no coverage of Finnie's Balls during the 1950s.
54. E. Franklin Frazier, *Black Bourgeoisie* (Glencoe, IL: The Free Press, 1957), 195.
55. Ibid., 201–02.
56. "Female Impersonators," 64.
57. "Female Impersonators Hold Costume Ball," *Ebony*, March 1952: 62–67.
58. *The Chicago Defender*, November 5, 1955, 3.
59. Jacques Cristion, Telephone interview by author, February 21, 1994, tape recording in possession of author.
60. Jim Darby, Interview by author, January 9, 1994, Chicago, tape recording in possession of author.
61. "Gay Affair Names Queen," *Jet*, November 15, 1957: 63; *The Chicago Defender*, November 5, 1953, 1.
62. Cristion interview.
63. "Female Impersonators Hold Costume Ball," 62–67.
64. John Fiers (pseudonym), Telephone interview by author, February 17, 1994, tape recording in possession of author.
65. Fiers and Darby interviews. I thank George Chauncey for assisting me with this formulation.
66. "Female Impersonators Take the Stage," *The Chicago Defender*, November 10, 1951, 28.
67. Rev. Adam Clayton Powell, Jr., "Sex in the Church," *Ebony*, November 1951: 27–34; "Can Science Eliminate the Third Sex?," *Jet*, November 22, 1953: 47–50; Gladys Bentley, "I Am a Woman Again," *Ebony*, August 1952: 92–98.
68. Derby and Banyard interviews.
69. Banyard interview, *emphasis added.*
70. "Female Impersonators," 67.
71. Martin Duberman, *Stonewall* (New York: Dutton, 1993), especially 167–213.
72. Ibid., 196.
73. Ibid., 200–01.
74. For an impressive theoretical/historical analysis of the repudiation by post-gay/lesbian liberation activists of the gender inversion model, see Carole-Anne Tyler's essay, "Boys Will Be Girls: The Politics of Gay Drag," *Inside/Out*, 32–70.

The "Fun Gay Ladies"

Lesbians in Cherry Grove, 1936–1960

Esther Newton

In 1953, Audrey Hartmann, then twenty-three years old, was staying in the summer resort of Ocean Beach when she heard that there were lesbians in nearby Cherry Grove. Determined to find them, but afraid her roommates would hear about it if she took a beach taxi, she hiked five miles down the beach. What she saw there changed her life:

> The houses were all gas lamps, charming little houses . . . it was so wooded, and so beautiful, a canopy of trees wherever you'd walk, and you could look in the windows and I remember seeing women by candlelight sitting there, and thinking "Oh, I wish this were I!" I so well remember that . . . I just said, "I *have* to come back and live here."[1]

Cherry Grove is a predominantly gay summer community in the New York metropolitan area. Located on Fire Island, an Atlantic barrier island a few miles off the east coast, the "Grove" today consists of about 275 beach houses, a small commercial center, and a sweeping ocean beach. You can walk all around the community on boardwalks—there are no roads or cars—in a few minutes.

First arriving in the 1930s, gay summer renters from New York City were becoming homeowners by the 1950s. They created an underground mecca which sheltered and nurtured those lesbians and gay men who were lucky enough to find it; in the virtual absence of social, political, or economic organizations, gay people could only communicate by means of personal "grapevines."[2]

Under the wing—and in the shadow—of gay male power and culture, an intrepid group of lesbian homeowners and renters and a larger number of "day-trippers" established a fragile presence. My subject is the small, close-knit group of white upper-class and upper-middle-class women who made up the resident lesbian population from about 1936 to 1960.[3]

For many female (and some male) narrators, gay Cherry Grove was founded by, or at least coalesced around, two gay women[4]: Natalia Danesi Murray (1902–1993), the longtime companion[5] of the late Paris correspondent for the *The New Yorker* Janet Flanner (1892–1978), and a wealthy, beautiful woman named Kay (1903–1989).[6] Audrey Hartmann told me that Natalia Murray, a "coterie of women," and a couple of men from the theater world came out in a speed boat from Sayville "because they had heard of this wonderful place called Cherry Grove where all the theater people were hanging out.... They were just looking for a little hideaway, a place where they could be, quote, 'themselves.'[7] In the hotel bar, "just like that" Natalia recalled, they met John Mosher, the *The New Yorker* film critic and short story writer, who would later introduce Natalia to Janet Flanner. Natalia rented that summer and every summer until she had her own house floated over in 1945.[8]

Natalia Murray was an Italian-born aspiring actress and singer who, after divorcing her American husband, became the Italian language broadcaster for the Voice of America on NBC radio, and was later an editor for the Italian publisher, Rizzoli.[9] "By all accounts," wrote Flanner's biographer, "Natalia was stunning, a dark-haired, handsome woman whose ready laughter and volatile enthusiasms charmed many who met her,"[10] an opinion shared by several Grove narrators who had been part of her circle.

Two summers after Natalia discovered the Grove, Kay was visiting friends in Ocean Beach when her lover suggested that they go five miles east to Cherry Grove to visit her friends Marty Mann, the founder of the National Council on Alcoholism, and Priscilla Peck, an attractive woman who was art editor at *Vogue* magazine.[11] Sitting on the shady deck of her Cherry Grove cottage during her 85th birthday party, Kay still remembered knowing during that very first visit to Peck and Mann's house that "Cherry Grove is where I want to live!"

Kay had come to New York in 1926, where she quickly got a job as a publicist for Paramount Pictures. She also seems to have parlayed family money into more wealth in the booming stock market of the mid–1920s. In 1938, she was thirty-five years old, still an exceptionally beautiful natural blonde with vivid large blue eyes. Flying small airplanes, driving fast cars and speedboats, Kay was a risk-taker and a legendary seductress; much more of a party girl than the intellectually inclined Natalia Murray, her Grove friend and sometime lover,[12] Kay's real affinity had been with the sophisticated Jazz Age speakeasies. Among her friends and conquests were pretty showgirls like Dottie Justin, who had danced in the Ziegfeld Follies and at Texas Guinan's Prohibition speakeasy, where she and Kay had met. Another friend was the "human dynamo" Peggy Fears, a

> [v]ery personable and very pretty showgirl from Texas, one of the first ones to affect the bleached streak in her hair. She did a nightclub act, she played the Rainbow Room at the top of Radio City Music Hall, and came down those stairs with a book on her head singing "Pretty Peggy."[13]

Despite her subsequent marriage to a rich man named A.C. Blumenthal—Grove wits sometimes called Fears "Mrs. AC/DC"—her woman companion was the "ravishingly beautiful" Teddy Thurmond, who announced the weather on the radio. According to another Grove resident: "You couldn't have been gayer than they were. And they spent the entire time hurling champagne bottles at each other. It was a wonderful atmosphere—I mean, nobody ever got bored."[14]

The presence of women like Peck, Mann, Murray, Kay, and Fears assured that, from the start, gay women as well as men would be attracted to the Grove. There is a common shape to the stories that gay women told about their years in the Grove, narratives which were both collective markers of time and parables of the founders most cherished values, represented most often in the figure of their leading member, the fabulous and beautiful Kay.

"We Came to This Magical Place"

Cherry Grove's natural beauty and social advantages were irresistible to the founding narrators. As Natalia Murray told me, "[t]his place, so close to New York, you can breathe the fresh air; when we found it [in 1936] it seemed so secret, wonderful. You see people just leaving Sayville, they breathe freer."[15]

Then in their thirties and forties, Kay, Natalia, and their friends were energetic white women with independent incomes, professional occupations, or both. Their jobs included work as an employment agency publicist, an advertising copywriter for a women's magazine, and a designer for a department store; most were connected to or identified with the theater world. Members of what was called Cafe Society, they had been part of a young urban elite—ancestral to the Jet Set and our present day Glitterati—which had emerged from the First World War and clustered in New York City. Artists, writers, intellectuals, and theater people, members of this generation founded such postwar institutions as the Theatre Guild and *The New Yorker* magazine, which by the 1930s constituted the U.S. intellectual establishment.[16]

The Grove crowd of the late thirties and the forties included, at one time or another, writers like Janet Flanner, Jane Bowles, Patricia Highsmith, and Carson McCullers; legitimate actresses like Betty Garde; and the founder of the Group Theatre and Actor's Studio, Cheryl Crawford, and her companion, Ruth Norman. There were also the "follies girls" in Kay's circle like Peggy Fears and Dottie Justin. These women were more than a random group of summer renters, and more, even, than a haphazard group of lesbians; they constituted a lesbian circle of friends and colleagues, an artistic elite who played major roles in U.S. cultural life.[17]

As a group, Grove women and men, Natalia Murray thought, were "Interesting, talented people . . . who had so much fun!" There was no organized nightlife on the island, nothing to do but enjoy the pleasures of the beach and bay, and entertain each other. Heavy drinking was a feature of these first cocktail parties, and so were costumes, sometimes elaborate, sometimes just clever. Natalia remembers "the first party" in the late 1930s, to which Arthur Brill, an interior designer, came dressed, significantly, as the Statue of Liberty.[18]

While Natalia Murray and Kay, members of a gay and bisexual theatrical elite, were looking for a little "hideaway" close to New York, the lesbian narrators like Ann Leone who came just after World War II had heard from other gays, often men, "that Cherry Grove was the place that gay people can go and feel free and enjoy themselves and have a ball."[19] Part of the vastly expanded gay life of the postwar years, most—but not all—of these women were, like the prewar crowd, professional or wealthy and sometimes both. Cris flew a seaplane to commute from her bay house to supervise her factory, Laura came from plenty of old money, and Mary Hecht was the heir to a New York City department store fortune.

Used to getting what they wanted, these women could be haughty. During a hurricane in the mid-fifties, Laura, her then-companion Ann, Peggy Fears, and her companion Teddy Thurmond were evacuated from the Pines by Bob Pokorney, owner of the ferry service who, much to his annoyance, was almost immediately detoured by a message that Kay was stalled out on the Great South Bay on her own motorboat, *Cagey*. If Kay, who once told me that she adored hurricanes, had wanted to experience the storm up close or simply to evacuate herself, she had undue confidence in her seamanship; *Cagey* had already sunk once before and had to be pulled up, so Pokorney's irritation was understandable.

Eventually, Laura, Ann, Peggy, and Teddy wound up in the Patchogue Motel on the mainland for three days without any electricity or water, and were so cold they survived by piling into bed with each other. Laura had brought nothing with her but her toothbrush and a bottle of scotch. They also had very little cash on them:

> Peggy Fears went to the manager and said, "I too am in the hotel business and have been all my life." This was a lie; she had only just started the Botel [a dockside hotel] in the Pines. "If you want these ladies and other Fire Island people to frequent your motel"—of course, we would never have returned there for any reason—"what you should do is send them all up double martinis, and not charge them." He was so impressed with Peggy, who had an authoritative tone and always got what she wanted, that he did just that.[20]

But even these resourceful and imperious women had to be discreet in everyday life. Mary Hecht married and had a child, Laura married a gay man from her social set to keep up appearances, and they all felt forced to lie and hide their sexual orientation, which meant their entire personal lives, from their families, friends, and coworkers. Under these conditions, the Grove meant much more to them than a pleasant summer spot. Laura explained:

> It was terribly exciting to be in a place that was totally gay ... [T]o wear slacks and to be with and talk to other people like yourself was for us, at that age, a simply extraordinary feeling of freedom and elation ... because [outside the Grove] there was nothing.[21]

I asked Peter Worth, who had escaped from Nazi Germany and then from occupied France, what she liked about the Grove when she arrived in 1946. "The homosexuality!" she exclaimed. "I felt, *finally* I am in the majority—ah! this was my world and the other world was not real."[22] For Ann Leone, a pretty youngster from a working-class background, it was "another world; it was just beautiful, because as fake as it was, it was exactly what [she] needed in [her] life." "Why 'fake?'" I asked.

> Well, my girlfriend Flo, she embroidered stories. I won't say she lied, but they were all out of her head, like she said she was the daughter of a prince—and I loved it! ... Why was it fake? Because it seemed so unstable ... the word "gay" seemed to mean that that's what they wanted to be, and not be responsible—well, they all had responsible jobs—but certainly not be responsible for a thing like marriage and children ... [They] wanted no part of anything that was binding, and that's why they went to the Grove, for complete freedom. And that's where it was.[23]

Even the threat of male heterosexual harassment and violence was left behind on the mainland. In the Grove, women could move about outdoors, even at night. Peter Worth found that "[y]ou could go out at night in the dark and, if there were any boys, they were only disappointed you were not another boy and they never bothered you."[24] Propositions from the decreasing number of straight men were brushed off—some lesbians remember being aided by "our boys"—and, for the most part, police harassment, a chronic problem until 1970, targeted only gay men. The most notable exception occurred during a period of intense harassment in the late forties, when Kay, Camilla Munklewitz—a local Long Island woman of eccentric and perhaps bisexual inclination—and a third woman from Chicago were arrested for nude sunbathing in the dunes.[25] But Kay's arrest was the exception proving the rule that all women were safe in the Grove. The Grove offered lesbians a breather from the strains of continual concealment, and from straight men's unwanted sexual attentions, in a glorious, natural setting.

"We Had Such Fun"

The gay people who came to Cherry Grove in this period made their livings in New York City. The Grove was a pleasant, weekend summer place, the antithesis of the hot, dirty, and crowded city. This is true of most summer vacation spots, but closeted Grovers had desperate reasons to go someplace where they could be what they felt was their authentic selves. In the Grove they could be free, which meant they could be openly gay—expressive, honest, and sexual. As Laura put it, "[y]ou could do everything you couldn't do in the city. We would throw off our girdles, dresses, and heels."[26] Here they could let their hair down and melt away the mask in a martini glass. Parties, relaxing, fun—early Grove social life revolved around the local bar and an incessant round of cocktail parties.

From 1938 to 1956, Duffy's Hotel—a ramshackle wooden structure with a restaurant, bar, dance floor, and rooms for rent—was the venue for gay and lesbian social life on weekend nights. The proprietor, Edward Duffy, though heterosexual and married, was sympathetic to the gay crowd. He let the "girls" dance together at any time, and even the "boys" could do so late in the evening after the last ferry left. While men could meet each other cruising or at the huge parties they threw, Duffy's provided the only public lesbian social space and the only entree for new women to see and be seen. Audrey Hartmann remembered vividly when, after that hike down from Ocean Beach, "I walked in, the very first time, to Duffy's, this huge, cavernous room, and saw all these women on the floor. And I was quite overwhelmed. There were so many."[27]

Although lesbians were invited to the men's big costume parties—though by all accounts their costumes tended to be less elaborate—smaller parties were sometimes all "boys." But "girls" too had their dinners, cocktail parties, and buffets. Laura recalled the all-women's parties in the middle '50s as "quite elegant.... I can remember having a catered brunch for thirty ladies, and that was considered sort of par for the course. And, of course, all the people would be mixed up, I mean the Kays and the Natalias would be there."[28]

By the 1950s, the founders—Kay, Natalia, and their friends—were in their forties and fifties and a second cohort, the "young crowd," was coming in. Although from similar social backgrounds, the younger "girls" often partied separately and, for the most part, were sexually involved with each other. Laura recalled: "One could sort of run around amongst oneselves ... but certainly one did not invade the love lives, the sacred marriages, of the older group."[29]

The younger group was more committed to butch and femme identities than Kay's generation. Kay, who "prided herself on being 'adaptable,'" as Peter Worth put it, was always made up and wore elegant dresses and suits as well as slacks. Yet Ann Leone insisted that "Kay might not have made that distinction [of calling herself butch], but that's what her approach was." She recalled a weekend when "Somehow I wound up sleeping with Kay. [She] was so determined and aggressive ... she was very, very, very strong. And I had a wonderful night of just making love. And *she* made all the love."[30]

The younger crowd used gendered terms self-consciously and assertively, but they were careful to distinguish themselves from the kinds of working-class lesbians they had left behind in New York's gay bars of the fifties. Ann Leone explained the intricacies of the system:

> There was a big distinction between femmes and ... the masculine ones [who] were called "dykes," or "butch" was used more. "Dyke" was used more as a derogatory statement, like Mary [Hecht] was called a "dyke." That means, [laughs] "forget about it." A butch was more [points to me]—you're a real typical butch. "Dyke" was reserved for people that they didn't like, that were seedy and crummy looking and maybe very fat ... It's like saying "the lousy Jew or the Yid—Guinea."[31]

Laura and especially Cris were cited by others as having been "very butch" or "mannish." Cris was a "wonderful looking gal, stunning" who reminded Ann Leone of Stephen Gordon in *The Well of Loneliness*, "tall, blonde, lean, and *gorgeous*." She and her girlfriend, Agnes Browning, were always elegantly dressed, and Cris frequently wore a jacket and tie, looking, according to one male Grover, "just like [the movie star] Ronald Coleman."[32] "Cris was very good looking," Peter Worth agreed, adding with a laugh, "The boys adored her—they loved to dance with her, she was such a good lead."[33]

Although the older "ladies" pursued lesbian relationships with relish, they were more ambivalent than their younger friends about claiming a lesbian identity. Natalia Murray began an interview by telling me how much she disliked labels and Kay always tried to dissuade me from writing a book about Cherry Grove with a "gay slant." Both of these women and several others of their generation often or always used their married names preceded by "Mrs."[34] Fewer of the younger crowd ever married; they chafed more under the restrictions society imposed, and their collective pride was celebrated in the ritual of "Lithuanian flag raising day," which lasted for several years during the 1950s. A Lithuanian flag was hoisted to a chorus of "Hail Lithuania, Lithuania rules the waves" sung to the tune of "Hail Brittania." People told me many slightly different versions of the origins of this tradition. According to Laura's,

> Alice and Alyson were at Duffy's and they heard these two little old ladies from Sayville discussing the men and the ladies, and the authoritative lady said, "They are"—about the men—"homosexuals," and the other little old lady pointed to two [of our] ladies and said, "And what are they?" and the authoritative lady said, "*They* are Lithuanians." So Alice and Alyson from then on had Lithuanian flag raising every 4th of July.[35]

Despite differences between the generations, the older women did not entirely exclude the younger ones. Kay especially was accessible because of the parties she threw and because her legendary powers of seduction led her across social boundaries of age, ethnicity, and class. Explaining why she found working-class women attractive, she once told a friend, "[t]hat kind don't have the same inhibitions that we do." And while Grove lesbians generally practiced serial monogamy, Kay was a happy-go-lucky flirt who moved from conquest to conquest and whose attentions were greatly desired. Alice and Alyson, whose house "We Three" was the site of the Lithuanian flag raising and who were would-be social arbiters for the younger crowd, once organized a game of "post office" at their house, which Kay attended. Peter Worth recalled Alyson saying reverentially, "If it weren't for that party, I would never have had occasion to kiss Kay."

Although Audrey Hartmann felt that Natalia Murray "brought us up," for almost all female (and many male) narrators, Kay, more than the more intellectual and socially selective Natalia, epitomized the ideals of the Grove's "golden age." When she died in the summer of 1989, she was eulogized by the priest who presided over her memorial service, a male Grover, as "our queen." When I asked people, "Who struck you particularly in those years?" Laura summed up many responses: "Kay, there was no question ...

She was really the grande dame . . . Her elegance, she was older than the rest of us and she was more suave."[36]

Until the 1970s, Kay was a bountiful party giver; one lesbian narrator recalls her giving a mixed cocktail party for one hundred people followed by a buffet brunch for a somewhat smaller group. This may have been the annual Halloween or pumpkin party Kay hosted in her larger house, "Katherine the Grape," which was painted all purple. One year for the party, George Fiehl, a decorator for several large department stores, made giant spider webs complete with spiders to drape Kay's house in.[37]

She was revered not only for giving parties, but also for her ingenuity, what Laura called "her good ideas." Laura remembered the birthday party Kay held for her toy poodle. Eighteen "ladies" and their dogs were invited:

> There was a huge birthday cake made of hamburger, and hot dogs as candles, and she gave every dog in that tiny house of hers a slice of cake and a marrow bone as a present. So, of course, big dogs like mine swallowed the whole thing in one second, and the little ones were still gnawing hours later, and I thought to myself, only Kay would throw all these dogs together in this tiny house, and *know* that there wouldn't be an argument. And there wasn't. There wasn't one dog that made a face at another dog.[38]

But not everyone was in the inner circle. Ann Leone, the pretty working-class girl from a Brooklyn Italian family, was not invited to the dog birthday party. From her perspective, "[t]here were a lot cliques. You were either in or out. . . . They were mostly based on how successful you were . . . money was the measuring stick."[39] Grove social life revolved around parties, and if you couldn't afford to throw your own, you were "only a taker," as Ann put it. But wealth, though necessary to social prestige, was not enough. Natalia Murray and Kay were looked up to for reasons that went beyond the fact that they were older, relatively wealthy, and homeowners in an era when even many privileged lesbians could only afford to rent.

Kay's opposite was Mary Hecht, the department store heiress and owner at that time of an imposing house on the bay, who was, according to Cris, also a "fun, crazy party person." Yet many saw her as "gross looking and gross acting." For Stephan Cole, Mary Hecht was "a monster, a woman who was ugly as sin."[40] She was "terrible, completely obnoxious, overweight," Ann Leone recalled, adding,

> she had a lot of money . . . [so] she did what she damn well felt like doing. . . . She kept herself quite aloof . . . maybe go to the bar and pick one out and take her home . . . I don't think she would ever accept me so I never even tried. She

> only wanted to associate with people who would mean something . . . she was a social climber.[41]

The story of how Mary Hecht threw her girlfriend's clothes into the bay is also often recounted. Moreover, although she picked up other people's bar and restaurant tabs, she was reputed to be a mean drunk and seems to have had many acquaintances but few friends.[42] How Mary Hecht's behavior or her reception in the Grove might have been affected by being Jewish in a primarily WASP circle is hard to evaluate.[43]

But Kay was not admired *because* she was a Gentile. Her virtues were apprehended as a luminous whole. Kay represented—she *was*—elegance, beauty, "good ideas," generosity, sexual prowess, and the ability to hold her liquor. Forty years after the end of their affair, Natalia Murray visibly warmed to the mention of Kay's name. "She was a very, very beautiful girl," she told me, smiling. "Kay is a grand . . . fun, party girl."[44]

To say that someone was a "fun person"—indeed the Grove's unwritten charter was to be a "grand, fun, party" place—during the gloomiest era of gay American history was high praise. Grove sensibility, which challenged adversity and denigration with a flippant, witty remark, was given dramatic expression once the Cherry Grove Arts Project was founded in 1948, just two years before Senator Joseph McCarthy's attack on homosexuals in the State Department ushered in the most homophobic decade in the nation's history. The theater quickly became a social center to complement Duffy's Hotel. Grove gay "ladies" Kay, Cheryl Crawford, Peggy Fears, and Betty Garde were among the founders of this community organization,[45] which put on light musical reviews written and acted by Grovers for Grovers. Every skit had a gay slant conveyed primarily through double entendres and drag. Programs from the early 1950s show that most numbers were written by men but acted by both genders. For example, Maggie MacCorkle recalled that the 1950 show, called *Berthe of a Nation*, was about how the actress Bertha Belmore and her theatrical friends got lost in the fog on the Great South Bay and, at last finding themselves on Fire Island, "gave birth to the nation of Cherry Grove."[46]

Most of the skits featured about the same number of men and women, like a take-off on Ziegfeld's Floradora girls, in which, MacCorkle remembered, the men played the girls and the women played male escorts dressed in "morning trousers and cutaway coats."[47] But *Berthe of a Nation* also featured one "all-girl" number, titled "Bill Ronin's All-Girl Orchestra."[48] Laura remembered a Lithuanian number from the mid-fifties where the women wore white t-shirts that spelled out "Lithuanians Unite!" or something like it. But until the late '50s, the theater was basically a mixed-gender project which celebrated the camp virtues of parody, gender bending, and spontaneity.

There was some tension, however, between the gay men and lesbians, especially in the late '50s. Laura remembered the "boys" becoming hostile toward women's participation in the theater after the success of an "all-girl" number. Peter Worth laughed recalling that when the "girls" started a *thé dansant* Sunday afternoons at Duffy's: "There were two boys behind me and one of them said, 'Mark my words, the girls are taking over.' "[49]

Grove "girls" and "boys" in the '30s, '40s, and '50s shared similar class backgrounds and tastes. Collectively they called themselves "homosexuals." Often they were good friends and were part of the same crowd, and occasionally they even married to give each other "cover." But compared to heterosexual groups, what generally *was not* between them—mutual sexual interest, bona fide marriage, children, kinship ties, economic interdependence—was more striking. "Girls" and "boys" didn't always see eye-to-eye over such issues as men's cruising and promiscuity, and women's equality, either. But where there were differences, the "boys" set the tone and would have resented any challenge to their predominance.

Yet, in general, the "girls" and "boys" co-existed harmoniously and in the spirit so valued by all the founders—the spirit of fun, a way of diffusing stress and differences by teasing and poking fun, what anthropologists call a "joking relationship." Grovers handled gender conflict through such customs as holding a "field day" on the beach following the Lithuanian flag raising. One event was a mock softball game between an all-male team in drag and a lesbian team. And the Lithuanian flag raising day that male and female narrators enjoyed the most was one in the mid-fifties when:

> The boys . . . decided to invade the Lithuanian flag raising party . . . They carried these large banners that said things like, "Would you want your sister to marry one" and "Lithuanians go home" . . . and they all marched down on us, and of course we beat the living daylights out of them because we all came out—there must have been fifty of us in that tiny little house of Alice and Alyson's—and attacked the boys and threw them off the boardwalks into the sand. Of course, they were all dressed in drag and we had on our slacks, and we had a *marvelous* time. . . .[50]

"It Got Tacky"

During the 1940s and '50s, the lesbians formed an exceptionally homogeneous group. As Laura said, "I don't think there *were* any strange outside people . . . all the gay ladies were equally fun-type gay ladies that all got along beautifully together."[51] And, as another narrator put it, "In those days, the Grove was like a very private gay country club."[52]

But in 1956, Duffy's Hotel burned to the ground in a fire that Grovers believed was set by the Mafia. Within a year the current hotel was built on the same spot, and the new management brought with it the burgeoning gay and lesbian bar culture of the mainland in the late 1950s.[53] Lesbians started coming, and staying, whom the "gay ladies" viewed with horror. The new hotel manager was a "Mafia guy and his girlfriend" whom Maggie MacCorkle had seen in all the New York gay bars. The new hotel, as she and her friends saw it, attracted "all the worst elements in both the gay and straight world."[54]

In the early fifties, when the "young crowd" arrived, they were welcomed and assimilated by the older generation, but for years there was no mixing between the "ladies" and the working-class newcomers of the late fifties on. Unlike many Grove "boys," most "ladies" (Kay excepted) claim never to have been lured over class lines by sexual attraction. When I asked one "lady" to name some of the "toughies," as she put it, she answered, "I don't know, I only knew them from looking the other way." Another referred angrily to those "diesel dykes," who were "big and fat and mannish," women from the Sea Colony, a working-class lesbian bar in New York City.[55] "They all had attitudes," she continued. There was always "dyke drama," always some femme in a fight with another femme. She hadn't wanted any part of it.[56]

Heavy drinking, butch/femme "roles," bottle throwing, and slaps—even Kay had reportedly once thrown a chair across Duffy's dining room in a jealous fit—all these played a part in the founders' way of life, too. The difference was style, money, education, and interests: "A different class of people came in who were younger, less attractive. It got tacky, that's what it did . . . the way the people looked . . . I mean *we* were gay, but . . ."[57]

The trend toward more intensive development was accentuated in 1961 when electricity and running water were put in. Construction doubled and tripled. The old-timers looked on aghast as the "unspoiled" natural setting of their "gay country club" was "raped," as Natalia Murray put it. Many more men than women had the money to take advantage of the boom. The drag became far more serious and commercial; cruising went on day and night. Many of the women were deeply offended. Audrey Hartmann complained, "The men had just taken over, cruising and sex everywhere, in the Meat Rack [the outdoor male cruising area], on the boardwalks, just *everywhere*."[58]

"We Left"

Most of the lesbian founders responded to the male and working-class influx of the late fifties and early sixties by leaving the Grove for what they saw as more congenial surroundings further from the city. Only the wealthiest like Kay, Natalia Murray, Cris, and Mary Hecht were homeowners. Some of the renters, who had less to lose, left in the late '50s, and even Natalia Murray took to renting her house out in July and August. Only Kay and a few others stayed put through the '60s. As early as 1960, the founding "ladies" had mostly given up their cottages, their parties, their yachts. Lois McIntosh, who arrived to work as a bartender that year, told me vehemently, "There were no women when I came." "Yes," I said, "there have been women here since the beginning." "Maybe in their houses," she answered, "but they weren't around, they didn't come out."[59]

In the 1960s, many "ladies" became part of the "Bermuda shorts triangle"[60]—an imaginary line connecting their winter apartments on the Upper East Side of Manhattan and their summer places in the Hamptons on Long Island's East End, or around Westport, Connecticut. As a young lesbian hanging around the Hamptons in the mid-sixties, I knew them as the "Blazer Dykes," from the blue blazers they wore with white slacks or Bermuda (knee-length) shorts. The 1960s were to be the era of a nearly all-male Grove until a new set of lesbians began arriving toward the end of the decade.

The older cohort of Grove "gay ladies" belonged to the generation of well-off, cultured, and accomplished lesbians who succeeded the Paris circle of Natalie Barney, Gertrude Stein, and Radclyffe Hall.[61] Janet Flanner, Jane Heap, Margaret Anderson, and Solita Solano are some of the more well-known members of the generation to which Kay, Natalia Murray, and Cheryl Crawford also belonged by age, class, sensibility, and, to a degree, personal friendship. A lesbian named Spivy, Laura explained, who frequented the Grove:

> was a legend among the ladies . . . [Her nightclub, Spivy's Roof,] was where all the really elegant ladies [went], this was a fun type thing before what I call the many crew-cutted bulldyke ladies came around. It was more like the Bloomsbury group, more like Liane de Pougy—well, of course, it wasn't as intellectual as all that, as Virginia Woolf.[62]

Liane de Pougy was not only Natalie Barney's lover but also a celebrated Parisian courtesan.[63] "Ladies" though they undoubtedly were by background, the founders were also lesbians and therefore sexually unorthodox. Most of them frequented bars and nightclubs more than their heterosexual peers, and some of them had backgrounds which were positively racy. Kay, the "grande dame" and "party girl," had sexual relationships and friendships with the "follies girls" like Dottie Justin and Peggy Fears who figure in Grove history. Twentieth-century lesbian history will be the story of settlement houses, women's colleges, literary salons, *and* speakeasies, nightclubs, and the *demi-monde*—the marginal subculture that services the publicly unacknowledged desires of respectable society.[64]

But Grove history also shows how status and money differences kept lesbians separate. Over a fifty-year period, lesbians came to the Grove from Park Avenue apartments and Greenwich Village bohemia and working-class neighborhoods. The "ladies'" privileged position allowed them to be a special minority in a male realm. No one was more aware of this than the few women of more modest means who somehow gained entrance to the "gay country club." Myrna Wiese had been working in a defense plant when she first came to the Grove in 1944. When I asked if she thought there were more women in the Grove in the 1980s than ever before, she answered: "I don't *think*, I know. I know. And I know why. Because women have more money now. When I first started coming out here they just couldn't afford it."[65]

The working-class ethnic women who first began to come around 1960 had almost all worked as bartenders or waitresses in gay bars; naturally they had a very different outlook from the "ladies," who frequented these same bars only to go slumming. So it really makes no sense to talk about "*the* lesbian community" or "lesbian history" in abstract generalities. And although lesbians (and some bisexual and straight women) played critical roles in founding the gay Grove, the common framework of Grove lesbian history has been provided by gay men—without their ongoing determination to create gay space, there would have been no turf in the later '60s for a new generation of lesbians to claim.

And yet, despite our painful differences, we lesbians are also compelled by what we have in common: stories that cross and recross, roots and destinies entangled. Audrey Hartmann, who as a twenty-three year old had hiked to the Grove from Ocean Beach, left in the '60s—only to miss it so much that she reconciled herself to the changes and came back in the '70s, when "[the Grove] was notorious . . . everyone knew it was gay, and it was all types of gays, by then." All these years she had told people at the office that she was going to Ocean Beach. Only when she came back and built her own house did she begin to say, "I live in Cherry Grove and that's that."[66] And Cris, the "Ronald Coleman" type who held onto her house on the bay until the late '60s, because, she said, "Cherry Grove still had its charms," always returned to visit with longtime friends. Until the last summer before her death, she fantasized about coming back to live because, she said, "I still think of the Grove as my real home."[67]

Acknowledgments

This essay is dedicated to Peter Worth.

Notes

1. Audrey Hartmann, Interview by author, June 19, 1986. This essay is based primarily on interviews with nine lesbians whose ages ranged from fifty-five to eighty-five at the time of the interviews (1986–89), and who rented or owned in the Grove between the years 1936 and 1960. During the field work, I also interviewed twenty-six gay men who discussed the same time period. The second reference to interview material is abbreviated "IBA."
2. Gay people were only mentioned in the press when they were arrested. Although this negative publicity probably helped gay people find each other, all narrators—I prefer this term for Grovers who gave me interviews to the more traditional anthropological "informant," which conjures up unpleasant images of police spies—reported hearing about the Grove in gay bars or through the "grapevine."
3. I have elicited the full names of thirty-five regular lesbian residents during this twenty-five year period; the total number is a much larger but unknowable figure. I am more sure about their number at any one time. According to one estimate, during an average summer week after World War II, there were about one hundred men and women in the Grove. Using another lesbian's guess that women comprised about 40 percent of the total population, and at least 40 percent of these women were lesbians, I estimate fifteen lesbian residents during the week. Assuming the numbers quadrupled on weekends, we get a figure of sixty lesbians on a weekend, which matches well with the figure of fifty present at a Lithuanian flag raising (see below) in the mid-1950s. Presumably there were more women present at Duffy's Hotel because it was public.
4. Older Grovers almost never call themselves "lesbian," preferring instead "(gay) girls" or, less often, "(gay) ladies." I use these terms more or less interchangeably in quotes to convey Grovers' perspective. When I am describing them, I sometimes use "gay women"; as a feminist, I am put off by calling grown women "girls." For Grovers, though, "girl" and "boy" connoted "gay," as opposed to words like "man," "woman," and "guys," which implied "straight." Thus the statement "The girls liked to go to Fire Island" was a code for "Lesbians liked to go . . ."
5. Virtually all Grovers over fifty prefer the word "friend" to describe a relationship now generally signalled by the word "lover." They can generally tell by the context or the inflexion what kind of friend is meant. Not caring for the use of quotation marks to set off the word "friend," I use "companion" (with no quotation marks) to signify a committed couple relationship. This old-fashioned usage has been adopted by *The New York Times* in their obituaries and I find it felicitous.
6. Kay wished to have only her first name used in this account.
7. Hartmann, IBA. According to Raymond Mann (Interview by author, July 16, 1987), there was only one other woman, perhaps, among the gay men in Natalia's original group. Sayville is the Long Island town from which the ferry for the Grove departs.
8. Natalia Danesi Murray, ed., *Darlinghissima: Letters to a Friend* (New York: Random House, 1985), 83.
9. Ibid., 3.

10. Brenda Wineapple, *Genet: A Biography of Janet Flanner* (New York: Ticknor and Fields, 1989), 168.
11. The biographical information on Mann and Peck is in Virginia Spencer Carr, *The Lonely Hunter: A Biography of Carson McCullers* (New York: Doubleday and Company, 1975), 361.
12. According to Kay and other Grovers, the two were lovers for a period around 1948. Kay often said that, despite their "really hot affair," Natalia was too bossy for her, a real "general" who "like[d] things done exactly her way." One night in the summer of 1948, Kay called a man whom she knew had two lots and a house on the then undeveloped East End and told him she'd buy them for $5,000. He agreed, and she said she wanted to move in that night and he said sure, there was a bed there. So she walked out of Natalia's house that day and ended the affair.

    This picture is rather at odds with Natalia's self-portrait in *Darlinghissima* as a kind of devoted grass widow to Janet Flanner, who insisted on living in France. When I mentioned this to Kay, she snorted and said, "I'm very fond of Natalia but, honey, she was no widow!" Janet harbored no rancor toward Kay over the affair and "just didn't want to know about it." Kay, Janet, and Natalia remained good friends, Janet even staying with Kay in the Grove occasionally. Natalia attended Kay's memorial service in 1989.
13. Mann, IBA.
14. Laura, Interview by author, September 7, 1986. Fears also belonged to the circle of torch song singer Libby Holman and her sometime lesbian lover, Louisa Carpenter. A 1932 party at Holman's husband's estate, Reynolda, was described by an eyewitness as "'little more than a convention of homosexuals.' That night he met Clifton Webb, Blanche Yurka, Louisa Carpenter, and a man from California named Bobby Froelich . . . the following week, Libby invited Clifton Webb, Bea Lillie, and Peggy Fears down for a long weekend." See Jon Bradshaw, *Dreams that Money Can Buy: The Tragic Life of Libby Holman* (New York: William Morrow and Company, 1985), 106.
15. Natalia Murray, Interview by author, April 25, 1987.
16. On *The New Yorker*, see Dale Kramer, *Ross and the New Yorker* (Garden City, NY: Doubleday, 1951). For two first-hand accounts of the Theatre Guild, and its offshoot, the Group Theatre, see Harold Clurman, *The Fervent Years* (New York: Da Capo Press, 1983); and Cheryl Crawford, *One Naked Individual: My Fifty Years in the Theatre* (Indianapolis: The Bobbs-Merrill Company, 1977). For Cafe Society, see Lewis A. Erenberg, *Steppin' Out: New York Nightlife and the Transformation of American Culture, 1890–1930* (Westport, CT: Greenwood Press, 1981).
17. The friendship of Flanner, Crawford, Bowles, and McCullers (although both of the latter were married, they seem to have been bisexual) dates at least from the days of George Davis and W.H. Auden's famous Brooklyn house at 7 Middagh Street in 1940–1941, which was made up largely of homosexual artists; Bowles and McCullers both lived in the house. See Carr, *The Lonely Hunter*, 123, 125; and Crawford, *One Naked Individual*, 146.

    Crawford (1905–1986) was one of the most important theatrical producers of this century. She founded the Group Theatre and co-produced, with Elia Kazan and Howard Clurman, most of its plays; she also produced *One Touch of Venus* (1943), *Brigadoon* (1947), and *The Rose Tattoo* (1951), for which she won a Tony. Crawford cravenly nullifies her sexuality and her primary relationship with

Norman in her 1977 memoir. And except for one fleeting reference to reading the script for *Brigadoon* on the beach in Fire Island (151), she never alludes to the Grove or the Arts Project, of which she was a founding and active member in 1948. "My low voice and the ability to ape men, learned from my brothers, always won me male roles [at Smith College]," writes Crawford (15), while going out of her way to lie about her private life: "I had [none] to speak of, just occasional evenings with colleagues. A social life, not to mention a love life, takes time, and I had none to spare. It was a high price to pay . . . Man's best friend became this woman's best friend" (112).

For Carson McCullers's frequent visits to stay with Marty Mann and Priscilla Peck in the Grove during the late forties and early fifties, see Carr, *The Lonely Hunter*, 361. Several narrators mention that Bowles and Highsmith, though not central or longtime participants, were in and out of the Grove scene; the latter, author of the lesbian novel *The Price of Salt* under the name "Claire Morgan" (New York: Coward-McCann, 1952), had an affair with Kay, who also remembered Jane Bowles climbing a ladder to try to get into her bedroom.

Peggy Fears and Betty Garde, besides being mentioned by narrators, are listed in numerous Arts Project documents from the late forties and fifties. Garde (1905–1989) was primarily a radio actress but had appeared in the original Broadway production of *Oklahoma!* See Obituary, *The New York Times*, December 28, 1989.

Three other actresses mentioned by narrators are Thelma Ritter (1905–1969), Kay Ballard, and Nancy Walker. I have not found Ritter's name in Grove documents of the period, but feel confident of her residence because Stephan Cole who, as Tallulah Bankhead's manager knew the theater world intimately, said:

> Donald Cook and his wife went up and bought a piece of land [in the Pines]. And she sat around on the deck of the Botel and saw some ladies playing canasta. And she came back and said, "I want to sell those lots, Donald. I'd much rather be in the Grove and see Thelma Ritter dancing around in drag." [laughter] Thelma Ritter lived *right there.*

Cole, a reliable and knowledgeable informant, was not contradicted by any of the other old-timers in this group interview. (Group 2 [twelve narrators], Interview by author, August 16, 1986). Although an obituary noted that Ritter owned or rented a "six-room place on Fire Island," it went out of its way to foreground her marriage, children, and housewife role (Obituary, *The New York Times*, February 5, 1969, 45).

Kay Ballard is mentioned as having frequented the Grove during the fifties; she attended at least one of the Lithuanian flag raising days (Maggie MacCorkle, Interview by author, September 6, 1986). She also performed at Jimmy Merry's Club Atlantique during the 1960s (Robert A. "Rose" Levine, Interview by author, June 21, 1986).

Stephan Cole and one other narrator (Bob Adams, Interview by author, March 9, 1990) named actress Nancy Walker as having appeared in early Arts Project revues; she definitely starred in "The Cherry Grove Follies of 1948" along with Fears and Garde (Program, author's collection).

Nevertheless, the sexual preferences of these three women must still be considered an open question, since living in the Grove and participating in its theater does not prove lesbianism, especially in the thirties and forties. Broadway actress Bertha Belmore appeared in several shows of the time, including the 1948 Follies; the 1950 revue, *Berthe of a Nation*, was even named after her. Yet all narrators agree that Belmore, who was married, was heterosexual. (In this era, marriage neither proves nor disproves sexual orientation). Even after gay predominance in the Grove, from about 1949 on, a straight minority has continued on for economic reasons, because of historic attachment to the place, or because they simply like a gay atmosphere.

18. Murray, IBA.
19. Ann Leone, Interview by author, March 13, 1987.
20. Laura, IBA.
21. Ibid.
22. Peter, who is slight and feminine, took her first name (which she used in gay contexts but not at work) to signify that she *was* gay; for the same reason, as a young woman, she wore a tie. Peter Worth, Interview by author, August 29, 1986.
23. Leone, IBA.
24. Worth, IBA. I have never heard of violent crime against lesbians in the Grove over a fifty-year period except for several assaults by mainland men during clearly homophobic incidents. Considering that Grove men have been in the vast majority and that men and women have always lived there as close neighbors and sometimes even housemates, I find this extraordinary. It suggests a return to early feminist analyses of heterosexuality and the family as the sources of women's oppression—I am thinking of Shulamith Firestone, for instance, *The Dialectic of Sex: The Case for Feminist Revolution* (New York: Bantam Books, 1970), especially Chapter 6.
25. This episode was often mentioned by narrators including Kay, who looked back on it with glee. Unfortunately, I have not been able to find a reference to it in the local newspapers.
26. Laura, IBA.
27. Hartmann, IBA.
28. Laura, IBA.
29. Ibid. Peter Worth felt that the putative sanctity of the older women's relationships was overblown. Kay in fact fell in love and spent the last twenty years of her life in a relationship with a member of the young crowd.
30. Leone, IBA.
31. Ibid. The reference to me illustrates her usage; one would not call a college professor a "dyke" in this system.
32. Thirty years later, both Laura and Cris brushed off interview questions on this matter. "Role playing was a big deal to some people," Cris commented. "Agnes needed to feel she was with a 'man.' Playing the 'man' did not matter to me" (Cris, Interview by author, August 9, 1987). By 1987, when I met her, Cris looked like an outdoorsy, wealthy matron, not a lesbian butch. This metamorphosis probably says more about aging than about how Cris might have felt in the fifties.
33. Worth, IBA.
34. Kay married three times, the last during the homophobic 1950s to a wealthy, older man with whom she lived happily each winter until his death many years later. Her husband had his own interests and did not object to Kay's tastes—the relationship was essentially social, financial, and companionate. "He was beyond all

that [sex]," she told me. As if to emphasize that the summers were hers, she named her Grove house "No Man's Land."

35. Laura, IBA.
36. Ibid.
37. George Fiehl, Interview by author, July 14, 1986.
38. Laura, IBA.
39. Leone, IBA.
40. Stephan Cole, Interview by author, August 20, 1986.
41. Leone, IBA.
42. Stephan Cole saw a good side to Mary Hecht that did not, however, impress lesbian Grovers. He "thought better" of her upon hearing that when Hecht went out on her yacht with her captain, Mr. Oakley (the father of two brothers who are still local contractors and carpenters), "[s]he used to go out and pick up a couple of girls, one for him and one for her. She was a tough broad. . . . She tried to be nice, and she was nice at times. She had a lot of hangers-on, of course . . . she had plenty of money" (Cole, IBA). Mary Hecht also insisted that a boardwalk through a parcel of land she owned be named "Maryland Walk."
43. Narrators do not spontaneously mention who was Jewish. I only realized that Mary Hecht was Jewish after two summers of research because of a throwaway comment by Ann Leone; as an Italian among the WASPs, she was much more self-conscious and forthright about ethnicity. Anti-Semitism was present in the Grove as it was in the country at large, and because there were Jews who moved in the same social and professional circles as Gentile Grovers, and who indeed lived in the Grove, anti-Semitism—unlike racism, since people of color were safely distant—was a personal and present issue. I have a sense that for most founders, Gentile and Jewish alike, being Jewish was one of those embarrassing facts that could be overlooked on an individual basis, but in any case should not be mentioned in polite society.
44. Murray, IBA.
45. "Roaring 20's Party," program for a winter 1948 fundraiser for the Arts Project, author's collection, 3. The four women are among twelve people listed as members of the "Advisory Board" of the Arts Project.
46. "Program," author's collection. Bertha Belmore (1882–1953), an English actress, had a long career, primarily in musical theater, including the Ziegfeld Follies, where she starred with W.C. Fields and Will Rogers. She was married to actor George Belmore; they owned a Grove house named "By Jupiter" after her Broadway hit play of the period. See *Who Was Who in the Theatre 1912–76*, Vol. 1 (Detroit: Gale Research Company, 1978), 178–79. As mentioned above (note 18), Belmore was heterosexual, one of those larger-than-life female personas around whom gay men gather.
47. MacCorkle, IBA.
48. It was a take-off on a 1930s all-women orchestra which was conducted, as was this Grove number, by a man, here Bill Ronin, a longtime Grover and narrator. The women dressed like "Vassar prom women," played imaginary instruments, and mimed "Take Me Back to My Boots and Saddle," according to Maggie MacCorkle (IBA).
49. Worth, IBA.
50. Laura, IBA.

51. Ibid.
52. MacCorkle, IBA.
53. Madeline D. Davis and Elizabeth Lapovsky Kennedy, "Oral History and the Study of Sexuality in the Lesbian Community: Buffalo, New York, 1940–1960," in *Hidden From History: Reclaiming the Gay and Lesbian Past*, eds. Martin Bauml Duberman, Martha Vicinus, and George Chauncey, Jr. (New York: New American Library, 1989), 426–40. Davis and Kennedy's work has now been published in its entirety (*Boots of Leather, Slippers of Gold: The History of a Lesbian Community* [New York: Routledge, 1993]), giving lesbian studies its first detailed community history.
54. MacCorkle, IBA.
55. See Joan Nestle's essays, "The Bathroom Line" and "Esther's Story," in *A Restricted Country* (Ithaca: Firebrand Books, 1987), 37–39, 40–45, for sympathetic recollections of the Sea Colony in the fifties.
56. MacCorkle, IBA.
57. Laura, IBA.
58. Hartmann, IBA.
59. Lois McIntosh, Interview by author, August 27, 1986.
60. Bea Kreloff, personal communication.
61. For a valuably detailed account of this Paris circle (which is marred by a doctrinaire cultural feminist perspective), see Shari Benstock's *Women of the Left Bank: Paris, 1900–1940* (Austin: University of Texas Press, 1986).
62. Laura, IBA.
63. See Karla Jay, *The Amazon and the Page: Natalie Clifford Barney and Renée Vivien* (Bloomington: Indiana University Press, 1988).
64. The work of Joan Nestle ("Lesbians and Prostitutes: A Historical Sisterhood," in *Sex Work: Writings by Women in the Sex Industry*, eds. Frédérique Delacoste and Priscilla Alexander [Pittsburgh: Cleis Press, 1987], 231–47) and Lisa Duggan ("The Crisis in Lesbian History," Paper presented at the Sex and the State Conference, Toronto, Canada, 1985) first made me think about the historic connection between lesbianism and the domains of prostitution and risque entertainment and to look for it in my own data. When Kay, Camilla Munklewitz, and Kay's friend from Chicago were arrested for nude sunbathing in the late '40s, the friend gave the address of a Chicago brothel as her own in order to confound the police.
65. Dr. Myrna Wiese, Interview by author, September 2, 1987.
66. Hartmann, IBA.
67. Cris, IBA.

7. The Changing Face of Lesbian Bars in Detroit, 1938–1965

Roey Thorpe

The very first lesbian bars I ever visited in the early 1980s were, from the outside, unrecognizable as such. Each attempt to find a new bar, on the directions of friends, felt like an initiation into the secret society of lesbians. The address would take me to a deserted block in an obscure location of whatever city I was in, where I would find what looked like an abandoned building with the front all boarded up. Careful scrutiny, however (fueled by frustration and a desperate desire to meet other women like myself), would reveal a back entrance with a street address or the name of the bar in small letters. Persistence was usually rewarded by the broad smile of the woman bouncer, but the message was clear: this space was not for the casual interloper.

A few years later, as I read Joan Nestle's memories of lesbian bars, along with the beginnings of Elizabeth Kennedy and Madeline Davis's study of Buffalo, New York, I wondered why the early bars seemed so public compared with the bars I had worked so hard to locate.[1] The idea of a neighborhood bar that catered to a lesbian clientele seemed so appealing that I was unsure why it had been replaced by what seemed like an unnecessarily secretive site. Why, when gay and feminist movements were making lesbians more visibile, would bars become hidden? And why would lesbian bars be more hidden than bars for gay men, or bars for a mixed gay and lesbian clientele? This essay is an attempt to answer that question, using oral history interviews with lesbians in Detroit, Michigan.[2] It reveals a complicated matrix of gender and class that caused lesbian bars to change their physical characteristics in order to respond to political and social oppression.

From 1939 to 1975, Detroit was home to at least twenty different bars whose main clientele was lesbians and bisexual women.[3] Some of these bars, like the Sweetheart Bar and the Palais, stayed in business for over twenty years. Others, like Fred's, Mary's Memory Bar, the K9 Bar, and the Golden Slipper, lasted only a few years. The bars that I'm discussing in this essay had predominantly white clientele and owners. African-American lesbian bars, which first opened in the mid-1960s, faced different sets of problems that I've described elsewhere.[4] One thing that all of the bars with a largely a white clientele had in common was the racial segregation practiced in them, which was an important component of their attractiveness to most white lesbians. Many Black narrators believed that white lesbians would not have tolerated more than a few token lesbians of color in their bars at any one time.[5]

For lesbian bars to survive in mid-twentieth-century Detroit, the owners and clientele had to grapple with certain problems that were unique to lesbian spaces. First, the bars had to alleviate somehow the discomfort that many women felt upon entering a lesbian bar. Lesbians felt uncomfortable for many reasons, including the risk of exposure in going to a public homosexual space, and the strangeness of being in such a place at first, despite possibly feeling relieved at meeting other lesbians.[6] Second, in order to survive, the bars sought to expand their clientele to include more women with money to spend on drinks and entertainment. Because middle-class women were unlikely to visit places regularly where harassment and exposure were strong possibilities, bars changed their physical location, appearance, and interior layout over time to try to attract a more middle-class clientele. Third, bars had to walk the fine line of the law, which forbade homosexual establishments. Keeping their businesses open and free from vice raids required creativity and subtlety.

Perhaps most importantly, the lesbian clientele of these bars often had to share the space with heterosexuals, who were a fixture of early bar life. Heterosexual couples visiting a bar to watch homosexuals interact was a widespread practice in the 1940s and '50s. According to Billie Hill, "They'd have a date and they'd take their girlfriend down to see a queer. You know, that was a big thing then."[7] Brandy Maguire acknowledges the humiliation that accompanied being on display to heterosexuals, as well as the need to make the best of the situation:

> [Y]ou just got to the point where you, if you wanted to enjoy yourself, you had to ignore them because they really never said anything to you, they would just sit there and be amused. I mean, we were their x-rated, sort of like, back in the fifties, sixties. We'd be the x-rated version of a videotape now, you know, seeing women caressing and kissing and dancing together. . . . But everybody . . . got false ID to go because there was no place else to go.[8]

The presence of heterosexuals in the bars served a purpose for some women, who had secret motives for visiting lesbian bars. Bev, who had been sexual with other girls since junior high, asked boyfriends to take her to gay bars. In fact, she first found out about gay bars by participating in heterosexual dating. She muses, "I wanted to go there, and he'd take me. . . . I was interested in knowing about it, but I didn't know anything. Now how did I know to even go to a gay bar? How'd I know that was a gay bar? Unless somebody talked about it or, you know, said something about it."[9] C.B. describes heterosexual couples who would cross the Canadian border from Windsor, Ontario, in order to visit gay bars, claiming that "A good lot of the Canadians came in to gawk at the rest of us. . . . And it was odd to note that on one weekend you would see a man and wife come in together, or boyfriend and girlfriend, and the following week one or the other would be coming in alone!"[10] A heterosexual date was a safe way for people to experience a gay bar for the first time, and for some of these people, it was a step toward entering the bar in search of a same-sex relationship.

But some heterosexual men in the bars posed a serious threat to the lesbian clientele. Rampant sexism, which limited the mobility of women in public spaces, particularly at night and particularly in places seen as "date spots" for heterosexual couples, gave men license to approach women and physically threaten those who refused their advances. It was this violence, both actual and threatened, that caused the bars to undergo major changes in location and layout in order to try to protect their lesbian patrons.

The Sweetheart Bar

The earliest of Detroit's lesbian bars was the Sweetheart Bar, which opened in 1939.[11] Several women remember it as the first lesbian bar that they went to, and have fond memories of both the bar and its owners, Anna and Irving "Izzy" Ginsberg. The Sweetheart was located at 3928 Third Street, in the heart of what was Detroit's manufacturing center. On the outside, the Sweetheart looked like any neighborhood bar, but on the inside, it was divided into four sections, each with its particular clientele and activities. The front of the bar, the area closest to the entrance, seemed like other nearby bars, where heterosexual men and women from the surrounding neighborhood came to have a drink and socialize. At the back of this section stood a pair of double doors, behind which stretched a large space where the floor show, usually a drag performance, alternated with time for dancing. By convention, this space was divided according to sexuality. Billie Hill describes the back room as follows:

> [T]wo women could dance or two men could dance together there. So the straights would come in and sit on the one side just so that they could see all

> this, you know, what was going on. . . . Then the middle section was more or less for the bisexuals and they'd go men or women, you know. Then over in this side it was the gays, mostly girls but boys too, but mostly girls.[12]

The physical layout of this bar served several purposes. It provided a space for heterosexual people in the neighborhood to use, which no doubt undercut the animosity they would have felt toward a bar where they were not welcome. Their patronage also helped keep the bar in business. The double doors provided a barrier that need not be crossed by clientele uninterested in observing homosexuals and bisexuals, and thus also provided a bit of privacy for those who frequented the space behind the doors. This privacy meant that same-sex couples could dance together, an unusual privilege even in gay bars of the time.[13] The social organization of that rear space also served practical functions; in particular, it allowed for specific forms of socializing while avoiding embarrassing and possibly dangerous situations. People could display their intentions and their interests by positioning themselves in a selected third of the back room.

Separate sections also meant that while heterosexuals could watch lesbians and gay men from a distance, they were courting danger by crossing over into homosexual territory. The existence of the bisexual space in the center of the room meant that there was a buffer between heterosexual observers and women who were exclusively lesbian. It protected lesbians from some of the staring and pointing of heterosexuals who had come to the bar as their form of entertainment for the evening.

These sections were not always enough to keep heterosexual men away from lesbians, however. Billie Hill recalls that although "the guys knew if they went over and ask a girl to dance [and] she said no, that was it—leave her alone," as early as 1945 or 1946, men were ousted from the Sweetheart for harassing lesbians. She explains:

> [I]f a straight guy come up and kept insisting on dancing then they just got put out. . . . And then they'd wait outside, try to beat you up. That's where all the fights started. . . . They'd, you know, bounce a couple guys outta there for bothering the girls and they'd wait outside until the bar closed and jump the girls and beat 'em up. And we got so that when we'd leave the bar we'd leave, you know, four and five of us together, then if a guy jumps, we can handle 'em.[14]

The need to address harassment became a powerful force in shaping lesbian bar culture. It was a considerable challenge to keep lesbian social space separate from heterosexual men. But doing so was crucial for creating a space that was safe for white, working-class lesbians, since their refusal to dance or go home with heterosexual men left them vulnerable to physical attack. Lesbians also had to learn to fight in order to protect themselves when physical separation in bars failed.[15]

The Palais

In 1949, ten years after the Sweetheart first opened its doors, another lesbian bar emerged that would also play a major role in the history of Detroit lesbians. The Palais, also known as "The Pit," was more than just a place to drink or dance on weekend nights; it served as a social center for white, working-class lesbians during its twenty-five years in business, sponsoring parties, picnics, and other social events. Billie Hill describes a "great big snifter glass sitting on the bar" into which customers would drop their spare change. When the glass got full, the bartender would use the money to buy supplies for a picnic. This responsibility fell to the bartender because, as Billie explains, "Back then, most all the bar owners were straight."[16] The bartender or manager, always a lesbian, would go the extra mile for her community. Billie recalls the extensive preparations made for one such picnic:

> [The bartender] would be in charge of it and she would go and get hot dogs and buns and . . . chicken. I know the one time she bought seventy-five, a hundred small frying chickens and they took 'em all to the bar and cut 'em all up and then we all went out to a park and they build a barbecue and they had hot barbecue chicken dinner out there, you know. They . . . bought a couple packs of potatoes and somebody made potato salad and . . . somebody made coleslaw and then took all these chickens out to this park and had big barbecue chicken. There would be maybe seventy-five, a hundred people at these things.[17]

These picnics had a special significance, since they required a far more public presence than even the bars did. Parks were not only public, they were outdoors. To take lesbian bar culture out of the darkness of the bar and quite literally bring it into the daylight required courage and mutual support. The threat of violence was very real. Brandy vividly evokes one frightening incident:

> We went to this Hines Park, it's a big long winding road. . . . There was like a hundred of us, I say seventy-five-to-a-hundred of us, for some reason got all together on a holiday, and . . . we had been playing ball. Now, I didn't . . . notice if they were kissing and necking or anything, but all of a sudden, about fifteen

> guys started approaching and calling us all kinds of names. And some of the girls picked up the bats and about fifty of 'em chased these fifteen guys . . . a half-mile down the road and nobody bothered us the rest of the day.[18]

Brandy recalls that this picnic was "the only time I remember doing anything outside of the Palais back then" with a group of lesbians. The possibility was too great that, as Brandy put it, someone "would sense, when they seen that many women together, something was wrong."[19] Occasional picnics drew large numbers of women, which made the outings somewhat safer, and the consistency of the bartender in charge, just as she was at the bar, added stability to the events.

The Palais also provided the space and audience for social rituals that were usually arranged by and restricted to heterosexual families. The Palais sponsored birthday parties, lesbian and gay weddings, and even baby showers for regular patrons of the bar. The first time that Carole ever went to a gay bar, a friend took her to the Palais on the night of a lesbian wedding. She describes the scene: "The night that Marilyn took me, there was a wedding there, and one was in a tuxedo and one was in a wedding gown. For a first experience, it was unbelievable! Unbelievable what we walked into!" Bev recalls Carole's reaction at the time this way:

> They went to the Palais and I guess there was a marriage ceremony going on, and one of the women wearing a tux and the other one was in a white gown, and she said, "They actually had a ceremony. They think they're married! Can you believe it? Two women?"[20]

Part of the magic of bars like the Palais was that major social markers like marriage did seem possible there. The importance of these rituals cannot be overstated, since much of the internalized homophobia and self-hatred of lesbians, then and now, has been predicated on the belief that lesbianism excludes a woman from the events that indicate that she is not only "normal," but a contributor to society: marriage, childbirth, anniversaries. By holding such rituals within its walls, the Palais sustained and nurtured its clientele, and gave a vital authenticity to their lives.

The Palais was located at 655 Beaubien, just a few blocks north of the Sweetheart, and like the Sweetheart, it looked on the outside like an ordinary neighborhood bar. The interior organization of the Palais, however, represented a step forward for the lesbians who frequented the bar. Unlike the Sweetheart, which could only separate lesbians from heterosexuals by social custom, the Palais provided clear physical boundaries. Billie explains, "[D]own at the Palais, the back part was just gays and mostly girls and then the front part was for sightseers or the gay boys."[21] The existence of a separate space for lesbians gave them a clearer physical turf to defend. Although heterosexuals could enter the rear part of the bar, if they harassed the lesbian customers, they would be asked to leave. According to Billie Hill, who worked as a bouncer at the Palais, heterosexuals were told, "Either you stay in your side of the bar or get out."[22] In contrast to the Sweetheart, the Palais employed big, tough lesbians as bartenders, waiters, and bouncers. These women were responsible for asking heterosexual men who stepped out of line to leave the bar, and resorting to physical violence if they refused. Not only did working for the bar give a few of the most hard-core butches a means of supporting themselves without compromising their butch personas, but patrons of all sexual orientations had the unique experience of seeing lesbians whose job was to maintain a safe lesbian space. Heterosexuals were not excluded, but their behavior was regulated by lesbians.

Even with tough bouncers and physical barriers, lesbians still had to put up with heterosexuals observing their every move. Lesbians who became regulars at the Palais had to develop a strong sense of themselves and a thick skin to protect themselves against the comments of heterosexuals. Billie Hill recalls a conversation that she had while waiting tables at the Palais with a heterosexual woman who had come in with her date:

> I went over to take their order and the one girl just sit at the table and she's looking, you know, just looking, and I said, "Now will you think you'll know me next time you see me?" She said, "I don't believe it. . . . You're so pretty." I said, "Well, what did you expect? A horn coming out or one eye growing out of my forehead or something?" Well she said, "I thought queers were different." I said, "Honey, I'm the same as you are, I got the same things that you have."[23]

Frequently, violence erupted when heterosexual men harassed lesbians, who felt a vital need to protect the only turf that they could call their own. B. Koz reflects on the buildup of tension caused by the combined effect of living a secret life and heterosexuals crossing the boundaries into lesbian space:

> You'd get a lot of straight guys in and they'd try and make out with the girls. . . . I suppose the girl would have to get up and take care of the girl she was with and fight off these straight guys. But there was always a lot in there. They had to watch it carefully. And I think a lot of it was the tension of going to where you, when you went you had to be secretive. . . . And it was a constant battle. You were always lying. And I think that's the hardest [thing].[24]

Billie Hill confirms this explanation, recalling: "There was so many fights and that down there because so many of the sightseers would come down, figure, you know, they could take this gal and show her what the hell life was all about, you know, and they's always getting into fights."[25] As Elizabeth Kennedy and Madeline Davis have pointed out in their study of Buffalo, fighting became an integral part of bar life and tough lesbian identity. This was necessary because lesbian turf was so vulnerable to encroachment by heterosexuals.[26]

Sometimes, however, the fighting in the bars turned lesbians against one another. Violence became a common and integral part of life in the bars; brawls were not at all uncommon. Brandy Maguire remembers that the first time she ever went to a gay bar, a fight broke out. She describes the scene and her reaction to it:

> As soon as we got in there, my girlfriend disappeared and I'm sitting there at this table, and I had never seen people dancing together and . . . kissing like this, you know, and this was so traumatic for me. Then all of a sudden a fight broke out, and I mean a fight. These girls were hitting each other, they were knocking tables over, chairs, shoving across the room. They even went out in, fought into the street. I'm sitting there wondering where my girlfriend was, who was supposed to be there so I would be alright. . . . Right after the fight breaks up, this girl comes up to me dressed in black . . . and asked me if I'd like to dance. And I'm sitting there saying [to myself], "Oh my god, if I don't, she probably bust my head open."[27]

This incident so influenced Brandy that years later, when she worked as a bouncer at a lesbian bar, she always went out of her way to make sure that new women felt safe and welcome. B. Koz remembers tensions between gay men and lesbians, pointing out: "The gay guys didn't like the girls and the girls didn't like the guys. It's not as bad now. They seem to get along."[28] C.B. explains that women were barred from LaRosa's and the K9 Bar because of fighting. She acknowledges that "for a while, they did let women in, but then it seemed like the women caused a ruckus. They were inclined to get in fights more readily with one another and cause mayhem."[29] And Billie Hill claims that one of the things that made her a good bouncer at the Palais was that "if the girls would get into fights, I could talk 'em out of it . . . and there wouldn't be any fighting. . . . I'd just . . . kinda talk 'em out of it, just by starting to laugh and joke and, you know, talk to 'em."[30] The Palais was a place where fights, both with heterosexual men and between lesbians, were common. The fact that violence was woven so closely into the fabric of lesbian bars, right alongside the lasting friendships and the ongoing support offered there, is testimony to the difficulty of maintaining lesbian space and the pervasiveness of internalized homophobia.[31]

Although toughness and fighting were able to be incorporated into an attractive butch image, what white, working-class lesbians really wanted was their own space, free from harassment. Additionally, an environment that included fistfights—a decidedly working-class activity—and allowed anyone to enter, and therefore offered only a limited amount of privacy, was not acceptable to middle-class lesbians. Detroit's lesbian bars would undergo yet another transformation in the attempt to provide both physical safety and anonymity for their lesbian clientele.

Fred's Bar

In 1952, only five years after the Palais opened, Fred's Bar provided an upscale alternative to the Palais and the Sweetheart. Fred's represented a new phase for lesbian bars in several ways: its location, the quality of its interior, its appeal to middle-class lesbians, and its exclusively lesbian clientele. Fred's was located in the northeast section of Detroit, still near downtown, but closer to the rapidly growing suburbs than either the Palais or the Sweetheart. Why did Fred's appear on the lesbian landscape of Detroit when it did? No one seems to know, but a number of historical factors seem to have played a part, including postwar prosperity, the beginning of white migration from the urban center to newly forming suburbs, and the rapidly solidifying need for lesbian-only space in the public sector.[32]

Unlike the Sweetheart and the Palais, Fred's attracted a middle-class lesbian clientele. Its location contributed to this appeal, but perhaps more importantly, Fred's was a larger, cleaner bar than the others. Judy Utley, who only went to Fred's at the time, describes it as having "just bare wooden floors, and they had a big pool table, and they had a big dance floor and there was a bar . . ."[33] In contrast to the Sweetheart and the Palais, both of which were small spaces that could feel cramped on a busy weekend night, Fred's, according to Bev, was "a great big barny place, had pool tables and [was] friendly. It's just a place to go sit and talk and dance."[34] C.B. claims that Fred's was,

> to my way of thinking, the best bar of all. . . . They had a great dance floor, good music, the bartender was a gay girl, the owners were very nice to us, couldn't have been nicer, and they kept the prices the same as they had been before we ever went in. They didn't double the prices because it was a gay bar.[35]

Women who frequented Fred's do not describe memorable "characters" they met in the bar, with the exception of Mac, the bartender; instead, Fred's seems to have offered a measure of anonymity that could not be provided by smaller, neighborhood-style bars.

This anonymity was important, since middle-class women often held jobs that were particularly vulnerable to charges of homosexuality. Teachers, nurses, librarians, and secretaries all depended to a great extent on their perception as "acceptable" women in society. Teachers especially feared that being discovered as lesbians would raise the specter of pedophilia, a common stereotype about gay men, bisexuals, and lesbians. While a woman who worked on the assembly line in a Ford factory might lose her job if anyone knew that she was gay, a teacher definitely would. The factory worker was far more likely to be harassed or even physically attacked by her coworkers, but the schoolteacher would be quickly and summarily fired. Many of the women who were regulars at the Palais were taxi drivers or factory workers, occupations that were nontraditional for women, where gender roles were less likely to be reinforced.

Even those women who wanted to move up in factory work felt pressured to keep their lesbianism out of public view. Judy Utley, who was promoted several times until she eventually became a plant superintendent in a metal factory, puts it most eloquently:

> [Y]ou were just petrified that . . . you were going to get caught in one of those places, you know, and it would be written up in the paper or something. You would get thrown in jail and lose your job because you couldn't go to work if you were in jail. Or your family would find out because you were in jail. "What are you doing in jail? Why did they arrest you?" You know . . .[36]

Other middle-class lesbians echo this concern, with some of their primary memories of lesbian bars centering on evenings when they unexpectedly saw someone they knew at the bar (none of the working-class women whom I interviewed spoke about similar incidents). Even though all women were incriminated by their presence in the bar, middle-class white women had less trust in the lesbian code of silence than their working-class counterparts. B. Koz recounts the story of a future employer spotting her in a lesbian bar. B. had already been hired for a summer camp job when her boss saw her in the bar. She remembers, "[the employer] said to her friend, 'My God . . . that's my assistant waterfront director!' And her friend said, 'Well, Jesus, if she's here and you're here, what are you worried about?'"[37] This logic eased her boss's worries, and the two eventually became fast friends. But this fear was enough to keep Bev and her lover Carole, a physical education teacher, out of the bars for years. Bev recalls:

> [I]n the first years of our relationship, we used to go to the bars quite often, just to meet people and dance and socialize. And one night, in the first few years of Carole's teaching, she went into the bathroom at GG's [another middle-class lesbian bar] and ran into one of her students. And this was not a past student, this was a kid that she had in class every day. In fact, I think she was a gym assistant that she saw all the time.... And then we just stopped going to the bars because Carole was just petrified of meeting one of her students.... And boy, that was like a Friday night and that weekend it was like, what is she gonna do on Monday? What is she gonna do? What is she gonna say? And we thought of all kinds of things.... And she went to the school on Monday and that kid never said a word. Just like she never saw her.[38]

For white, middle-class lesbians, the desire to be in the company of other lesbians was always countered, and often outweighed, by the risk of exposure.

Fred's went a step further than the Palais did in trying to ensure the anonymity that many middle-class women desired. Rather than providing separate rooms for heterosexuals and lesbians, Fred's excluded heterosexuals altogether by having a back door entrance. Billie Hill identifies this hidden entrance as one of the major changes that bars underwent at that time:

> [A]t Fred's, the front was boarded and blocked up ... there was no front door to it. You'd go down this little alleyway and knock on the back door ... so that the people [in the] neighborhood and that, they didn't even know there was a bar there, see.... You had to go and knock on the back door and identify yourself before they'd even let you in.[39]

Judy Utley remembers that Fred's "had a big bulldyke that was the bouncer" whose responsibility was to make sure that only lesbians could come into the bar.[40]

Excluding heterosexuals from Fred's served other purposes too. Women did not have to defend their turf against the advances of straight men, which cut down on the fighting that was a regular part of an evening at the Sweetheart and the Palais. C.B. states: "There just wasn't any fights that I can remember. And I was there a lot."[41] This lack of violence was partly due to the class divisions that will be discussed below. But it was also an important element in making the bar into a safe place for middle-class lesbians, most of whom were not accustomed, nor were they willing, to engage in fist fights over public space. For these women, fighting was too high a price to pay for an evening out.

Fred's only lasted five years; it closed in 1956, ostensibly because of the owner's illness. There may have been other reasons, however, why Fred's failed to remain open. First, the bar was located in an area in which many women did not feel safe. The anonymity of the bar did not help matters, since if a woman ran into trouble, she could not automatically count on the support of other bar patrons. Judy Utley recalls one incident when she and her sister B. were coming out of the bar and two men tried to grab B.'s purse as she got into the back of Judy's car. She describes the scene:

> I finally got the car started and just pulled away from the curb. And he's hanging on, the door's halfway open, and she's screaming, and there's two of them in the car when we finally started pulling away.... It's at closing time, and [we're] screaming and yelling and everything. And [the women coming out of the bar] just ... weren't going to get involved, you know. We finally got away. It was a mess![42]

Bev also remembers an incident where a man tried to grab her lover's purse.

> As we got out of the car, and some guy came up and grabbed Carole and they started kind of tussling and she's swearing and I'm screaming, and he grabbed her purse and she's fighting to keep her purse.... And I was hysterical, I mean, I could have helped, but I just stood there and just screamed and screamed. And this guy stole her purse, took off with it.[43]

In neither of these instances did anyone come to help the women who were victims of robbery. Getting involved might have resulted in being mentioned in a police report or a newspaper, which many women saw as too risky. Plus, white, middle-class women were often unaccustomed to jumping into the middle of a physical confrontation. And, perhaps most importantly, the anonymity that made Fred's feel safer to middle-class women in some ways, failed to protect them in others. Unlike the Palais, where women defended each other as a matter of course and where the code of ethical behavior demanded that lesbians help out other lesbians, even if it involved risk of physical harm, patrons at Fred's were on their own. In the end, many middle-class women felt that the neighborhood was too rough, even if Fred's was a great place to socialize.

Fred's also lacked other aspects of working-class lesbian bar culture that might have attracted a more regular clientele—what enabled the Sweetheart and the Palais to remain open for so many years. This is evident in working-class lesbians' descriptions of Fred's, which are as revealing about class differences as their depictions of the Palais. The interplay of class values in these interviews tells a great deal about divisions between lesbians in Detroit. Billie Hill didn't care for Fred's, even though she remembers that "if you had a date and you wanted to go and dance, you know, to a nice place, you'd take your girl to Fred's. But if you were out houndin' around and whorin' around, then you went to the Palais." It wasn't just her preferred form of socializing that drew Billie to the Palais, however. She recalls:

> A lot of 'em that would, if you'd meet 'em at Fred's, you wouldn't even know 'em, the difference in 'em from Fred's to the Palais. At the Palais, you know, they'd curse and carry on. When you go out to Fred's, they were just little, pissy little, you know. That's why I never went to Fred's much. 'Cause I didn't believe in being that two faced. I really didn't.[44]

For Billie and for most of the other blue-collar women whom I interviewed, honesty and the space to be themselves were important values. What Muriel Crisara and other middle-class women saw as the niceties they expected, both in environment and behavior, working-class women tended to see as annoying pretenses. This was especially true when it came to expressing butch-femme roles, since Billie, a self-described "daddy butch," which was the very "butchest" of butches, considered fighting and swearing essential to her expression as a butch.[45]

While Muriel was also extremely butch—she bought all her clothes except for her bra in a men's clothing store and considered herself a man in a woman's body—she expressed her butch identity in distinctly middle-class ways. Because she always wore stylish suits, she was nicknamed "Dude." But she did not fight or swear, since expressing anger in such public, violent ways was contradictory to her class background.

Muriel also only had sex with women she was involved with, and was disdainful of the one-night stands that other women in the bars enjoyed. When asked about these differences, she replied, "You see, you're talking about two kinds of people here. I'm talking about a bar that's in the slums, and you're talking about relationships. Slum bars don't have long relationships. Middle-class people have longer relationships . . ."[46] For Muriel, fidelity was important in relationships, and between relationships, it was equally important that people not give away sex freely. To her, sex was for intimate, lasting relationships only, and one-night stands were a symbol of moral degeneracy. Because she associated lesbians with the relaxed sexual codes of the bars, she chose to become involved mostly with middle-class, straight-identified women who shared her class perspective and were not connected with the bar scene. For Judy, the bars were difficult places to meet lovers because she "was never one that could ever go to a bar and pick somebody up and go home with them," which was a pattern that she associated with the bars.[47]

Class-based traditions help to explain the disparities between the social lives of white-collar and blue-collar lesbians. Lesbians grew up in families that spent their leisure time in ways that were consistent with their classes. Leisure activities were class appropriate not only because a family could afford them, but because the activities were judged by whether or not they reinforced class-based beliefs about gender behavior and morality.

Moreover, blue-collar and white-collar lesbians often had different ideas and needs when it came to the question of safety. For middle-class lesbians, safety typically meant a clean, nice place with as little chance of exposure to heterosexuals as possible, little or no exposure to other forms of vice, anonymity (so that one's status and privacy could remain unbreached), and the company of other women with similar values. Safety also included financial stability and a respectable profession. Lesbian oppression undercut some of the class privilege that middle-class white lesbians might have enjoyed had they been heterosexual. Many of the ideals associated with middle-class womanhood assumed a woman's heterosexuality: marriage, children, not working outside the home, deference to men, attending and organizing events with extended family, and adherence to traditionally feminine standards of appearance. All of these things kept middle-class white women "safe," far from the dangers of postwar threats, both political and moral, to families and nations.[48] For middle-class women, the dilemma of living a lesbian life centered around building the structures of an acceptable middle-class existence and, at the same time, finding friendship circles and love relationships with other lesbians.

For working-class lesbians, safety meant "turf" to call one's own, where a woman could go any time of the day or night and be herself. Acceptance on one's own terms was extremely important to blue-collar lesbians, since their self-expression often crossed the rigid lines separating masculinity from femininity. Physical safety was less of a need than was a group of comrades who could be counted on in a dangerous situation. Because they were lesbians, these working-class women were also exposed to vice that they might not have encountered otherwise. But the gap between them and the prostitutes and hustlers they met in the bars was often less than the chasm experienced by middle-class women, and their working-class traditions involved patronizing neighborhood bars, which meant that public space was an important component of community for these women. Yet the constant harassment and scrutiny of heterosexuals, along with the lack of privacy, must have been too much for some working-class lesbians to bear.

Conclusion

As bars became more institutionalized as sites for lesbians to meet, socialize, and court one another, they increasingly had to adhere to a new set of criteria for what constituted lesbian-positive spaces. The creation of bars that were invisible to heterosexuals, and even to lesbians who were unaware of their existence, meant that the bars were less widely known and talked about among heterosexuals, and that these spaces were patronized almost exclusively by a select group of women. They also lost one of the features that made working-class lesbians feel at home, namely the feeling of mutual support and the willingness to stand up for each other. Yet the changing physical features of the bars meant that more middle-class women would feel comfortable spending time in these places, since there was less harassment from heterosexuals, particularly men, and less reason for violence to be a defining characteristic of bar life. In addition, the lesbian bouncer became a job available to a few tough bar lesbians who had difficulty finding other work because of their physical appearance.

On a larger scale, these changes helped to redraw the boundaries between lesbians and heterosexuals. Lesbians (and bisexuals seeking same-sex partners) no longer socialized alongside heterosexuals, or allowed themselves to be the entertainment for a heterosexual date. While homophobia caused many heterosexuals to refuse to socialize with lesbians, and often to punish visible expressions of lesbian desire, the need and wish for privacy and control of their lives led many lesbians to frequent the bars that most excluded heterosexual men and prevented such violence. Thus, as bar owners changed their establishments to fit these needs, they reinforced growing sexual divisions in U.S. society.

Acknowledgments

Many thanks to the many people in my life who support me and make my academic work possible, including Lisa Roehl, Lesley Finch, Renee Perry, Leslie Allee, Sue Rochman, Vera Whisman, Tracy Morgan, and Katie Gilmartin. And thanks, too, to Brett Beemyn, who helped to put this essay together when it seemed impossible.

Notes

1. See Joan Nestle, *A Restricted Country* (Ithaca: Firebrand, 1987); and Elizabeth Lapovsky Kennedy and Madeline D. Davis, *Boots of Leather, Slippers of Gold: The History of a Lesbian Community* (New York: Routledge, 1993) and "Oral History and the Study of Sexuality in the Lesbian Community: Buffalo, New York, 1940–1960," in *Hidden from History: Reclaiming the Gay and Lesbian Past*, eds. Martin Bauml Duberman, Martha Vicinus, and George Chauncey, Jr. (New York: New American Library, 1989), 426–40.

2. These interviews were conducted for a larger study, a dissertation about lesbian life in Detroit during the mid-twentieth century, that is still in progess. The dissertation focuses on the ways that race and class affect lesbian lives historically.
3. Neither "lesbian" or "bisexual" would have been widely used at the time by the women in the bars. I use these terms to mean women who went to certain bars specifically to seek the company of other women who shared their sexual and other desires. Seen from the vantage point of the current lesbian, gay, and bisexual political movement, some of these women's life histories appear to be "lesbian," and others "bisexual." For the purposes of this essay, I use the term "lesbian" in an inclusive sense, that is, to mean that the "lesbians" in the bars were women who, regardless of the choices they would make the following year, or the following evening, were in the bars because they desired friendship, society, romance, and sex with other women. In this essay, I am obscuring the differences in life trajectories of individual women because I believe the larger problems of harassment by heterosexual men and class differences between women were experienced by all of the women in the bars who were there seeking the company of other women. Many thanks to Brett Beemyn for sharing his thoughts on this issue.
4. See my essay, "'A House Where Queers Go': African-American Lesbian Night Life in Detroit, 1940–1975," in *Imagining Lesbian Cultures in America*, ed. Ellen Lewin (Boston: Beacon, 1996).
5. Detroit bars have never been completely desegregated, remaining mostly separate for Black and white lesbians to this day. The larger African-American and white communities are so separate that many whites come to the city only to work, while many African-Americans rarely leave their neighborhoods. As a result, it is possible to live and work in or near Detroit and never actually interact or make friends with someone of a different race. With the exception of workplace acquaintances, Blacks and whites rarely mix in Detroit.
6. This point sheds light on one of the questions I raised above, namely why bars for gay men or for both gay men and lesbians would have less need for extreme anonymity. Unlike men who went to lesbian bars for the purpose of harassing lesbians, a man not accompanied by a female date would have felt less comfortable entering a bar that included gay men, since he would be presumed to be homosexual by people both in and outside the bar. This taboo may have been enough to discourage many harassers from entering bars frequented by gay men.
7. Interview with Billie Hill, January 24, 1992.
8. Interview with Brandy Maguire, June 23, 1992.
9. Interview with Bev, February 8, 1992.
10. Interview with C.B., February 7, 1992.
11. *Detroit City Directory*, 1939.
12. Interview with Billie Hill.
13. Elizabeth Kennedy and Madeline Davis make the same observation about lesbian bars in Buffalo. *Boots of Leather, Slippers of Gold*, 48–49.
14. Interview with Billie Hill.
15. In the past few years, scholars have begun to explore the ways that lesbians and gay men interact with urban geography and create their own "public" spaces. See, for example, D. Bell, "Insignificant Others: Lesbian and Gay Geographies," *Area* 23 (1991): 323–39; Samuel R. Delany, "Street Talk/Straight Talk," *differences* 3:2 (1991): 21–38; Lawrence Knopp, "Sexuality and the Spatial Dynamics of Capital-

ism," *Environment and Planning D: Society and Space* 10 (1992): 651–69; L. Peake, "'Race' and Sexuality: Challenging the Patriarchal Structuring of Urban Social Space," *Environment and Planning D: Society and Space* 11 (1993): 395–413.

16. Interview with Billie Hill.
17. Ibid.
18. Interview with Brandy Maguire.
19. Ibid.
20. Interview with Bev.
21. Interview with Billie Hill.
22. Ibid.
23. Ibid.
24. Interview with B. Koz, July 22, 1992.
25. Interview with Billie Hill.
26. Kennedy and Davis, *Boots of Leather, Slippers of Gold*, 90–93.
27. Interview with Brandy Maguire.
28. Interview with B. Koz.
29. Interview with C.B.
30. Interview with Billie Hill.
31. To what extent fighting was the result of lesbians defending their turf and to what extent it reflected more mainstream, predominantly heterosexual, working-class bar life is hard to say. Certainly, despite the physical changes that bars have undergone, and the relatively protected space within most lesbian bars, fights still break out among some groups of lesbians.
32. Many thanks to Lisa Roehl for her insights into the importance of Fred's.
33. Interview with Judy Utley, June 25, 1992.
34. Interview with Bev.
35. Interview with C.B.
36. Interview with Judy Utley.
37. Interview with B. Koz.
38. Interview with Bev.
39. Interview with Billie Hill.
40. Interview with Judy Utley.
41. Interview with C.B.
42. Interview with Judy Utley.
43. Interview with Bev.
44. Interview with Billie Hill.
45. Ibid.
46. Interview with Muriel Crisara, June 23, 1992.
47. Interview with Judy Utley. Contrary to what Judy may have observed, my research shows that women who engaged in "one-night stands" were frequently looking for a longterm relationship.
48. For a thorough examination of this subject, see Elaine May, *Homeward Bound: American Families in the Cold War Era* (New York: Basic Books, 1988), especially 16–36.

8. A Queer Capital

Race, Class, Gender, and the Changing Social Landscape of Washington's Gay Communities, 1940–1955

Brett Beemyn

World War II was a watershed event for gay life, resulting in a large increase in the number of lesbians, gay men, and bisexuals in cities such as Washington and a dramatic rise in the number of bars, restaurants, and other meeting places that they could frequent.[1] As historian John D'Emilio states, "the unusual conditions of a mobilized society allowed homosexual desire to be expressed more easily in action. For many gay Americans, World War II created something of a nationwide coming out experience."[2] But, while histories of lesbians and gay men typically present the wartime migration only in terms of its positive contributions towards the growth of explicitly gay communities and social institutions, research on Washington during this period demonstrates that it had negative effects as well.

In the nation's capital, the massive influx often had a deleterious impact upon the atmosphere within existing gay bars and led to the establishment of new bars that excluded African Americans, members of the working class, and/or women. This resulted in the entrenchment of race, class, and gender segregation among gays in the city. Still, the migration of African Americans and whites to Washington during and after World War II was instrumental to the formation of same-sex sexual communities, which developed both within and outside of existing, predominantly heterosexual, communities. More than at any previous time, those attracted to people of the same sex had opportunities to find each other and to socialize publicly together. Besides the proliferation of bars and the continued popularity of parks and other cruising locations, a growing number of house parties, late-night cafeterias, and out-of-town drag balls provided gays with places to meet in the 1940s and early '50s.

As the center of U.S. military planning and one of the major points of war production and training, Washington was inundated with servicepeople and newly hired civilian workers during World War II. The population nearly doubled, and many of these migrants remained after the war, increasing the size of the city by more than fifty percent by 1950. A large number of lesbians, gay men, and bisexuals were among those who were stationed at military installations in or near Washington, or who migrated to the capital to find work during or immediately following the war.[3] "Scott Harrison," for example, came to Washington soon after the U.S. entered World War II to work for a local chapter of the USO as a musician. He found that the large wartime influx, coupled with the tremendous popularity of USO centers, made it easy to pursue relationships with both women and men; he became involved with several men during the war before falling in love and marrying a woman in the late 1940s. For "Ed Wallace," the move to the capital came after the war; he settled in the area in 1948 to attend college after serving in Germany as part of the U.S. army's postwar occupying force. Having had a number of sexual relationships with men while in the military, he quickly found an active social life in D.C. and became a regular at bars patronized largely by gays.[4]

The extent to which military personnel crowded nightly into Washington bars with a mostly or exclusively gay clientele is demonstrated by the experiences of "Haviland Ferris." Moving to D.C. in the late 1930s, Ferris began the practice of having all of the people who visited him sign their names in a guest book. With the commencement of the war, he began to meet men from the armed forces in the city's gay bars and brought a number of them home with him; among the people listed in his guest book for the year 1939 are servicemen who were stationed at Fort Myer (an Army base across the Potomac River from Washington), the Arlington Cantonment (an Army installation), Quantico (a Marine base in Northern Virginia), and the city's Marine Barracks.[5]

"Every Friday and Saturday Night": Bar Life in the Nation's Capital[6]

The presence of so many military personnel, some of whom settled in Washington after the war, led to a significant rise in the number of bars with a lesbian, gay, and/or bisexual clientele in the 1940s and early '50s. Also contributing to this increase was D.C.'s strict liquor law, which Congress passed following Prohibition, ironically to try to limit the growth of bars and drinking in the capital. Under the new regulations, there were technically no bars in Washington, only restaurants that had liquor licenses to serve alcohol as an adjunct to their businesses. To ensure that the sale of liquor was secondary to food purchases, the law required patrons to be seated at a counter or table to drink beer and wine and only at a table to consume mixed drinks.[7] Restaurants which sought to function more like bars were able to skirt the requirements by having very limited menus, but they still had to have fully equipped kitchen facilities, thereby decreasing the size of their dining space. The need for patrons to be seated also reduced the number of people who could be served. Consequently, many bar-restaurants had relatively small capacities, leading to the creation of additional bar-restaurants to accommodate the tremendous migration during and after the war.

During World War II, the number of bars with a large gay clientele increased from five to about seven; by 1950, there were more than eleven, and in 1955, at least fifteen.[8] Most of these establishments, though, did not serve gays specifically or exclusively, and even the bars that were patronized entirely by lesbians, gay men, and/or bisexuals at night were "straight" dining facilities during the day. The fact that a number of bars had very disparate clienteles at different times was often known by straight patrons, who were sure to leave before gays started arriving around 6 or 7PM. However, when they were unaware of the changeover, conflicts sometimes arose.[9] Another problem was the possibility of being "outed" to friends or family members. In the late 1940s and '50s, "Frederick Schultz" was a regular customer of the Chicken Hut, a bar patronized exclusively by gays at night. Once, though, he was taken there for lunch by unsuspecting straight coworkers, who introduced him to his evening waitress. Fortunately for Schultz, she did not let on that she knew him.[10]

Located at 1720 L Street, Northwest, two blocks from Lafayette Square, the Chicken Hut was the most popular bar among white middle-class gay and bisexual men in the postwar period. Men in their twenties and thirties who were more open about their sexuality were particularly attracted to the Hut because of the campy atmosphere provided by Howard, its gay pianist for more than thirty years. Known to the bar's gay clientele as Miss Hattie, Howard played show tunes and satirical renditions of popular ballads to which almost everyone sang along. A number of the songs had campy lyrics; for example, "The Sun Shines Nellie" poked fun at a mother whose son becomes gay, and "I Wonder Why" joked about someone no longer being cruised because they looked too queer. When Jack Nichols first entered the Chicken Hut, patrons were singing "Somewhere Along the Way"—which included the line, "our hearts were carefree and gay"—letting him know that he had found a place patronized by others like himself.[11] Howard also gave regular patrons of the Hut their own theme songs, which he would play whenever they entered the bar. "Michael Borchert," whose theme was "St. Louis Woman" because he liked to wear flamboyant clothing, notes that this practice made him and many other gay and bisexual men feel at home in the Chicken Hut and kept them coming back each weekend.[12]

The most popular bar among white lesbians and bisexual women in the late 1940s and early '50s was an establishment at 1628 L Street, NW, four blocks from the Chicken Hut. Opened immediately following the war, the bar was originally known as the Maystat because it was halfway between the Mayflower and Statler Hotels. And just as the bars in those two hotels were gathering places for many white middle-class gay and bisexual men during the war, the Maystat's clientele initially consisted largely of white men who were looking to meet other men for sex. According to M. Tilden-Morgan, men would often move between the three locations on weekends, seeing what the atmosphere was like in each. White lesbians and bisexual women began to frequent the Maystat in increasing numbers in the late 1940s following the closing of the Showboat, the principal women's bar in Washington from the mid–1930s to the mid–1919140s.[13] As the Maystat's clientele was changing, so too was its name; in the early 1950s, it became first the Jewel Box and then the Redskin Lounge.

White lesbians and bisexual women rarely went to any of the other bars in Washington in the immediate postwar period, in part because it was still not considered respectable for a woman to be in bars without a male escort. But even in the city's gay bars, where women unaccompanied by men would not be viewed with disdain, the exclusion of women was widespread nevertheless. For example, few of the white men interviewed for this study remembered seeing *any* women in the bars that they frequented in the 1940s and early '50s, and partly as a result, almost none had lesbians and bisexual women as friends during these years. The bars with a substantial white gay and bisexual male clientele had a number of practices that kept women out. Some, like the "men's bars" of the Mayflower and Statler Hotels, openly denied admittance to women, while others did so less explicitly through atmospheres that were uninviting to women. In particular, the tradition of singing campy songs for hours each weekend at the Chicken Hut and later at Johnnie's in Southeast Washington had a strong appeal to many white gay and bisexual men, but seems to have generated little interest among white lesbians and bisexual women. In contrast, the Redskin Lounge was well-liked by these women because it featured a butch lesbian performer singing and telling jokes and bands playing contemporary music.[14]

Another reason why the Hut, Johnnie's, and similar bars were not popular with women was the simple fact that they were completely full of men, assuring that women would always be a small, isolated minority in these places. Consequently, when the Showboat closed, women began frequenting bars that were not male dominated, but which still had gay-supportive atmospheres, such as the Redskin Lounge and David's Grill (which had been a popular bar among lesbians, gay men, and bisexuals in the 1930s when it was called the Horseshoe). How an establishment could attract lesbians and bisexual women is demonstrated by Joanna's, a bar that opened in the late '50s in the 400 block of 8th Street, SE, one block away from Johnnie's. It was intended to appeal more to women than its male-named predecessor, and since Joanna's had no well-established male clientele, it did become a principal gathering place for lesbians and bisexual women.[15]

Just as most of the bars with a large gay and bisexual male clientele excluded women, so too were they racially segregated during and after World War II. Not until 1953, when the Supreme Court ruled that Washington, D.C. restaurants could not discriminate against African Americans, did most downtown establishments begin to serve Blacks. But even then, many bars and restaurants continued their discriminatory practices. For example, when Ed Wallace went to the Chicken Hut soon after the Supreme Court's decision, he found that the management had put "reserved" signs on the tables, so that if any African Americans came in, they could be told that there was no available seating.[16]

Faced with hostility in the downtown bars with a substantial gay clientele and wishing to socialize with others like themselves, African American gays established their own bars within the city's Black neighborhoods of Shaw and Columbia Heights. In the late 1940s, the most popular gathering place for African American gay and bisexual men was the Cozy Corner, a second-story bar (the first floor was a restaurant with a largely heterosexual clientele) located several blocks from Howard University. Not only did Black men go there, but also a few whites who were looking to meet Black sex partners.[17] The other main bar, Nob Hill, began as an upscale private club for Black gay and bisexual men in Washington's Columbia Heights section in 1953. It continued to be patronized largely by middle-class African Americans when it opened publicly in the mid–1950s. During those years, Pat Hamilton, a working-class Black drag queen, never went to Nob Hill because he felt that its clientele was color and class prejudiced:

> They wanted you to be light; they wanted you to be a postal worker, or a doctor, or something in that area. They were very "snooty" because they were mainly men [in] suit and tie, [with] briefcase. Nobody really knew they were gay.[18]

African American lesbians and bisexual women, as well as working-class gay and bisexual men who felt excluded from the Cozy Corner and Nob Hill, often frequented neighborhood bars that did not have a specifically gay clientele. Since many Black lesbians, gay men, and bisexuals identified at least as strongly as African American as they did as gay, this fact should not be surprising.[19] And because "everybody knew everybody" in Washington's Black community, they were rarely made to feel unwanted in these places and were generally accepted by other patrons. Most African American gays, however, did not press the issue. At least within predominantly straight bars, they were not entirely open about their sexuality, although they still frequently socialized together.[20]

The opening of a large number of gay bars that excluded women, African Americans, and/or working-class people contributed to the entrenchment of gender, race, and class segregation among gays in Washington, D.C. in the 1940s and early '50s—divisions which persist today in the city's gay bars. Most general histories of lesbians and gay men, though, ignore these forms of segregation, which were particularly prevalent in Southern cities like Washington, and their effects on the development of gay communities.[21] For example, John D'Emilio states in *Sexual Politics, Sexual Communities: The Making of a Homosexual Minority in the United States, 1940–1970* that bars with an "all-gay environment" served as "seedbeds for a collective consciousness that might one day flower politically" as gays "dropped the pretension of heterosexuality." Similarly, Lillian Faderman argues in *Odd Girls and Twilight Lovers: A History of Lesbian Life in Twentieth-Century America* that the proliferation of exclusively gay bars in urban centers "fostered a sense of community," leading to the beginnings of an "incipient political consciousness" among lesbians.[22] Both historians overlook the fact that many Black lesbians, gay men, and bisexuals did not frequent bars with a primarily gay clientele or socialize just with other gays. And since many African Americans already had a "collective consciousness" and were politically active as Blacks, the centrality assigned to all-gay bars in the formation of personal identities and "a sense of community" is applicable to only a segment of white lesbians, gay men, and bisexuals in the mid-twentieth century.

By constructing a metanarrative that centers upon a process of coming out in postwar gay bars, histories of lesbians and gay men not only fail to account for the very different experiences of many African Americans, but also overemphasize the role of gay bars. Clearly, the creation of bars that were patronized mostly or exclusively by lesbians, gay men, and bisexuals was a significant development in gay history and a transformative moment for women and men who had previously felt isolated or believed that they were "the only one." But, as demonstrated above, many lesbians, gay men, and bisexuals were excluded from gay bars or did not feel welcomed there. Others preferred more private social spaces which did not entail publicly disclosing their sexual orientation and where they did not have to run the risk of encountering coworkers, bosses, friends, and family members to whom they were not "out."

Focusing on the growing number and popularity of gay bars during and after World War II also ignores the negative impact that these changes could have on previously existing bars and their patrons. For example, the Showboat, once a leading bar for white lesbians, gay men, and bisexuals, went out of business during this period, while another gay bar, Carroll's, lost much of its regular clientele. Before the war, Carroll's was popular with Army, Navy, and Marine personnel stationed in or near Washington and with local gay and bisexual men interested in meeting men in uniform. Because the military population in the city was relatively small and stable during this period, the local patrons of Carroll's, with the help of the bar's two supportive waitresses, were able to learn quickly the names, backgrounds, and even reputations of the service personnel who came there. As a result, sailors, marines, and soldiers had to be sure to maintain good reputations if they expected to find sexual partners; those who mistreated the men who took them home became known to others and were unofficially banned from the bar. One of the regular local patrons, Haviland Ferris, remembers that anyone in the armed forces whom the waitresses "knew to have robbed or beaten up one of the gays was soon effectively ostracized, and by a series of small discriminations and total inattention, was made aware that Carroll's was not for him." Ferris himself once had a typewriter stolen and pawned by a young marine whom he had met at Carroll's. He recovered the typewriter and, by writing to the man's mother, was reimbursed for the expense. The marine never went back to the bar, it seems, because he knew that he would have a bad reputation and likely be shunned by its patrons.[23]

However, in Ferris's words, "when the war came, that changed everything." Not only was there a large increase in the number of military personnel in Washington bars, but this population was constantly changing as members of the armed forces were sent overseas. At Carroll's, this situation meant that men in uniform were not absorbed into the bar community and that neither the local patrons nor the waitresses knew their reputations, making it much more dangerous for gay and bisexual men to pick up soldiers, sailors, and marines. As a consequence, many regular prewar customers like Ferris stopped socializing there, and it began to be known as a "rough trade" bar—that is, a place where a number of the patrons were straight-identified and might turn violent during a sexual encounter.[24]

Social Opportunities Outside of Washington Bars

In their study of mid-twentieth-century lesbian life in Buffalo, New York, Madeline Davis and Elizabeth Lapovsky Kennedy found that Black lesbians went to both predominantly straight neighborhood bars and to primarily white gay bars, which they pushed to desegregate in the 1950s. However, they often preferred house parties over either type of bar because they could openly socialize with other Black lesbians, gay men, and bisexuals at parties and avoid the racism prevalent in white-dominated bars. Holding house parties was a way for them to remain in Buffalo's Black community, yet still have a gay social life.[25]

African American lesbians, gay men, and bisexuals in Washington likewise regularly attended house parties within the city's Black neighborhoods in the 1940s and '50s. Some of these parties were hosted by and consisted primarily of heterosexual African Americans; others were specifically for lesbians and bisexual women, gay and bisexual men, or both groups. Frequently, these gatherings took the form of rent parties, a popular tradition among Black gays and heterosexuals alike in U.S. cities dating back to the early twentieth century.[26] In Washington, according to Esther Smith, "a lot of people had those, where you would pay maybe $3 or something like that to go in. They would have sodas or something for you to drink. Some people might have food like fried chicken and stuff like that." By the end of the night, the host would have enough money to make their rent payment. In addition to rent parties, Black lesbians, gay men, and bisexuals also hosted and attended card parties, where participants played whisk, spades, or other games, as well as danced and socialed together.[27]

Racial, gender, and class segregation in Washington bars contributed to the popularity of house parties among African Americans, especially among Black women, but another important attraction was the ability to socialize freely without the threat of harassment from heterosexuals or the police. Esther Smith puts it succinctly:

> You could be yourself . . . If I invite you to my house, you can come in here and do anything that you want to do. You can dance, you can eat, you can talk to who you want to talk to. If you just want to talk to a female, you can do that. If you just want to talk with a male, you can do that.

Since even D.C. bars with an exclusively gay clientele prohibited same-sex dancing through the 1950s—for fear that undercover police would shut them down, as was the case in other cities[28]—the ability to dance at house parties was not a small consideration for Black lesbians, gay men, and bisexuals.

The chance to be able to dance together and to socialize more openly than in most bars also made private parties popular with many white gays. Another reason why parties were attractive to whites had to do with the particular social constraints placed upon the sale of alcohol in the nation's capital. Fearing a return to unfettered drinking following the lifting of Prohibition in 1933, temperance forces in Washington succeeded in passing regulations that required bars in the city to close at midnight on Saturday and Sunday nights, while they could remain open until 2A.M. the rest of the week.[29] But rather than discouraging drinking and all-night carousing, the early closure gave rise to a tradition among white gay and bisexual men—the primary patrons of downtown gay bars—of hosting and attending weekend after-hour parties. As Frank Kameny states:

> What developed was a pattern, which was very well-established when I arrived here in Washington [in the mid–1950s] and remained for many years thereafter, of Saturday night parties in private homes after the bars closed. If you arrived in the bar anytime after about ten o'clock in the evening, the first question you would inquire was "Where is the party tonight?" There were usually a small number of *enormously* overcrowded parties. You would quickly find out where the one or perhaps two—or once in a great while on a weekend, three—parties were. These were BYOB or BYOL parties. The liquor stores were open till midnight [on Saturdays], so, between eleven and midnight, people would go rushing out for quick trips to the liquor stores to buy their six pack or whatever, and come back to the bar until closing time and then go on off to the parties, which went on long into the night. That was very, very much the pattern . . .[30]

Because the address of a party was often widely disseminated to patrons at the Chicken Hut, Johnnie's, or another bar with a largely gay clientele, the host would sometimes know few of the men who showed up at his doorstep.

For some middle-class men, though, such open parties were too dangerous. Their job security and social status depended upon an image of respectability that could be maintained only through keeping their sexuality publicly invisible, and parties at which "you'd never know what you would get" were a serious threat to such concealment. Moreover, since the police had an undercover presence at times in bars that were patronized largely by gays, an open invitation to a party could inadvertently result in an officer attending. As a consequence, a host sometimes wouldn't admit strangers unless they were accompanied by someone they knew or would quietly ask their acquaintances whether they were familiar with unknown guests.[31]

The fact that Washington bars closed early on Saturdays and Sundays also helped establish traditions among white gay and bisexual men of patronizing late-night cafeterias and travelling to Maryland bars, which did not have the same closing-time restrictions. The two D.C. restaurants that attracted a mainly gay clientele after midnight—the California Kitchen near Dupont Circle and Britt's in Georgetown—not only provided men from the bars with an opportunity to continue socializing, but also to find a sexual partner if they hadn't met anyone in places like the Chicken Hut. For that reason, the California Kitchen was known among gay and bisexual men as the "Last Chance Cafe." According to Ed Wallace, a regular there:

> If you had not been successful—you had made the major rounds in the bars and nobody was interested in you—you might be able to pick up something at the California Kitchen. All the people came out of the clubs and went into this place on Connecticut Avenue. You could get waffles and eggs. They did a business like you wouldn't believe. They were almost lined up at the door. If you hadn't gone to a party and you were still hoping to be able to meet somebody, that was the place to go.... Everybody knew that was where the gay crowd would end up.[32]

The other cafeteria, Britt's, was only a block down the street from the Georgetown Grill, a bar that began to attract a significant number of gays in the 1950s, and when the Grill and other bars closed for the night, many went to "Britt's for grits." Part of the attraction of Britt's for Michael Borchert and his friends was that "the owner was sensitive to gays. He really appreciated our business and protected us a lot."[33]

Lesbians, gay men, and bisexuals of all races who wanted to continue drinking on Saturday nights in the postwar period often patronized bars in the Maryland suburbs of Washington or made the thirty-six mile drive to Baltimore, since Maryland bars remained open every day until 2 A.M. Frequently, a group of white gay and bisexual men from the capital would make the trip together, leaving from Johnnie's, the Grill, or another downtown bar at closing time. African American gays travelled to Baltimore bars for late-night partying as well, but they also went to the city for day trips and weekend stays.[34]

As in earlier decades, both white and Black gay and bisexual men also drove to Maryland in the 1940s and '50s to view and participate in drag events. Perhaps the most anticipated event of the year, however, was in New York: the annual Fun Makers Ball, which was held in some of Harlem's most lavish dance halls each Thanksgiving beginning in 1945. For D.C. drag queens, part of the big appeal of the Fun Makers Ball was simply the fact that it occurred at all. While police in the nation's capital prevented drag balls from taking place there, New York police gave "official sanction for one night of the year to men dressing as women in public" and even provided crowd control to ensure that a melée like the one that broke out after the banning of a Washington drag ball in the 1930s did not mar the New York event. Because the event was legal, it was the only ball that Pat Hamilton participated in each year, but also important to him was the fact that the drag queens there really tried to be successful crossdressers: "they gave you what we say is confusion. You had to really look good, and you had to work. You had to definitely be glamorous."[35]

The large number and diversity of spectators and participants was another important attraction of the Fun Makers Balls for many Washington drag queens. During the early 1950s, between two-to-three thousand people came to see or be seen at the balls, with nearly equal numbers of Blacks and whites, and a mixture of working-class and middle-class gays. According to *Ebony* magazine, which provided extensive and largely favorable coverage of the 1952 and 1953 balls, "Park Avenue rubbed shoulders with 125th Street and bankers laughed gaily with artists from Greenwich Village."[36]

Although drag queens could not hold balls for their own pleasure in Washington in the 1940s and early '50s, they were able to perform as female impersonators to entertain largely non-gay audiences, and many did so because it was a way that they could cross-dress and still earn a living, albeit a difficult one.[37] Pat Hamilton, who had regularly worn "women's" clothing since he was about eight years old because he "felt like [he] should have them on," performed in a number of largely straight, largely Black clubs in Washington in the 1950s. He remembers that at these bars,

> You had to really work. They weren't paying us much in them days. I think we did two shows on the weekend, it was like $27 we'd get. And you had to be able to do everything. You had to sing, you had to dance, you had to be able to wait on tables, you had to go back there in the kitchen, you had to do everything. That's what they required.

Being successful as a female impersonator also required a drag queen to be "real," to be able to pass as a traditionally feminine woman—the more glamorous the better. Hamilton notes that audiences "wanted to see you made up, [with] nice hairdo, and lovely gowns on. That's what brought the men in, the women [too]. They loved it."[38]

On the surface, it may appear paradoxical that men in drag would be condemned and rendered invisible in one location—the drag ball—yet celebrated and made the center of attention in another—the heterosexually coded bar. But it is precisely because of the difference in setting that these seemingly similar transgressions of gender norms produced such contrary responses. Drag balls were sites in which the participants themselves were in control and could celebrate themselves for one night without fearing arrest or being made to feel like an oddity. As a result, these events affirmed the gay community and provided gay and bisexual men with a sense of empowerment and belonging. This empowerment was especially significant for

Black gay and bisexual men, who were able to exercise a measure of authority that was frequently denied to them elsewhere in society. It was thus not surprising that the D.C. police—in charge of maintaining and enforcing state power—would see drag balls as threatening and prevent them from being held, as they did in the 1930s.

Drag queens who performed before an overwhelmingly heterosexual audience, in contrast, were not considered threatening; they were isolated individuals who, rather than receiving validation for their cross-dressing, were often seen as a curiosity or laughed at for it. And while they may have received a certain level of acceptance as female impersonators, it was only as long as they remained a form of exotic entertainment, as long as their "gender bending" was limited to a heterosexually controlled space. Drag that was performed in front of a gay audience could not be contained in this way, and for that reason, Washington bars with a largely gay clientele rarely offered drag acts in the 1940s and early '50s, fearing that the police would arrest the performers—a worry not shared by "straight" bars because of their presumed heterosexuality.

But, no matter what the context in which they wore drag, all drag queens had to be concerned about police harassment. In the 1950s, the D.C. police commonly beat up men whom they recognized as being in drag in public or arrested them for disorderly conduct. According to Hamilton, "you paid $10 to get out for disorderly. And this could happen two or three times a night if [the police] wanted to. So you always carried $10 with you."[39] Hamilton was eventually forced to leave Washington because he experienced so much police brutality. The story he tells demonstrates both the resistant spirit of many drag queens and the comraderie between the "sisters":

> I left Washington in '59 because I was having problems with the police. They liked to just jump out on you and [making thumping sound] do you any way—tear your clothes off, take your wig off. It didn't matter. And I said I wasn't having it. You weren't going to abuse me. So I got into several fights, and I was a little teeny thing too—a size nine until I got into my thirties. And I was carrying on so bad with the police that my sisters, they asked me to leave because they didn't want me to get killed. They said, "I know you are fighting these policemen too much and one of them is going to shoot you. You have a couple of friends in New York, go there. Calm yourself." So I went.... [A] couple of more kids went with me.

In New York, Hamilton formed a drag group with "the kids" called Les Girls and, by "working three nights, two shows, for $250," made a decent living through tours of East Coast and Southern cities.[40]

Cruising Men in the Postwar Period

Besides visiting bars, late-night parties, after-hours restaurants, and drag balls in other cities, Washington's gay and bisexual men had opportunities to meet through a variety of different cruising areas, just as they did in earlier decades. But what distinguished cruising during the late 1940s and early '50s from the practice in previous years was the wider range of available sites, particularly for whites, and the greater number of gay and bisexual men who frequented these locations. Such growth seems evident in the city's dramatically rising arrest figures: in the late '40s, an average of two men a day were charged with "indecent acts" or "disorderly conduct" with other men, and more than a thousand per year were apprehended by the early '50s.[41] While the large number of arrests can partly be attributed to the tremendous postwar population influx and to greater police surveillance and prosecution, it also demonstrated the heightened prominence of Washington's gay communities during this period—a visibility which had led local authorities to step-up attacks on cruising in the first place.

Besides the police crackdown, the larger society's increasing recognition of gays was reflected in the more extensive and often more sensational media coverage given to homosexuality. A prime example was Jack Lait and Lee Mortimer's *Washington Confidential*, the best-selling book of 1951. One in a series of reactionary tabloid-style exposés on different cities, *Washington Confidential* sought to demonstrate how a growing government bureaucracy had spawned corruption and vice, turning the capital into "a cesspool of drunkenness, debauchery, whoring, homosexuality . . . among anomalous situations found nowhere else on earth." Lait and Mortimer especially singled out gay men for attack, warning that "they have their own hangouts, visit one another, and cling together in a tight union of interests and behavior" and, "with more than 6,000 fairies in government offices," were ensconced in the civil service.[42]

Yet, despite its hostile and often belittling attitude toward gays, the text provided a detailed geography of postwar gay life in the capital and inadvertently served as a guide for lesbians, gay men, and bisexuals who were new to the city or who were just beginning to recognize their attraction to others of the same sex. For example, a chapter describing the prevalence of cruising in Lafayette Square—entitled "Garden of Pansies"—made the significance of the location known to a number of gay and bisexual men, including Jack Nichols and Jack Frey. Both subsequently found out for themselves that it was a principal site for meeting other men.[43]

Although Lafayette Square was the leading outdoor cruising area in the 1940s and early '50s, a number of other parks gained in popularity, particularly as the police began to target the Square for surveillance. None of the city's parks, however, were exempt from regular police patrols, and arrest statistics show that the Washington Monument grounds, Franklin Park, Dupont Circle, and Meridian Hill Park, among others, were common sites for cruising.[44] According to Nichols, Franklin Park and Dupont Circle were especially active locations. As a young high school student in the early 1950s, he would often take a bus from his mother's home in Chevy Chase, Maryland, to Dupont Circle, where he would wait for someone to "come right up to [him] or walk right by and let [him] know somehow that they were looking at [him]." Among those "looking" was Frey, who, like an increasing number of gay men, had recently moved to the Dupont Circle neighborhood and took advantage of the area's popularity as a cruising area. In characterizing those years, Frey states: "it [was] a wonder I ever got my degree because I would write four pages on the term paper and go out and trick, then go back in."[45]

In addition to the tree-lined park located at the Circle itself, cruising routinely occurred on Connecticut Avenue, the neighborhood's main street and a principal commercial district of the city. One of the reasons that Connecticut Avenue was a popular cruising location, in fact, was its many retail businesses, specifically the street's large number of display windows.[46] The development of elaborate display windows in turn-of-the-century America enabled the middle-class, particularly "respectable" white women, to loiter on the street without censure, provided they remained tied to the new consumer culture. As Susan Porter Benson argues, "department stores created new public space for women, providing a socially acceptable way for them to enjoy the excitement of urban downtowns and a woman-oriented center of comfort and amenity." Members of the working-class were not as concerned about social acceptability, but they could still legitimize their presence on the street by viewing the latest consumer products, even if purchasing them was frequently beyond their means. For gay and bisexual men, however, the display window often had an altogether different meaning. Under the subterfuge of shopping for goods, they could meet one another in front of display windows without drawing undue public attention to themselves.[47]

The use of a series of subtle questions, gestures, and mannerisms also enabled gay and bisexual men to remain largely unnoticed by other pedestrians, and helped ensure that they did not approach heterosexual men or an undercover police officer. The initial move was simply to catch someone's attention through prolonged eye contact as they were looking at a display window or walking down the street. This was effective because, in Bill Youngblood's words, "men usually don't look at other men, they look at women." Therefore, it was a positive sign "if a man watches you and sees you are watching him."[48] At this point, a verbal greeting might be exchanged, which, according to Ed Wallace, was particularly common among African Americans, who did not have the luxury of remaining inconspicuous in a segregated neighborhood like Dupont Circle. If the two men were standing in front of a display window, they would then usually discuss its contents. Wallace describes a typical experience:

> Pretty soon it's all right to say, "That's beautiful, I wish I could afford that" or "What's that? Oh, that right there." The next question is usually, "Are you from here?" [and then,] "Do you come around here very often?" There was a regular ritual form. Those were the first two questions. You don't ask where you live—that's bad. You don't ask too many personal questions. "Do you come around here? Are you here very often?" This was a very good key. You could also ask some things relating to the display in the window, if you know anything. You had to go beyond just saying "it's pretty" or "I wish I could afford it." . . . These are the verbal behaviors that I learned.[49]

Not only was it against the unwritten rules of cruising to ask questions that were too personal or too overt, but, particularly among middle-class whites who feared losing their social standing, it was also considered inappropriate to use "any gestures that would appear to be at all effeminate. . . . They would say 'that's too flaming.' . . . You did not want to be marked off as being gay [in] behavior, clothes, appearance, anything."[50]

Ironically, although many men did not want to be read as "gay" by the larger society, one of the means by which they could recognize each other was through utilizing the word "gay." In the mid-twentieth century, "gay" as a term for men who were attracted to other men was primarily unknown by those outside the group. For example, both Black and white newspapers in Washington used the word in the 1940s and '50s to refer exclusively to an event that was exuberant or mirthful; in contrast, they described men who pursued same-sex sexual relationships as "twilight men," "the lavender set," "sex perverts," "sexually aberrated males," and "sex offenders."[51] Thus, because of the different meanings of "gay," it could be included in a conversation by gay and bisexual men to determine whether another man was similarly interested in people of the same sex. "If you get a spark of recognition," says Frank Kameny, then "you know. And if you didn't get any recognition at all, either the person was being excessively guarded or there was nothing there."[52]

For some gay and bisexual men, though, it wasn't a question of being cautious; they simply were unfamiliar with the word. While "gay" began to be used extensively as an in-group term in the 1930s, particularly among younger men, it was not known in some gay circles in Washington until a decade or more later.[53] "Wilson Burke," for example, did not hear the term until 1954, when another gay Washingtonian used it while the two were serving in the Army together in Germany. Ed Wallace likewise first heard the word while stationed in Germany; after a traumatic break-up with a Polish man in 1946, he was visibly depressed, leading his sergeant to ask him whether he was gay. When the meaning of the word was explained to him, Wallace was concerned about being discovered, but the sergeant was also gay and invited him to a secret party for men interested in meeting other men socially.[54]

Some gay and bisexual men in Washington were familiar with the word "gay" in the 1940s and early '50s, but preferred other terms to describe themselves and their community, even in predominantly straight settings. "Queer" and "queen," for example, were commonly used by both Black and white gays, especially among older men and those who wore drag. However, these words were also widely employed as terms of derision by the larger society, so they could not be utilized as code words. Instead, some gay and bisexual men used euphemistic expressions like "he's a friend of Mrs. King"—a reference to "queen"—or "oh, are you like that" to identify each other.[55]

Trying to discover someone else's sexual orientation without directly revealing one's own not only involved the use of in-group terminology, but also depended upon recognizing the significance of specific locations. Since certain places in Washington were coded as "gay" by those who patronized or knew of them, an effective cruising technique was to mention the name of a bar or other setting frequented by gays to someone to gauge their reaction.[56] Similarly, the presence of a person in one of these spaces indicated that they were likely interested in others of the same sex, which could then be confirmed through verbal clues and body language. Thus a man lingering by himself in front of display windows on Connecticut Avenue would be read as gay, particularly if he was subtly watching and making eye contact with men passing by.[57]

Frequenting other areas and places in the capital could also mark someone as gay, such as the commercial streets of Georgetown, where display windows often served a similar function, and the main branch of the local YMCA, which was a principal site for white men to meet for brief sexual encounters in the postwar period. M. Tilden-Morgan, a regular patron in the early '50s, remembers that

> [the YMCA] was wonderful because it had a pool and, of course, in those days it wasn't mixed, so there was nude swimming. It had a men's room downstairs, which became dangerous because the vice squad kept checking it. And so

> people from out of town who just heard that there was a "gay" men's room at the "Y" would go down there and oftentimes get picked up by the vice squad. All of us locals knew that was not the place to go. You went upstairs to the roof, which was wonderful for sunning. Of course, the pool and showers were very active—I can remember some interesting underwater encounters there. There was also a steam room on the floor above. That got very crowded and very steamy.[58]

The men's bathroom at the downtown YMCA, which *Time* magazine labelled "a notorious hangout for deviates,"[59] was far from the only Washington rest room that served as a popular rendezvous for men seeking sex. Known as "tearooms" (short for "toilet rooms") in gay argot, washrooms in parks, theaters, bars, department stores, bus stations, and other locations became popular sites for homoerotic activity throughout the country because, according to sociologist Laud Humphreys, they offered "the advantages of both public and private settings." Particularly in public parks, active tearooms were easily recognized by and accessible to men interested in same-sex encounters, while remaining largely unknown and invisible to the larger society.[60] The anonymity of rest rooms also made them appealing; men who feared being seen in a bar with a largely gay clientele, or who were unaware of such bars because they did not immerse themselves in a gay culture, could patronize most tearooms without unduly risking public exposure. For this reason, they were particularly popular with men who were married and those who did not identify as gay. Michael Borchert, for example, became active in the city's gay life, which included patronizing tearooms, while still married, and it was this involvement which forced him to acknowledge his attraction to other men.[61]

What Humphreys calls the "tearoom trade" was ironically aided by moral reformers, who advocated the construction of outdoor washrooms in U.S. cities in the late nineteenth and early twentieth centuries to improve health conditions for the urban poor. In Washington, public comfort stations were built in the city's main parks, many of which were already popular gay cruising areas: Lafayette Square, Dupont Circle, Franklin Park, the Washington Monument grounds, and Meridian Hill Park. Not surprisingly, men who frequented public parks in order to meet other men readily incorporated these washrooms into their cruising practices; they no longer had to engage in sexual activities in the shadows of a park or to travel to one of their homes or a nearby, cheap hotel to ensure a level of privacy. The D.C. police sought to prevent this gay appropriation of park comfort stations by increasing patrols and, in the late 1940s, by installing and monitoring peepholes and one-way mirrors, but even the Assistant U.S. Attorney admitted that "90 percent of [sex] offenses [were still being] committed in men's rooms operated by the Federal government." In desperation, the police ordered the closing of most park rest rooms in 1950, despite strong protests from African Americans, who did not have the alternative of using the lavatories of segregated downtown restaurants, hotels, and other establishments.[62]

The Construction of Racialized Gay Identities

As I have shown in this essay, racial segregation in Washington often led African Americans and whites to establish different sites for pursuing relationships with people of the same sex and contributed to the development of separate communities. African American gays remained closely linked to the city's Black communities in the 1940s and early '50s because of the prevalence of racism among whites, as well as the strength of their emotional and economic ties to other African Americans. White gays, on the other hand, did not have the same compelling needs to maintain such racial bonds; nevertheless, the communities that they created were also structured by race, a result of both racial exclusion and white racial privilege.

White gay communities are typically defined by same-sex sexual attraction and are rarely examined through a racial lens, which implies that race plays no role in these communities, that they are racially neutral. But, as Ruth Frankenberg makes clear, race does personally impact upon whites, informing their everyday experiences and structuring their identities. In her study of thirty white women in the U.S., Frankenberg found that

> race privilege translated directly into forms of social organization that shaped daily life (for example, the de jure and, later, de facto residential, social, and educational segregation that characterized most of these women's childhoods), and that these in turn shaped the women's perceptions of race.

Racial privilege also meant that the women in her study saw white cultural practices as normative and were largely unaware of the effects of racism upon their lives.[63]

In Washington, racial privilege, combined with class and gender privilege, enabled white middle-class gay men to dominate the sexual geography of most of the city and to do so without having to question their right to control this landscape. They thus saw the bars, after-hours places, tearooms, and other locations that they patronized as exclusively and undoubtedly "theirs," even though African Americans frequented some of these same spaces and were kept out of others only through legalized segregation. The fact that Black gays were still generally not welcomed as part of this sexual geography when segregation in the capital's public facilities was ruled unconstitutional in the early '50s demonstrates the extent to which the terrain had become racially coded. Ironically, at a time when the state was barring gays from its institutions—the government and military—because they were considered outside of the "natural order," white gays were naturalizing whiteness to keep African Americans from occupying "their" social spaces.

Further evidence that white gay male identities in Washington were grounded upon racial exclusivity can be found in the nearly complete absence of African Americans from these men's personal lives. Few of the white gay and bisexual men interviewed for this study knew any Black gays, much less had any Black gay friends, in the decade following World War II. The only exception were whites (like Ed Wallace) who specifically sought out Black men as sexual partners by frequenting the Cozy Corner bar and other places where African Americans gathered.[64] But in terms of their attitudes towards race, these men were often not any less critical of the system of racial exclusion than those who consciously or unconsciously equated being gay with being white. Contemporary accounts by Black gay men, for example, have pointed out that whites who look for African American sexual partners at night—perhaps believing in the stereotype of the Black man as supersexual stud or exotic "other"—typically ignore them when the sun rises. Consequently, many whites, both then and now, were "not seriously concerned with the existence of black gay men except as sexual objects."[65]

Here, the experiences of M. Tilden-Morgan are telling. His "first introduction to Blacks" was while staying with white gay friends in Washington, one of whom had a Black lover. Being told that he would "see something pretty," Tilden-Morgan was invited by the other housemate to watch the couple having sex, a racist objectification which he found "sort of interesting."[66] He also patronized the Cozy Corner with these and other white men who were seeking interracial sexual relationships, but he denied having the same intentions, saying that it was primarily the bar's cheap food which attracted him. Later in the interview, though, he admitted to being involved with one of the Black men he met, a fact which he explained by denying any racial difference between him and the man: "he was so light and so white in his mannerisms and speech that it didn't bother me."[67]

Tilden-Morgan's comments suggest the multiple ways in which racism shaped the identities of white gay and bisexual men in Washington in the 1940s and '50s. On the one hand, they viewed African American gays as exotic tokens, an "interesting" diversion because of their perceived otherness. On the other hand, Black gay and bisexual men could be largely invisible and not worth mentioning, unless they were seen as differing substantially from the white racial norm. In that case, they could "bother" whites by upsetting the conflation of same-sex sexual attraction with whiteness.

Obviously, such racism had a tremendous impact upon the identities of Black gay and bisexual men; combined with de jure and, later, de facto segregation, the hostile and demeaning attitudes of many whites meant that African American gays rarely frequented social spaces outside of Black neighborhoods. Instead, they participated in the vibrant nightlife of the city's Black community. "We didn't really have to go downtown," according to Pat Hamilton, "because we had everything up here [in the Black section of Northwest Washington] we needed—all of the theaters . . . [and] many, many movies and plenty of clubs." So much were the social lives of African Americans often separate from those of whites that, looking back, "Edith Parker" thought that African Americans were a majority in Washington in the immediate postwar period when, in fact, the city was less than one-third Black. By socializing primarily with other African Americans, Black gays like Hamilton and Parker were able to maintain both a strong sense of racial identification and close links to the city's Black community at large.[68]

Another factor that kept African American lesbians, gay men, and bisexuals rooted in the Black community was the significance of familial ties. White gays typically left their families to pursue same-sex sexual relationships; for example, Ed Wallace went cruising in downtown Washington when he could get away from his parents' home in Maryland, and Thomas "Dusty" Keyes moved to the capital because he "had to get out of Connecticut" to explore his sexuality.[69] In contrast, as bell hooks stresses about the Southern Black community in which she was raised, "sheer economic necessity and fierce white racism, as well as the joy of being there with the black folks known and loved, compelled many gay blacks to live close to home and family."[70] This was also the case with the African Americans I interviewed: all of them grew up in D.C., while none of the white narrators did.

Because Black lesbians, gay men, and bisexuals often remained in or near the Washington neighborhoods in which they were raised, they lived out their sexual preferences within the confines of their home communities, making it difficult to conceal their same-sex sexual attraction from families and friends. Fortunately, the African Americans with whom I spoke were largely accepted by relatives and peers, sometimes even receiving their strong support. Edith Parker, for example, "could bring every gay person in Washington to [her] mother's house." The validity of this statement, and the extent to which her mother stood behind her, is illustrated by the following incident:

> One night there was about twenty of us there and she was cooking for us. And a friend of hers came in. . . . My mother said to her, "Is there something wrong?" She never said a word. My mother said, "I'll tell you what. Anything you see in here that you don't like—you go home. This is her house, she can bring who she wants to here." But I wasn't living at home. But that's the relationship that my mother and I had.[71]

Similarly, during the time that Pat Hamilton was dressing and performing in drag in Washington's Black community, he was living at home with his brothers and sisters. But he "never had any problems out of them about [his] being gay. The only thing they drilled in [his] head [was] 'You have to stand up and fight and don't let anybody take advantage of you.'" This advice served Hamilton well in school, where it seems that he was initially considered "easy prey" by bullies because of his cross-dressing. After he fought back, though, the other students soon left him alone, and many actually became close friends: "I couldn't get rid of them. . . . They loved me to death."[72]

By focusing here upon the ways in which race structured the sexual identities of both white and Black Washingtonians, I do not mean to suggest that it was the only—or even necessarily the most important—factor shaping their lives. Clearly, as I have sought to demonstrate, gender and class also had significant effects on how lesbians, gay men, and bisexuals experienced their sexualities. But what makes race stand out is the way in which it often served as an impermeable barrier: while gays commonly crossed gender and class lines to socialize together in Washington in the 1940s and early '50s, particularly the African Americans who went to parties, bars, and other social events in the Black community, African Americans and whites rarely occupied the same social spaces in the city unless they were specifically looking for interracial sex. Even the one event at which Black and white Washingtonians could regularly intermix—drag balls—were largely limited to men and held only in other cities, making them inaccessible to all but a handful of gays from the capital. Thus racial exclusion played a significant role in the social lives of lesbians, gay men, and bisexuals in Washington, and any examination of their sexual identities must consider the centrality of race and racial difference.

Most historical texts in queer studies, though, naturalize whiteness by failing to see white people as having a racial identity. Consequently, unless specifically discussing the lives of "people of color," these works ignore race and, at times, assume that the experiences of whites are applicable to other racial groups. For example, in *Sexual Politics, Sexual Communities*, D'Emilio describes how World War II led to the creation of sex-segregated environments which enabled women and men to gain a measure of independence from their families. But such a paradigm ignores the experiences of many African Americans, who frequently maintained their roots within Black communities and led their social lives within Black neighborhoods. In a similar way, *Gay New York*, despite its thoroughness and otherwise groundbreaking examination of an urban community, largely limits discussions of race and racial difference to its treatment of Harlem and rarely extends this analysis to the rest of the city. As a result, the experiences of whites are often not named as such, granting them a false universality.[73]

Clearly, historians cannot treat white people as racially neutral, as if race and racial privilege play no part in their everyday lives. From my study of lesbians, gay men, and bisexuals in Washington, it is evident that racism had a profound effect upon both Black and white gays. Segregation and racial exclusivity shaped not only the social spaces that each community established in the 1940s and early '50s, but also how individuals within these communities organized their sexual identities. Moreover, given the fact that racism remains prevalent in many white gay communities today, it is even more important that historians recognize and examine the ways in which sexual identities are racialized. Challenging heterosexist assumptions and the invisibility of lesbians, gay men, and bisexuals should not mean reinforcing the dominant racial order.

Acknowledgments

For their support and assistance, I owe a great thanks to Loraine Hutchins, Leslie Schwalm, Martha Patterson, Roey Thorpe, Mickey Eliason, David Johnson, and the Washingtonia Collection of the Martin Luther King, Jr. Public Library in Washington, D.C. I am particularly grateful to the narrators; their moving stories both inspired me and laid the groundwork for this essay.

Notes

1. I use the phrase "lesbians, gay men, and bisexuals" to refer to all people who had some level of same-sex sexual involvement. For the sake of brevity, I also use the word "gay" in this manner. As will be discussed in this essay, "gay" often served as an in-group term in the 1940s and early 1950s for people who pursued same-sex sexual relationships.
2. John D'Emilio, *Sexual Politics, Sexual Communities: The Making of a Homosexual Minority in the United States, 1940–1970* (Chicago: University of Chicago Press, 1983), 24. A similar perspective is provided by Lillian Faderman in *Odd Girls and Twilight Lovers: A History of Lesbian Life in Twentieth-Century America* (New York: Columbia University Press, 1991), 120–30.
3. David Brinkley, *Washington Goes to War* (New York: Knopf, 1988), 227–28; Allan Bérubé, *Coming Out Under Fire: The History of Gay Men and Women in World War Two* (New York: Plume, 1990), 123–24.

4. Personal interview with "Scott Harrison," June 2, 1994; personal interview with "Ed Wallace," May 25, 1994.
5. Personal interview with "Haviland Ferris," May 16, 1994.
6. Quoted from personal interview with "Michael Borchert," May 31, 1994.
7. District of Columbia Alcohol Beverage Control Act, *Statutes at Large of the United States of America from March 1933 to June 1934*, Volume XLVIII, Part I (Washington, DC: Government Printing Office, 1934), 325–26; Jack Lait and Lee Mortimer, *Washington Confidential* (New York: Crown, 1951), 42; "Ban on Standing at Bars Sought to Block 'Old-Time' Saloon," *Washington Evening Star*, April 9, 1941; "Barry Proposes City Update Liquor Laws, Extend Selling Hours," *Washington Evening Star*, January 23, 1979; personal interview with Frank Kameny, March 20, 1994; telephone interview with Otto H. Ulrich, Jr., May 24, 1995; Borchert interview; Ferris interview.
8. For the rest of this essay, I will use the word "bar" to refer to restaurants that functioned largely as bars and reserve the term "restaurant" for cafeterias, diners, and other facilities which did not serve alcohol.
9. Personal interview with Peter Morris and Jack Frey, March 22, 1994; personal interview with "Hugh Crane," June 8, 1994; personal interview with "M. Tilden-Morgan," May 23, 1994; Borchert interview; Ulrich interview.
10. Diary of "Frederick Schultz," viewed May 25, 1994.
11. Jack Nichols, *A Few Kisses Ago: A Chevy Chase Boy Grows Up Gay* (unpublished autobiography), 9–10; Lige Clarke and Jack Nichols, *I Have More Fun with You than Anybody* (New York: St. Martin's Press, 1972), 75–76; telephone interview with Jack Nichols, May 20, 1995; personal interview with Bill Youngblood, June 1, 1994; Borchert interview; Morris and Frey interview.
12. Nichols, *A Few Kisses Ago*, 9–10; Borchert interview. The campy atmosphere of the Chicken Hut, though, wasn't attractive to all white middle-class gay and bisexual men. Being a classical pianist, Ted Richards "thought most of the music that [he] heard at the Hut was just trash," and couldn't relate to the "way people were just sort of into this song or that song and having [Howard] play something again." Telephone interview with Ted Richards, May 24, 1995.
13. Personal interview with Ralph Jarnagin, June 6, 1994; Tilden-Morgan interview; Nichols interview; Lait and Mortimer, *Washington Confidential*, 93; Kennedy Smith, "Walk on Washington," *Washington Blade*, April 23, 1993: 119.
14. Nichols interview.
15. Youngblood interview; Nichols interview; Borchert interview; *International Guild Guide* (Washington, DC: Guild Press, 1969); Smith, "Walk on Washington," 125.
16. "Top Court Rules D.C. Cafes Must Serve Negroes," *Washington Evening Star*, June 8, 1953: A1; "Police Set to Enforce Integration Law in District Restaurants," *Washington Evening Star*, June 10, 1953: A1; Wallace interview.
17. Personal interview with Pat Hamilton, January 13, 1995; Wallace interview; Tilden-Morgan interview; Morris and Frey interview.
18. Personal interview with Esther Smith, June 9, 1994; Hamilton interview.
19. For more on Black gay identities, particularly the "gay first" versus "Black first" debate, see Gregory Conerly, "The Politics of Black Lesbian, Gay, and Bisexual Identity," *Queer Studies: A Lesbian, Gay, Bisexual, and Transgender Anthology*, eds. Brett Beemyn and Mickey Eliason (New York: New York University Press, 1996).
20. Personal interview with "Edith Parker," June 9, 1994. For a discussion of the

historical treatment of African American gays within Black communities, see, for example, Audre Lorde, *Zami: A New Spelling of My Name* (Trumansburg, NY: Crossing Press, 1982); and bell hooks, "Homophobia in Black Communities," *Talking Back: Thinking Feminist, Thinking Black* (Boston: South End Press, 1989), 120–26.

21. Although Washington is often seen simply as the nation's capital, and thus as devoid of any regional affiliation, its population in the 1940s and '50s, as well as its location, rooted D.C. in the South. Significantly, many of the people interviewed for this study referred to Washington in those years as a "small Southern town" without provocation. See, for example, Ferris interview; Morris and Frey interview; Nichols interview; Harrison interview.
22. D'Emilio, *Sexual Politics, Sexual Communities*, 33; Faderman, *Odd Girls and Twilight Lovers*, 127–28. Allan Bérubé likewise contends that exclusively gay bars "helped shape a sense of gay identity that went beyond the individual to the group." *Coming Out Under Fire*, 271.
23. Haviland Ferris, "An Extract from Washington History," *Washington Blade*, September 11, 1980: A5; Ferris interview.
24. Ferris interview; Borchert interview; Wallace interview; Morris and Frey interview.
25. Elizabeth Lapovsky Kennedy and Madeline D. Davis, *Boots of Leather, Slippers of Gold: The History of a Lesbian Community* (New York: Routledge, 1993), 129.
26. Eric Garber, for example, documents a rich tradition of rent parties in Harlem in the 1920s and '30s. Garber, "A Spectacle in Color: The Lesbian and Gay Subculture of Jazz Age Harlem," *Hidden from History: Reclaiming the Gay and Lesbian Past*, eds. Martin Bauml Duberman, Martha Vicinus, and George Chauncey, Jr. (New York: New American Library, 1989), 321.
27. Smith interview.
28. Although police action was taken against establishments in other cities where same-sex dancing occurred, there apparently were no such incidents in Washington. In fact, when questioned, the D.C. police chief said that he would permit same-sex couples to dance, provided that they did not "grope each other." Following this discovery, bars in the city began to ease their dancing prohibition in the early 1960s. Kameny interview; Ulrich interview. For limits placed on same-sex dancing in other cities, see Kennedy and Davis, *Boots of Leather, Slippers of Gold*, 48–49; and Sherri Cavan, *Liquor License: An Ethnography of Bar Behavior* (Chicago: Aldine, 1966), 71–72.
29. Brinkley, *Washington Goes to War*, 228; Lait and Mortimer, *Washington Confidential*, 123; Kameny interview.
30. Kameny interview; Richards interview.
31. Ferris interview; Wallace interview; Nichols interview; Clarke and Nichols, *I Have More Fun with You than Anybody*, 63.
32. Wallace interview; Tilden-Morgan interview; Morris and Frey interview. George Chauncey, Jr. notes that certain cafeterias in New York were likewise known among gays as "The Last Chance" or "The Last Stand." Chauncey, *Gay New York: Gender, Urban Culture, and the Making of the Gay Male World, 1890–1940* (New York: HarperCollins, 1994), 415.
33. Borchert interview; Youngblood interview; Ulrich interview.
34. Jarnagin interview; Youngblood interview; Smith interview; Ulrich interview; personal interview with Thurlow Tibbs, Jr., May 24, 1994.

35. Jarnagin interview; Hamilton interview. Hamilton distinguishes between an older generation of impersonators who did glamour or serious drag and a younger generation who were less concerned with looking glamorous and more interested in camp. For more on this division, see Esther Newton, *Mother Camp: Female Impersonators in America* (Chicago: University of Chicago Press, 1972), 46–56.
36. "Female Impersonators Hold Costume Balls," *Ebony*, March 1952: 63; "Female Impersonators," *Ebony*, March 1953: 64. *Jet* magazine also reported on the balls, but provided less extensive coverage. See "Male or Female?," *Jet*, December 13, 1951: 34–35; "2,500 Impersonators Frolic," *Jet*, December 10, 1953: 16–17; "Hefty Funmaker," *Jet*, December 9, 1954: 20. A more personal description of a Fun Makers Ball in the late '40s is provided by Donald Webster Cory, *The Homosexual in America: A Subjective Approach* (New York: Greenburg, 1951), 129–34.
37. As is common in many gay and transgender communities, I am using "female impersonators" to refer to men who cross-dress in front of largely heterosexual audiences for a living and 'drag queens' to designate gay and bisexual men in particular who cross-dress."
38. Hamilton interview.
39. Ibid. Washington drag queens who were charged with soliciting a police officer received a substantially higher penalty: a $50 fine or thirty days in jail. "Nab Female Impersonator Who Solicited Policeman," *Jet*, May 28, 1953: 23; "Cops Nab D.C. Busboy Who Poses as Woman," *Jet*, July 1, 1954: 17.
40. Hamilton interview.
41. "Male Pervert Arrests Rise in District," *Washington Post*, November 7, 1948; D'Emilio, *Sexual Politics, Sexual Communities*, 49.
42. Lait and Mortimer, *Washington Confidential*, ix, 90, 95. For a more detailed analysis of the gay stereotypes in *Washington Confidential*, see David K. Johnson, "'Homosexual Citizens': Washington's Gay Community Confronts the Civil Service," *Washington History* 6 (Fall/Winter 1994–1995): 45–63.
43. Ibid., 90–98; Nichols interview; Morris and Frey interview. The fact that Lafayette Square remained a principal site for cruising is also demonstrated by arrest figures. In just one night in September 1947, the police arrested sixty-five gays there. Max Lerner, *The Unfinished Country: A Book of American Symbols* (New York: Simon and Schuster, 1959), 318.
44. "Annual Report of United States Park Police," Office of National Capital Parks, National Park Service, Washington, D.C. Reports for 1947–1948, 1949, and 1950.
45. Nichols, *A Few Kisses Ago*; Nichols interview; Morris and Frey interview; Ulrich interview. See "Dupont Circle: A Totally Urban Experience," *Washington Blade*, July 28, 1985: 1, 5–6, for more on the development of Dupont Circle as a white gay neighborhood.
46. Morris and Frey interview; Ferris interview.
47. William Leach, *Land of Desire: Merchants, Power, and the Rise of a New American Culture* (New York: Pantheon, 1993), 55–70; Susan Porter Benson, *Counter Cultures: Saleswomen, Managers, and Customers in American Department Stores, 1890–1940* (Urbana: University of Illinois Press, 1986), 18, 84. Display windows often played a similar role among gay and bisexual men in New York. Chauncey, *Gay New York*, 189–90.
48. Nichols interview; Youngblood interview.
49. Wallace interview.

50. Ibid.
51. An example of "gay" being synonymous with "merry" was a February 25, 1950 article in the *Washington Afro-American* entitled "Gay Birthday Party." For the characterization of gay people in the capital's newspapers, see, for instance, George T. Jay, "No Real Cure for Sex Pervert," *Washington Afro-American*, November 9, 1940: 16; "Strange Love Brings Murder," *Washington Afro-American*, July 9, 1949: 1; "Morals Detective Rebuked, Assault Conviction Reversed," *Washington Post*, July 15, 1953; "Male Pervert Arrests Rise in the District," *Washington Post*, November 7, 1948. Further evidence for the in-group nature of the term "gay" is provided by a glossary of "homosexual slang" compiled by Gershon Legman in 1941. It lists "gay" as "an adjective used almost exclusively by homosexuals . . ." Quoted in Jonathan Ned Katz, *Gay/Lesbian Almanac* (New York: Harper and Row, 1983), 577.
52. Cory, *The Homosexual in America*, 108–09; telephone interview with Robert Ricks, May 19, 1995; Nichols interview; Richards interview; Kameny interview.
53. Ferris interview; Cory, *The Homosexual in America*, 107–08; Chauncey, *Gay New York*, 19. Before then, according to Chauncey, the word "gay" was used primarily by effeminate men in the United States to describe anything that was flamboyant, including their own dress and speech.
54. Telephone interview with "Wilson Burke," June 6, 1994; Wallace interview.
55. Chauncey, *Gay New York*, 14, 19; Hamilton interview; Tilden-Morgan interview; Smith interview; Wallace interview.
56. Nichols interview.
57. At the same time that many gay and bisexual men were using code words and subtle gestures to find others like themselves, lesbians and bisexual women were often relying upon highly visible aspects of femme and butch style and appearance to recognize one another. Whether in bars, at parties, or on the street, butches in Washington and other cities were easily identified by their use and manipulation of masculine-coded gestures, stances, and apparel that, according to Esther Smith, included "slacks with key chains, ties, [and] men's hats or caps." For femmes, recognition by the larger society typically came through their association with butches, but other femmes and perceptive butches could often spot a femme through familiar body language and knowing glances. Femme and butch identities were seemingly ubiquitous in Washington in the 1940s and '50s, especially among Black lesbians, who commonly used the words "femme" and "butch" to refer to one another. I am currently researching femme and butch identities in the capital and intend to provide a longer discussion in my dissertation, "A Queer Capital: Lesbian, Gay, and Bisexual Life in Washington, D.C., 1890–1955."
58. Ferris interview; M. Tilden-Morgan interview. The danger of sexual encounters in the basement men's room of the YMCA was vividly demonstrated by the apprehension there of Walter Jenkins, the "right hand man" of Lyndon Johnson, in 1959 and 1964 for "disorderly conduct (pervert)" and "disorderly conduct (indecent gestures)" respectively. The arrests were made by two vice squad officers who stationed themselves at peepholes behind the door of an abandoned shower room "that gave them a view of the washroom and enabled them to peep over the toilet partitions." According to a published report, "there [were] two peepholes in this and several other washrooms in the area because two corroborating officers are required in such cases." The 1964 arrest of Jenkins made national headlines,

resulting in his resignation and admittance to a Washington hospital for "high blood pressure and nervous exhaustion." See "The Senior Staff Man," *Time*, October 23, 1964: 19–23; "The Jenkins Report," *Newsweek*, November 2, 1964: 26; "The Jenkins Affair: Arrest of Johnson's Aide Could Bolster GOP's Election Day Chances," *Wall Street Journal*, October 16, 1964: 1, 14. A discussion of the Jenkins case and how it figures into representations of the gay male body is provided by Lee Edelman's "Tearooms and Sympathy, or, The Epistemology of the Water Closet," *The Lesbian and Gay Studies Reader*, eds. Henry Abelove, Michèle Aina Barale, and David M. Halperin (New York: Routledge, 1993), 553–74.

59. "The Senior Staff Man," 21.
60. Laud Humphreys, *Tearoom Trade: Impersonal Sex in Public Places* (Chicago: Aldine, 1975), 3.
61. Borchert interview. Although his research was not very scientific, Humphreys found that 54 percent of his interviewees were married, and had chosen tearooms partly to avoid the possible disclosure of their sexual encounters to their wives and families. Similarly, Chauncey states that a quarter of the men arrested for homoerotic activity in New York in 1920–21 were married, and many had children (*Gay New York*, 200). Some of these men were undoubtedly gay, but had married because of convenience or necessity; others were truly bisexual and used tearooms to explore a part of themselves that was proscribed by society.
62. "Night Closing of Comfort Stations Urged," *Washington Post*, October 17, 1950; "Reader Irked about Closed Rest Rooms," *Washington Daily News*, January 20, 1953: 12; "Trial Reveals Comfort Station Peepholes for Indecency Arrests," *Washington Evening Star*, February 27, 1951; "Keep the Comfort Stations," *Washington Afro-American*, October 21, 1950. Although the *Washington Afro-American* urged the government to keep public comfort stations open to give the city's Black community access to downtown bathroom facilities, the newspaper was supportive of the police's efforts against gay and bisexual men, stating: "Race prejudice itself is a form of perversion and on our books the two evils should be stamped out simultaneously."
63. Ruth Frankenberg, *White Women, Race Matters: The Social Construction of Whiteness* (Minneapolis: University of Minnesota Press, 1993), 11.
64. Wallace interview.
65. Essex Hemphill, Introduction, *Brother to Brother: New Writings by Black Gay Men*, ed. Essex Hemphill (Boston: Alyson, 1991), xviii.
66. Tilden-Morgan interview.
67. Ibid.
68. Hamilton interview; Parker interview.
69. Wallace interview; personal interview with Thomas "Dusty" Keyes, May 30, 1994.
70. hooks, "Homophobia in Black Communities," 120.
71. Parker interview.
72. Hamilton interview.
73. D'Emilio, *Sexual Politics, Sexual Communities*, 29. See, for example, Chauncey's treatment of the formation of queer identities among middle-class men, a discussion which fails to account for the fact that the people in question are almost exclusively white (*Gay New York*, 99–127).

9. Place and Movement in Gay American History

A Case from the Post–World War II South

John Howard

> In the postmodern world the notion of culture as something located in a specialized venue will be . . . no longer operable; culture will increasingly come to us and not vice versa. It will no longer be a question of congregation but of circulation, no longer of venues but of avenues. . . . Culture, in short, is something which "happens" to us increasingly at home—in, as they say, our own space. . . .
>
> —Gilbert Adair

Difficulties in researching and uncovering the history of lesbians, gay men, and bisexuals in the United States are compounded when the inquiry is focused on a section that has been particularly hostile to sexual difference—the American South.[1] Archivists and university administrators often express reservations about the validity of the field; families seeking to preserve the "good name" of their relatives routinely deny access to materials; and, as in any other part of the country, traditional historical sources remain largely silent with regard to homosexuality prior to the 1960s.[2] Thus, oral history serves a vital role in reclaiming the lesbian, gay, and bisexual past, especially in the South.

Barry Kline (not his real name) is one of only a handful of older Alabamians who, given the state's persistent legal and societal strictures, is willing to discuss frankly his experiences as a gay man of the South.[3] A resident of Birmingham since his birth in 1917, Kline "came out," as he terms it in retrospect, at the age of twenty-eight just after returning home from serving in World War II. Kline's story exemplifies many of the major themes outlined by gay historians. As in other parts of the U.S., urbanization, economic independence, public space, the gay bar, friendship networks, casual sex, and intimate relationships all were central to the formation of gay cultures and gay identities in Birmingham. However, the events from Kline's life complicate some of the leading assumptions surrounding U.S. gay life in the twentieth century, particularly the significance of the religious and medical professions.

Race, class, gender, and the attendant levels of social and physical mobility figure prominently in Kline's description of mid-twentieth-century gay life. The ability to travel, both to nearby rural areas and to other cities, provided a means of escape from familial pressure and police persecution—factors that, though prevalent in other parts of the U.S., were especially restrictive in the Deep South in the postwar period. Moreover, and perhaps most significantly, Kline's story encourages us to re–think the role of place and movement in U.S. gay history. It helps us to reconsider the predominant theoretical model in the field—what I call the urban capitalist model of identity and cultural formation—which, although quite useful and descriptive, also serves to marginalize and exclude large numbers of people, notably many Southerners and rural folk throughout the U.S.

Based on interviews conducted with Barry Kline, this article examines white gay male culture in Birmingham, Alabama, through the experiences of one individual and a community of friends, foes, and family members. Focusing on the twenty–five years immediately following the Second World War, the essay demonstrates that this was an era of gay cultural formation in the South, despite negative mainstream attitudes toward homosexuality and a heightened level of repressive activity by those in positions of power. The lived experience of Kline and others like him forms the historical foundation of a culture that continues to evolve, forging increasing levels of freedom and solidarity for lesbians, gay men, and bisexuals in Alabama and throughout the South.

Coming Out, Finding Community

Upon his return in 1946 from Europe, where he served as a lieutenant in the U.S. Army, Barry Kline began to build a friendship with a boyhood acquaintance, Robert Holley. "Here I had 120 days of [paid] leave and all of that," says Kline, "so I wasn't anxious to get down to work." Holley, who was employed in his family's dry goods business, "didn't go to work until ten o'clock in the morning," so the two were free to stay out late into the evening and explore the nightlife of a postwar Southern city.

Kline recalls how his friendship with Holley suddenly developed into a romance:

> We eventually, one night, wound up out by what was Edgewood Lake and got in a very serious discussion. And I had no idea what it all amounted to. But somehow or other I began to shake.... It wasn't because I was cold. It had to do with what we were talking about. I don't remember. But he took the bull by the horn and says, "I'm going to kiss you." And I didn't object.

Though he had experienced several homosexual encounters during his youth and early adulthood, Kline views that particular night as his coming out. Holley differed in important ways from Kline's previous partners, who typically were strangers he met during his travels or childhood pals of a lower socioeconomic class.

The fact that class distinctions structured Kline's own sense of identity is evident in his description of Robert as compared to two sex partners from his youth, a flamboyant set of twins. The twins, according to Kline, "really never did earn a good living. I mean, they were never successful. They did menial jobs, odd jobs." Their open avowal of homosexuality inevitably led Kline to ponder his own sexual orientation: "It was a great big question in my mind as to whether I was or wasn't. [But] I just couldn't be like those twins." Robert, on the other hand, represented a type and class of person with whom Kline could readily identify:

> Well, ... I was older. I was twenty-eight by that time, twenty-seven. I was doing this thing with somebody who was, I guess, a respected member of the community. And I began to meet other people who were doing the same sort of thing. It made me realize that I was not the only one in the world.

Indeed Holley, who at age thirty-three had long since accepted his gay identity, was able to introduce Kline to the white gay male culture that was emerging in and around Birmingham.

Gay life existed on the margins of so-called mainstream culture in Alabama. A small, select circle of Kline's friends, "circumspect I guess you would say," would occasionally gather for parties in homes or apartments, usually late at night. If they ventured into more public realms, gay white men frequented straight establishments only outside of regular or peak operating hours, or they found clubs that catered to a homosexual clientele but that typically were located on the outskirts of town. In downtown Birmingham, the Bouvet and the Jewel Box at the elegant Tutwiler Hotel, the Red Room at the Redmont Hotel, and the Stirrup Cup at the Thomas Jefferson Hotel all tolerated groups of gay men, provided they understood the primacy of heterosexual patrons. According to Kline, the Stirrup Cup, for example, would become a hub of activity only after a measure of secrecy and safety was assured:

> I remember one Saturday. You know everybody would go in there and have drinks and sit around the tables. Had two black waiters who didn't know what was going on.[4] One Saturday night I remember, ... I guess it was around ten o'clock. Well, the last straight couple left out of there, and somebody stood up and said, "The meeting will come to order. Will the secretary read the minutes of the last meeting?" Up until that time, everybody was only involved in talking to their immediate companions. And then of course after that everybody got chummy-chummy.

Kline remembers an unnamed, tarpaper shack honky-tonk southwest of the city on the Bessemer Superhighway "where the owner would let us dance together." And "from time to time, there were things over the mountain in Homewood," including the Little Southerner, which featured a lesbian pianist from New Orleans who played classics and boogie-woogie. But such bars were short-lived, says Kline, and most, like the Little Southerner, eventually "changed ownership, and gradually they ran everybody away."

As in other Southern cities during the late forties and fifties, men also congregated in public parks after dark to find friends or sex partners. In Woodrow Wilson Park (later renamed Linn Park), situated between City Hall and the Public Library, a man out walking might subtly proposition another by asking for a match. Or a man circling the park in his car might first establish prolonged eye contact with a passerby, then stop to strike up a conversation. Kline says that "any and all kinds" of people could be found in the park, but this diversity was largely limited to white men of varied socioeconomic classes. Many women were reluctant to walk downtown after dark unless escorted, and blacks would not have been found there, as city parks were racially segregated by law. Thus "cruising," like so much of homosexual interaction in and near Birmingham, was predicated on a complex web of forces, not the least of which were gender and race.

Parents, Pastors, Politicians, Policemen, and Physicians

In Cold War America, a public preoccupation with the "dangers" of homosexuality became apparent in both the scientific and popular media.[5] The medical profession asserted authority over the treatment of what were referred to as sexual perverts and psychopaths.[6] Politicians hysterically warned that homosexuality threatened not only the nation's domestic stability but also its international security. Under such conditions, police crackdowns on homosexual activity in U.S. cities were commonplace. Religious leaders spearheaded community attempts to clean up the streets, while families and neighborhoods were urged to remain alert to the potential threats within their midst.

Physicians, particularly psychiatrists, played an important role in the development of lesbian, gay, and bisexual awareness and identity through the increasing medicalization of homosexuality in the late nineteenth and early twentieth century.[7] Medical authorities also were critical agents in the expanding discourse on homosexuality during the Second World War, when millions of U.S. armed service recruits were asked about the nature of their sexual relations in routine pre-induction interviews, and numerous enlisted women and men were interrogated in occasional post-induction purges.[8] Yet doctors might have had less influence than previously thought on the lives of individual lesbians, gay men, and bisexuals.[9] Barry Kline recalls only once mentioning his perceived sexual problems to a physician, a military doctor, when he considered getting married prior to leaving the U.S. for active duty:

> I met a girl . . . in Alexandria [Louisiana] that I liked very, very much, and we dated and carried on. . . . It was Camp Livingston, which was north of Alexandria. . . . I said, "You know, I don't know what's going to happen with this war." Maybe it was after Pearl Harbor that I said, "No, I'm not going to get married because I just don't know what's going to happen." This was early '42. I did talk to one of the battalion physicians. I said, "Hey Doc, you've met Ella Barnes. You know I like her very, very much, but the idea of getting a hard-on—it just doesn't get to me." And he says, "Oh, . . . there's nothing wrong." He says, "If we were back in Philadelphia, I'd know who to send you to, but . . . I wouldn't worry." He says, "You're away from home. It's a different life. You don't have big pectorals. So you're not queer."

Kline placed little faith in such assessments. Eventually, he grew to ignore the pronouncements on homosexuality made by medical professionals. Although he might have self-identified as gay within the broader context of an extensive scientific discourse, it was without the advice, counsel, or consternation of any particular physician or psychiatrist.

Unlike many other gay men of the postwar South, Kline also seemed unaffected by the region's pervasive religious fervor, which is especially distinctive in the Southern lesbian, gay, and bisexual experience.[10] An upper-middle-class Jew in a historically poor and Protestant state, Kline never mentions having consulted a rabbi or other cleric. He doesn't recall any religiously based condemnations of homosexuality in sermons or in the press. Nor does he remember any concerted efforts by the churches and synagogues of Birmingham to persecute lesbians, gays, and bisexuals.

Foremost among the concerns of Barry Kline were being arrested by the police and being discovered by his and his friends' relatives. The fear of disclosure often persisted even after death. Such was the case with Kline's longtime partner, Robert Holley. "We were a thing for several years there," according to Kline. And while the two suffered their share of lovers' quarrels, resulting primarily from Kline's dalliances while Holley was away on business in New York, the two remained close until Holley's life was cut short in 1957.

Even today, Kline's anxiety over the events surrounding Holley's funeral continues, reflecting the clandestine, conspiratorial nature of homosexual relationships vis-à-vis families:

> Robert died. . . . Had a cerebral hemorrhage in a hotel in New York on one of his trips. I don't know what his family thought. You know, the times he used to leave the Cadillac convertible for me to drive. . . . But when he died, they didn't ask me to be a pallbearer. His sister [Susie] couldn't stand me. She tolerated me but she could not stand me until the day she died. Although one, her youngest son . . . calls me Uncle Barry to this day. And Susie's husband was very cordial to me, Robert's brother was cordial to me, but Susie and his mother were not that cordial. I think they figured out what was going on and resented it very much. And it was not my fault, it was Robert's—it was—but. . . .

That Kline would feel it necessary to assign blame for the romance is less an indication of his own misgivings about the affair than of the tremendous societal pressure that was brought to bear on Southern lesbians, gays, and bisexuals in the 1950s.

Among gay men in general, the possibility of being found out fostered intense feelings of anxiety, shame, and self-loathing—emotions which may have contributed to the suicide of one of Kline's friends in the late fifties. According to another gay Alabamian of the same generation, the South proved markedly inhospitable to gay men at mid-century: "I've had a lot of miserable experiences with being gay in the course of my life, and I feel a little bit bitter. . . . In the early days we scurried around in the dark and were afraid."[11]

Despite the safeguards they took, like locating many gay establishments outside of the city limits, gay men nonetheless ran up against law enforcement officers who were determined to thwart the growth of gay social networks and maintain the marginalization of sexual deviants. In the early fifties, after neighbors burned down a suburban house noted for its late night parties in the ironically named Queenstown Lake development, Barry Kline and his friends began to frequent a private-home-turned-gay-hot-spot in Shelby County, roughly forty miles southeast of the city. County officials raided the property, arresting the owner and citing several patrons for liquor violations. As Kline describes it:

> [A] young fellow came here as an automobile salesman. He was not making a living, and he rented a house down in Shelby County. He says, "Well I'm going to throw some Saturday night parties and see if I can't make ends meet by charging a dollar," which he did. I went down there a couple of times....
>
> [One night,] probably around eleven thirty, I ran into somebody who said, "Let's go down to Biff's in the next county, Shelby County, to the house for a party." And I said, "Oh, I don't know." But then I said, "Okay, I'll go.... Let me get some alcohol." I carried a flask of Canadian Club in my glove compartment. I said, "I don't know whether I want a drink, but I'll just take it in case I do." So I put it in my coat pocket and got in Scott's car, and we drove down there. And the minute we turned off of Highway 280, there was a car parked. He flagged us down. Turned out to be the sheriff and his men. Well, they opened the trunk and poured out all Scott's whiskey—he had about five quarts in there—and gave him a ticket. If I hadn't had that flask on me, I wouldn't have gotten a ticket. But they took my flask and poured out the whiskey and gave me the flask back and gave me a ticket.... Of course, that was the end of Biff's place down there. [The sheriff] had been there before. And they had already made the raid.... [T]hey arrested Biff, ... he [got] out on bond, ... [and] he skipped town.

But it wasn't until several years later, the summer of 1962, that Kline was involved in a police action that he says "changed [his] life." Two men from Nashville, who had been contracted to renovate a dwelling on 31st Street on Birmingham's more affluent Southside, decided to give an after–hours party in the house, where they lived while construction was underway. On that hot Saturday evening, neighbors heard the noise through open windows and called the police. A paddy wagon arrived and carried four loads of men, thirty–eight in all, to jail. Arrested along with the others on charges of disorderly conduct and visiting a disorderly house, Barry Kline was freed after posting a bond. He later paid a fine. But the most damaging result of the incident happened a few days later with the listing of the arrestees' names and addresses in a local daily newspaper.[12] Moreover, when Kline returned to the site of the party to pick up some things left behind, he was subjected to more intense interrogation by the police, who likewise had returned to the scene of the crime.

Birmingham's infamous police chief and politician Eugene "Bull" Connor turned the event to his advantage, publicly boasting that the police force had successfully squelched a homosexual "convention." Apparently noticing that the hosts were Tennesseans and a few of the party guests were out–of–state residents—mostly former Birminghamians who had moved on—Connor concluded that the queer gathering was the work of outsiders, just as he mistakenly construed civil rights unrest as the stirrings of the ubiquitous "outside agitators." Nevertheless, the police crackdown on homosexuality had lasting repercussions for natives such as Barry Kline, who feels "it traumatized [him]." Afterwards, even when he travelled to relatively safe havens such as Chicago, he would be "scared to death" that the gay bars he visited would be raided and his sexuality would be exposed to the folks back home.

Home Making and Trip Taking: The Benefits of Class Privilege

Circumventing the police and eluding familial control required creative solutions, many of which were possible only through economic means. Barry Kline enjoyed considerable class privilege; he had assumed the management of his family's business within a few years of his return from World War II, and many of his gay friends were similarly well-situated. To escape the watchful eye of his mother and the long arm of the law, Kline, like many upper-middle-class gay Birminghamians, used his financial clout to secure opportunities for sexual liberty.

While his only sibling married in 1942 and his father died in 1951, Kline continued to live with his mother in his childhood home. Consequently, he had to explain away his social comings and goings, since his mother apparently remained unaware of his sexual orientation even after the gossip generated by his arrest in 1962. Kline did not move out of his mother's home and into an apartment of his own until 1966, at the age of forty–eight.

However, in the late 1950s, Kline pooled his resources with his friend Burton and rented an apartment, which they called "the trick house."[13] As Kline remembers:

> I would never stay there [overnight]. He did. He furnished it up with a bed, whatever, this, that, and the other. And then later [we] took a coachhouse up in Cliff Alley here, and that's when he went off to school in Tallahassee, and I started going to the bar and bringing people home at night: "You want to party? Come on, let's go home. Let's go up to the coachhouse and we'll have a little party for a couple of hours."

These "parties" for two or more often developed into larger gatherings of numerous friends and acquaintances, as the bar crowd sought a place to congregate after commercial liquor sales halted at midnight. The parties were often rowdy and festive:

> [These were] just after-hours parties that I started doing. Even one night when it snowed, a few people would get there. I don't know how, but they did. The alley was above the homes down on Cliff Road. And sometimes when they'd left the party, [they would shout] "Where are you going?" "I'll meet you at the Waffle House," or something like that. That began to disturb those people down there. So [the owners] would not renew the lease.

Yet, over the years, Kline continued to keep one apartment or another—his "pad" he called it, a safe space away from home—until he left his mother's house and moved into the apartment he already rented on 33rd Street, South. By this time, Kline had convinced several friends to lease the other apartments in the eight-unit building, likely making it the first all-gay apartment complex in the state of Alabama. Friends jokingly referred to it as "the Kline Building" in "Homo Heights," in light of its strategic location just up the street from a popular gay bar in "Homo Flats."

Travelling extensively from a young age, Kline met gay men from other cities as early as the 1930s, when as a teenager he and his family spent their summers in Miami. As an adult, Kline took regular trips out of town thereby reducing—if only temporarily—the pressures of life in a hostile environment.[14] After World War II, he regularly made at least one major excursion out of Birmingham each year. Though many of these were business trips, as he became a board member and then an officer of a national trade association, he made time during the meetings and conventions to explore the gay nightlife of his destinations, and met a number of men with whom he developed satisfying, if fleeting, sexual relationships. In the late forties and fifties alone, he visited Miami, Orlando, Richmond, Philadelphia, Atlantic City, New York, Boston, Buffalo, Cleveland, Chicago, New Orleans, Dallas, Los Angeles, and San Francisco, among other cities. In addition, with groups of friends he often drove down to the Gulf Coast of Florida.

Such excursions, and the sexual opportunities they enabled, were direct functions of Kline's race, class, and gender. Whereas scholars Elizabeth Kennedy and Madeline Davis found that working-class lesbians' "defiant," nothing-to-lose attitudes fostered a direct, combative "community of resistance" in 1950s Buffalo, a significant segment of white gay male culture in Birmingham—the monied elite—utilized class prerogatives wherever possible to sidestep confrontations with intrusive police officers, irksome family members, and acrimonious townspeople.[15] Most poorer gays in Birmingham could not have afforded the automobile that allowed men like Barry Kline to patronize gay establishments on the city's outskirts, much less could they have born the cost of train or plane fares to distant cities or paid the rent on a "trick house." Lesbians in Birmingham faced not only economic marginalization, but also gender obstacles, including limits on their mobility which made the development of a women's community along the lines of the gay male culture unthinkable.[16] And blacks in the Jim Crow South were burdened with oppression of a different sort; the police and the media focused on the Civil Rights Movement and the heroic attempts to overturn racial segregation, while the struggles of the African-American community's lesbians, gays, and bisexuals were further eclipsed, made even more marginal.[17] Kline and his friends built one of the Deep South's early homosexual cultures upon a foundation of white, male, upper-middle-class privilege. With legal and political persecution of lesbians, gays, and bisexuals widespread throughout the U.S., these strategies appear to have been very effective for the few who could pursue them.

Conclusion: At Home in the Urban South

According to the urban capitalist model of identity and cultural formation, urbanization proved an essential element in the development of lesbian and gay cultures and identities in the U.S.[18] As industrial capitalism took root in the late nineteenth century, new wage laborers and salaried employees left the family farm behind and pursued economic independence in large cities. Men and women who recognized their same-sex affections and erotic interests could more easily find others like themselves in these crowded urban settings. Communities were thus formed, and gay identities emerged. But because the South remained a predominantly agrarian society long after other parts of the country had mechanized, urban enclaves of lesbians and gay men in this section may have developed more slowly. By the end of World War II, however, the requisite population movements had taken place in the South, causing lesbian and, especially, gay male cultures to become increasingly visible in the larger cities of New Orleans, Atlanta, and Birmingham.[19]

Barry Kline did not move to the city for economic or sexual reasons, as was the case with many gay migrants.[20] Born in Birmingham, his need for mobility arose out of a need to free himself of family obligations and the possible threat of police persecution. Yet Kline's identity as a gay man was established and reinforced by his connection to his hometown and friends, most of whom belonged to the same socioeconomic class. Kline insists that he accepted his homosexuality after discovering, through Robert Holley and his social circle, that he was "not the only one in the world." But surely Kline had known this before. He had had sporadic homosexual liaisons for over ten years in various parts of the world. Significantly, however, the ability to categorize himself as gay and to identify with other gay men came only after an intense attachment to a fellow Birmingham native, Robert Holley, and an increasing involvement in a structured, localized gay community. While others found community by moving to the city, Kline found it, after travelling the globe, only by returning home. Yet home, as always, became transformed as a result of experiences in different places.

The prevalent theoretical model among lesbian and gay historians—a model that is distinctly modernist in its totalizing, linear construction[21]—would have us view cities as centrifugal forces, magnets that pull isolated individuals from the hinterlands into large urban centers, where they could recognize their sexualities, find one another, and become a community. This causal schema, a long-term historical trajectory mirroring innovations in transportation and communication, denies rural people the ability to act and think—that is, to attach meanings to their sexual desires and behaviors.

Barry Kline's life suggests the need for a new postmodern gay history in which cities would be seen as centripetal forces—locations from which emanate any number of forays and journeys, many which were short-term, leading to a variety of opportunities for encounters, meetings, and rendezvous. Of course, such movements and interpersonal connections need never involve cities at all, such that we can begin to see avenues rather than venues, spokes rather than hubs. Certainly for those friends of Barry Kline who relocated to Birmingham from small-town and rural Alabama, life did not begin with the move. Their wanderings and wonderings preceded the rural-to-urban exodus and likely included a number of different sexual situations.

In the mid-century South, there functioned a sense of space markedly at variance from that of the dense, congested landscape of the East Coast, for example, and these instances of coming together, often one-on-one, regularly involved automobiles. Cars thus were conduits—tangible, material manifestations of a more accurate sexual mapping of the United States.

While class privilege eased movement and greatly facilitated the construction of gay identity for Kline and his friends, economic advantage cannot be construed solely as a means for circumventing oppressive forces or for avoiding confrontations. In Birmingham, throwing a party, patronizing a bar, driving the roads, or even walking the streets could precipitate a contentious encounter with the police. As a result, resistance in the 1950s often took subtle, but still empowering, forms.

> [W]e started going to a place called . . . the Rose Room, which was on 22nd and 5th Avenue North [in the heart of downtown]. It was a restaurant that on Saturday night catered to a clientele that turned out to be gay. They had a little band that played, led by one Harold Welch. He played a . . . clarinet. . . . And of course one of their big hits was "When the Saints Go Marching In." And they would come down off the bandstand and march out the front door and down 22nd Street and in the back door and back up on the stage. . . . Everybody would follow them out there, which of course for Birmingham was quite risky.

Barry Kline and successive generations of gay Birminghamians assumed the risks, and despite the obstacles, their community expanded, holding out hope for even greater freedom and equality in the years to come.

Acknowledgments

Portions of this essay were presented to the Oral History Association Conference in Birmingham, Alabama, November 6, 1993, and to the Seminar on Homosexualities at Columbia University, New York, New York, September 7, 1995. A shorter version of this essay appeared in *CrossRoads* 3 (Fall 1994/Winter 1995): 20–35. For invaluable assistance in this project, I am grateful to Barry Kline and to Patrick Cather, Martin Duberman, Margaret Rose Gladney, Nancy Koppelman, Joyce LaMont, Catherine Nickerson, Mary Odem, Allen Tullos, Candace Waid, and Marvin Whiting.

The epigraph, from Gilbert Adair's *The Postmodernist Always Rings Twice: Reflections on Culture in the 90s* (London: Fourth Estate, 1992), 20, 24, is quoted in Paul Delany's introduction to *Vancouver: Representing the Postmodern City* (Vancouver: Arsenal Pulp Press, 1994), 4. While Adair is speaking primarily of traditional cultural institutions, Delany extends the analysis to the city:

> The centre is . . . the place that sets the cultural clock: events originate in the capital, and in the provinces there are only echoes and reflections—everything happens belatedly, unfashionably, and as a lame copy of the metropolitan "real thing." Postmodernism reverses this modernist centralism, into a dispersal and decentering—not least of the metropolis itself.

Notes

1. David Greenberg summarizes survey research from the early 1980s which shows that in the U.S., "respondents from the South, from small towns, and from rural areas, who [we]re older, poorer, and less well-educated, [we]re more likely to think homosexuality morally wrong and to oppose gay rights." *The Construction of Homosexuality* (Chicago: University of Chicago Press, 1988), 468. The presidential election year surveys of the University of Michigan's Survey Research Center from 1972 to 1984 indicate that white Southerners' ill feelings toward lesbians and gays were exceeded only by their distaste for radical students, black militants, and marijuana users. For black Southerners, negative reactions toward lesbians and

gays exceeded those for all other categories. Cited in Earl Black and Merle Black, *Politics and Society in the South* (Cambridge, MA: Harvard University Press, 1987), 62, 69.

2. Martin Duberman discusses South Carolinian archivists' reluctance to provide access to letters revealing homosexual affairs in "'Writhing Bedfellows' in Antebellum South Carolina: Historical Interpretation and the Politics of Evidence," in *Hidden from History: Reclaiming the Lesbian and Gay Past*, eds. Martin Bauml Duberman, Martha Vicinus, and George Chauncey, Jr. (New York: New American Library, 1989), 153–68. In the course of editing the letters of Georgian Lillian Smith, Margaret Rose Gladney spoke of her difficulty in securing the family's permission to publish letters disclosing Smith's relationship with Paula Snelling. See *How Am I to Be Heard? Letters of Lillian Smith* (Chapel Hill: University of North Carolina Press, 1993).
3. This essay and the quoted passages within are drawn from six hours of interviews conducted by the author with Barry Kline (pseudonym) on September 5, 1992 and January 12, 1993. Additional information was gleaned from numerous subsequent conversations and correspondence. Cassette tape recordings and partial transcriptions of the interviews are on deposit at Special Collections, Gorgas Library, University of Alabama, Tuscaloosa. In accordance with restrictions placed upon the materials by Barry Kline, all proper names of individuals have been changed.
4. That the "two black waiters . . . didn't know what was going on" seems unlikely. Perhaps they loathed or resented the late-night patrons. Or perhaps one or both felt a sense of complicity or camaraderie, despite the color line.
5. Adopting the term "moral panic" from Jeffrey Weeks, Gayle Rubin compares this period of recodification in the relations of sexuality with 1880s England and late 1970s America. "Thinking Sex: Notes for a Radical Theory of the Politics of Sexuality," in *Pleasure and Danger: Exploring Female Sexuality*, ed. Carole S. Vance (Boston: Routledge and Kegan Paul, 1988), 267–319.
6. Estelle Freedman, "'Uncontrolled Desires': The Response to the Sexual Psychopath, 1920–1960," in *Passion and Power: Sexuality in History*, eds. Kathy Peiss and Christina Simmons (Philadelphia: Temple University Press, 1989), 199–225; John D'Emilio, "The Homosexual Menace: The Politics of Sexuality in Cold War America," in *Making Trouble: Essays on Gay History, Politics, and the University* (New York: Routledge, 1992), 57–73.
7. Mary McIntosh, "The Homosexual Role," *Social Problems* 16 (1968): 182–91; Jeffrey Weeks, *Coming Out: Homosexual Politics in Britain from the Nineteenth Century to the Present* (London: Quartet, 1977); Michel Foucault, *The History of Sexuality, Vol. 1. An Introduction*, trans. Robert Hurley (New York: Vintage, 1990).
8. Allan Bérubé, *Coming Out Under Fire: The History of Gay Men and Women in World War Two* (New York: Plume, 1991).
9. See, for example, George Chauncey, Jr., "Christian Brotherhood or Sexual Perversion? Homosexual Identities and the Construction of Sexual Boundaries in the World War I Era," in *Hidden from History*, 294–317.
10. In "The Library, the Park, and the Pervert: Public Space and Homosexual Encounter in Post-World War II Atlanta" (*Radical History Review* 62 [Spring 1995]: 166–87), I argue that legal, political, and media persecution of white gay men in Atlanta during the 1950s was indelibly linked to religious oppression.

Specifically, I contend that conservative Protestant Christianity, particularly as articulated by Southern Baptist leaders, enabled and supported the 1953 crackdown on homosexual sodomy in the rest room of the Atlanta Public Library, resulting in the arrests and convictions of twenty men, as well as the 1953–1956 regulation of homosexual and heterosexual activity in Piedmont Park. I suggest that religious complicity in the multipronged attack on homosexuality represented a potentially defining feature of lesbian and gay experience in the South. In another essay, I discussed the deep religious convictions of many lesbian and gay Southerners, as well as the religious roots of oppression; "'Homosexuals Invade Jackson': Lesbian and Gay Sexuality and Protestant Religiosity in Mississippi, 1973–1983," paper presented at the annual meeting of the American Historical Association, Chicago, Illinois, January 6, 1995.

11. Keith Vacha, *Quiet Fire: Memoirs of Older Gay Men* (Trumansburg, NY: Crossing Press, 1985), 168.
12. *Birmingham Post–Herald,* July 3, 1962. A brief account also appeared in the evening paper, *Birmingham News,* July 4, 1962. That this was a gay (male) party could only be deduced from subtle hints in the *Post–Herald* account, which noted that only "three girls" were present at the party. Jail records and court documents show that all thirty–eight arrestees were white men between the ages of eighteen and fifty–six. While the median reported age was twenty–six, Kline says that some of the younger men declared themselves to be older than they were. *Docket, Recorder's Court No. 4 of the City of Birmingham, Ala.*, Case Nos. K 22226–7, 22230–5, 22237–42, 22244–5, 22248–51, 22253–60, 22262–5, 22269–70, 22277–8, 22282–301, 22303–6, 22310–7, 22319–20, 22322, 22324–6. *City of Birmingham, Alabama, Warden's Docket—Avenue "F" Prison*, Docket Nos. 846–83.
13. In this case, "trick" does not refer to a paying client, as sex workers often use the term, but rather to a friend or, more commonly, a new acquaintance with whom one has casual sex.
14. One study from the era described Birmingham as "conservative . . . sometimes to the point of reaction," and further noted "considerable moral prudishness" in the city. *The Birmingham Metropolitan Audit: Preliminary Report, 1960* (Louisville: The Southern Institute of Management, 1960), 17, 22. For recent scholarly accounts of Birmingham in the twentieth century, see Edward Shannon LaMonte, "Politics and Welfare in Birmingham, Alabama: 1900–75," Ph.D. diss., University of Chicago, 1976, and Glenn Thomas Eskew, "But for Birmingham: The Local and National Movements in the Civil Rights Struggle," Ph.D. diss., University of Georgia, 1993.
15. Elizabeth Lapovsky Kennedy and Madeline D. Davis, *Boots of Leather, Slippers of Gold: The History of a Lesbian Community* (New York: Routledge, 1993), 2, 4.
16. For one lesbian's account of growing up in postwar Birmingham, see Toni McNaron, *I Dwell in Possibility: A Memoir* (New York: Feminist Press, 1992).
17. Noted gay cartoonist Howard Cruse, a native Alabamian now residing in New York, has produced a graphic novel, set in Birmingham and historical in nature, if not directly autobiographical. *Stuck Rubber Baby* (New York: Paradox Press, 1995). According to Cruse, "the story I'm telling takes place largely in 1963, which was close to the period when I came out and ventured into Birmingham's gay subculture." It includes significant material on black gay life in Birmingham. Letter from Cruse to author, March 16, 1993.

18. John D'Emilio, *Sexual Politics, Sexual Communities: The Making of a Homosexual Minority in the United States, 1940–1970* (Chicago: University of Chicago Press, 1983), 11.
19. On the limits of the urban capitalist model of identity and cultural formation, especially as pertaining to rural Southerners who engage in homosexual activity but do not self–identify as lesbian or gay, see Donna Smith's insightful essay, "Remodeling the Closet: Theorizing Lesbian/Gay Identity Pre–Stonewall," paper presented to the annual meeting of the Oral History Association, Birmingham, Alabama, November 6, 1993.
20. Of the twenty men arrested in the rest room of the Atlanta Public Library in 1953, for example, three out of four were migrants to Atlanta. They were born in the rural areas, towns, and smaller cities of Alabama, Florida, Georgia, Mississippi, North and South Carolina, and Tennessee.
21. Scott Bravmann, "Telling (Hi)stories: Rethinking the Lesbian and Gay Historical Imagination," *OUT/LOOK* 8 (Spring 1990): 68–74.

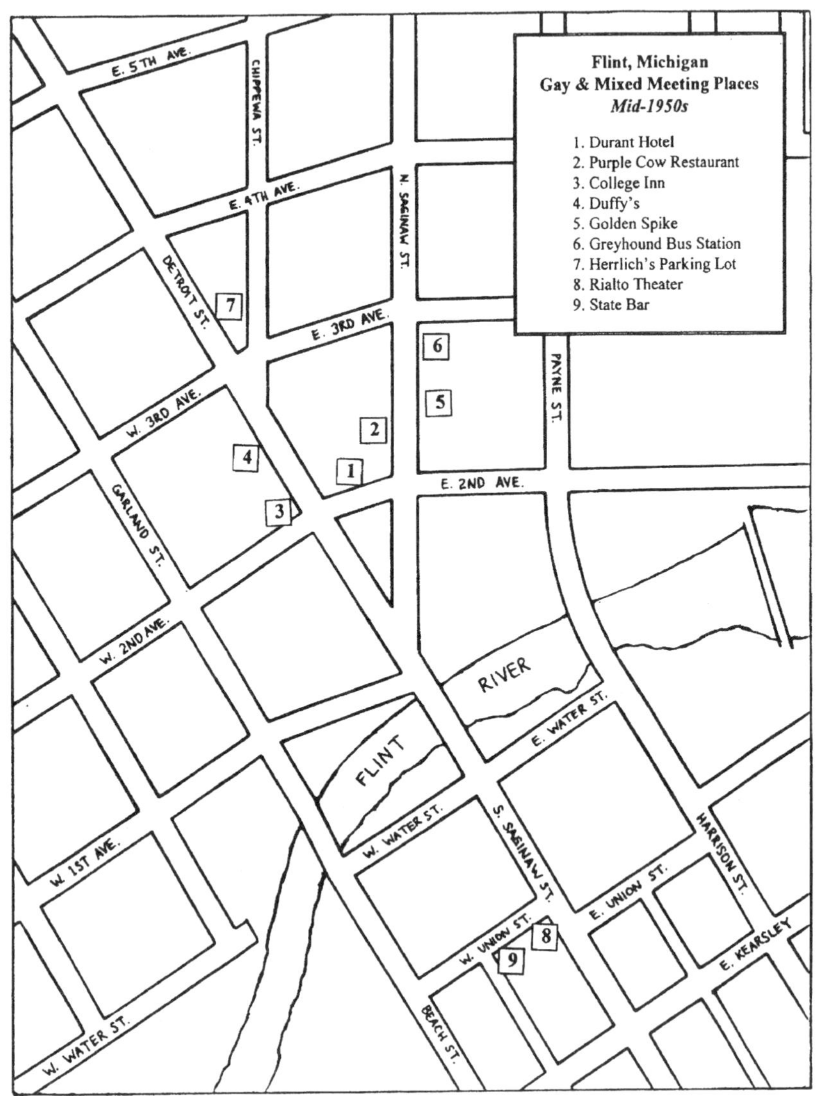

Flint, Michigan Gay and Mixed Meeting Places, Mid–1950s

10. Cars and Bars

Assembling Gay Men in Postwar Flint, Michigan

Tim Retzloff

"Shouldn't be hard for a stud like you to hitch a ride . . ."

—Queen of the Road[1]

"The automobile . . . allows its passengers to move through the public sectors of the city encased in a cocoon of private space."

—Lyn H. Hofland, *A World of Strangers*[2]

On the early morning of June 11, 1950, in Flint, Michigan, two men were having anonymous sex on the sofa-like seat of a parked Chevrolet coupe. Perhaps suspicious of steamed-up windows or alerted by an unfamiliar car parked in the blue-collar East Side neighborhood, police discovered them shortly after 2:30 A.M. One of those caught, P.M.,[3] a Fisher Body employee, was dressed in female attire. Police arrested him for gross indecency, a felony under state law. After six weeks of incarceration, P.M. was examined by psychiatrists under an order from the judge in the case. In diagnosing the twenty-five-year-old African-American autoworker as an "Active Homosexual," the three examiners wrote:

> He states "I was born a queer." Further, he states that since the age of eight he has practiced the use of his mouth as a sex organ with other men and claims that he has frequently practiced the use of his anal region for use as a sex organ with other men. Since the age of eleven, he has frequently garbed himself for the intent purpose of enticing men. . . .[4]

Using the 1939 Goodrich Act, under which people apprehended for "sex crimes" in Michigan could be defined as "criminal sexual psychopaths" and confined to a mental hospital for an indeterminate time, the judge ordered P.M. committed to Ionia State Hospital on August 29, 1950.[5] He was paroled two years later, despite being evaluated by doctors as "not recovered." Supervised by the Department of Mental Health, P.M. worked as a press operator for the next five years at an automotive factory in nearby Pontiac. He was formally discharged from custody in 1959. The second occupant of the car, a power company employee who later married, denied consenting to any sex act. He was not examined by psychiatrists, nor was he ever brought up on felony charges.[6]

The surviving details of the incident suggest that P.M., a transgendered and homosexual man, had appropriated the automobile as a vehicle for covertly acting on his sexual identity. Like other men in Flint throughout the 1950s and '60s, P.M. learned to negotiate homosexual desire through different layers of concealment. Cross-dressing, anonymity, cross-town travel, and the painted steel body of the Chevrolet were all intended to shield P.M.'s encounter from social agents like the Flint Police Department who were hostile toward homosexuality.

By the 1950s, despite persistent social policing, a distinct gay male culture had assembled in this midwestern automotive center. Homosexual men, and bisexual men interested in homosexual encounters, met in locations marked as gay, locations largely determined and significantly shaped by privately owned motor vehicles. A homosexual milieu nearly invisible to heterosexual Flint took shape not only in newly accessible gay and semi-gay bars, but literally *on* the streets, in moving and parked cars. In forging a gay life in Flint, men such as P.M. used the very product that they and their heterosexual coworkers manufactured.

Discernible gay cultures predating the automobile were evident in major metropolitan areas during the late nineteenth century. Often in demographically turbulent U.S. port cities, these bar-centered homosexual enclaves, which arose in part because of urban migration and the mobility afforded by urban transit, affected the homosexual communities which emerged in the 1940s and '50s in smaller places like Flint, a city with a population never greater than 200,000. The rise of smaller, bar-centered homosexual communities has been attributed in part to the mass mobilization precipitated by World War II. Wartime developments, however, do not completely explain the rapidity with which such communities spread across the United States. John Howard, in his study of 1950s Atlanta, attributes the emergence of lesbian and gay communities to "changes in postwar modes of living." One of the newer modes, automotive mobility, suggests one explanation for how and why these communities emerged at this particular historical moment, especially in the hinterland.[7]

One such postwar bar-centered gay community arose in Flint, Michigan, a blue-collar company town named by *Look* magazine as an All-American City in 1954. The case of Flint sheds new light on the historical developments which gave rise to such communities, shining highbeams on the influence that mobility—as manifested in transience, travel, and especially transit—had on nurturing community and identity formation at midcentury. The car made Flint, and the car made Flint's gay community.[8]

The birthplace of General Motors in 1908 and an economic boom town for the first six decades of this century, Flint exemplifies the classic American success story. During the 1950s, General Motors, at the height of its power, captured fifty percent of the automotive market. GM's prosperity meant that jobs were plentiful in Flint, attracting an influx of newcomers. In Ronald Edsforth's words, "During the automobile boom, the progressive business class in Flint . . . offered working people both the dream [of] and access to a new, more affluent and more secure way of life." Flint's population grew from only 13,000 at the turn of the century to over 156,000 by 1930, dipped to 151,000 in 1940, rose again to 163,000 by 1950, and peaked at 197,000 in 1960. The population increases included infusions of unskilled blacks and whites from the rural South, as well as sizable emigrations of Poles and Hungarians.[9]

The automobile not only propelled Flint's economy, it also permeated the city's civic culture. Lavish parades down the city's main street celebrated the fifty-millionth GM car in 1954, the city's centennial in 1955, and the corporation's fiftieth anniversary in 1958. These pageants of chrome, painted steel, and tail fins featured the spectacle of dancing spark plugs and such celebrities as Dinah Shore, who pitched Chevrolets on her Sunday-night television show. A "culture of abundance" in the 1950s encouraged consumption; the cornerstone of that consumption was the automobile. In Flint, workers had survived the hardships of the Depression, won decent wages for members of the United Automobile Workers following the landmark 1936–37 Sit-Down Strike, and produced armaments for World War II. In the postwar years, they achieved working-class prosperity. A car in the driveway was the reward for years of sacrifice.[10]

Nightcaps and Hubcaps

Flint, Michigan's prosperity, and its product, were necessary for the growth of a bar-centered gay community. In a city spread out over thirty-two square miles, access to gay meeting spaces, even in private homes, required transportation. In Flint, where laborers could attain one of the highest wages in the U.S. for unskilled work, social mobility provided the means for buying a car. The car offered its own brand of mobility, enabling Flint residents to fulfill homosexual longings in a manner not previously available to them.

By the Depression, before automobiles became widely owned beyond the middle class, a rudimentary and vulnerable gay presence had already surfaced in Flint. It existed within a geographic area whose limits were established by streetcars and walking. Jack Pierson, for example, had numerous homosexual encounters throughout the 1930s in downtown public rest rooms and movies theaters that were readily accessible by public transit. Pierson also met his lifelong partner, Robert Purcell, while walking downtown near Willson Park, a covert homosexual rendezvous, in 1938, when both men were in their twenties.[11] Other traces of Flint's early homosexual underground further suggest a gay life determined by the bounds of pedestrian mobility. One of the few officially documented cases of adult homosexual behavior prior to 1950 involved a white twenty-nine-year-old former autoworker who was arrested and nearly sterilized for soliciting a young man in the Strand Theatre balcony in 1938. During police interrogation, he disclosed that he frequently strolled downtown to pick up strangers for homosexual encounters. The full extent of Flint's prewar homosexual underworld is unknown, but historical material such as this suggests an underworld demarcated by the available modes of transportation.[12]

In both its proliferation and its impact, the car came into its own during the 1950s. Postwar prosperity swiftly extended automobile ownership to most of the U.S. population. Many less affluent Americans, including Flint's working class, could now afford to purchase a car. In 1941, only half of U.S. households owned an automobile. This figure jumped to sixty percent in 1950, seventy-seven percent in 1960, and eighty percent in 1970. Not surprisingly, the rate of car ownership in Flint was much higher. In 1950, the ratio of cars to people in the Flint area was 1 to 3.3, surpassing the U.S. average of 1 to 4.2. Ten years later, Flint boasted one car for every 2.7 people, compared to 1 to 3.1 nationwide. Not merely a product of blue-collar labor, the automobile had become a tangible indicator, sometimes fabricator, of a rising standard of living, the very symbol of blue-collar aspirations. Like other manufactured commodities, the car, with its wide range of differently priced models, gave a member of the working class a means to "'pass' as a higher status individual."[13]

At the same time that people across the U.S. were adopting a system of consumption centered around car ownership, they were also embracing an ideology of marital heterosexuality and sexual conformity. Concurrent with the virulent anticommunism of the McCarthy era, a powerful "breadwinner ethic" dominated American society which glorified traditional gender roles and stigmatized same-sex sexuality, with right-wing ideologues engineering a campaign to purge gays from the government, military, and public sphere. Fears of a "homosexual menace" served as part of what historian John D'Emilio describes as a "widespread effort to reconstruct patterns of sexuality and gender relations shaken by depression and war."[14]

Michigan, automotive center of the nation, joined other states in countering the perceived homosexual threat with increased social control. Beginning in 1948, state liquor regulations prohibited "licensed premises to be frequented by or to become the meeting place, hangout, or rendezvous for known . . . homosexuals."[15] The next year, G. Mennen "Soapy" Williams, deodorant heir and Michigan's newly elected pro-labor governor, established the Commission on the Deviated Criminal Sex Offender, a panel dominated by psychiatrists whose self-described mission was to safeguard children from "sex deviates." Its 1952 report, published the year of P.M.'s release, advocated stiffer penalties for "sex crimes," including sodomy. In a widely distributed booklet issued under the auspices of the Commission, a physician from Flint's neighboring city of Saginaw warned:

> Because of the human unhappiness, discouragement, and neurotic anxiety that homosexual tendencies and acts cause; because of the very large number of broken homes, divorces, and suicides resulting from homosexuality; and because of the large number of individuals who lose faith in God and men, and finally drift into a life of worthlessness as a result of it, homosexuality far exceeds, in its social importance, all the crimes that are committed by sexual deviates.[16]

Against this backdrop of nationwide and statewide antagonism toward homosexuality, Flint's gay bar community emerged in the 1950s. As the automobile ascended in importance within the lives of working-class people and as ridership on public transportation plunged, the city's gay culture became less private and more visible. In the decade following World War II, gay men staked out territory on the edge of downtown, parking their cars and walking to various bars centered around the premier Durant Hotel. North of the Flint River, the Durant faced a small triangular park where Saginaw Street, the city's heavily trafficked main thoroughfare, met Detroit Street. The hotel's public lavatory served as an active tearoom, and the Purple Cow restaurant, inside the hotel and next door to a Marine Corps recruiting station, became a favorite gay meeting place. Within a three block radius of the Durant, amongst storefront businesses, all-night coney-island restaurants, a Buick dealership, and a Sears department store, a small cluster of bars attracted a nightly homosexual patronage. A bus station and a drugstore parking lot in the vicinity also drew men seeking sexual encounters with men, lured there by the twenty-four-hour activity (see the map on the following page). The area, less than a mile from the giant Buick installation where wartime plane engines had been made, remained the fixed, if contested, nucleus of semipublic, semi-gay socializing into the 1960s. Alan Banks, a regular visitor to the neighborhood's several mixed gay and straight bars, depicts the area fondly: "That was sort of the hub of it. People used to walk between them, and you'd see everybody you knew there, on that corner."[17]

What Banks calls the "hub" consisted of the Loner Bar, Duffy's, the College Inn, the Golden Spike, and the State Bar, all primarily white bars. Before moving to the area in 1946 from Rochester, Michigan, Maurice heard that the Durant Hotel's Loner Bar was a place to meet other homosexuals. Sure enough, he made friends with a man there who introduced him into a gay circle. Similarly, Alan Banks befriended the pianist at Duffy's, a bar which hosted drag shows and sing-alongs, across Detroit Street from the Durant. It attracted gays until it closed in the mid-1950s. Through a coworker at the Fisher Body plant, Bruce Globig heard about the College Inn, a businessman's bar a few doors down from Duffy's, which also had a substantial gay patronage. Customers with same-sex interests soon learned, by accident or from others, that gays congregated at the bar, not at booths or tables. Ralph Stallings liked to visit the College Inn because of its gay clientele, but did not cruise there for fear of losing his job at the Durant. On the other side of the Durant from the College Inn, on Saginaw Street, "a greasy spoon that had a liquor license" called the Golden Spike had a more working-class clientele. Marty Rudman favored the Spike to other bars, but remembers the disdain of its straight proprietor: "With the Golden Spike you always felt like the owner was spitting on you all the time he was selling you the booze, because you were dirty rotten perverts. But he was very happy to get our money."[18]

None of the bars near the Durant, however, attained the prominence of the State Bar, located a few blocks away and across the river from the hotel. Situated next to a pawn shop and a taxi company on Union Street, the State would evolve into the preeminent institution of gay life in Flint for the next four decades. According to local folklore, Melva Earhart, a white thirty-six-year-old lesbian, bought the bar after the owner banished her from the premises. Originally from Sault Ste. Marie, nearly three hundred miles north of Flint in Michigan's Upper Peninsula, Earhart worked for ten years at the Fisher Body plant before opening a tailor shop which made uniforms for the Flint police. Perhaps because her charisma and factory background endeared her to customers, she received one of the city's few available liquor licenses and was successful in the bar business. She expanded twice in the

1950s, adding her old tailor shop to the bar in 1954 and annexing an adjacent space three years later. As a tribute to her success in these boom years, Budweiser's Clydesdale horses paid a promotional visit to the State in the late 1950s when the bar was one of the brewer's top-selling outlets.[19]

Like the bars near the Durant, the State was not yet strictly gay during the 1950s. Earhart herself described the tavern in those years as a "rough, redneck, hillbilly" place. But while the State was on a "very skid row" street, Alan Banks remembers the bar affectionately. "It's where some people [went], well-dressed and poorly dressed, well-fed and poorly fed," he recalls. "Often those were their real families, because that's where they got their support. . . . People really cared for each other." Seating less than a hundred but often packing in twice that, it featured country and western performers who appealed to the many southern migrants working in Flint factories. During the day, the bar relied on a pedestrian patronage of derelicts, prostitutes, ex-cons, and cab drivers from the taxi company next door, but at night most of its clientele drove there from other parts of the city. Since Earhart and several employees were lesbian, gay women and men began to gather at the State, and the tavern became known as a place that welcomed homosexual patrons. In contrast to the seating pattern at the more discreet College Inn, bartenders at the State reserved booths and tables for the "gay kids," while relegating straight patrons to the stools at the bar, where they couldn't bother the gay clientele. According to Betty Underwood, a former State Bar manager who dated Earhart beginning in 1957, "Melva, she wouldn't let 'em bother us, because she was pretty tough." Outside of the State, however, customers were cautious about displaying the slightest hint of their sexuality. Earl, who worked as a cook in several downtown restaurants during the 1950s, recalls that he and a male companion always paired up with lesbians to avoid drawing attention to themselves when they walked to their cars from the safety of the bar.[20]

Driving downtown for an after-work beer or nightcap provided an important escape from the tedium of the assembly line and the social expectations of family and coworkers. Most gay men in Flint maintained a double existence, separating their factory lives from their social lives. Since the mixed-gay-and-straight bars in the hub were presumed to be heterosexual, these businesses provided an inconspicuous refuge for gay and bisexual men who sought to keep their sexuality hidden from the larger, straight society. Locales like the State thus preserved a level of plausible deniability, augmenting other strategies for avoiding exposure, such as driving across town in order to socialize with other gays and having anonymous sexual encounters in cars.[21]

Flint's gay population, too small to congregate into an identifiable neighborhood, was dispersed throughout the city and county. As a result, even socializing in homes required access to a car. In the 1950s, most of Flint's gay professionals remained wary of the more public nature of mixed commercial establishments, preferring instead to socialize and seek sex partners at private house parties, which provided a greater sense of security. Some get-togethers, like the spontaneous African-American gay parties that Clint remembers frequenting in the city's black neighborhoods, could be attended on foot. Others necessitated a vehicle. Maurice, a local gay, white businessman, entertained friends in an abandoned library building he owned in a nearby village, with gatherings modeled after the secretive gay "dollar parties" he attended in Detroit during the Depression. Maurice dubbed these gatherings the "Literary Society," playing on the library location and offering a possible excuse that men could give their families to explain their whereabouts. Doctors, lawyers, and teachers from Flint and elsewhere had to drive backroads to reach the remote location, but gladly did so in order to dance, drink beer, and cuddle free-of-charge—and free from harassment. Bruce Globig, who had married on the advice of a psychiatrist to try to curb his homosexual urges, would make some excuse to his wife to attend. "We felt secure being in a private home. Much more so than in the bar. When you're in the bar, everybody walks in the door and you're uptight," Globig explains.[22]

The proliferation of motor vehicles, coupled with improved road systems, enabled the gay residents of Flint to pursue new travel-related social and sexual possibilities. For example, in the 1950s, a Chevrolet or Dodge provided Flint gays with regular access to the more robust bar communities in other cities, particularly Detroit, sixty miles to the south. Then the fifth largest U.S. city and ten times the size of Flint, Detroit had a rich gay culture which dated back at least to the 1920s.[23] Exclusively gay bars like the Rio Grande, the Diplomat, the Palais, the Silver Dollar, LaRosa's, and the Woodward drew homosexuals from Flint and elsewhere, sometimes by the carload, because they offered out-of-towners a taste of gay life in Detroit's fast lane. Other men found a satisfying and more secure sexual outlet in several Detroit-area bathhouses.[24]

For gays from Flint, a one-hour jaunt provided exposure to a gay culture unavailable at home, like gala drag shows and the comedic antics of ChiChi, Detroit's notorious camp performer. Such trips became a regular part of the lives of many gays from Flint. Andrew met his sweetheart James Johnson while visiting the Palais, where Johnson sang. Maurice, who kept an apartment in Detroit because of regular business dealings, felt that the larger city offered greater anonymity: "If I got into trouble with the law I'd rather get in trouble in Detroit, in a big city, than I would in a small town like Flint." Maurice once had a close call with the Detroit police, evading arrest only by speeding away in his car.[25] Even the drive down to Detroit could prove rewarding. Before the construction of Interstate 75 in the early 1960s, men interested in same-sex encounters could stop for a "quickie" at a popular roadside rest area on the Dixie Highway.[26]

Cruising the Main Drag

Not all spaces appropriated for homosexual activity in Flint, Michigan during the 1950s were stationary. The car not only allowed gay men and women to congregate in downtown bars, but also became an additional site for many men to act on homosexual desires. Sexualized since its inception, the automobile has long been acknowledged as a ready avenue for heterosexual passions. But its use for same-sex liaisons is perhaps more significant, for it enabled gay and bisexual men in cities like postwar Flint to subvert the societal norms which sought to deny them social and sexual outlets.[27]

The car served as an entrance into a gay world and a ready getaway in case of danger, but unlike bars, it was a gay space typically dominated by men. In a city with around-the-clock automobile production, it was not unusual to see cars on the street at all hours, and since the automobile was traditionally considered to be a male domain, gay men driving at night would not be seen as suspect in the way that lesbians, as women, would. Gay men could thus use their male privilege to covertly transgress bounds of accepted sexuality.[28]

The appropriation of the automobile for intimate sexual exchanges was analogous to the rise of the tearoom: both functioned as sites for fleeting, risky, anonymous sex and provided opportunities for cross-class socializing, becoming a means for teachers to interact with autoworkers, salesmen with college students, and factory supervisors with grocery clerks. The car, however, had the added feature of offering an interior that was specifically designed to be homelike. Moreover, teenagers living at home, married men, and laborers who could not afford motel rooms could use their cars for sexual encounters, and if a gay man did not have his own car, he could look for sexual partners who did. Thus, for many gay men in Flint, acquiring a license to drive also gave them a license to frolic. To borrow a phrase that George Chauncey has applied to poorer gay men in the 1920s, "privacy could only be had in public."[29]

The sense of privacy, however, was often illusionary. The Flint police routinely contested this same-sex "auto-eroticism," and most of the local arraignments for consensual sodomy and gross indecency involved cars. For instance, in January 1951, county deputies caught a thirty-three-year-old Chevrolet supervisor and a nineteen-year-old bowling alley pinsetter having sex in an Oldsmobile at a roadside park outside the city. The two men, both white and neighbors on the same street, had had previous sexual encounters in the car. But the probation officer assigned to the case, noting that the younger man had been drinking the night of the offense, had no criminal record, and his "reputation" was "good," urged the court to keep the case out of the newspaper so as not to jeopardize the repentant man's employment. The Chevrolet supervisor was also remorseful and, according to a psychiatrist's assessment, "motivated to seek medical assistance." The judge, apparently viewing the crime as an accidental slippage, gave both men two years probation. The pinsetter married soon after; the other man left the area following his probation. As this case shows, cars might have been a convenient vehicle for sex, but they did not shield gay men from danger. On the contrary, they often made them more vulnerable.[30]

Besides being a popular, mobile site for sexual activity, cars interacted dynamically with fixed spaces such as bars and other geographic landmarks in the hub. For example, on Detroit Street, a block north of the College Inn, a parking lot next to Herrlich's pharmacy became a "very famous" place for gay and bisexual men to meet, including male hustlers and a flamboyant youth who, perched on the back of a pink convertible, hooted to passersby. "I had a friend, his car I think it had auto-pilot," remembers Dennis, who came of age in the early 1960s. "He couldn't go across town without going by Herrlich's." Clint discovered the Herrlich's lot by chance one Friday night when he happened to have use of his brother's vehicle after his second-shift factory job. He went to the drugstore and someone standing beside it asked him for a cigarette. As they smoked and chatted, the young man asked Clint for a lift, saying that "[he'd] do anything for a ride home." En route, they took a sexual detour to Clint's apartment. Clint learned a great deal about the parking lot scene from the youth and, after buying his own car, became a regular there.[31]

The Herrlich's lot was not without dangers. "I stayed away from there because it was too much vice infested," Earl says. Clint confirms this: "I remember the police cruised that area quite a bit. But we were pretty much aware of the time [of night] they would start cruising and to what extent." Clint and other men were wary of unfamiliar cars, approaching a vehicle new to the lot only after witnessing its driver interact with someone known to the lot scene. By being so cautious, Clint managed to avoid any police officers in unmarked cars.[32]

Another man was not so lucky. Cruising the streets near Herrlich's in his 1955 Chevrolet one night in June 1959, L.N., a fifty-seven-year-old black custodian, blinked his lights hoping to attract the notice of other drivers. The local gay community knew the signal was an indication that he desired a homosexual encounter, but evidently, so did the police. Instead of a sexual partner, the man picked up a member of an undercover vice team and was arrested when he drove the officer to the parking lot of Flint Junior College for what was to have been a quick sexual exchange. Although L.N. had a long history of anonymous same-sex encounters, he also sang in his church choir and was "not viewed as dangerous," so the judge gave him three years' probation plus a fine.[33]

Another notable gay appropriation of the automobile involved what Ralph O'Reilly remembers as "a brisk trade in hitchhikers" at night on Saginaw Street. One of the hitchhikers, Andrew, discovered the sexual possibilities of looking for a ride while still in high school. Since his family lived out in the country, he travelled to Flint only a couple of times a month by bus, and then relied on strangers to drive him home after the buses stopped running at night. Cruising the sidewalks and sometimes standing in front of the Golden Spike, he invariably got rides, as well as sexual encounters. "If you were downtown, all you had to do was walk from one end of South Saginaw to the other end of South Saginaw and you would be picked up," he recalls. If he saw someone attractive driving by, he would start a conversation, perhaps asking if they'd like to go for coffee or a hamburger at the Purple Cow, with the hope of more to follow. Andrew got his "own wheels" in 1950 at the age of sixteen and began to take trips to downtown Flint "two or three times a week." To save money, however, he rarely cruised from the driver's seat. "I parked my car and walked. Let 'em use *their* gasoline." And even with his own automobile, Andrew still sought rides.[34]

After nightfall, Saginaw Street became a veiled promenade for a specialized form of gay cruising. Ironically, at a time when J. Edgar Hoover was warning of the perils of picking up hitchhikers, many drivers in Flint pursued them, seeking passengers for sex. While car cruising was also favored by heterosexual male youths, it took on a distinctive, campy flavor with the gay and bisexual men who drove up and down the twelve blocks of downtown Saginaw Street eyeing potential male partners. Some gay participants referred to this slow crawl through the central business district, which was ironically the same route as GM's gala parades, as "Dragging the Gut." With a smile, Alan Banks recalls one drive-by encounter: "There was a kid [who] we often saw on the Gut, on Saginaw Street. He was carrying a big buck rabbit. So people that day commented on the rabbit and stroked the rabbit and so forth. And I said, 'For God's sake, what are you doing with that rabbit?' And he said, 'Getting attention.'" Ordinarily, drivers seldom made contact with foot traffic on the sidewalk, but for these gay drivers the very purpose of "Dragging the Gut" was to interact with pedestrians. The primary hazard was soliciting someone who was straight, especially someone who might react with hostility. "Now and then things got a little tangled because . . . certain people didn't know how to do it properly, and there would be a little disruption," Walt Lewis remembers. Earl saw the entire process as "a dangerous habit, because it could be some local cop in that car you were cruising."[35]

The police remained a constant threat, in uniform as well as undercover. On February 10, 1956, state police caught J.C., a man in his forties, performing oral sex on a fifteen-year-old boy in the back seat of the man's 1953 Chrysler sedan. In a statement to the police, the youth divulged a similar sexual pickup, with another stranger, the year before. He then recounted his recent wintertime car trysts:

> Q. Where and when did you first meet [J.C.]?
> A. I was hitchhiking in front of the, I think it's the Summerfield Chevrolet [dealership] on Saginaw Street in Flint two weeks ago Tuesday I think. He stopped and picked me up. He started talking filthy and then asked me if I wanted to go out on a side road. We went on the same road we got caught on tonight. He did the same thing to me then.
> Q. Did he do it any other time after that before tonight?
> A. Yes, once before. He told me to meet him the following Saturday night in front of the Rialto Theater in Flint at 8:30 P.M. I went there and he wasn't there. I walked down to the Summerfield lot and started hitchhiking again. He came along and picked me up. We went out onto the same road and he did the same thing.[36]

In addition to highlighting the youth's knowledge of Flint's gay cruising grounds, this case points to increasing anxieties felt toward teenagers and cars. John Howard argues that the entry of middle-class youths into the public sphere for courting in postwar Atlanta ultimately affected other groups, such as homosexual men, who had long used public spaces. As more adolescents acquired cars and took to the road in the 1950s, their new freedoms exposed them to a homosexual underground also utilizing the same pavement. This convergent use of the automobile by gays and youths justified campaigns against homosexual activity.[37]

Evidence suggests that the entire area surrounding the Durant Hotel was regularly policed, but like authorities nationwide, law enforcement officials in Flint could not eradicate homosexual activity. They did attempt, however, as George Chauncey argues, to "contain it by prohibiting its presence in the public sphere."[38] In Flint, periodic police crackdowns in the 1950s focused on homosexual behavior in public arenas. But despite their desire to render homosexuality invisible, authorities in the city seemed reluctant to impose harsh penalties. Arrest statistics and court documents indicate that most infractions were handled as misdemeanors and dispatched in municipal court, treated as a routine nuisance, much like prostitution. Only occasionally did such cases appear before circuit court judges, and even then they rarely resulted in confinement. Still, continuous arrests during the 1950s provided a constant threat aimed at deterring homosexual activity.[39]

For example, Officer Kenneth Allard, on "special assignment" with the Flint Police Department Morals Squad, often worked in the vicinity of the Durant Hotel, Herrlich's Drugstore, and the Greyhound Bus Station "for the purpose of checking on the activities of homosexuals." One night in August 1957, Allard was approached by a "repeatedly smiling" deaf mute man. J.G., a twenty-three-year-old graduate of the Michigan School for the Deaf, a state facility located in Flint, passed notes back and forth to Allard. The plainclothes officer feigned interest in the man for several hours, until J.G. exposed Allard's penis in a 1953 Buick sedan. Allard arrested J.G. for "attempting to procure an act of gross indecency," remarking in his description of the case that "the defendant smelled strongly of perfume." Confused by the legal procedures, J.G. did not plead guilty in municipal court and, as a result, the case landed in circuit court, the only one of seven cases from this particular crackdown that was not handled at the lower-court level. A psychiatrist assessed J.G.'s "homosexual trend" as "scarcely out of control" and surmised that the arrest itself would serve as a deterrent, so the judge ordered the charges dropped.[40]

Situated in close proximity to the Durant and nearby bars, the Greyhound Station, where J.G. met Allard, was perhaps the most closely monitored homosexual rendezvous in Flint. Bruce Globig discovered the station's tearoom when he drove a taxicab for a short time before finding employment in the auto industry. James Johnson, who sang at the Palais—a bar popular among Detroit lesbians—observed constant activity around the men's rest room as he waited in the station for the bus to his Saturday night engagements. Disapproving of such boldness and promiscuity, he found the traffic unsavory. Whereas the bars were subdued, the bus terminal represented for him the most notorious and sordid of the gay spots in the hub. Greyhound terminals across the country typically had reputations for attracting "hoodlums, pickpockets, and perverts," and Flint's station was especially enticing for men seeking same-sex encounters. It was open twenty-four hours and served as the entry point for many single men arriving from Missouri, Arkansas, and Tennessee looking for work in Flint's auto plants.[41]

Driven Out

In the 1960s, the automobile contributed increasingly to the decentralization of Flint's landscape. Greater numbers of General Motors workers, sustained by continuing good times, settled in the suburbs and relied on their cars to commute on Flint's recently built expressways. Meanwhile, new suburban shopping centers, drive-in theaters, and fast-food restaurants siphoned business away from downtown. From 1958 to 1963 the central business district lost twenty-two percent of its retail establishments. Efforts to revitalize the city's center included a 1960 proposal to close off Saginaw Street and convert it to a pedestrian mall to compete with the shopping plazas on Flint's outskirts. However, according to journalist Richard Hébert, who has described the car's impact on Flint, "Merchants were hardly likely to support banning the city's chief product, automobiles, from the main street of the downtown area."[42]

The geographic dispersal of Flint in the 1960s also changed the contours of its developing gay world. With the rapid decline of the downtown area, the bars near the Durant ceased being homosexual institutions and were replaced by other commercial establishments further from the city's center. Only the State Bar survived the decade as a gay bar, but even it was forced to relocate and change its character significantly in order to remain in business.[43]

In 1960, Melva Earhart found herself caught in the urban renewal effort to revitalize downtown. The State Bar was slated for demolition, forcing her to move to a different location. With earnings from the business, Earhart secured property on West Kearsley Street along the river. Between a warehouse and the Chevrolet Manufacturing Plant, she built a $100,000 establishment that she named the Poodle Lounge. The 7,200 square foot facility included a large stage, dressing rooms, a forty-eight-foot-long bar, a screened terrace, a pink neon sign, and parking for four hundred cars. In publicizing the 1961 grand opening, *Hi-Spots*, a local, mainstream bar guide, told its readers to "be prepared for pleasurable pleasure" at the Poodle. Earhart also did her own publicity, using her car. As Earl recounts: "She used to pull up in front of Uncle Bob's [Diner] on Harrison [Street] in a pink Cadillac with two pink-dyed poodles in there, with blue ribbons in their hair."[44]

The new showbar atmosphere of the "Pink" Poodle (whose name returned to the State in 1962) marked a sharp departure from the seediness of the previous location. Earhart lost much of her unseemly clientele, pedestrians who had patronized the Union Street site because it had been a convenient place to drink. She now catered more to the car-owning market, bringing in top entertainers like Count Basie and Dinah Washington and expecting men to don sports jackets and women to wear dresses. The leap from skid-row tavern to elegant club, with an ambiance of flashy elegance, allowed Flint's gay and lesbian working class to dress up for a night out and to experience being of a higher class—the same effect many sought with their vehicles.[45]

At her new location, the automobile provided the means for Earhart to further immerse the bar in gay culture. The State began to present touring floor shows of female impersonators, including Gilda "the Golden Girl," Princess Pamecan, Jerri Daye, and, "direct from Hollywood," Mr. Bunny Bates, acts which usually traveled from city to city by road. The performers, however, had to wear pants underneath their female attire while driving to the State because a Flint ordinance forbade cross-dressing, except on the stage. Sponsoring cross-dressing entertainment, Earhart embraced a decidedly gay institution, what Esther Newton terms "an illegitimate junction of the homosexual and show business cultures." The traveling entertainers were often joined by many locals, aspirants to fame in the big-time female impersonation circuit. Dennis, an underage working-class youth whom Earhart took under her wing when he snuck into the State in the early 1960s, subsequently entertained in Chicago as a professional female impersonator. Another State regular, Kim August, later performed at the renowned Club 82 in New York and appeared with Rod Steiger in the film *No Way to Treat a Lady*, although he was not identified as a man in the credits.[46]

Like the Union Street location, the clientele at the West Kearsley site were a blend of heterosexuals and homosexuals, but now the gay crowd—a significant portion of the patronage—was on display like never before. Straights were onlookers more than customers. "It got to be a tourist trap," Hal Lawson recalls. "Everybody knew the Pink Poodle was where the queers hung out." *Hi-Spots* promised mainstream audiences that there was "never a dull moment" at the State Bar, and Earhart encouraged their patronage. At the peak of its popularity, the State attracted visitors who drove to Flint from Detroit, Pontiac, and Lansing to witness the lavish flamboyance of Earhart's club.[47]

Meanwhile, the hub around the Durant ceased to be a major locus for local gays. The College Inn started discouraging homosexual visitors and the Golden Spike went out of business. Other establishments appeared in their place, but were less centrally located. Bill Dakota, an industrious Flint native in his twenties, opened Studio D, an all-gay after-hours club, in the early 1960s. Above a motorcycle repair shop in a run-down area about half a mile from the hub, it was Flint's first commercial gay space to be so far from downtown. Another establishment, the Sports Bar, was a jazz club with a gay/straight mix located in a downtown alley, and Sub's Inn, a bar in Flint's North End, replaced the State in popularity during a brief span when Earhart's bar was out of business.[48]

In July 1967, when the State Bar's novelty had worn off and attendance had dropped, Earhart was forced to close. Betty Underwood explains: "It was too big. It sat 475 people. That's too much. You can't pack a place like that every night." Even with the car, Flint's size limited the extent to which the city could sustain gay institutions. But the maturing barkeeper (now fifty-three years old) faced obstacles in trying to reopen elsewhere. An attempt to transfer her liquor license to a smaller establishment on South Saginaw Street, near the path of the planned I-69 expressway, was stalled when neighbors protested the new bar, a delay which placed a financial strain on Earhart. "I have been out of business nearly four months in which I had only one month to move," she wrote to the Michigan Liquor Control Commission. "This is my only livelihood." Nevertheless, the state licensing panel denied Earhart's appeal, forcing her to look for a site beyond the downtown area.[49]

Earhart reopened the State nearly a year later at a location on Dort Highway, toward the southeastern city limits. The new spot, a developing commercial strip with no sidewalks, was even more difficult to reach without a car. But with the move, the State completed its transformation into an exclusively gay bar, packing in weekend crowds and becoming the "first establishment in Flint to allow men to publicly dance together," as Earhart would later boast. The new building was big enough to accommodate Flint's gay community, but not so large as to bankrupt the owner. In fact, it proved rather lucrative, enabling Earhart to buy a top-of-the-line car and to attain a version of the American dream that was ultimately unavailable to most of her working-class customers.[50]

The area around the State Bar became a significant gay institution as well. Soon after the State opened on Dort, the neighboring dirt parking lot began to be as popular as the bar itself, particularly on warm summer nights. With the hub in decline, the traffic from the Herrlich's lot migrated to Dort Highway. People cruised the State's lot until the early hours of the morning, with drivers slowly circling the area in their vehicles and flashing their brake lights. Parking spaces became trysting places, and the police left the new cruising grounds alone. Without the constant threat of arrest, the principal mobile and stationary spaces of 1950s Flint gay life were thus able to merge.[51]

Even today, in the mid-1990s, the State remains firmly entrenched in the local gay culture, still operating ten years after Melva Earhart's death. "She wanted a safe place for the kids," Betty Underwood declares. "That was her goal, I guess her goal in life, to have a nice safe place." In the small, rust-belt city of Flint, a former "redneck" bar has survived as the principal space where lesbians and gay men can openly meet, adapting itself to its customers' increasingly mobile lives.[52]

Wheels of Change

Elizabeth Kennedy and Madeline Davis argue that when Buffalo grew to more than 500,000 in 1950 it reached a critical mass, whereby the lesbian population was large enough to forge important community institutions even before gay liberation. The evidence of enduring, active gay, lesbian, and bisexual institutions in Flint, Michigan, with its population of barely 200,000, implies a need to reassess such estimates of critical mass. Communities smaller than Buffalo, and sometimes smaller than Flint, could and did emerge before Stonewall. Future research may explain how the population base for community building might have varied in different regions, depending on specific historical and local conditions.[53]

Automobile ownership was one such historical condition in Flint. Motor vehicles transformed U.S. society, putting increased power—horse power—into the hands of individuals and altering the landscape with new patterns of urban growth. In Flint, the car allowed gay and bisexual men to assemble like never before, and these men gave new meaning to the concept of driving for pleasure. Flint's experience showcases the unrecognized, instrumental significance of the automobile, both in the lives of individual gay men and in the spread of homosexual communities across the U.S., especially to less densely populated areas. Increased surveillance at mid-century was aimed at halting the expanding communities and driving them underground, but authorities were helpless to apply the brakes.

George Chauncey, Jr. contends that the capacity of gay men "to build a gay world covertly in the midst of a hostile straight world should be considered a form of resistance, since it was their very ability to keep parts of the gay world invisible that allowed them to circumvent the prohibition of that world." This capacity for resilient resistance was clearly at work in Flint. Homosexual life shifted gears from private networks to public commercial establishments almost as soon as cars came off the city's assembly lines. A new gay world based on a collective gay identity emerged in bars distant enough from home to provide anonymity to customers. Therefore, the concealment and mobility afforded by the automobile greatly enhanced the ability of gay men to find each other. Driving also introduced working-class gay men to vibrant gay communities in larger cities. The car thus gave men access to gay spaces both local and distant, became a gay space itself, and helped shape stationary gay spaces as they evolved during the 1960s. Although Flint felt the car's impact in an exaggerated way, the experiences of the city's gay men nonetheless signal a need to examine the automobile's historical role elsewhere, particularly in places like Los Angeles, which had its own well-developed car culture and which was where the homophile movement began in 1950.[54]

The impact of the automobile on gay men nationwide is most evident in the unmistakable manner in which the car was part of the broader gay culture, such as its incorporation into the term "cruising," a gay slang word dating back at least to the 1930s.[55] Like tearooms, baths, and bars before them, car cruising, car sex, and homosexually active parking lots all became acknowledged sites where gay and bisexual men could claim public spaces as their own.[56] Roadside rest areas also became prominent, if sometimes scorned, homosexual institutions.[57] The seemingly high prevalence of homosexual men thumbing or offering rides suggests that hitchhiking was another deliberate pickup strategy, which helps explain why it was a common theme in gay male pulp fiction of the 1960s.[58] Often far away from urban areas, these various car-centered institutions provided men with possibilities for homosexual encounters and ways to create gay identities. By the beginning of the 1970s, phrases such as "carhop" (to solicit passing motorists from the sidewalk), "curb service" (a gay man on foot who cruises drivers), and "road queen" (a gay hitchhiker) were entrenched in homosexual argot.[59]

The phenomenon of gay car culture raises additional questions about the effects that technology has on lesbians, gays, and bisexuals, and on other oppressed peoples. The entry of lesbian, gay, and bisexual people into bars, into automobiles, and more recently into cyberspace shows that stigmatized sexual groups have an uncanny ability to commandeer different kinds of spaces, quickly "queering" those sites to make them their own.[60]

Acknowledgments

Grateful thanks to Nora Faires, George Chauncey, Marc Stein, Roey Thorpe, Chuck Coggins, Brett Beemyn, and J Katzeman for their help at different stages of this effort. Thanks especially to the men and women who generously allowed me to interview them, several of whom have since died.

Notes

1. *Queen of the Road*, 2. The only known copies of this undated, anonymously written 1960s pulp novel are held by Special Collections at the Michigan State University Libraries and the New York Public Library.
2. Lyn H. Lofland, *A World of Strangers: Order and Action in Urban Public Space* (New York: Basic Books, 1973), 136.
3. Strict respect for self-disclosure and confidentiality is essential to researching gay history in smaller cities. Consequently, although criminal records in Michigan are public, this study will use initials in reference to individuals identified in case files.
4. Information, Criminal Record no. 12109 (1950), Genesee County Clerk files, Flint, Michigan (hereafter cited as GCC files). An "information" is a legal document, similar to an indictment, formally charging an individual with a crime.

Additional data come from Flint Police Department, Circuit Court Record and Application for Warrant, Flint Law Department files, Flint, Michigan, obtained separately under the Michigan Freedom of Information Act, requested and received in June 1995. Gross indecency convictions under Michigan law could result in up to five years imprisonment, sodomy convictions up to fifteen years; see Michigan, *Public Acts* (1931), no. 138, sections 158 and 328, effective September 18, 1931.

5. R. Gordon Brain, M.D., Joseph Shapiro, M.D., and A. Tayber, M.D. to Judge Clifford A. Bishop, August 2, 1950; Proceedings before Bishop, July 27 and August 29, 1950, Criminal Record no. 12109, GCC files; Michigan, *Public Acts* (1939), no. 165, effective September 29, 1939. A review of its passage appeared in the *Detroit News*, November 20, 1949, A16. Michigan enacted the law in the wake of a Depression-era sex crime panic which swept the U.S.; see Estelle Freedman, "'Uncontrolled Desires': The Response to the Sexual Psychopath, 1920–1960," *Journal of American History* 74, no. 1 (June 1987): 83–106. The Goodrich Act was applied to homosexuals in Genesee County, where Flint is located, in only two other instances; see Criminal Record no. 10999 (1947) and Criminal Record no. 12209 (1950), GCC files.
6. Reports of Psychiatrists, undated; John G. Hearer, M.D. and Alfred Birzgalis, M.D. to Judge Stephen J. Roth, December 2, 1958; Order of Roth, January 30, 1959, Criminal Record no. 12109, GCC files. The other party's occupation and later marital status were found in the *Flint City Directory*, 1950 and 1955 (Detroit: R.L. Polk).
7. John Howard, "The Library, the Park, and the Pervert: Public Space and Homosexual Encounter in Post-World War II Atlanta," *Radical History Review* 62 (Spring 1995): 166–87. On prewar developments, see George Chauncey, *Gay New York: Gender, Urban Culture, and the Making of the Gay Male World, 1890–1940* (New York: BasicBooks, 1994); John D'Emilio and Estelle B. Freedman, *Intimate Matters: A History of Sexuality in America* (New York: Harper and Row, 1988), 226–28; John D'Emilio, *Sexual Politics, Sexual Communities: The Making of a Homosexual Minority in the United States, 1940–1970* (Chicago: University of Chicago Press, 1983), ch. 2; Allan Bérubé, *Coming Out Under Fire: The History of Gay Men and Women in World War Two* (New York: The Free Press, 1990). Studies of postwar gay and lesbian communities have focused primarily on coastal cities. See John D'Emilio, "Gay Politics and Community in San Francisco Since World War II," in *Hidden from History: Reclaiming the Gay and Lesbian Past*, eds. Martin Bauml Duberman, Martha Vicinus, and George Chauncey, Jr. (New York: New American Library, 1989), 456–73; Marc Stein, "Sex Politics in the City of Sisterly and Brotherly Loves," *Radical History Review* 59 (Spring 1994): 60–92; and David K. Johnson, "'Homosexual Citizen': Washington's Gay Community Confronts the Civil Service," *Washington History* 6, no. 2 (Fall/Winter 1994–95): 44–63. A remarkable exception to the emphasis on the coasts is Elizabeth Lapovsky Kennedy and Madeline D. Davis, *Boots of Leather, Slippers of Gold: The History of a Lesbian Community* (New York: Routledge, 1993), a pioneering look at women in Buffalo, a city roughly three times the size of Flint.
8. Chauncey, *Gay New York*, introduction, ch. 1–3; Kennedy and Davis, *Boots of Leather, Slippers of Gold*, 10. For Flint's selection as an All-American City, see *Look*, February 9, 1954, 52–53.

9. Ronald Edsforth, *Class Conflict and Cultural Consensus: The Making of a Mass Consumer Society in Flint, Michigan* (New Brunswick: Rutgers University Press, 1987). Edsforth provides a good discussion of Flint's industrial development and the paternalistic role of General Motors. See also David Halberstam, *The Fifties* (New York: Villard Books, 1993), 118–30. Population characteristics are drawn from *Statistical Abstract of the United States, 1961*, 82nd ed. (Washington, DC: Government Printing Office, 1961), table 14; Robert G. Schafer, *Producing a Human Mosaic: Immigration and Economic Change in the Development of Genesee County's Population, 1820–1987* (Flint: University of Michigan-Flint Archives, 1989), 33–43.
10. The phrase "culture of abundance" comes from Warren I. Susman, *Culture as History: The Transformation of American Society in the Twentieth Century* (New York: Pantheon Books, 1984), xxix. On Flint in the 1950s, see *Flint Journal*, souvenir ed., November 22, 1954; centennial ed., September 4, 1955; souvenir ed., August 14, 1958; "Flint and the American Dream," permanent exhibit at the Alfred P. Sloan Museum, Flint, Michigan, opened November 10, 1993. On the Sit-Down Strike, see Sidney Fine, *Sit-Down: The General Motors Strike of 1936–1937* (Ann Arbor: University of Michigan Press, 1969). On Flint's part in World War II, see *Buick at Its Battle Stations* (Flint: Buick Motor Division, 1944).
11. Jack Pierson, interviewed March 10, 1990. Unless otherwise indicated, interviews were conducted in Flint.
12. See also Flint Police Department Circuit Court Record and Application for Warrant; Proceedings before Judge E.D. Black, September 30, 1938, Criminal Record no. 7431 (1938), GCC files. Documentation on gay life in Flint prior to the 1930s has yet to be uncovered. The full extent of this prewar experience awaits further research.
13. John B. Rae, *The Road and Car in American Life* (Cambridge, MA: MIT Press, 1971); H.F. Moorhouse, "American Automobiles and Workers' Dreams," *Sociological Review* 31 (August 1983): 403–26; *Automobile Facts and Figures* (Detroit: Automobile Manufacturer's Association, 1951), 25; also 1961 ed., 23, 33; 1971 ed., 46.
14. John D'Emilio, "The Homosexual Menace: The Politics of Sexuality in Cold War America," in *Passion and Power: Sexuality in History*, eds. Kathy Peiss, Christina Simmons, and Robert A. Padgug (Philadelphia: Temple University Press, 1989), 226–40. See also Elaine Tyler May, *Homeward Bound: American Families in the Cold War Era* (New York: BasicBooks, 1988); Barbara Ehrenreich, *The Hearts of Men: American Dreams and the Flight from Commitment* (Garden City, NY: Anchor Press, 1983), ch. 1–2.
15. Rule 436.3d, Michigan, *Administrative Code* (1944), supplement 14, 7, effective August 18, 1948.
16. Samuel W. Hartwell, M.D., *A Citizen's Handbook of Sexual Abnormalities and the Mental Hygiene Approach to Their Prevention* (Lansing: State of Michigan, 1950), 4–6. Hartwell's definition of "sexual deviate" compared homosexuals to exhibitionists and child molesters. On the Study Commission, see George Chauncey, "The Postwar Sex Crime Panic," in *True Stories of the American Past*, ed. William Graebner (New York: McGraw-Hill, 1993), 160–78; *Report of the Governor's Study Commission on the Deviated Criminal Sex Offender* (Lansing: State of Michigan, 1951). In response to the Commission's recommendations, the legislature enacted a measure providing up to life imprisonment for repeat sex offenders; Michigan, *Public Acts* (1952), no. 73, section 1, effective September 18, 1952.

17. Alan Banks [pseud.], interviewed February 14, 1991. See also Ralph O'Reilly, letter to author, June 30, 1993; Bill Dakota, letter to author, May 19, 1995. The hotel was named for William Crapo Durant, founder of General Motors. In 1957, a man accosted an undercover police officer in the Durant rest room; see Information, Criminal Record no. 16271 (1957), GCC files. Additional information about the area is drawn from *Flint Telephone Directory* (Detroit: Michigan Bell Telephone Company, 1959), 92, 254, 255; *Flint City Directory*, 1947, 1950, 1952, 1954, 1957 (Detroit: R.L. Polk). On the rapid decline in bus ridership following the war, see Richard Hébert, "Flint: GM's Mark of Excellence," in his *Highways to Nowhere: The Politics of City Transportation* (Indianapolis: Bobbs-Merrill Co., 1972), 3–37.
18. Marty Rudman [pseud.], interviewed March 4, 1991; Maurice, interviewed in rural Genesee County, April 7, 1995; Banks interview; Bruce Globig, interviewed in Los Angeles, September 26, 1990; Ralph Stallings, interviewed in Holly, Michigan, October 2, 1993. Kennedy and Davis discuss mixed bars and their occasional transformation into full-scale gay spaces; *Boots of Leather, Slippers of Gold*, 40–42, 48–50, 70–73.
19. *Metra*, December 18, 1980, 21; Betty Underwood, interviewed in Inkster, Michigan, May 13, 1995; Banks interview. See also License Issue Record for Melva M. Earhart Estate, File no. 6239, Michigan Liquor Control Commission files, Lansing (hereafter MLCC files), obtained under the Michigan Freedom of Information Act, requested and received February 1992; *Hitting the Hi-Spots*, April 14, 1950, 14; *Flint News-Advertiser*, June 5, 1953, 1. Further biographical information is from Earhart's obituary in *Flint Journal*, January 17, 1985, C3.
20. Underwood interview; Earl, interviewed August 22, 1995; Banks interview; Rudman interview. See also *Metra*, March 31, 1983, 33; *Hitting the Hi-Spots*, April 14, 1950, 17.
21. Lesbians in Buffalo in the 1940s and 1950s exercised the same caution; Kennedy and Davis, *Boots of Leather, Slippers of Gold*, 54–62. Although many men involved in Flint's gay community were married to women, whether any of them adopted a gay or a bisexual identity in the 1950s and '60s is unclear.
22. Globig interview; Clint, interviewed July 26, 1995; Andrew, interviewed in Burton, Michigan, July 23, 1995; Maurice interview; Arthur Zimmer [pseud.], interviewed March 23, 1991. For the car's effect on individual travel, see John A. Jakle, *The Tourist: Travel in Twentieth-Century North America* (Lincoln: University of Nebraska Press, 1985), ch. 9.
23. A full examination of gay Detroit remains to be done. For evidence of its pre-World War II homosexual life, see Jonathan Katz, *Gay American History: Lesbians and Gay Men in the U.S.A.* (New York: Thomas Y. Crowell, 1976), 144, 395–97. Maurice recalls that during Prohibition he visited a gay "blind pig," or speakeasy, in Detroit called Mother Bea's; Maurice interview.
24. For more information on Detroit in the 1950s, see Roey Thorpe, "'Feminine Would Be Very Hard to Recognize': Lesbian Silence and Visibility in Detroit, 1950–75," paper presented to the American Historical Association, San Francisco, 1994; Bramwell Franklin [a.k.a. ChiChi], interviewed in Detroit, July 8, 1993; Tom McClain, "Gays in Detroit," *Cruise*, August 24, 1984, 28; Joseph Raphael, "'Tonights the Night!': An Interview with Andy," *Gayzette*, July 1973, 8–9. On Detroit bars, see "The Lady Jai Recommended List," copy in possession of author. Its compiler dates the listing as 1954; see Jai Moore, interviewed in Detroit, June 14, 1993, and in Flint, November 17, 1993.

25. Maurice interview. On Flint excursions to the Motor City, see Andrew interview; Zimmer interview; Clint interview; Banks interview. Author Seymour Kleinberg, who taught at Flint Junior College from 1959–62, noted that he left town to experience gay life: "I reserved my homosexuality for excursions to New York, Chicago, Detroit, and Ann Arbor, and to occasional pickups of local working-class men." *Alienated Affections: Being Gay in America* (New York: St. Martin's Press, 1980), 32. For background on gay baths, see Chauncey, *Gay New York*, ch. 8.
26. The stretch of I-75 from Flint to Detroit first appeared on state highway maps in 1963; see *Official Transportation Map of Michigan* (Lansing: Michigan State Highway Commission, 1962 and 1963). In recounting their histories, both Ralph O'Reilly and Arthur Zimmer mention the Dixie rest area; see O'Reilly, letter to author; Zimmer interview. The car also gave individuals from Flint contact with the small, pioneering homophile organizations of the 1950s and '60s. A.K., a Flint man who had corresponded with the New York chapter of the Mattachine Society, was put in touch with the Detroit Area Council, a short-lived, middle-class effort to organize homosexuals in Michigan. He joined the group, visited on occasion, and provided his mimeograph machine for the organization's newsletter. When Hal Lawson, Detroit Mattachine's chair, started a romance with a man from Flint, he migrated from Detroit. His relocation contributed to the demise of the Detroit chapter of Mattachine in March 1960; Hal Lawson, interviewed November 23, 1990. See also my "Detroit Mattachine," *Between the Lines*, June 1995, 13.
27. On the eroticization of the automobile, see Stephen Bayley, *Sex, Drink and Fast Cars* (New York: Pantheon Books, 1986); Grady Gammage, Jr. and Stephen L. Jones, "Orgasm in Chrome: The Rise and Fall of the Automobile Tailfin," *Journal of Popular Culture* 8 (1974): 132–47. For the car's role in heterosexual courting, see Beth L. Bailey, *From Front Porch to Back Seat: Courtship in Twentieth-Century America* (Baltimore: Johns Hopkins University Press, 1988); David L. Lewis, "Sex and the Automobile: From Rumble Seats to Rockin' Vans," in *The Automobile and American Culture*, eds. David L. Lewis and Laurence Goldstein (Ann Arbor: University of Michigan Press, 1983), 123–33; D'Emilio and Freedman, *Intimate Matters*, 240, 257–60. A double standard was also employed during the same period in Atlanta, where city officials campaigned against teenagers using automobiles for heterosexual petting, asserting that the mobile space was public, even though cars had long been seen legally as only semi-private. Authorities in the city ultimately gave limited sanction to heterosexual "spooning" behind the wheel, while at the same time curtailing public displays of homosexuality on the footpaths of Atlanta's parks. See Howard, "The Library, the Park, and the Pervert." (Howard, though, does not address homosexuals in cars). Flint authorities apparently gave tacit approval to other-sex liaisons as well. No such incidents in cars were prosecuted as felonies in Genesee County during the 1950s and '60s. The legal question of the car's privacy was partly settled in the 1920s when the U.S. Supreme Court ruled in a Michigan case that automobiles were not protected from searches in the same manner as dwellings; see *Carroll v. United States*, 267 U.S. 132 (1925).
28. On the car as distinctive territory, see F.A. Whitlock, *Death on the Road: A Study in Social Violence* (London: Tavistock Publications, 1971), ch. 10. On the car as a male domain, see Clay McShane, *Down the Asphalt Path: The Automobile and the American City* (New York: Columbia University Press, 1994), ch. 8; Virginia

Scharff, *Taking the Wheel: Women and the Coming of the Motor Age* (New York: The Free Press, 1991), 138–40.

29. For a discussion of the motivations of tearoom participants, see Laud Humphreys, *Tearoom Trade: Impersonal Sex in Public Places* (Chicago: Aldine Publishing, 1975). Humphrey's method of study utilized license plates and motor vehicle registrations. Kennedy and Davis make the important observation that, based on differences in privilege and oppression, gay male history in some ways contrasts strikingly with lesbian history; *Boots of Leather, Slippers of Gold*, 381. George Chauncey's discussion of street-life dynamics has been crucial to my understanding of Flint's gay car culture; *Gay New York*, ch. 7.
30. Genesee County Sheriff's Department Circuit Court Record and Application for Warrant; Report of Investigation to Court by William H. Coleman regarding B.M., March 15, 1951; Report of Investigation to Court by William H. Coleman regarding F.S., March 15, 1951; Joseph Shapiro, M.D. to Coleman, February 9, 1951; Proceedings before Judge Philip Elliot, April 24, 1951; Order of Discharge from Probation, March 6, 1953, Criminal Record no. 12385 (1951), GCC files. See also *Flint City Directory*, 1950, 1952, 1955, 1961 (Detroit: R.L. Polk).
31. Dennis, interviewed by Deborah Larsen, June 7, 1993. My thanks to Larsen for sharing her tape recording. See also Clint interview; Banks interview. Interestingly, Herrlich's was also noted for having the busiest pay telephone in the city, with as many as 140 calls a day; see *Flint Journal*, January 10, 1960, 17.
32. Earl interview; Clint interview.
33. Proceedings before Judge Philip Elliot, November 2, 1959; Flint Police Department Circuit Court Record and Application for Warrant, Criminal Record no. 17094 (1959). Hours after L.N.'s arrest, the same officers apprehended a twenty-nine-year-old sales manager in his brand-new Pontiac in almost identical circumstances; see Flint Police Department Circuit Court Record and Application for Warrant, Criminal Record no. 17118 (1959), GCC files.
34. O'Reilly, letter to author; Andrew interview.
35. Walt Lewis [pseud.], interviewed in Detroit, July 8, 1995; Earl interview; Banks interview. On Hoover's warnings against hitchhikers, see *New York Times*, June 2, 1951, 11, and July 4, 1957, 15. Chauncey examines cruising in its better known form—on foot—in *Gay New York*, 180–84.
36. Statement of W.S., February 10, 1956; Michigan State Police Report to Prosecuting Attorney, Criminal Record no. 15223 (1956), GCC files.
37. Peter Marsh and Peter Collett, *Driving Passion: The Psychology of the Car* (Boston: Faber and Faber, 1986). See also Bailey, *From Front Porch to Back Seat*; Howard, "The Library, the Park, and the Pervert."
38. Chauncey, *Gay New York*, 9.
39. Almost half of the one hundred arraignments on felony gross indecency or sodomy charges in Genesee County from 1950 to 1969 were same-sex situations involving consenting adults or entrapment. In contrast, only three of the forty cases from 1934 to 1949 were for consensual adult homosexual activity. The exact number of arrests for homosexual "accosting and soliciting," a misdemeanor, is unknown since such records are not permanently retained; see Michigan, *Public Acts* (1931), no. 328, section 448, effective September 18, 1931. Police statistics offer some clues here, however. Complaints for "other sex offenses," a category likely to comprise mostly homosexual arrests because it excluded prostitution and

rape, reached as high as 226 in 1954. Throughout the next fifteen years, the figure rarely dipped below 130 per year. Available arrest reports corroborate this pattern. Prostitution, by comparison, was less consistently enforced, registering a low of 64 complaints in 1953 and a high of 317 in 1954; see *Flint Police Department Annual Report*, 1953–1969.

40. Flint Police Department Circuit Court Record and Application for Warrant; R.A. Jaarsma, M.D. to Robert A. McKenney, January 16, 1958; Proceedings before Judge John W. Baker, February 17, 1958, Criminal Record no. 16246 (1958), GCC files.
41. Bruce Globig, letter to author, August 6, 1990; James Johnson [pseud.], interviewed in Burton, Michigan, July 23, 1995. See also O'Reilly, letter to author; Carlton Jackson, *Hounds of the Road: A History of the Greyhound Bus Company* (Bowling Green, OH: Bowling Green University Popular Press, 1984), 83–85. On the migration of Southerners to Flint during the 1950s, see *Flint Journal*, December 25, 1988, A1. The arrest of a Buick autoworker for approaching another man at the bus station in January 1959 was a typical case; see Information; Proceedings before Judge Philip Elliot, February 24, 1959, Criminal Record no. 16937 (1959), GCC files.
42. Hébert, "Flint," 15.
43. The Durant itself barely survived the decade. It closed in September 1973, and has since remained vacant; see *Flint Journal*, September 30, 1973, D1.
44. *Hi-Spots*, May 19, 1961, 1. *Hitting the Hi-Spots* (later *Hi-Spots*) was published weekly in Flint from 1939 to 1975. The most complete known holdings are owned by the Genesee Historical Collections Center, University of Michigan-Flint. Further data on the Poodle is from License Issue Record for Melva M. Earhart Estate, File no. 6239, MLCC files; Property Data Sheet for 712 West Kearsley Street, Box 3, Gerald Healy Papers, Genesee Historical Collections Center; *Flint Journal*, June 19, 1960, 13; June 26, 1960, 13.
45. Underwood interview.
46. Esther Newton, *Mother Camp: Female Impersonators in America* (Chicago: University of Chicago Press, 1972), 7; *Hi-Spots*, August 7, 1964, 10; May 21, 1965, 10; June 16, 1967, 1; Underwood interview; Dennis interview. See also *No Way to Treat a Lady*, dir. Jack Smight (Paramount Pictures, 1968). On the 82 Club, see Joe E. Jeffreys, "Who's No Lady? Excerpts from an Oral History of New York City's 82 Club," *New York Folklore* 19, nos. 1–2 (1993): 185–202. For the local prohibition on cross-dressing, see Ordinance no. 1277, approved May 16, 1955. In urging passage of this ordinance, Vice-Mayor Carl W. Delling asked that "something be done to rid Flint streets of men who walk the streets posing as women." He said he was "getting sick of looking at them." His comments were reported in *Flint News-Advertiser*, April 12, 1955, 1.
47. Lawson interview; *Hi-Spots*, June 16, 1967, 34. See also Bob Damron, *The Address Book*, 3rd ed. (San Francisco: Bob Damron, 1966), 33; *IN Guide* (New York: IN Guide, 1966), 24. Such guides saw their debut in the early 1960s, another sign of increased car travel among gay men; see "'Gay Sexualist' Hal Call," in Eric Marcus's *Making History: The Struggle for Gay and Lesbian Equal Rights, 1945–1990, An Oral History* (New York: HarperCollins, 1992), 59–69. While extremely useful in documenting the burgeoning pre-Stonewall bar culture, these guides are scarce. The Gay and Lesbian Historical Society of Northern California, the New York Public Library, and Bob Damron Enterprises all hold significant collections.

48. Bill Dakota, letters to author, May 19 and June 13, 1995; Dan, interviewed June 7, 1995. In 1964, Studio D was raided; see *Flint Journal*, December 14, 1964, 9. Dakota was later imprisoned on allegedly trumped-up charges of having sex with a fourteen-year-old boy; see Criminal Record no. 20231 (1965), GCC files. For information on other gay establishments, see *International Guild Guide, 1965* (Washington, DC: Guild Book Service, 1965), 53; *Directory 43*, 3rd ed. (Minneapolis: Directory Services, 1965), 53; *International Guild Guide '69* (Washington, DC: Guild Press, 1969), 42; *Bob Damron's 1970 Address Book*, 6th ed. (San Francisco: Bob Damron, 1969), 45; *Flint City Directory*, 1960, 1964, 1965 (Detroit: R.L. Polk).
49. Underwood interview; Melva M. Earhart [to Liquor Control Commission, November ? 1967], File no. 6239, MLCC files. See also *Proceedings of the Flint City Commission*, November 6, 1967, 605; November 13, 1967, 621; Memorandum from Rosemary Lipkovitz to Roger J. Rosendale, January 23, 1968; Memorandum from Roger J. Rosendale to License Division, February 26, 1968; License Issue Record for Melva M. Earhart Estate, File no. 6239, MLCC files; Donald R. Cronin, interviewed May 11, 1995.
50. Earl interview. The start of men publicly dancing together in Flint was indicated in *Metra*, March 31, 1983, 33. See also *International Guild Guide '69*, 42. Earhart left an estate exceeding $120,000; see Order Settling Contested Matters, September 3, 1987, File no. G-85–117722, Genesee County Probate Court files, Flint, Michigan.
51. The State's parking lot scene, as enduring as the bar itself, was featured in *Flint Journal*, July 28, 1991, A1. See also Jack Struby, interviewed June 14, 1991; Jack Horton, interviewed in Genesee County, April 14, 1995; Dan interview.
52. Underwood interview.
53. Kennedy and Davis, *Boots of Leather, Slippers of Gold*, 10. By at least the early 1960s, Michigan cities such as Ann Arbor, Battle Creek, Kalamazoo, Pontiac, and Port Huron, all smaller than Flint, each had places specifically identified as gay. See *The Lavender Baedeker* (San Francisco: Guy Strait, 1963), 15–16; and the other early gay guides cited previously.
54. Chauncey, *Gay New York*, 374n. On the overall impact of the automobile on U.S. society, see Rae, *The Road and Car in American Life*. On the special relationship between Los Angeles and the automobile, see Martin Wachs and Margaret Crawford, eds., *The Car and the City: The Automobile, the Built Environment, and Daily Urban Life* (Ann Arbor: University of Michigan Press, 1992), ch. 13–17. On the Los Angeles beginnings of the homophile movement, see D'Emilio, *Sexual Politics, Sexual Communities*, ch. 4; Stuart Timmons, *The Trouble with Harry Hay, Founder of the Gay Movement* (Boston: Alyson, 1990), ch. 8. One study of Los Angeles found that car arrests for homosexual activity in the mid-1960s were second only to rest room arrests; Martin Hoffman, *The Gay World: Male Homosexuality and the Social Creation of Evil* (New York: Basic Books, 1968), 87–89.
55. To "cruise," according to G. Legman's 1941 compilation of gay slang, meant "to walk or drive in an automobile through the streets, aimlessly but in certain specific and likely areas, looking for . . . a companion for homosexual intercourse, whether for money or *pour le sport*;" see "The Language of Homosexuality: An American Glossary," in *Sex Variants*, ed. George W. Henry (New York: Paul B. Hoeber, 1941), vol. 2, appendix VII, 1161–62.
56. On car cruising, see Andrew Holleran, "Car Sex: Meaningless Sex Should Not

Require a Half-Tank of Gas," *Christopher Street*, no. 84 (January 1984): 10–13; David Bell, "Perverse Dynamics, Sexual Citizenship, and the Transformation of Intimacy," in *Mapping Desires: Geographies of Sexualities*, eds. David Bell and Gill Valentine (New York: Routledge, 1995), 304–07. On parking lots, see Meredith R. Ponte, "Life in a Parking Lot: An Ethnography of a Homosexual Drive-In," in *Deviance: Field Studies and Self-Disclosures*, ed. Jerry Jacobs (Palo Alto: National Press Books, 1974), 7–29.

57. For a discussion of rest areas as gay spaces, see Richard R. Troiden, "Homosexual Encounters in a Highway Rest Stop," in *Sexual Deviance, Sexual Deviants*, eds. Erich Goode and Richard R. Troiden (New York: William Morrow and Co., 1974), 211–28; Jay Corzine and Richard Kirby, "Cruising the Truckers: Sexual Encounters in a Highway Rest Area," *Urban Life* 6, no. 2 (July 1977): 171–92. In Michigan, rest areas have continued to be popular sites for homosexual activity, as well as for police surveillance; see *Gay Liberator*, February 1972, 1; *Metro Gay News*, September 1976, 1; *Flint Journal*, February 29, 1980, A1; *Detroit News*, October 28, 1984, A3; *Lansing State Journal*, March 19, 1986, A1.

58. One investigator conducting field research in the late 1960s and early '70s found that only 120 of the 525 hitchhikers he picked up were heterosexual. Three hundred eighty "considered themselves bisexual," while twenty-five identified themselves as being homosexual; see Walter F. Weiss, *America's Wandering Youth: A Sociological Study of Young Hitchhikers in the United States* (Jericho, NY: Exposition Press, 1974), 47. For examples of hitchhiking in gay male pulp fiction, see James Harper, *Another Room—Another Brother* (Los Angeles: Echelon Book Publishers, 1968), Special Collections, Michigan State University Libraries; *The Hitchhiker* (Washington, DC: Guild Press, 1969), Special Collections, Stanford University Libraries. An earlier, more literary treatment is Donald Windham, *The Hitchhiker* (Florence, Italy: privately published, 1950). Hitchhiking later became a popular theme in gay male pornographic films, as well; see *Pacific Coast Highway*, dir. William Higgins (Catalina Video, 1981); *Flashpoint*, dir. John Rutherford (Falcon Studios, 1994). The relationship between sexuality and hitchhiking deserves further study.

59. These examples of gay slang are from Bruce Rodgers, *The Queen's Vernacular: A Gay Lexicon* (San Francisco: Straight Arrow Books, 1972), 42, 58, 172; see especially the various jargon listed under "wheels," 212–13.

60. On the entry of lesbians, gays, and bisexuals into cyberspace, see Donald Morton, "Birth of the Cyberqueer," *PMLA* 110, no. 3 (May 1995): 369–81; Barbara Presley Noble, "Wired for the Revolution," *New York Times*, June 26, 1994, F21; Kennedy Smith, "A Whole New (Gay) World: As Internet Expands, So Does Its Resources for the Community," *Washington Blade*, July 21, 1995, 43.

11. "Birthplace of the Nation"

Imagining Lesbian and Gay Communities in Philadelphia, 1969–1970

Marc Stein

The *Oxford English Dictionary*'s (*OED*) first definition of "nation" is "an extensive aggregate of persons, so closely associated with each other by common descent, language, or history, as to form a distinct race or people, usually organized as a separate political state and occupying a definite territory."[1] Are lesbians and gay men, then, a nation? Are they two nations, one female and one male? Are they multiple nations, defined in racial, class, or geopolitical terms? Are there bisexual, transgendered, and queer nations as well? Extensive in number, lesbians and gay men have often associated closely with each other. And lesbian and gay studies scholarship has confirmed what members of these groups have known for a long time—that lesbians and gay men share a number of traditions, languages, and histories and constitute distinct peoples with unique places in the social, cultural, political, and geographical landscape.

Lesbians and gay men, however, have rarely conceived of themselves as a nation. More commonly, they have articulated their senses of collective identities by describing themselves as a class, community, culture, ethnic group, family, interest group, lifestyle, people, race, society, subculture, tribe, or world. For example, the 1915 edition of Havelock Ellis's *Sexual Inversion* refers to the large "*world* of sexual inverts" in U.S. cities as a "*community* distinctly organized—words, customs, traditions of its own." George Chauncey explains in *Gay New York* that gay people before World War II spoke of "coming out into what they called 'homosexual *society*' or the 'gay *world*'" (my emphases).[2]

Although lesbians and gay men have not often thought of themselves as a nation, nations have thought about them. George Mosse's *Nationalism and Sexuality* and Andrew Parker, Mary Russo, Doris Sommer, and Patricia

Yaeger's edited anthology *Nationalisms and Sexualities* have explored the historical "interplay between nation and sexuality." As the editors note, "Whenever the power of the nation is invoked . . . we are more likely than not to find it couched as a *love of country*: an eroticized nationalism."[3] This work builds upon Benedict Anderson's insight in *Imagined Communities: Reflections on the Origin and Spread of Nationalism* that "the nation is always conceived as a deep, horizontal comradeship." Parker and his colleagues point out that "typically represented as a passionate brotherhood, the nation finds itself compelled to distinguish its 'proper' homosociality from more explicitly sexualized male-male relations." Ruthann Robson's *Lesbian (Out)Law* suggests that nations have also, if differently, thought about lesbians, who have been "both outside the law and within it."[4]

While they have rarely represented themselves as a nation, and nations have often attacked them, lesbians and gay men have deployed discourses of nationalism in their political struggles. According to *Nationalisms and Sexualities*, "That it is the nation rather than other forms of imagined collectivity that carries today this immense political freight has meant, of course, that disenfranchised groups frequently have had to appeal to national values precisely to register their claims as political."[5] So while discourses of nationalism have tended to mask, mystify, and exacerbate internal social cleavages and inequalities, they have also been mobilized in the service of liberal reform and counterhegemonic revolution. Liberal movements for suffrage, military service, and integration in the United States, for example, have often celebrated national ideals. From the Confederate, Aryan, and Christian Nations on the right, to the Black, Lesbian, and Queer Nations on the left, radical political movements in the United States have also turned to the rhetoric of nationalism.[6]

This essay will examine five episodes in Philadelphia lesbian and gay history in the period immediately surrounding New York City's 1969 Stonewall riots.[7] Linked geographically and chronologically, these events were also all marked by conflicts over meanings of nationalism. Each section of this essay explores a particular convergence of lesbian/gay nationalisms. Taken as a whole, the essay moves forward chronologically, tracing a genealogy of more recent nationalisms. Named the "City of Brotherly Love" by William Penn and called the "birthplace of the nation" because the U.S. Declaration of Independence was adopted there in 1776, Philadelphia is a rich site for exploring historical intersections between homoeroticism and nationalism. Setting up a productive tension between a study of a local community and a study of nationalism, this essay also argues for integrating community studies and cultural studies by placing emphasis on the cultural symbols associated with particular cities.

By "nationalism," I mean something narrower in one sense and broader in another than the definition commonly used today. Although the term is often equated with separatisms of various types, as when Lisa Duggan writes that "nationalisms have a long history in gay and lesbian politics and culture," I use it in a more historically specific sense.[8] Nationalism here refers to the articulation of collective identity through the term "nation" or through language that is understood to be culturally central to a formation labelled a "nation." Insofar as I do not regard all articulations of distinct lesbian/gay identities and communities as nationalist, my use of the term is narrow. Insofar as I regard as nationalist all rhetoric that celebrates a nation's values, patriotism, and citizenship, my use of the term is broad. As the *OED* defines it, nationalism is "devotion to one's nation; national aspiration; a policy of national independence"; "'a national idiom or phrase.'"[9] Whether the nation at issue is the U.S. nation, the lesbian/gay nation, or both, I regard all of these discourses as nationalist. In the end, I am less interested in the general question of whether lesbians and gay men *are* a nation than in the historical questions of when, how, in what ways, for what reasons, and with what effects lesbians and gay men have deployed discourses of nationalism.

Repression and Liberation

About eight weeks before the Stonewall riots, Clark Polak announced suddenly that *DRUM* magazine, which he had founded in 1964, would cease publication. *DRUM* was produced by the Philadelphia-based Janus Society of America, which described itself as a "national" organization with a "national" membership.[10] Aspiring to be a "gay *Playboy*, with the news coverage of *Time*," *DRUM* combined male physique photography with hard-hitting news and features. Challenging the predominantly "respectable" U.S. homophile movement by embracing the sexual revolution, *DRUM* emerged from what one historian has called "the private city" to become the most widely circulating homophile magazine in the country.[11]

Polak's magazine rejected accommodationist appeals to straight readers, declaring in response to homophile critics that the magazine was published "by male homosexuals for the information and entertainment of other male homosexuals."[12] In other words, the magazine imagined the existence of a national community of gay men entitled to autonomous cultural space and a shared network of politics and desire. Written in a gay language with gay-coded photographs for a gay audience, *DRUM* confirms Anderson's argument that "the most important thing about language is its capacity for generating imagined communities, building in effect *particular solidarities*." As Anderson explains and *DRUM* illustrates, print media have played a central role in the development of national imagined communities.[13]

While building gay solidarity, Polak began working to advance gay interests vis-à-vis the national state. With proceeds from *DRUM*, he created the Homosexual Law Reform Society (HLRS), which provided funds and legal support for court cases addressing fundamental U.S. values. In one of HLRS's cases, *Val's v. Division of Alcoholic Beverage Control* (1967), the New Jersey Supreme Court affirmed the rights of "well-behaved apparent homosexuals" to assemble in bars. In a second major HLRS case, *Boutilier v. Immigration and Naturalization Service* (1967), the U.S. Supreme Court upheld immigration restrictions for "homosexuals." Immigration law had long been a site of struggle between competing discourses of U.S. nationalism; now the Court ruled that lesbians and gay men were not welcome in the nation.[14]

While Polak struggled within U.S. political structures, the national state and its local allies worked actively against his movement. Frank Donner has argued that "practices associated with the term *police state* abound in the United States" and that "among such subsequently disclosed police state patterns, Philadelphia's is outstanding." For this reason, Donner calls Philadelphia a "police city."[15] The Federal Bureau of Investigation (FBI), which began monitoring homophile groups elsewhere in the 1950s, initially did so in Philadelphia in 1963. Within a year, the nation's law enforcement apparatus moved strongly against Polak, *DRUM*, and Janus.[16] Direct harassment began when postal inspectors visited Polak to investigate a "series of classified advertisements offering booklets on homosexuality" and advertisements for a "correspondence club." Although officials acknowledged that "none of the pamphlets offered for sale appear to be in violation of Obscenity Statutes," Polak "voluntarily discontinue[d]" the club.[17]

Government agencies soon began conducting a coordinated campaign of surveillance against Janus activists and *DRUM* readers. Richard Schlegel, the founder of a Janus chapter in Harrisburg, lost his job as the Pennsylvania Department of Highways' director of finance in 1965 after the results of postal monitoring of his mail were revealed to his superiors.[18] U.S. Customs blocked Polak's attempts to import "obscene" publications.[19] Warned that publishing "Tropic of Crabs," a parody of Henry Miller's *Tropic of Cancer*, would leave *DRUM* open to obscenity charges, Polak removed the article from all newsstand copies.[20] In 1966, the Buffalo Postmaster temporarily withdrew an entire run of *DRUM* from the mails while he forwarded samples to the Department of Justice for possible obscenity prosecution.[21]

Polak did not fail to respond to these assaults. In addition to reporting on these developments in *DRUM*, he published articles that criticized government practices ("How to Handle a Federal Agent" and "I Was a Homosexual for the FBI") and defended sexual photography ("Frontal

Nudes" and "The Story Behind Physique Photography").[22] (Ever vigilant, postal officials helped the FBI obtain a copy of the parody of the Bureau.[23]) In 1965, Polak also began to include nude centerfolds in copies of *DRUM* sent to subscribers and Janus members. He worked with the American Civil Liberties Union to mobilize support for Schlegel and others victimized by state repression, a strategy that yielded an article in *The New Republic* entitled "Mail Snooping," a congressional investigation, and a change in postal surveillance policy.[24] Ever the profiteer, Polak labelled the *DRUM* issue containing "Tropic of Crabs" "censored" in advertisements for back copies of the magazine, which ensured that this was one of the first issues to sell out.[25] And, in addition to founding the respectable HLRS, Polak created two pornography businesses (Trojan and Beaver Book Services) and bought three adult bookstores.[26]

Interestingly, legal harassment continued despite the fact that high-level officials acknowledged that *DRUM* was not obscene. In 1966, Assistant U.S. Attorney General Fred Vinson, Jr. wrote to Chief Postal Inspector Henry Montague that Janus appeared to be "an 'official' spokesman of proclaimed homosexuality and it would seem, judging by 'Drum' magazine, to take a serious position on homosexuality." Vinson recommended further investigation only if Janus mailed "other homosexual material of a more prurient nature."[27] Similarly, a Philadelphia postal inspector wrote that "the magazine does not appear to be in violation of the federal or Commonwealth of Pennsylvania Obscenity Statutes."[28] Presumably justifying their continued surveillance on the grounds that a magazine that was "speaking" for "proclaimed" homosexuality was presumptively proto-obscene, officials were preemptively striking out, not against same-sex sexual activity but in opposition to public expressions of gay male language.

The Post Office continued to build its case between 1967 and 1969, systematically monitoring Polak's mail, using test purchases, and examining the contents of "broken" packages.[29] Meanwhile, local and state officials, led by then-Philadelphia District Attorney (now U.S. Senator) Arlen Specter, pursued Polak as well. In March 1967, police obtained a search warrant for Polak's house and found approximately "75,000 books and periodicals dealing with homosexuality" and a mailing list "conservatively estimated to contain over 100,000 names." Polak was promptly arrested on obscenity charges. A year later, a local judge ruled that the search warrant had been faulty.[30] In April 1969, Polak was found guilty on new obscenity charges and received a one-to-two-month sentence, which he then appealed.[31]

These, then, were the circumstances immediately surrounding Polak's decision to terminate *DRUM* in May 1969.[32] Polak's troubles, however, were far from over. Two of his bookstores were raided on May 27 and Polak and three of his clerks were arrested on obscenity charges.[33] On July 2, the last day of the Stonewall riots, Philadelphia's postal inspector provided a U.S. Attorney with additional evidence against Polak.[34] Nine days later, he was found guilty of displaying obscene films and fined $550.[35] In October, a grand jury returned an eighteen-count indictment against Polak for violating federal obscenity laws. After an Assistant U.S. Attorney and eight postal inspectors seized 250,000 brochures and a mailing list of approximately 75,000 names from his offices, Polak was then indicted on twenty-one additional obscenity counts.[36]

In February 1970, U.S. District Court Judge Thomas Masterson ordered the police to return the "instrumentalities" seized, declaring that although he was sympathetic to the "attempt to control this sewer effluent" and believed that Polak's "dirty business" would "meet any test of obscenity," he still opposed the government methods used because there had been no prior adversary determination of obscenity.[37] In March, Polak placed a series of advertisements in *Screw* magazine, announcing "Trojan's going back into business sale." Claiming that there had been a fire at Trojan on February 19 (the very day that his offices had been raided and the twenty-one new indictments handed down), the advertisement noted that Trojan's "complete mailing list was destroyed" and that old and new patrons should write for new brochures and new orders, since "miraculously, all of our stock of paperbacks, male nudist magazines, gay movies and other specialty items was saved."[38]

The return of Polak's materials did not mean that federal obscenity charges against him had been dropped. Shortly after terminating *DRUM*, Polak left Philadelphia for southern California. In 1972, in a plea-bargain arrangement, Polak finally agreed to abandon his pornography businesses, pay a $5,000 fine, and be placed on probation for five years.[39]

While activists around the country worked to harness the political energies unleashed by Stonewall, state repression of Polak's activities received little attention.[40] Nevertheless, these developments suggest that we re-think the meaning of the riots. Focusing too much attention on this individual instance of New York police harassment has deflected attention away from the systematic state repression of Richard Nixon's America. Moreover, contrasts between activists in the 1960s and activists in the 1970s are simplified when we make the history of pre-Stonewall gay sexual liberationism disappear and thus contribute to the success of state repression. We also need to continue exploring the critical roles played by language and media in the cultural imagination of local, national, and transnational lesbian and gay communities. If we understand "obscenity" to be the government's term for gay language, the state campaign against "gay English" suggests that the stakes in the struggle to imagine a national gay community were quite high. Finally, it is crucial that we place the efforts of activists to mobilize nationalist discourse in the context of national state repression.

Independence

On Independence Day, 1969, just days after the Stonewall riots and in the midst of the state campaign against Polak, between forty-five and one hundred-fifty activists participated in the fifth "Annual Reminder" demonstration at Independence Hall.[41] As forms of political action, the contrast between drag queens and other bar patrons rioting in Greenwich Village and well-dressed lesbians and gay men peacefully picketing in the "Quaker City" could hardly have been greater. Demonstration leaders, including Philadelphia's Barbara Gittings, spoke to reporters in a language of patriotic respectability: "We are here today to remind the American public that in its homosexual citizens, it has one large minority who are still not benefitting from the high ideals proclaimed for all on July 4, 1776."[42]

Another striking contrast to draw here is between the campy and playful nationalism of Ed Burke's *Berthe of a Nation*, performed in the gay resort of Cherry Grove, Fire Island in 1950, and the earnest and sincere nationalism of the Annual Reminder, performed at a leading Philadelphia tourist attraction in the 1960s. Esther Newton has described two major gay sensibilities: the "camp/theatrical" one, which she sees in *Berthe*, and the "egalitarian/authentic" one, which we can see at the Independence Hall demonstrations. While some spectators undoubtedly saw the Reminders as a big joke, the prevailing tone was quite serious.[43]

Activists in Philadelphia's Mattachine Society (1960–61), Janus Society (1962–70), Daughters of Bilitis (1967–68), and Homophile Action League (1968–72) frequently deployed discourses of patriotism, Americanism, and citizenship. For example, Polak and Janus fought against the exclusion of homosexuals from the military, helping to organize nationally coordinated demonstrations on Armed Forces Day in 1966. Ten thousand leaflets distributed at the Philadelphia Naval Yard declared that "we don't dodge the draft; the draft dodges us." While the Vietnam War was leading many to question U.S. values, homophile activists mobilized patriotic rhetoric to advance their cause.[44] (They did so under the watchful eye of the FBI, which monitored the Reminders and the Armed Forces Day demonstration.[45])

Lesbian and gay activists worked with two U.S. political languages in this period. A libertarian discourse drew on the long tradition of resistance to state infringements of individual rights. This tendency even led Polak to flirt with the idea of endorsing Barry Goldwater for President in 1964. "As the Federal establishment supplies more of the goods and services required for daily living," Polak wrote in *DRUM*, "each of us pays the price in terms of erosion of private liberties. So, Goldwater's cry for limited government is not only appealing, but seems a necessity for the maintenance of the United States as a democratic republic."[46]

More commonly, activists turned to a discourse of minority rights.[47] As we have seen, there were a variety of ways that lesbians and gay men might have articulated their senses of collective identity. At this historical juncture, however, when many in the United States had come to support equality for the African-American "minority," claiming status as a minority group had a great deal of rhetorical power. Minority discourse was particularly useful for lesbians and gay men, who could combat the notion that they were seeking to recruit, convert, or seduce straight people by adopting the common belief that minority groups were biologically, socially, and culturally distinct. Ironically, Philadelphia lesbian and gay activists turned to this discourse despite the fact that they were criticized in *The Philadelphia Tribune*, an African-American newspaper, for sponsoring a lecture that had no African Americans (other than the reporter) in the audience and only one distributing pamphlets.[48]

As had been the case with previous Reminders, the predominantly white picketers in 1969 appropriated the language of the civil rights and Black Power movements. "Gay is Good" buttons were modelled on the "Black is Beautiful" slogan.[49] Gittings told the *Tribune*'s reporter that homosexuals were the country's second largest minority and that "in many ways the homosexual population is the most persecuted (and prosecuted) minority group."[50]

Whether or not this was true, African-American politics offered a variety of models for lesbian/gay appropriation. Polak had earlier compared his struggle against the "respectable" homophile movement, whose politics he decried as "Aunt Maryism," with the fight of the "hip Negro" against the "square Negro," who in other contexts was called an "Uncle Tom."[51] Covering the 1969 Reminder, the national lesbian magazine *The Ladder* was ambiguous about which model it considered most appropriate: "Is it, therefore, impossible to win your rights without violence? Are the only groups to achieve freedom those who carry guns? We are asking into society, not out of it, and more and more, we are wondering why our cry is not heeded. Can it be that we are using a 'language' that cannot be understood?" Offering a vision of integrated and peaceful lesbians and gay men, *The Ladder* simultaneously threatened to turn to a different kind of "language," one that might echo with the sounds of violence that had come to be associated with innercity African-American communities.[52]

In its account of the 1969 demonstration, *Distant Drummer*, a local leftist newspaper, reported on a dispute that erupted when "two girls" began "holding hands on the picket line."[53] Challenging an older generation that had been responsible for the Reminders since 1965 was a younger group much affected by Stonewall, the counterculture, and the women's movement. Demonstration leader Frank Kameny from Washington, D.C. approached the women, "slapped their hands," and said, "You can't do that!"[54] Gittings agreed: "There is a time and a place for holding hands.... On a picket line—no." New York's Craig Rodwell, however, objected: "Our message is that homosexual love is good." Rodwell then began "defiantly marching hand in hand" with his lover. Soon two young female couples did likewise.[55]

Holding hands was not the only bodily transgression frowned upon by organizers. A number of activists who had participated in previous Reminders boycotted the 1969 one in opposition to a dress code that required "neat coat and trousers for men, neat dresses, skirts, or suits for women." Mattachine New York's Dick Leitsch explained that "we cannot support a demonstration that pretends to reflect the feelings of all homosexuals while excluding many," including "drag queens, leather queens," and "groovy men and women whose wardrobe consists of bell-bottoms, vests, and miles of gilt chains."[56]

Holding hands and dressing casually or outrageously threatened the strategy of heterosocial respectability that had been central to the Reminders since their inception. As Mosse's *Nationalism and Sexuality* would lead us to expect, activists combined discourses of nationalism and sexual respectability in the Independence Hall demonstrations.[57] Challenging the cultural effeminization of male homosexuality, the masculinization of female homosexuality, and the pathologization of homosexual bodies, activists presented idealized images of feminine lesbians, masculine gay men, and heterosocial couples in much of their political work. Unlike Polak, whose imagined single-sex community of gay men was founded upon sexual desire, these activists imagined a mixed-sex community of lesbians and gay men founded upon a desexualized social identity. Holding hands proved so controversial in part because the moment that two bodies sexed as "the same" touched, the disembodied and asexual lesbian/gay dyad was revealed to be a strategic construction.

While Reminder activists clashed over the place of heterosocial respectability within a politics of integrationist nationalism, they agreed that lesbians and gay men ought to seek improvements in their status by embracing U.S. national values. New gay liberationists were not walking hand in hand at Independence Hall to signal their rejection of the United States. In a period in which mass movements against the Vietnam War and for Black Power had raised fundamental questions about the nature of U.S.

values, these activists were celebrating the national Fourth of July holiday by taking the liberty of walking together in same-sex pairs, hand-in-hand, before one of the central symbols of U.S. identity. And they were doing so in an "orderly" way that would earn them a commendation from Police Commissioner Frank Rizzo.[58] While generational conflict erupted at the 1969 Reminder, both younger and older activists at the "birthplace of the nation" were claiming what they saw as the rightful place for lesbians and gay men within the United States.

Dominion, Freedom, and Self-Determination

Several months after the final Annual Reminder, in November 1969, gay liberationists from New York, now organized in the Gay Liberation Front, clashed with homophile activists at a meeting of the Eastern Regional Conference of Homophile Organizations (ERCHO) in Philadelphia. Debate focused on the future of the Reminder, antiwar mobilizations, and a series of radical resolutions. ERCHO decided unanimously to replace the Independence Hall demonstrations with an annual Christopher Street Liberation Day that would commemorate the Stonewall riots.[59] The symbolism could hardly have been clearer—the movement's largest annual actions would no longer be held on the nation's birthday in the nation's birthplace, but would instead mark gay liberation's birthday in *its* birthplace.

Although ERCHO met in a city long known as a center of pacifist, antiwar, and peace activism, radicals were less successful with their antiwar proposals.[60] While ERCHO approved a call for lesbians and gay men to take part in the November antiwar mobilization in Washington, D.C. and "to do so as homosexuals," the Conference refused to endorse the mobilization.[61] Still in favor of using the politics of respectable nationalism, ERCHO drew back from attacking the nation's policies abroad.

In fact, ERCHO proved quite willing to use national political discourse, although in ways different from the earlier employment of libertarian and minoritarian rhetoric. Resolving that it considered certain "inalienable human rights above and beyond legislation," ERCHO mobilized natural rights discourse from the Declaration of Independence and the U.S. Constitution. Significantly, the first of these rights was "dominion over one's own body," which included "sexual freedom without regard to orientation" and freedom to use birth control, abortion, and drugs. Whereas the United States had challenged European and American Indian claims to dominion over the land of the North American continent, ERCHO challenged the state's dominion over the bodies of individuals.[62]

The second right, "freedom from society's attempts to define and limit human sexuality," adapted libertarian political discourse. Whereas this discourse traditionally opposed state restrictions on freedom of human action and expression, lesbian and gay activists now challenged social restrictions on freedom of sexual action and expression. Interestingly, the language used here reveals a fundamental tension that marked the politics of gay liberation. For while the first right invoked the concept of sexual "orientation" and the third used the notion of "minority groups," the second opposed social definitions of and limitations on sexuality. But were not the concepts of sexual orientation and minorities a product of "society's attempts to define and limit human sexuality"? While the first and third rights suggested the existence of a group of people whose desires were oriented in particular directions, the second implied the existence of a universally shared polymorphous sexual desire.

The third right, "freedom from political and social persecution of all minority groups," was said to include "the right of self-determination of all oppressed minority groups in our society." Moving beyond the assertion of minority rights within the United States, ERCHO called for the rights of oppressed minorities to be self-determining. This formulation adapted the rhetoric of self-determination from the Declaration of Independence and joined it in embracing the paradoxical notion of *self*-determination by the collective.

In adopting these resolutions, ERCHO was using the time-honored radical strategy of using U.S. revolutionary rhetoric against the state. Calling for self-determination for oppressed minority groups and dominion over individual bodies, ERCHO was simultaneously seeking to limit the power of the state and establish bases for individual and community sovereignty. Although the decision to replace the Reminders represented a step away from U.S. national iconography, these resolutions worked within a now sexualized but still familiar national idiom.

In the wake of the ERCHO conference, Homophile Action League (HAL) leader Carole Friedman wrote that "we hear the call, the appealing call, to commit ourselves to alliances with other minorities, to throw in our lot with the radical left, to strive not for equality within the system, but for a new liberty to be obtained by destroying the system, which is viewed as inherently evil, oppressive by nature, unable to respond fairly to our demands." Friedman explained, however, that "it is our feeling that the radical, humanist, libertarian principles and guarantees built into the U.S. Constitution are still viable, that they still offer the best protections of individual freedoms we know of."[63] Friedman also believed in working within capitalism, calling for the "emancipation of homosexuals from economic dependence" through "gay capitalism" and "gay economic self-determination."[64] By early 1970, the League, along with five other groups, had dissociated itself from a number of ERCHO's radical resolutions.[65] (Despite this fact, the FBI soon was monitoring HAL as part of its surveillance of the women's liberation movement.[66])

While scholars have ignored evidence of radical gay sexual liberationism in the 1960s, we have also failed to consider the possibility that much of the post-Stonewall movement has continued in the tradition of the respectable and patriotic homophile movement. Seen in this light, Stonewall and the gay liberation movement of 1969–70 were brief episodes, and the story of lesbian/gay politics is more continuous than we have wanted to believe. Moreover, although homophile activists in late 1969 favored strategies that involved a less radical reformulation of U.S. national values than what gay liberationists advocated, both groups employed nationalist rhetoric, which suggests an additional example of historical continuity. And this rhetoric shaped not only their conception of lesbian and gay rights but also their notions of lesbian and gay sexualities.

Life, Liberty, and the Pursuit of Happiness

In the summer of 1970, HAL was joined by a new Gay Liberation Front (GLF) in Philadelphia. Like GLFs elsewhere, Philadelphia's group distinguished itself from its homophile predecessors, as was clear in its statement of purpose:

> Homosexual love is the most complete form of expression between two members of the same sex. Philadelphia Gay Liberation Front is struggling to build self-liberating alternatives to society's channeling and limiting of sexual, personal, and political energies. Our fight against homosexual oppression is one with the revolutionary struggle of all oppressed peoples for life, liberty, and the pursuit of happiness.[67]

Rejecting the notion that homosexuality represented a perversion of same-sex relations, GLF celebrated lesbian and gay relationships as more "complete" than their non-sexual homosocial counterparts. In effect, GLF was challenging the boundaries that separated straight women from lesbians and straight men from gay men. As GLF leader and Japanese-American human rights activist Kiyoshi Kuromiya declared in the *Philadelphia Free Press*, "Personally I don't care what heterosexuals do in bed . . . as long as they stop bothering ME and start loving me as a person, fraternally, emotionally AND physically."[68] (And Kuromiya had been "bothered." Born in a Wyoming concentration camp for Japanese-Americans during World War II, Kuromiya was indicted in 1968 on federal and local obscenity charges for his "Fuck the Draft" poster, which was distributed at the Chicago

Democratic Party convention.[69]) Calling for the liberation of same-sex desires in all people, GLF attacked the notion that its struggle was that of a minority group seeking rights and instead encouraged everyone to deepen their same-sex relationships.

GLF's opposition to hegemonic sexual categories was influenced by developments in gay liberation elsewhere and by the lesbian feminist ideas outlined in Radicalesbians-New York's paper, "The Woman-Identified Woman," which was reprinted in Philadelphia's *Gay Dealer.*[70] But it was also informed by GLF's multiracialism and the existence of distinct sexual cultures among people of color, whose opposition to the dominant racial order shaped and was shaped by their opposition to the dominant sexual order. GLF's multiracialism in turn helps explain its commitment to "the revolutionary struggle of all oppressed peoples."

Unlike HAL, which was predominantly white, GLF was multiracial from its inception. A series of "gay dances" sponsored by HAL and GLF in 1970 were the first local movement events to attract large numbers of lesbians and gay men of color.[71] Along with other developments in the histories of various peoples of color in the United States, these dances contributed to the multiracialization of the organized lesbian and gay movement in Philadelphia. While racial conflict led people of color in GLF-NY in the summer of 1970 to form Third World Gay Revolution, GLF-Philadelphia remained multiracial. Kuromiya recalls that the local GLF was "about 30 percent Black, 30 percent Caucasian, 30 percent Latino, and 10 percent Oriental," while another account estimates that the group was 50 percent African-American.[72]

While GLF was multiracial, it did not attract many lesbians of any race. This is not to say that GLF was not feminist. In identifying sexism, capitalism, and racism as the sources of gay oppression, GLF was the first predominantly gay male group in Philadelphia to use feminist rhetoric. Moreover, much of the language used by GLF suggests that it was joining Radicalesbians-New York in calling upon its followers to become women-identified. Yet while GLF understood itself and its goals in feminist terms, it did not work to create a mixed-sex group. Conceiving of itself as part of a movement parallel to women's liberation and lesbian feminism, GLF instead took the lead in helping an isolated lesbian member to form Radicalesbians-Philadelphia in 1971.[73]

Radical in its opposition to hegemonic sexual categories, racism, and sexism, GLF also opposed the earlier nationalist discourses of the homophile movement. Writing in the leftist *Plain Dealer*, Kuromiya likened the Reminders' calls for ending military and federal employment discrimination to petitioning President Nixon "to form a new S.A. [Sturmabteilung—storm troops] as in Nazi Germany."[74] GLF's rejection of integrationist nationalism makes it all the more striking that its statement of purpose concluded by endorsing the struggle for "life, liberty, and the pursuit of happiness," a phrase it appropriated from the Declaration of Independence. When it came time for GLF to define what it had in common with other radical movements, it turned to the revolutionary rhetoric of "Founding Father" Thomas Jefferson.

GLF also joined other revolutionaries in turning to one of the most traditional bases of nationalist claims, the defense of land. Appropriating a term from African-American discourse, GLF was the first group to talk of a "gay ghetto" in Philadelphia's Center City and thus to offer a territorial conception of the gay community in the "City of Neighborhoods." For example, when "homosexuals in Philadelphia's gay ghetto" were "subject to an increasing number of physical attacks and intensified harassment by straights and the police," GLF called for an end to "these incursions."[75]

By late 1970, then, Philadelphia featured HAL, which was predominantly white and lesbian-led and fought for the rights of sexual minorities, and GLF, which was multiracial and predominantly male and encouraged everyone to come out as lesbian or gay. The former sought to transform the nation by working within the structures of the U.S. Constitution, while the latter used the founding rhetoric of the U.S. nation to define the goals of a new revolution.

Constituting the Nation

In September 1970, gay liberationists and lesbian feminists attended the Revolutionary People's Constitutional Convention (RPCC) in Philadelphia.[76] In announcing the Convention, the Black Panther Party called upon African Americans to address the question of their "National Destiny." "If we are to remain a part of the United States," the Panthers explained in a "Message to America" reprinted in the *Philadelphia Free Press*, "then we must have a new Constitution that will strictly guarantee our Human Rights to Life, Liberty, and the Pursuit of Happiness. . . ." ". . . If we cannot make a new arrangement within the United States," the Panthers warned, "then we have no alternative but to declare ourselves free and independent of the United States." For the time being, however, Panther nationalism included an effort to remake the U.S. nation.[77]

Nearly two hundred years before, delegates from thirteen British colonies had gathered in Philadelphia, the largest city in the colonies, to consider independence. Having won that cause, thirteen states then sent delegates to Philadelphia, their capital, to write the U.S. Constitution. By 1970, although Philadelphia's population had fallen to fourth largest among U.S. cities, the percentage of African Americans had risen to 34 percent, and the Panthers could count on the support of important allies among local non-African-American leftists and Quakers.[78] And the Party recognized that the city had gained much symbolic power as the "birthplace of the nation."

The presence of gay liberationists and lesbian feminists at the RPCC followed a period in which gay and lesbian radicals had divided on the question of supporting the Panthers because of what many considered the Party's "anti-gay sexism."[79] For example, in a July 1970 *Black Panther* article attacking Philadelphia's "Pig Mayor Tate and Fascist Rizzo," local Panther "Mumia" described Rizzo as "a product of perversion" who also "produced perversion," both in "the leniency shown to the murders on the Philly Pig Force" and in his "homosexual son." Claiming that "this trend of perversion" had led Rizzo to "send the storm-troopers into the heart of the Black community and conduct the colonization process," "Mumia" also called George Fencl, the head of Rizzo's civil disobedience unit, "Georgey boy faggot Fencl" and "the primal licker" of Rizzo's "boots."[80] These kind of comments made the position of lesbian and gay Panthers difficult and created obstacles to the building of alliances between the Panthers and non-Panther lesbian and gay radicals.

Just weeks before the Convention, however, *Black Panther* published "A Letter from Huey [Newton] to the Revolutionary Brothers and Sisters About the Women's Liberation and Gay Liberation Movements."[81] Reprinted in Philadelphia's *Plain Dealer*, *Free Press*, and *Distant Drummer*, the Panther leader's letter referred to homosexuals and women as "oppressed groups" and called upon his followers to "unite with them." Presuming that his readers were straight males, Newton admitted that "sometimes our first instinct is to want to hit a homosexual in the mouth and to want a woman to be quiet." He explained that this was because "we're afraid we might be homosexual" and that a woman "might castrate us or take the nuts that we may not have to start with." While Newton appeared to recognize the fluidity of identities based on sex and sexuality, he quickly moved to solidify them by pluralistically stating that "we must gain security in ourselves and therefore have respect and feelings for all oppressed people." Homosexuals, he argued, "might be the most oppressed."

In modelling his analysis of sexuality on his understanding of race, Newton largely missed or rejected the anti-minoritarian impulses of gay liberation and lesbian feminism.[82] The Panthers' vision of a transformed U.S. nationalism was based upon the rights of groups with clear identity boundaries—African Americans, women, lesbians, gay men. In fact, RPCC's schedule featured Saturday meetings for "social groupings," which included third-world peoples, women, GIs, students, workers, female homosexuals, male homosexuals, welfare people, street people, and "head workers." ("Topical workshops" would be held on Sunday.)[83] This agenda forced those with multiple identities to choose which one to privilege. Moreover, boundaries between "social groupings" were rarely as clear as they seemed. When a Philadelphia *Inquirer* reporter noticed that 40 percent of the 6,000 people at one session were white, he cleverly suggested that apparently "the meaning of the word black has changed dramatically."[84] A *Tribune* story quoted one local African-American man as saying that he did not consider whites who attended the RPCC to be white.[85]

Although Newton may have thought of homosexuals as a sexual minority, this did not prevent gay or straight men from being drawn to him erotically. When Newton's letter appeared alongside a photograph of his shirtless body, as it did in the *Plain Dealer*, the erotic dimensions of Newton's leadership became more visible.[86] Alice Walker writes that "the charge of being a 'punk'" drove Panther men more than fear of the police or the FBI and she points specifically to a famous "pin-up" photograph that Eldridge Cleaver took that displays Newton as a "punk with revolutionary style." Walker concludes that "these men loved, admired and were sometimes in love with each other," that they might have had sex with men while in prison, and that they were "confused" by all of this.[87] In spite of this confusion, Newton called for "a working coalition" with gay and women's liberation. As we shall see, however, Newton's statement and developments at the RPCC did little to assure lesbian activists that they, too, would be encouraged to participate fully in making the new nation.

That the Panthers continued to believe in U.S. national ideals is all the more surprising when the state campaign against the Party is considered. Just days before the Convention, Philadelphia police raided Panther offices, arresting and beating fourteen men, some of whom were publicly strip searched and photographed bare-assed alongside shotgun-wielding police officers for the city and nation's newspapers and magazines.[88] After attending the Convention, the FBI concluded that there was "a connection between the Homosexual Movement and the Black Panther Party." And a connection there was—not the least of which was in their common experience of state repression.[89]

About sixty gay liberationists joined between 6,000 and 15,000 other delegates to draft the new constitution.[90] The multiracial Male Homosexual Workshop met in a Germantown church, where participants "were treated to the vision of two brothers fucking on top of the church's silk AmeriKKKan flag."[91] (Needless to say, for some this was the climax of the new gay nationalism.) The Workshop's statement was influenced by a "Third World" gay report, which confronted gay whites on racism and asked the

Workshop to "recognize Huey Newton's recently stated position in favor of Gay Liberation as being a tremendous advance in the revolution and that the Black Panther Party holds the most out-front position in terms of the struggle to give power to the people."[92]

As delegates arrived at Temple University's gymnasium to hear the workshop reports, the gay contingent began chanting "GAY POWER TO THE GAY PEOPLE, BLACK POWER TO THE BLACK PEOPLE, RED POWER TO THE RED PEOPLE, WOMAN POWER TO THE WOMEN PEOPLE." Kuromiya read the Workshop's statement to enthusiastic applause.[93] Challenging the delegates to question their sexual identities, the Workshop's statement, reprinted in the *Plain Dealer* and summarized in the *Tribune*, argued that "the revolution will not be complete until all men are free to express their love for one another sexually." According to Kuromiya, the statement "was carefully worded not to show or to present gay liberation as being an oppressed minority fighting for rights but more the process of a society in which people can come out and be all that it's possible to be." Most of the delegates, he recalls, "had never thought in terms of coming out themselves."[94] Just as the Panthers ambitiously wanted to reconstitute U.S. national values, gay liberationists and radical lesbians wanted to reconstitute the nation's sexual values.

Conceiving of anti-gay oppression within a feminist framework, the Workshop stated that "the social institution which prevents us all from expressing our total revolutionary love we define as sexism." The statement recognized the Panthers as "the vanguard of the people's revolution in Amerikkka" and demanded "the right to be gay, any time, any place," that "gays be represented in all governmental and community institutions," that "gays determine the destiny of their own communities," and the "abolition of the nuclear family because it perpetuates the false categories of homosexuality and heterosexuality."

"Oh, it was such a beautiful thing to hear Kiyoshi," one local African-American gay participant recalls, ". . . and to be acknowledged by people that we considered to be our peers and even our idols."[95] "Have you ever heard people say to radicals," one gay reporter wrote soon after the Convention, "'You just want to tear things down, but what do you want to replace it with?' The gathering in Philadelphia was designed to get all oppressed peoples together to answer that question. The new America, as spelled out by the various workshops, is a real turn-on."[96] Another reporter wrote in the *Distant Drummer* that the "most important" accomplishment of the RPCC was "the interracial makeup of the plenary session" and "the cooperative tie forged between the Panthers and the Women's and Gay Liberation movements."[97]

The "new America," however, turned out to turn off the predominantly white contingent of 20-to-25 lesbian feminists who formed the Lesbian Workshop. Initially, these women had been hopeful about the RPCC, particularly because of the role that Panther women played in forging new alliances. "When Afeni Shakur called the Radicalesbians asking them and Gay Liberation Front to Washington for a planning meeting," New York's Lois Hart later wrote, "I was charged with excitement. Afeni Shakur—beautiful Black woman, virile, revolutionary, nickname 'Power'—sexual excitement." Just as men were drawn homoerotically to Panther male leadership, women were drawn homoerotically to Panther female leadership.[98]

Hart later noted that she was a "white woman coming into the Panther presence" at a moment when she was developing a "growing consciousness of Women's and Gay oppression ... questioning the value of working with gay men and their infuriating unconscious sexism—ruling out straight men categorically as SUPER PIG." Hart had difficulties with the "super butch" Panthers, whom she described as "the brown, muscled, bare-armed, deep-voiced Afro-American," and "a straight man's trip in cinemascope and technicolor." The very erotic appeal that Panther men may have held for gay male, straight male, and straight female radicals could easily turn off lesbian feminists. But in meetings that led her to decide that her "real connection to the struggle to transform the Black Liberation movement was in the people of the THIRD WORLD GAY REVOLUTION," Hart helped to secure an agreement that there would be workshops on women's rights and sexual self-determination and a "chairwoman" and a "heavy woman speaker ... with a strong Woman's consciousness" at the Convention.[99]

Not long after the planning meeting, Newton's letter was published to mixed reviews by lesbian activists. While a group of New York lesbians wrote that they were "excited" by Newton's "written gesture of solidarity," Martha Shelley recalls thinking that the statement was "somewhat patronizing ... that homosexuals can be revolutionaries, too.... You know, the great Chairman Huey Newton gives his imprimatur. Thank you, Chairman Huey."[100]

For the most part, Newton's letter discussed the women's and gay liberation movements as if they were composed exclusively of straight women and gay men, respectively. At one point, however, he admitted that he had "hangups" about male but not female homosexuality. "I think it's probably because that's a threat to me maybe," he wrote, "and the females are no threat. It's just another erotic sexual thing."[101] Newton did not refer to the long history of straight male erotic fascination with lesbianism. Moreover, while lesbians might have competed with Newton for women or challenged his "manhood" in various ways (thus representing a real threat), Newton only imagined himself here as the subject or object of male homosexual desire. While lesbians might have welcomed Newton's lack of hangups about their identities, to the extent that he did not regard them as a threat, he might not have realized the distance he would need to travel to address their concerns.

At the Convention, between twenty and twenty-five predominantly white lesbians prepared a statement that in many ways offered a stridently sex-separatist vision of national transformation. "Women are the revolution," they declared in a statement reprinted in the *Plain Dealer*. As their presence at the Convention suggests, however, the Lesbian Workshop's participants were not opposed to working with men. In effect, they were making a bid to be the vanguard of the Convention. Moreover, the Workshop embraced the ideals of other movements, declaring that "women's revolution will be the first fundamental revolution because it will do what all the others aspired to." Demanding "complete control by women of all aspects of our social system," the Workshop called for "sexual autonomy," the "destruction of the nuclear family," "communal care of children," and "reparations" to redress women's status as a "dispersed minority." But the statement also held out a longer-term hope for "equalization of all power resources, so that someday human beings of all sexes can deal with each other on a more realistic level."[102]

The gay and lesbian statements offer revealing contrasts. Both called upon straights to deepen their same-sex relationships, but the men emphasized the sexual aspect of this. Both also pointed to sexism as the foundation of their oppression, but the Male Workshop thought that sexism victimized gay men as well as women. While the gay men asked for representation, the lesbians asked for "control." Both statements favored abolition of the nuclear family, but the men justified this on the grounds that the family perpetuates sexual categories while the women argued that women and children were "owned" by men within families, which they saw as a "microcosm of the fascist state." Finally, the Male Homosexual Workshop declared that the Panthers were the revolutionary vanguard, which the Lesbian Workshop did not support.

Lesbian Workshop members were not pleased with the Convention. Called "sex freaks" in one incident, these women were offended by Panther Michael Tabor's speech, which the *Plain Dealer* said used words that "oppress[ed] our gay comrades."[103] Lesbian criticisms increased when workshop sessions and an all-women's meeting were cancelled and when the "third world woman" scheduled to speak along with Newton was denied access to the building. The group of lesbians from New York reported critically that they listened to Newton "declaiming about the declaration of independence for Black manhood and promising to level the earth in pursuit of the goal of the dignity, glory and flowering of this same Black manhood." The newspaper *RAT* noted that "it was a great disappointment to many that he did not follow up on his earlier statements about Womens Liberation and Gay Liberation."[104]

Gendered as masculine, the Panther's new U.S. nationalism had little appeal for women-identified lesbians. After Newton's speech was followed by a talk by Boston's Sister Audry, whose "rap" they described as "totally devoid of any awareness of women's oppression and merely an echo of male Panther rhetoric," the lesbian delegates from New York began to feel that they were being "fucked over" and that "further relationships to the sexist, manipulative Panther convention" would be pointless. No doubt Panther women were not pleased to have one of their own criticized for "echoing" a Black man, and Panther men could scarcely have missed language suggesting that white women were being "fucked over" by Black men.[105]

The next day, at the Workshop on Self-Determination for Women, lesbian concerns increased further. As the New York group described it, the meeting was "presided over by a Panther woman with male Panther guards ringing the room and balconies." White lesbian demands for "the abolishment of the nuclear family, heterosexual-role programming and patriarchy" were met with "charges of racism and bourgeois indulgence." Calls for twenty-four-hour child-care centers, however, were labelled "right-on revolutionary." One Panther woman, Mother McKeever, who was said to have issued the "loudest" charges of racism, was criticized for referring to the lesbians as "men."[106]

If white lesbian activists failed to avoid racism in their interactions with Panthers, Panthers failed to avoid homophobia in their interactions with lesbians. As would happen many times in the coming years, alliances among straight, lesbian, and gay people of color; straight and lesbian white women; and gay white men foundered on the question of "the family." In the context of the long tradition of white attempts to damage and destroy families of color, straights activists of color tended to identify the family as a source of strength and a foundation for liberation. In the context of the long tradition of straight male domination in the family, white women's liberationists, lesbian feminists, and gay liberationists often pointed to the family as a source of oppression. At the RPCC, openly gay male activists of color apparently supported the Male Homosexual Workshop's indictment of the nuclear family, while women of color at the Workshop on Self-Determination for Women (none of whom have been publicly identified as lesbian) apparently opposed a similar proposal. In the coming years, lesbians of color, including Philadelphia's Anita Cornwell, would articulate their own distinctive positions in continuing debates about "the family."[107]

In the end, falling far short of the lesbian proposals, the Workshop on Self-Determination for Women called for "equal status." On the question of the family, the Workshop's statement declared that, within capitalist culture, the institution of the family has provided the foundation for "the private ownership of people." The Workshop encouraged the growth of "communal households and communal relationships and other alternative forms to the patriarchal family" and specifically demanded the "socialization of housework and child care." Critical of "the family" under "capitalism" and "patriarchy" (which should be understood in the context of the Daniel Patrick Moynihan-led attack on the Black "matriarchal" family), the statement was careful to avoid indicting "the family" in any form.[108] Martha Shelley accused the Panthers of believing that women's "function" was to "bear revolutionary babies" and that, "with regard to women, [the Party] is indistinguishable from the attitude of the German Nazi Party."[109]

The Workshop also declared that "every woman has the right to decide whether she will be homosexual, heterosexual, or bisexual." This minoritarian formulation was clearly at odds with the Lesbian Workshop's call for all "women-identified women" to deepen their same-sex relationships. Finally, the Workshop issued a demand for "equal participation in government," which fell short of the Lesbian Workshop's call for women to have "complete control." Shelley would soon write:

> the reason gay males were fairly well treated at the Convention was that they simply asked to be allowed to be gay and to fight alongside the Panthers. Women asked for "that amount of control of all production and industry that would ensure one hundred percent control over our own destinies." In short, women asked for *real* power, and the Panthers freaked out.[110]

After the self-determination workshop, the radical lesbians from New York decided to "split," attributing their decision to "threats of violence" and "the prevailing atmosphere of sexism." They concluded that their "efforts would be wasted in trying to deal with men without the power to validate our demands. We had attempted to negotiate on enemy territory and found it oppressive and unworkable." ". . . If women continue to struggle for their liberation within contexts defined by sexist male mentalities," these lesbians argued, "they will never be free." Lesbian feminists were issuing their own declaration of independence.[111]

At the final plenary, a Women's Liberation delegate and a GLF delegate "called attention to the absence of a Lesbian report," and urged "the inclusion of Gay women as a necessary part of a new Constitution."[112] By this time, however, it was too late. The New York lesbian feminists soon announced in the newspaper *Come Out* that "we women of a dispersed nation will build our community, speak in a woman's language born from our woman's oppression, grow strong together and explode in our women's revolution." At the Convention, women had been a "dispersed minority" fighting on what they described as "enemy territory." Influenced by the Convention, women were now a "dispersed nation," speaking a "woman's language."[113]

The Panthers left the Convention with bitter feelings toward white lesbian feminists and women's liberationists. One Panther told a reporter, "'We are being used by the whites.... They are trying to take over, forcing their mores on us.'" The reporter explained that this Panther and others "were specifically aiming their barbs at the Women's Liberation delegates."[114]

The next meeting of the Constitutional Convention, which took place in Washington, D.C. in November, met with more severe government repression and failed to overcome logistical problems. According to Philadelphia's *Gay Dealer*, the Male Homosexual Workshop proved to be "the largest such gathering to date, with over one hundred-fifty gay revolutionaries from all over the country."[115] Seven hundred women met and passed a resolution of support for the Panthers. Endorsing women's liberation, this statement attacked the role played by the group of white lesbian feminists in Philadelphia. These women, the resolution stated, "while blatantly overstepping their bounds as whites," sought to "invalidate the experience of Black women." "How relevant to Black women's lives are the white middle class women's demands for 'the abolition of the nuclear family' when Black families are being savagely uprooted . . .?" Arguing that Black women suffered from male and white supremacy, the resolution concluded that "since most Black women choose to struggle for liberation with Black men, can we not then assume that the overriding problem of Black women as they see it is that of white supremacy?"[116]

Not longer after it began, the Panther-led project of reconstituting the nation was over. A Panther statement explained that the Washington meeting was a gathering of "revolutionary peoples from oppressed communities throughout the world," not the nation. Declaring that U.S. imperialism had "transformed other nations" into "oppressed communities," the Panthers announced that they would no longer conceive of themselves as "nationalists" or "internationalists." Instead, the Party embraced what it called intercommunalism, a philosophy that simultaneously embraced the rights of communities to "write their own constitutions for self-governance" and sought to create "a new constitution for a new world."[117] The Panthers had effectively yielded the field of Black nationalism to others. Henceforth Black nationalism would be conceived of not as a project of remaking the U.S. nation but rather as the search to define a place for a nation within a nation, a nation that crosses other nations, or a new nation. These latter senses of nationalism would most strongly influence the development of "the lesbian nation" in the 1970s and the "queer nation" in the 1990s.

Imagining Non-National and Anti-National Communities and Histories

Lesbian and gay nationalism is no more a unitary phenomenon than is nationalism in general.[118] In just over a year and in only one urban center, lesbians and gay men encountered the power of the nation-state to apply force inside and outside its borders (as in the state campaign against Clark Polak) and to mobilize identifications and allegiances through language and symbols (as in the Declaration of Independence, the U.S. Constitution, and Independence Hall). *DRUM* magazine imagined a kind of community that has much in common with those imagined communities that Anderson links to the "origin and spread of nationalism." In legal strategies such as those employed in *Boutilier*, demonstrations on Armed Forces Day and the Fourth of July, and statements that endorsed "life, liberty, and the pursuit of happiness," lesbians and gay men deployed dominant discourses of U.S. nationalism. Even political revolutionaries in GLF and at the RPCC turned to ideas of nationalism in a general sense and to the idioms and iconography of U.S. nationalism more specifically in their efforts to create a new nation. Whether aiming for liberal reform within the *substance* of hegemonic nationalist discourse, radical revolution within the *forms* of hegemonic nationalist discourse, or declarations of independence to produce *new* nationalist discourse, lesbian and gay activists in Philadelphia after Stonewall were nationalists.

Deploying discourses of nationalism, lesbians and gay men in turn were themselves deployed by and within these discourses. U.S. nationalism shaped what it meant to be a lesbian or gay citizen, patriot, or "American" in Philadelphia and in the United States. It shaped what it meant to be a lesbian or gay conservative, liberal, radical, or revolutionary. It shaped what lesbians and gay men thought about relationships between and among their selves, societies, and states. It shaped the ways in which lesbians and gay men conceived of the sexualities of "other" cultures, including cultures of the past. And it even shaped lesbian and gay conceptions of their desires, bodies, relationships, sexes, genders, and sexualities.

Twice in the recent past, lesbians and gay men have explicitly and collectively conceived of themselves as nations. First was the Lesbian Nation, the Stonewall Nation, and the Gay Nation of the 1970s; more recently it was the Queer Nation of the 1990s.[119] As suggested above, however, lesbians and gay men have also articulated their senses of collective identities through means other than the language of nation and nationalism. In the homophile movement of the 1950s and '60s, for example, lesbians and gay men most often imagined their community as a "minority" or a "society." (Mattachine and Janus, after all, called themselves "Societies.") More recently, the March 1995 conference "Black Nations/Queer Nations?: Lesbian and Gay Sexualities in the African Diaspora" invoked (and questioned) not only the term "nation" but also the continental, transnational, and transcontinental "African Diaspora."

After the RPCC in 1970, the Panthers abandoned the languages of nation, nationalism, and internationalism in favor of the languages of community, communalism, and intercommunalism. Interestingly, a similar shift is underway in "U.S." lesbian/gay historical scholarship. In 1976, Jonathan Ned Katz titled his groundbreaking documentary collection *Gay American History: Lesbians and Gay Men in the U.S.A.* Seven years later, John D'Emilio's *Sexual Politics, Sexual Communities* was subtitled *The Making of a Homosexual Minority in the United States.*[120]

More recently, Esther Newton's *Cherry Grove, Fire Island: Sixty Years in America's First Gay and Lesbian Town*, Elizabeth Lapovsky Kennedy and Madeline D. Davis's *Boots of Leather, Slippers of Gold: The History of a Lesbian Community*, and George Chauncey's *Gay New York: Gender, Urban Culture, and the Making of the Gay Male World, 1890–1940* all fall within the genre of "community" or local studies.[121] This shift reflects a number of factors, including the tendency within U.S. historical scholarship for the production of general monographs to be followed by more specific studies that build upon and challenge earlier work until new syntheses are attempted. New interest in the politics of everyday life and culture has contributed to this process as well. Community studies also are taking advantage of a growth in local lesbian/gay libraries and archives. And community studies are proving to be appealing to large audiences because of the powerful role that "place" has in people's lives.

But there is an additional meaning that can be given to this shift, a meaning that relates to the signs of new localism, new nationalism, new transnationalism, and new globalism that are apparent as we approach the end of the twentieth century. While the power of nation states demands that oppositional political movements continue to organize nationally in some ways, the structures of local, transnational, and global power similarly demand local, transnational, and global historical analyses and responses. And in one sense, perhaps the measure of our success will be whether lesbian and gay "community" studies, either individually or collectively, prove to be intercommunal.

While historical trajectories can be traced from the Armed Forces Day and Annual Reminder demonstrations of the 1960s to the "gays in the military" struggle of the 1990s and from Black nationalism in the 1960s through Lesbian nationalism in the 1970s to Queer nationalisms in the 1990s, they can also be traced from Black Panther intercommunalism in the 1970s through the Rainbow Coalition of the 1980s to the struggle for multiculturalism in the 1990s. Having revisited the lessons learned by the Panthers twenty-five years ago, it is well worth beginning anew with the *OED*'s definition of "community":

> 1. The quality of appertaining to or being held by all in common. . . .
> 2. Common character; quality in common; commonness, agreement, identity. . . .
> 3. Social intercourse; fellowship, communion. . . .
> 4. Life in association with others; society, the social state. . . .
> 5. Commonness, ordinary occurrence. . . .
> 6. The body of those having common or equal rights or rank, as distinguished from the privileged classes. . . .
> 7. A body of people organized into a political, municipal, or social unity: a. A state or commonwealth. . . . b. A body of men living in the same locality. . . . c. Often applied to those members of a civil community, who have certain circumstances of nativity, religion, or pursuit, common to them but not shared by those among whom they live. . . . d. *The community*: the people of a country (or district) as a whole; the general body to which all alike belong, the public. . . .
> 8. *spec.* A body of persons living together, and practising, more or less, community of goods. . . .[122]

We might also turn to the *OED*'s first two definitions of "intercommune":

> 1. *intr.* To have mutual communion: to hold discourse or conversation with each other or with another. . . .
> 2. To have intercourse, relations, or connexion, esp. in *Sc. Law*, with rebels or denounced persons. . . .[123]

After explaining that "the nation is always conceived as a deep, horizontal comradeship," Anderson argues that "ultimately it is this fraternity that makes it possible, over the past two centuries, for so many millions of people, not so much to kill, as willingly to die for such limited imaginings."[124] Left unanswered is the question of whether such dangers lie as well in the fraternal and sororial bonds of non-national imagined communities, for which so many lesbians and gay men have longed so strongly and deeply.

Acknowledgments

The Center for Lesbian and Gay Studies (City University of New York Graduate Center) Ken Dawson Award, the University of Pennsylvania History Department, and an Andrew W. Mellon Postdoctoral Fellowship at Bryn Mawr College have supported work on this essay. I presented earlier versions at the Sixth North American Lesbian, Gay, and Bisexual Studies Conference in Iowa City, the Gay and Lesbian Studies Workshop at the University of Chicago, the "Black Nations/Queer Nations?" conference in New York, and the Mellon Seminar in the Humanities at Bryn Mawr College, and as "Approaching Stonewall from the City of Sisterly and Brotherly Loves," *Gay Community News*, June 1994, 14–15, 30. For their library and archival support, I thank Pat Allen, David Azzolina, Steven Capsuto, Douglas Haller, Brenda Marston, and Tommi Avicolli Mecca. For their comments and suggestions, I thank Henry Abelove, Christie Balka, Brett Beemyn, Rose Beiler, Stephen Best, Mary Frances Berry, Stephanie Camp, Chris Castiglia, George Chauncey, Steve Conn, Marla Erlien, Susan Garfinkel, Lori Ginzberg, Larry Goldsmith, Herman Graham, Chad Heap, Ed Hermance, Alison Isenberg, James Johnson, Michael Katz, Kevin Kopelson, Jay Lockenour, Jeff Maskovsky, Stephanie Poggi, Chris Reed, Leila Rupp, Liam Riordan, Nayan Shah, Carroll Smith-Rosenberg, Julie Sneeringer, Sharon Ullman, Rhonda Williams, and Kate Wilson. I thank my father for my *Oxford English Dictionary*. For political inspiration, I thank the members of Philadelphia's "Queer Action," 1990–91.

Notes

1. *The Compact Edition of the Oxford English Dictionary, Volume I* (Oxford: Oxford University Press, 1971), 1897.
2. Havelock Ellis, *Studies in the Psychology of Sex*, 4 vols. (New York: Random House, 1936), vol. 2, part 2, *Sexual Inversion* (3rd ed., 1915), 350–51; George Chauncey, *Gay New York: Gender, Urban Culture, and the Making of the Gay Male World, 1890–1940* (New York: Basic Books, 1994), 7.
3. George L. Mosse, *Nationalism and Sexuality: Respectability and Abnormal Sexuality in Modern Europe* (New York: Howard Fertig, 1985); Andrew Parker, Mary Russo, Doris Sommer, and Patricia Yaeger, eds., *Nationalisms and Sexualities* (New York: Routledge, 1992), 1, 4.
4. Benedict Anderson, *Imagined Communities: Reflections on the Origin and Spread of Nationalism* (1983; New York: Verso, rev. edition, 1991), 7; Parker, et al., *Nationalisms and Sexualities*, 6; Ruthann Robson, *Lesbian (Out)Law: Survival Under the Rule of Law* (Ithaca: Firebrand Books, 1992), 11.
5. Parker, et al., *Nationalisms and Sexualities*, 8.

6. On the "Lesbian Nation," see Jill Johnston, *Lesbian Nation: The Feminist Solution* (New York: Simon and Schuster, 1973); Lillian Faderman, *Odd Girls and Twilight Lovers: A History of Lesbian Life in Twentieth-Century America* (New York: Columbia University Press, 1991), 216–45; Alice Echols, *Daring to Be Bad: Radical Feminism in America, 1967–1975* (Minneapolis: University of Minnesota Press, 1989), 220–86; Arlene Stein, "Sisters and Queers: The Decentering of Lesbian Feminism," *Socialist Review* 22, no. 1 (January-March 1992): 33–55. On "Queer Nation," see Michael Warner, "Introduction: Fear of a Queer Planet," *Social Text*, no. 29 (1991): 3–17; Teresa de Lauretis, "Queer Theory: Lesbian and Gay Sexualities, An Introduction," *differences* 3, no. 2 (1991): iii-xviii; Lauren Berlant and Elizabeth Freeman, "Queer Nationality," *Boundary 2* 19, no. 2 (1992): 149–80; Allan Bérubé and Jeffrey Escoffier, "Queer/Nation," *OUT/LOOK*, no. 11 (Winter 1992): 13–15; Alexander S. Chee, "A Queer Nationalism," *OUT/LOOK*, no. 11 (Winter 1992): 15–19; Maria Maggenti, "Women As Queer Nationals," *OUT/LOOK*, no. 11 (Winter 1992): 20–23; Lisa Duggan, "Making It Perfectly Queer," *Socialist Review* 22, no. 1 (January-March 1992): 11–31; Michael Warner, ed., *Fear of a Queer Planet: Queer Politics and Social Theory* (Minneapolis: University of Minnesota Press, 1993). On late 1970 proposals for a "Stonewall Nation" and a "Gay Nation," see Donn Teal, *The Gay Militants* (New York: Stein and Day, 1971), 312–20.
7. See John D'Emilio, *Sexual Politics, Sexual Communities: The Making of a Homosexual Minority in the United States, 1940–1970* (Chicago: University of Chicago Press, 1983); Martin Duberman, *Stonewall* (New York: Dutton, 1993).
8. Duggan, "Making It Perfectly Queer," 16.
9. *The Compact Edition of the Oxford English Dictionary, Volume I*, 1898.
10. Clark Polak, "Memo on the Janus Society Board Meeting," October 28, 1964, Janus Society pamphlet, undated, Janus Society File, International Gay and Lesbian Archives (IGLA), West Hollywood, California.
11. Clark Polak, *Janus Society Newsletter* (February 1965): 2, International Gay Information Center Archives (IGIC), Rare Book and Manuscripts Division, The New York Public Library, New York, New York; Polak, "Memo on the Janus Society Board Meeting," IGLA. See also Marc Stein, "Sex Politics in the City of Sisterly and Brotherly Loves," *Radical History Review*, no. 59 (Spring 1994): 60–92; Marc Stein, "The City of Sisterly and Brotherly Loves: The Making of Lesbian and Gay Movements in Greater Philadelphia, 1948–72," Ph.D. dissertation, University of Pennsylvania, 1994. The reference to "the private city" comes from Sam Bass Warner, Jr., *The Private City: Philadelphia in Three Periods of Its Growth* (Philadelphia: University of Pennsylvania Press, 1968).
12. *DRUM*, nos. 18–19 (September 1966): 4.
13. Anderson, *Imagined Communities*, 133.
14. *One Eleven Wine and Liquors Inc. v. Division of Alcoholic Beverage Control* 235 A.2d 12 (N.J. 1967); *Boutilier v. Immigration and Naturalization Service* 387 U.S. 118 (1967). *Val's* was linked with *One Eleven*. On the HLRS's support, see *DRUM* and the *Janus Society Newsletter*, 1965–68, IGIC and the Lesbian and Gay Library/Archives of Philadelphia, Pennsylvania; Charles Alverson, "A Minority's Plea," *Wall Street Journal*, July 17, 1968, 1, 22, reprinted in *The Ladder* 13, nos. 1–2 (October-November 1968): 38–40; Marc Stein, "*Boutilier* Revisited: Lesbian/Gay Law Reform and the Limits of Sexual Liberalism on the Warren

Court," unpublished paper presented at the American Society for Legal History conference, Memphis, Tennessee, October 1993.

15. Frank Donner, *Protectors of Privilege* (Berkeley: University of California Press, 1990), 197.
16. In 1963, an FBI agent, Philadelphia Morals Squad members, and Philadelphia assistant district attorneys attended a Janus lecture by Donald Webster Cory. In the same year, the FBI obtained materials from the East Coast Homophile Organizations convention held at Philadelphia's Drake Hotel. SAC Philadelphia to FBI Director, February 4, 1963, FBI Mattachine Society File (HQ100–403320); SAC Philadelphia to FBI Director, September 27, 1963, FBI Mattachine Society File (100–33796). These materials are available at FBI headquarters in Washington, D.C. See also *The Ladder* 7, no. 7 (April 1963): 15; Larry Bush, "Has the FBI Been in Your Closet?," *Advocate*, no. 346 (July 8, 1982): 16–20, 24. On the campaign that began in 1964, see the results of a Freedom of Information Act request Polak filed in 1975, now in the possession of Polak's lawyer, Norman Oshtry, in Philadelphia. I thank Oshtry for sharing these materials with me and Claire Potter and John Noakes for helping me navigate the FBI's bureaucratic geography.
17. Report of Philadelphia Postal Inspector, June 30, 1965, Norman Oshtry Papers, Philadelphia, Pennsylvania; Interview with Lewis Coopersmith, June 9, 1993. Unless otherwise noted, I conducted all interviews cited.
18. Richard Schlegel Papers, Human Sexuality Collection, Rare and Manuscript Collections, Carl A. Kroch Library, Cornell University, Ithaca, New York; Oshtry Papers; 1965 correspondence (V29/FQ8000.22B, V1/FA1000–1001) and 1966 correspondence (V1/FA1001), American Civil Liberties Union (ACLU) Archives, Seeley G. Mudd Manuscript Library, Princeton University, Princeton, New Jersey; Clark Polak to Schlegel, March 31, 1965, Janus Society File, IGLA; Interview with Richard Schlegel, May 9–10, 1993.
19. Spencer Coxe to Clark Polak, January 28, 1965, Oshtry Papers; Hymen Schwartz to Janus Society, April 19, 1965 (V1/FA1000), ACLU Archives; Correspondence, depositions, and legal documents, November 17, 1965 through October 28, 1966 (V3/FA1003), ACLU Archives; *DRUM* 6, no. 2 (April 1966): 4.
20. Press release, undated, Mattachine Society Records (Box 7/F18), IGIC; *Janus Society Newsletter* (February 1965): 1–2, IGIC; Clark Polak to Dick [Schlegel], undated, Janus Society File, IGLA; Clark Polak, "The Legacy," *DRUM* 5, no. 3 (May 1965): 2.
21. Saul Mindel to Chief Postal Inspector, February 18, 1966, H. B. Montague to Fred Vinson, Jr., March 11, 1966, Report of Philadelphia Postal Inspector, March 15, 1966, Montague to Vinson, March 30, 1966, Oshtry Papers; Correspondence, March 17 through May 10, 1966 (V1/FA1001, V3/FA1003), ACLU Archives; *Janus Society Newsletter* (March 1966): 1, IGLA.
22. "How to Handle a Federal Agent," *DRUM* 4, no. 10 (December 1964): 15–16; "P. Arody," "I Was a Homosexual for the FBI," *DRUM* 5, no. 1 (March 1965): 14–15; Clark Polak, "Frontal Nudes," *DRUM* 5, no. 5 (July 1965): 2, 22; Clark Polak, "The Story Behind Physique Photography," *DRUM* 5, no. 8 (October 1965): 8–15.
23. D. J. Brennan, Jr. to J. J. Dunn, Jr., January 22, 1965, M. A. Jones to Mr. DeLoach, February 10, 1965, FBI Mattachine Society File, HQ100–403320.

24. "Mail Snooping," *The New Republic* 153, nos. 8–9 (August 21, 1965): 6–7; *DRUM* 5, no. 8 (October 1965): 5; Camden Postal Inspector to Henry Montague, August 5, 1965, Clark Polak to Bernard Fensterwald, Jr., August 5, 1965, Polak correspondence, September 1, 1965, Oshtry Papers; "The Watch on the Mails," *Newsweek* 67, no. 24 (June 13, 1966): 24. See also "New Attacks on Postal Censorship," *Publishers Weekly* 187, no. 5 (February 1, 1965): 63; "Mail-Tapping," *America* 112, no. 11 (March 13, 1965): 344; "House Repasses Bill to Stop 'Morally Offensive' Mail," *Publishers Weekly* 187, no. 16 (April 19, 1965): 69; "Showdown Coming on the Billion-Dollar 'Smut Industry,'" *U.S. News and World Report* 59, no. 23 (December 6, 1965): 68, 70.
25. See advertisements in *DRUM*, 1967–69.
26. Greg Walter, "Incest Is In," *Philadelphia Magazine* 59, no. 10 (October 1968): 78–79, 144–51; Arno Karlen, *Sexuality and Homosexuality: A New View* (New York: W. W. Norton, 1971), 540–41. See also extensive references to Trojan and Beaver in the *Janus Society Newsletter*, *DRUM*, the archival collections noted, Oshtry Papers, Interview with Schlegel, Interview with Norman Oshtry, May 25, 1993.
27. Fred M. Vinson, Jr. to Henry Montague, April 4, 1966, Oshtry Papers.
28. Report of Philadelphia Postal Inspector, June 30, 1965, Oshtry Papers.
29. Reports of Philadelphia Postal Inspector and Correspondence, 1967–69, Oshtry Papers. Postal reports provide historians with evidence for measuring the extent of Polak's operations. In 1969, for example, he purchased more than $30,000 worth of postage and, in one eight-day period, sent an average of 1,504 pieces of mail daily. Philadelphia Postal Inspector to Louis C. Bechtle, February 5, 1970, Philadelphia Postal Inspector to Chief Postal Inspector, February 24, 1970, Philadelphia Postal Inspector to Drew J.T. O'Keefe, May 5, 1969, Oshtry Papers.
30. Philadelphia Postal Inspector's Report, March 22, 1967; Philadelphia Postal Inspector to Chief Postal Inspector, March 27, 1968, Oshtry Papers. See also "Pornography Cache Found, Police Charge," *Evening Bulletin*, March 13, 1967, 32; "Burglary Arrests Lead to Smut Pinch," *Daily News*, March 13, 1967, 20.
31. Philadelphia Postal Inspector's Report, May 5, 1969, Oshtry Papers.
32. Clark Polak, "To All [Janus] Members And [*DRUM*] Subscribers," May 5, 1969, Janus Society File, IGLA.
33. "Police Raiders Arrest 6, Seize 2 Films as Obscene," *Evening Bulletin*, May 28, 1969, 17; "6 Are Arrested in Raids on 3 'Peep Shows,'" *Inquirer*, May 28, 1969, 53; Jim Smith and Tom Fox, "Six Charged, Films Seized in Midcity Obscenity Raids," *Daily News*, May 28, 1969, 6; "2 Men Charged with Contempt in Obscenity Case," *Evening Bulletin*, June 3, 1969 (not in microfilmed edition, but see Temple University Urban Archives, Philadelphia, clipping file for Clark Polak); "2 Men Held in Contempt," *Inquirer*, June 3, 1969, 31; "Judge Rules Two in Contempt for Withholding Films," *Daily News*, June 3, 1969, 26.
34. Philadelphia Postal Inspector to Louis Bechtle, U.S. Attorney, Eastern District of Pennsylvania, July 2, 1969, Oshtry Papers.
35. "One Convicted, Five Freed in Obscenity Case," *Evening Bulletin*, July 12, 1969, 3.
36. Grand jury indictments, *U.S. v. Clark P. Polak*, U.S. District Court for the Eastern District of Pennsylvania, No. 69–329, October 23, 1969; Memorandum in Support of Defendant's Motion to Suppress Evidence and Return Property, *U.S. v. Clark P. Polak*, No. 70–57, U.S. District Court for the Eastern District of Pennsyl-

vania; Grand jury indictments, *U.S. v. Clark P. Polak*, U.S. District Court for the Eastern District of Pennsylvania, No. 70–57, February 19, 1970; *U.S. v. Clark P. Polak*, U.S. Court of Appeals for the Third Circuit, Brief for the Appellant, Oshtry Papers; "Jury Charges Obscene Ads," *Inquirer*, February 20, 1970, 42; "Arch St. Dealer Indicted on Obscenity Charge," *Evening Bulletin*, February 20, 1970 (not in microfilmed edition, but see clipping in Oshtry Papers). At his office, Polak "had to be restrained by his attorney from abusing the inspectors with obscenities and insults." Philadelphia Postal Inspector to Chief Postal Inspector, February 19, 1970, Oshtry Papers. Oshtry would later claim in court that "this massive search and seizure has, to put it simply, wiped out the defendant's business" and had a "staggering impact on the exercise of First Amendment freedoms by the defendant and a large segment of the general public." Memorandum in Support of Defendant's Motion to Suppress Evidence and Return Property.

37. Hearing sur: Defendant's Motion to Suppress Evidence and Return Property, March 20, 1970, *U.S. v. Clark P. Polak*, U.S. District Court for the Eastern District of Pennsylvania, No. 70–57, Oshtry Papers. See also "U.S. Judge Voids Evidence Obtained in Obscenity Raid," *Evening Bulletin*, May 1, 1970, 27; "Press Freedom Applies to Ads, Judge Rules," *Inquirer*, May 2, 1970, 23. Masterson also wrote that the government's argument was "an extremely dangerous one because a projection of it would be if a man utters an obscenity you could seize his voice box." The government's appeal was denied on May 12, 1970 by the U.S. Court of Appeals for the Third Circuit.
38. Advertisements, *Screw*, March 15, 1970, 22; *Screw*, March 22, 1970, 26; *Screw*, March 29, 1970, 26.
39. Philadelphia Postal Inspector to Chief Postal Inspector, February 14, 1972, February 25, 1972, Oshtry Papers. Three years later, after filing a Freedom of Information Act request, Polak learned of the extensive state campaign against him. Oshtry Papers. In 1980, he committed suicide. *National Gay Archives Bulletin*, Fall 1983, IGLA.
40. Exceptions included Byrna Aronson's piece in the *Homophile Action League Newsletter* 3, no. 1 (September 25, 1970): 2, Lesbian and Gay Library/Archives of Philadelphia; Lige and Jack, "Poor 'ol Clark," *Screw*, February 16, 1970, 13.
41. Bill Wingell, "A Time for Holding Hands," *Distant Drummer*, July 10, 1969, 8; "150 Homosexuals Parade Before Independence Hall to Protest Maltreatment," *Tribune*, July 12, 1969, 5; Len Lear, "Confederate Flag Flies Atop White House," *Tribune*, July 15, 1969, 9, 28; *The Ladder* 14, nos. 1–2 (October-November 1969): 1, 39–40, 46. As has often been the case with media accounts of political demonstrations, estimates of the number of participants varied widely.
42. "150 Homosexuals Parade."
43. Esther Newton, *Cherry Grove, Fire Island* (Boston: Beacon Press, 1993), 85–88.
44. Clark Polak, "Homophile Conference," *DRUM* 6, no. 2 (April 1966): 25–26; *The Ladder* 10, no. 7 (April 1966): 4–5; Correspondence, April 1966, Mattachine Society Records (Box 3/F2), IGIC; "Homosexuals Open Drive to Serve in Armed Forces," *Evening Bulletin*, April 17, 1966, 35; *DRUM*, nos. 18–19 (September 1966): 27–28; *DRUM*, no. 23 (1967): 25; Janus Society, "Homosexuals and the Armed Forces—A Moral Dilemma," flier, Janus Society File, IGLA. For earlier work on this issue, see *JANUS* 4, no. 2 (February 1964): 6; *JANUS* 4, no. 4 (April

1964): 5–6, 15; *JANUS* 4, no. 6 (June 1964): 4, 16, Lesbian and Gay Library/Archives of Philadelphia.

45. SAC Philadelphia to FBI Director, May 6, 1966, FBI Philadelphia to FBI Director, May 22, 1966, SAC Philadelphia to FBI Director, May 23, 1966, FBI Philadelphia Report, May 23, 1966, FBI Philadelphia to FBI Director, June 21, 1966, SAC Philadelphia to FBI Director, July 28, 1966, FBI Philadelphia to FBI Director, July 4, 1967, FBI Mattachine Society File (HQ100–403320); FBI Philadelphia to FBI Director, July 3, 1967, SAC WFO to SA, July 3, 1967, FBI Mattachine Society File (100–33796).
46. Clark Polak, "Liberty in the Defense of Vice Is No Extreme," *DRUM* 4, no. 9 (November 1964): 2, 16. Polak wrote that because Goldwater's "stand for the good old morality is in direct contradiction to his own basic concept of freedom for the individual," he hoped he would be defeated.
47. See, for example, A. B. [Ada Bello] and C. F. [Carole Friedman], "Homosexuals as a Minority," *Homophile Action League Newsletter* 1, no. 7 (May 1969): 1–3, Lesbian and Gay Library/Archives of Philadelphia.
48. John Wilder, "Homosexuals See Hope for Selves by Negro Victory in Rights Drive," *Tribune*, February 25, 1964, 3; *JANUS* 4, no. 3 (March 1964): 3, Lesbian and Gay Library/Archives of Philadelphia; "Charles Philips" [Clark Polak], letter to the editor, *Tribune*, March 3, 1964, 5.
49. Wingell, "A Time for Holding Hands."
50. "150 Homosexuals Parade."
51. Clark Polak, "The Homosexual Puzzle, Part One," *DRUM* 5, no. 10 (December 1965): 13–17, 26–27; *Janus Society Newsletter* (September 1966): 1, IGLA. See also Gilbert Cantor, "Anticipations—Legal and Philosophical," Address at the East Coast Homophile Organizations (ECHO) Conference, September 25, 1965, ECHO Papers, Lesbian and Gay Library/Archives of Philadelphia.
52. *The Ladder* 14, nos. 1–2 (October-November 1969): 39–40.
53. Wingell, "A Time for Holding Hands."
54. Bill Weaver, cited in Teal, *The Gay Militants*, 30.
55. Wingell, "A Time for Holding Hands."
56. *Homophile Action League Newsletter* 1, no. 7 (May 1969): 4, Lesbian and Gay Library/Archives of Philadelphia; Dick Leitsch to Barbara Gittings, June 24, 1969, Mattachine Society Records (Box 2/F1), IGIC. See also *Mattachine Society of New York Newsletter* (July 1969): 9, Gay and Lesbian Historical Society of Northern California, San Francisco, California.
57. Mosse, *Nationalism and Sexuality*, 40–43.
58. J. Bradley, "Report on the Fall Homophile Conference," undated [1969], Schlegel Papers (Box 4).
59. ERCHO Minutes, November 1–2, 1969, cited by Toby Marotta, *The Politics of Homosexuality* (Boston: Houghton Mifflin, 1981), 164.
60. See, for example, Margaret Hope Bacon, *Mothers of Feminism: The Story of Quaker Women in America* (New York: Harper and Row, 1986) and *One Woman's Passion for Peace and Freedom: The Life of Mildred Scott Olmsted* (Syracuse: Syracuse University Press, 1993).
61. Bob Martin, "ERCHO Meeting Adopts Radical Manifesto," *Advocate* 4, no. 1 (January 1970): 24. See also Teal, *The Gay Militants*, 87; "ERCHO Spring Conference," *Gay Power* 1, no. 7 (1969): 6; Madolin Cervantes, "Autumn Confer-

ence of E.R.C.H.O. Meets in Philadelphia," *GAY*, no. 1 (1 December 1969): 3, 10. While Martin reported that this motion was finally adopted, 48–7 with 10 abstentions, *Gay Power*, Cervantes, Teal, and later references to this vote made no mention of this.

62. Ibid.
63. C. F. [Carole Friedman], "Whither the Movement," *Homophile Action League Newsletter* 2, no. 1 (November-December 1969): 1–2, Lesbian and Gay Library/Archives of Philadelphia.
64. Carole Friedman, "On Economic Independence for Gays," *Homophile Action League Newsletter* 2, no. 3 (March-April 1970): 1–2, Lesbian and Gay Library/Archives of Philadelphia.
65. C. F. [Carole Friedman], "ERCHO Report," *Homophile Action League Newsletter* 2, no. 2 (January-February 1970): 7, Lesbian and Gay Library/Archives of Philadelphia.
66. Letty Cottin Pogrebin, "The FBI Was Watching You," *Ms.* 5, no. 12 (June 1977): 76.
67. *Philadelphia Free Press*, July 27, 1970, 1; Tommi Avicolli Mecca Interview with Kiyoshi Kuromiya, March 15, 1983, Lesbian and Gay Library/Archives of Philadelphia.
68. Steve [Kiyoshi] Kuromiya, *Philadelphia Free Press*, July 27, 1970, 6.
69. Robert Vaughan, "The Defiant Voices of S.D.S.," *Life* 65, no. 16 (October 18, 1968): 90, 92; Mecca Interview with Kuromiya; John Quinn, "'Leading A Lewd And Immoral Life,'" *Au Courant*, April 26, 1993, 1, 11, 14–20.
70. Radicalesbians, "The Woman-Identified Woman," *Gay Dealer*, October 1970, 18–19, Lesbian and Gay Library/Archives of Philadelphia. The *Plain Dealer* was renamed the *Gay Dealer* after many staff members came out as gay. See Tommi Avicolli Mecca Interview with "Dijon," undated, Lesbian and Gay Library/Archives of Philadelphia; Mecca Interview with Kuromiya.
71. Hans Knight, "'Other Society' Moves Into the Open," *Evening Bulletin*, July 19, 1970, (Section 2) 1, 6; *Philadelphia GLF Newsletter*, undated [July 1970], Lesbian and Gay Library/Archives of Philadelphia; Rick Rosen, "Reflections," *Homophile Action League Newsletter* 3, no. 1 (September 25, 1970): 1, Lesbian and Gay Library/Archives of Philadelphia; *Homophile Action League Newsletter* 3, no. 2 (November 26, 1970), Gay and Lesbian Historical Society of Northern California, San Francisco, California; Arnold Eisen, "HAL Activists Move for Gay Liberation," *Daily Pennsylvanian*, February 1, 1971, 3; "Gay Lib Sets Dance," *Temple University News*, August 11, 1970, 2; "Gayla Affair," *Temple University News*, August 18, 1970, 2; "We're Not Gonna Take It!," *Plain Dealer*, September 3, 1970, 7; "Gay Soiree," *Plain Dealer*, September 3, 1970, 10; Interview with James Roberts, August 18, 1993; Mecca Interview with Kuromiya.
72. Mecca Interview with Kuromiya; Teal, *The Gay Militants*, 158, 212–14.
73. Interview with Miriam Rosenberg, May 14, 1994; Mecca Interview with Kuromiya.
74. Steve [Kiyoshi] Kuromiya, "Just a Kiss Away," *Plain Dealer*, June 4, 1970, 5.
75. GLF leaflet, undated [1970], Tommi Avicolli Mecca Papers, Lesbian and Gay Library/Archives of Philadelphia. See also "Gay Liberation Front," *Philadelphia Free Press*, August 31, 1970, 11; "Two GLF Members Beaten in Rittenhouse Square," *Philadelphia Free Press*, August 31, 1970, 11; "Gay Brothers Attacked in

Philly," *Plain Dealer*, September 3, 1970, 16; "Legal First Aid," *Gay Dealer*, October 1970, 6. Along the same lines, when GLF planned to establish a community center, it called the space "liberated territory." Basil O'Brien, "Gay Liberation Front Doesn't Want Your Acceptance," *Distant Drummer*, June 18, 1970, 5.

76. On the RPCC and the philosophy of intercommunalism discussed below, see *Black Panther* coverage beginning May 31, 1970; Philip S. Foner, ed., *The Black Panthers Speak* (Philadelphia: J. B. Lippincott, 1970), xxvii–xxviii, 50–66, 267–71; Franz Schurmann, ed., *To Die for the People: The Writings of Huey P. Newton* (New York: Random House, 1972), xviii–xx, 20–43, 156–62, 178–81, 207–14; Huey P. Newton, *Revolutionary Suicide* (1973; New York: Writers and Readers Publishing, 1995), 294–98; G. Louis Heath, ed., *Off the Pigs!* (Metuchen, NJ: The Scarecrow Press, 1976), 5, 21–23, 148, 151–58, 166, 172–73, 185–88, 219, 223–24, 227–29; Dick Cluster, ed., *They Should Have Served that Cup of Coffee* (Boston: South End Press, 1979), 45–46; Assata Shakur, *Assata* (Westport, CT: Lawrence Hill and Company, 1987), 216; Elaine Brown, *A Taste of Power: A Black Woman's Story* (New York: Pantheon Books, 1992), 277–85; John T. McCartney, *Black Power Ideologies: An Essay in African-American Political Thought* (Philadelphia: Temple University Press, 1992), 133–50; Angela Y. Davis, "Black Nationalism: The Sixties and the Nineties," in *Black Popular Culture*, ed. Gina Dent (Seattle: Bay Press, 1992), 317–24; David Hilliard and Lewis Cole, *This Side of Glory: The Autobiography of David Hilliard and the Story of the Black Panther Party* (Boston: Little, Brown and Company, 1993), 11, 302–21; Hugh Pearson, *The Shadow of the Panther* (Reading, MA: Addison-Wesley Publishing Company, 1994), 226–27, 234–35, 253. See also extensive coverage in Philadelphia's *Tribune*, *Inquirer*, *Evening Bulletin*, and *Daily News* in the weeks before and after the Convention.
77. Black Panther Party, "Message to America," *Black Panther*, June 20, 1970, 12–13, reprinted in *Philadelphia Free Press*, June 22, 1970, 7. This was decidedly at odds with the approach being taken at the same time by pan-Africanists, Black nationalists, African-American capitalists, and other leaders at the International Congress of African Peoples in Atlanta. See Charyn Sutton, "2,000 Blacks Meet in Atlanta," *Inquirer*, September 6, 1970, 9; "Snipers in Ambush: Police Under the Gun," *Time* 96, no. 11 (September 14, 1970): 13–14; Monk Teba, "African Congress in Atlanta, GA: Black Capitalism Ruins It," *Black Panther*, October 3, 1970, 15.
78. Adam Tait, ed., *1975 Bulletin Almanac* (Philadelphia: Evening and Sunday Bulletin, 1976), 218.
79. See Teal, *The Gay Militants*, 165–68; Marotta, *The Politics of Homosexuality*, 78–79, 82, 113, 126–28, 134–36, 142–43; Duberman, *Stonewall*, 216–17, 226–28, 250–51, 257–59. For Philadelphia examples, see Carol Friedman, "Between the Devil and the Deep Blue Sea," *Homophile Action League Newsletter* 2, no. 3 (March-April 1970): 7; Steve Kuromiya, *Philadelphia Free Press*, July 27, 1970, 6.
80. Mumia, "Occupation: Philadelphia, PA," *Black Panther*, July 4, 1970, 9.
81. Huey Newton, "A Letter from Huey to the Revolutionary Brothers and Sisters About the Women's Liberation and Gay Liberation Movements," *Black Panther*, August 21, 1970, 5, reprinted in *Plain Dealer*, September 3, 1970, 16; *Philadelphia Free Press*, August 31, 1970, 3; *Distant Drummer*, August 27, 1970, 5; *GAY*, September 14, 1970, 3, 12. See also Heath, *Off the Pigs!*, 225–26; Teal, *The Gay Militants*, 169–71. The text of Newton's letter varies; I use the *Plain Dealer* version.

82. For another example of this, see Pamala Haynes, "Delegates to Panther Meet Call for Guns and Sex Freedom for All," *Tribune*, September 12, 1970, 4, who wrote that the RPCC called for "freedom for homosexuals to pursue their own means of sexual gratification."
83. *Black Panther*, August 29, 1970, 9–10. The "topical workshops" would address self-determination for national minorities, women, and street people; rights of children; sexual self-determination; the family; control and use of the military and the police, the means of production, the educational system, the legal system, and the land; distribution of political power; internationalism; religious oppression and the new humanism; and drugs.
84. David Umansky, "Whites Constitute 40 Pct. Attendance at Black Convention," *Inquirer*, September 6, 1970, 9.
85. Len Lear, "New 'Constitution' for Poor Last Thing on Minds of Many Panther Delegates," *Tribune*, September 8, 1970, 2.
86. Huey Newton, "A Letter from Huey," *Plain Dealer*, September 3, 1970, 16.
87. Alice Walker, "Black Panthers or Black Punks?: They Ran on Empty," *New York Times*, May 5, 1993, A23. For the photograph, see also Schurmann, *To Die for the People*, after 106.
88. See extensive coverage and letters to the editor in Philadelphia's mainstream and leftist newspapers, August 31, 1970 through September 30, 1970; *Black Panther*, September 5, 1970, 1, 14–15; September 12, 1970, 3; September 19, 1970, 4, 5, 12–13; September 26, 1970, 19–20; October 3, 1970, 2; February 20, 1971, 4; "Philadelphia's Guerilla War," *Newsweek* 76 (September 14, 1970): 30–31; James Higgins, "Philadelphia Boomerang," *Nation* 211, no. 11 (October 12, 1970): 332–36; "Snipers in Ambush: Police Under the Gun," 14–15; Donald Janson, *New York Times*, September 1, 1970, 1, 25; "Bozo Rizzo Runs for Mayor," *Black Panther*, February 20, 1971, 4. See also Donner, *Protectors of Privilege*, 213–17; Interview with Reggie Schell, in *They Should Have Served That Cup of Coffee*, 64–66; Ward Churchill and Jim Vander Wall, *Agents of Repression: The FBI's Secret War Against the Black Panther Party and the American Indian Movement* (Boston: South End Press, 1988). On the Philadelphia Panthers, see also Heath, *Off the Pigs!*, 121, 148, 185; Interview with Reggie Schell, 47–69; Brown, *A Taste of Power*, 3. In addition to charging photographers, newspapers, and police with racism, critics accused them of "obscenity," "immorality," "pornography," "degeneracy," and "vulgarity," a counter-deployment of the very terms often used to attack those considered sexually different. Others wrote that the photographs proved that "Black is Beautiful." Some city officials charged that Panthers had intentionally dropped their pants, an accusation that may have been fabricated after police were criticized, or one that may indicate an effective Panther strategy for garnering public support. See local newspaper coverage.
89. Memorandum from SAC to FBI Director, August 21, 1970, Gay Liberation Front, HQ Cross Reference; Philadelphia to Director, September 5, 1970, Case 100–65673–12, cited in Martin Duberman, *Stonewall*, 312; Memorandum from SAC Buffalo to SAC New York, November 13, 1970, FBI File No. 100–14970.
90. Donald Cox, "On to Washington! Panther's New Battlecry," *Distant Drummer*, September 10, 1970, 3, 7; *Plain Dealer*, September 17–30, 1970, 10–11; "Gay Man in Philadelphia," *Come Out* 1, no. 7 (1970): 15; "Gay People Help Plan New World," *Gay Flames*, September 11, 1970, 1–2, 7; Teal, *The Gay Militants*, 173–77.

A number of the stories that appeared in local mainstream newspapers and in the *New York Times* referred to the gay presence.

91. "Gay People Help Plan New World." See also "Gay Man in Philadelphia"; Teal, *The Gay Militants*, 281.
92. "Gay People Help Plan New World." See also "3rd World Gay Revolution," *Come Out* 1, no. 5 (September/October 1970): 12–13.
93. "Gay Man in Philadelphia."
94. "Gay People Help Plan New World," 2, 7; Mecca Interview with Kuromiya. See also *Plain Dealer*, October 7, 1970, 17; Haynes, "Delegates to Panther Meet."
95. Mecca Interview with "Dijon."
96. "Gay People Help Plan New World."
97. Cox, "On to Washington!"
98. Lois Hart, "Black Panthers Call a Revolutionary People's Constitutional Convention: A White Lesbian Responds," *Come Out* 1, no. 5 (September/October 1970): 15. See also the photograph accompanying this article.
99. Ibid.
100. "No Revolution Without Us," *Come Out* 1, no. 7 (1970): 17; Martha Shelley, cited in Eric Marcus, *Making History: The Struggle for Gay and Lesbian Equal Rights, 1945–1990* (New York: HarperCollins, 1992), 185. See also Martha Shelley, "Subversion in the Womans Movement: What Is to Be Done," *off our backs*, November 8, 1970, 6–8.
101. Newton, "A Letter from Huey." Hart similarly reported that Panther David Hilliard told her at the Washington planning meeting that "he had nothing against lesbians getting their rights but he couldn't support male homosexuals because in prison they were 'snitches' and besides he had problems with his own masculinity." Hart, "Black Panthers."
102. "Lesbian Demands: Panther Constitution Convention," *Come Out* 1, no. 7 (1970): 16; "Lesbian Workshop Demands," *Plain Dealer*, October 7, 1970, 17. See also Echols, *Daring To Be Bad*, 222–24.
103. "Gay Man in Philadelphia"; *Plain Dealer*, September 17, 1970, 10–11.
104. "No Revolution Without Us"; "Philly Convention," *Rat*, 11–25 September 1970, 17. See also *Plain Dealer*, September 17, 1970, 10–11. For Newton's speech, see *Black Panther*, September 12, 1970, 1, 10–11.
105. "No Revolution Without Us." See Shelley, "Subversion in the Womans Movement," 6, for another reference to women being "fucked over" at the RPCC.
106. Ibid.
107. Anita Cornwell, *Black Lesbian in White America* (Tallahassee: Naiad Press, 1983).
108. *Plain Dealer*, October 7, 1970, 16. See also "Women and the Constitution," *Plain Dealer*, September 3, 1970, 6; "The Days Belonged to the Panthers," *off our backs*, September 30, 1970, 4; "YAWF Women's Statement," *Philadelphia Free Press*, December 7, 1970, 6–8.
109. Shelley, "Subversion in the Womans Movement," 5–6.
110. *Plain Dealer*, October 7, 1970, 16; Shelley, "Subversion in the Womans Movement," 6.
111. "No Revolution Without Us."
112. "Gay Man in Philadelphia."
113. "No Revolution Without Us."
114. Cox, "On to Washington!," 3.

115. Photo caption, *Gay Dealer*, October 1970, 17. See also "Panthers Hold the Line in Washington," *Philadelphia Free Press*, December 7, 1970, 7; "DC 12 Go Free, Put the Pigs on Trial," *Gay Flames*, no. 12 (1971): 6.
116. "YAWF Women's Statement."
117. *Black Panther*, December 5, 1970, after page 8; "It's Time for a New Constitution," *Philadelphia Free Press*, December 7, 1970, 6, 8.
118. See Parker, et al., *Nationalisms and Sexualities*, 2–3.
119. See footnote 6.
120. Jonathan Ned Katz, *Gay American History* (New York: Avon Books, 1976); D'Emilio, *Sexual Politics, Sexual Communities.*
121. Esther Newton, *Cherry Grove, Fire Island*; Elizabeth Lapovsky Kennedy and Madeline D. Davis, *Boots of Leather, Slippers of Gold: The History of a Lesbian Community* (New York: Routledge, 1993); Chauncey, *Gay New York.*
122. *The Compact Edition of the Oxford English Dictionary, Volume I*, 486.
123. Ibid., 1461.
124. Anderson, *Imagined Communities*, 7.

Afterword

Joan Nestle

Community studies are a profound way to explore the intricacies of U.S. lesbian, gay, and bisexual life in times different from our own. Filled with the drama of resistance and the splendor of invention, these stories of regional mores take on epic proportions, becoming pageants of survival and of celebration. But as these essays show, alongside the wonder lies the ordinary; in this second wave of lesbian, gay, and bisexual community studies, gay people are found within the larger national history, responding to changing economic and social systems along with the rest of society. In Flint, Michigan after World War II, automobiles become a site of gay lovemaking and socializing, just as they did for hundreds of thousands of other young Americans. Our early amazement at hints of a gay presence, born of so many years of narrative deprivation, is being replaced by the sense of an immensely possible story to be told.

In a little over twenty years, beginning with Jonathan Ned Katz's *Gay American History* (1976), we have gone from fragments, clues, and bones to sweeping social studies. We have discovered our own historical "truths"—the importance of World War II in the formation of public queer communities, the role of tough working-class lesbians in laying the groundwork for future liberation battles, the fairly recent construction of us as a "sexual other"—only to have them questioned by the next generation of gay scholars, who are well represented here. One of the first myths we dismantled about ourselves was that a vivid public life only began with Stonewall. And once we did that, our eyes fell upon the drag balls, the neighborhood hang outs, the resort havens, the tearooms, the factories, the buffet flats and bars on the wrong side of town, the communities waiting for us to push aside the debris of stigma, neglect, or bias. Because of community archives—and public libraries and college collections that have recognized the respectability of gay material—we have endless sources to fuel our discussions, our speculations. One feels that grassroots researchers and graduate students are moving about this country tracking down every gay voice over fifty. In twenty years, we have moved from shouts of joy in our archeological digs to rethinking whole cities.

In the concluding essay of this book, Marc Stein can now look over the decades and raise questions about how we have imagined community, the metaphors we have used—such as "an army of lovers cannot fail" and "the lesbian nation"—and what they say about our need for a historical place, how the words both came from within our own communities and from the national language of this country. All the documents we amass, all the copies of early gay journals we find, and all the t-shirts and buttons we save are giving us the opportunity to rethink, question, and analyze the journey of our own consciousness, and because of this, we are on a new frontier of what is possible in lesbian, gay, bisexual, queer, and transgender studies.

When, in my own archival work, I took Albert Memmi's words, "the colonized are condemned to lose their memory,"[1] as my challenge, I was thinking of the physical details of a life, of the faces I knew in the smoke-filled, police-haunted bars of the fifties, of how time and shame had made them ghosts. In the ensuing years, I have come to understand that the right to think about meaning is as crucial as remembering a name.

Our pioneering historians—Jeanette Foster, Jim Kepner, Jonathan Ned Katz, Allan Bérubé, Will Roscoe, Gloria Hull, John D'Emilio, Liz Kennedy, John Boswell, Madeline Davis, Arthur Evans, Judith Schwarz, Vito Russo, David Thorstad, J. R. Roberts, John Lauristen, the volunteers of the New Alexandria Lesbian Library (known today as the Sexual Minoritites Archives) and the Lesbian Herstory Archives, the grassroots researchers of the San Francisco and Boston Gay and Lesbian History Projects, Carroll Smith-Rosenberg, Lillian Faderman, Martin Duberman, Esther Newton, George Chauncey, Eric Garber, Barbara Smith, June Chan, Judy Grahn, Paula Gunn Allen, and all the others—have changed how gay people will live in history. They have given us the possibility of a dialectical process, where each new generation, each new difference of perspective, can refine, enlarge, or challenge the prevailing thesis, transforming the age-old gay tradition of pillow talk (where an older gay lover whispered survival secrets to a younger one as they lay in each other's arms waiting for sleep) into a body of complex and inclusive thought. As our ideas about ourselves thicken and grow, we will see more and more about what makes gay history unique and what about it is rich with connections to other communities, other historical journeys and analytical languages.

I have been lucky enough in my own life to have participated in the beginning moments of a people's movement from private history to public discourse. I remember the early meetings in Boston, Manhattan, Maine, San Francisco, and Toronto, where a handful of men and women gathered to share their discoveries and to agonize over how to find the money to continue, how to best share their work with the communities they were documenting, and how to balance the demands of privacy against the delight of revelation. I remember the flickering slide shows, capturing the lost faces and transformed streets of other gay times, and the stunned recognition of the audiences, meeting for the first time with their own public story. In those days, we were not always sure that this fledgling idea of lesbian and gay history would find a home in the world, but now, just twenty years later, the academy has made queer studies a thriving concern. I hope, however, that we continue to appreciate and support the grassroots researchers and institutions who pioneered the way, who out of passion and politics showed what was possible when a despised people took history into their own hands. We would do well to remember the words of Jean, a lesbian from Lowell, Massachusetts, who was part of a community of working-class women who socialized together at the city's Moody Gardens bar. In a letter to the Lesbian Herstory Archives commemorating the thirty-year reunion of the group in 1981, she wrote:

> Today there is hardly a TV program or book without the gay element used and our young sisters have come out boldly and with so much confidence because in a small way the world is making room for gay people, but not too many years ago, you felt so alone, you were the ugly duckling in a world of swans.
>
> When I was asked to play at the "Silver Star Cafe" in the 50s, there wasn't a place around for the gay people. We would get together but always felt that fear of being asked to leave a bar or of being physically hurt when you left the bar at night. But here was a chance to be myself and be accepted for what I was. We started playing Friday, Saturday, and Sundays all day, and within a short time you had to be there early to get a seat. The "kids" poured in and even though it was still a straight bar, we outnumbered the "straights" four to one and sometimes more than that. They came from all around, some travelling for two or three hours just for an evening with us. It was our "Mecca," we were family and we had found a home.
>
> So many of the kids ask—so what's special about Moody Gardens? To us it was our world, a small world yes but if you are starving you don't refuse a slice

of bread and we were starving—just for the feeling of having others around us. There, we were the kings of the hill, we were the Moody Gardens.

And today the word Moody Gardens is as much a part of our lives as it was then. There isn't a person today that was part of that era that doesn't remember the good times and the bad, the friends that even after thirty years still take time to come together and remember.

We are a small part of our history and that's why I have to write and tell our sisters of today if there hadn't been little Moody Gardens all over the world we wouldn't even be allowed to get together as we do today and feel in a small way, we are being accepted and we are not alone.

Note

1. Albert Memmi, *The Colonized and the Colonizer* (Boston: Beacon Press, 1967).

Notes on Contributors

A doctoral candidate in American Studies and African American Studies at the University of Iowa, Brett Beemyn co-edited, with Mickey Eliason, *Queer Studies: A Lesbian, Gay, Bisexual, and Transgender Anthology* (NYU Press, 1996). He is currently editing a collection of theoretical writings about bisexual men.

Nan Alamilla Boyd is an Assistant Professor in Women's Studies at the University of Colorado, Boulder, where she teaches courses in queer studies. She received a Rockefeller Fellowship in the Humanities from CLAGS, the Center for Lesbian and Gay Studies, for 1995–96. Her book, *Wide-Open Town: San Francisco's Lesbian and Gay History, 1933–61*, is being published by the University of California Press.

George Chauncey is an Associate Professor of History at the University of Chicago. He is the author of *Gay New York: Gender, Urban Culture, and the Making of the Gay Male World, 1890–1940* (1994), which won both the Frederick Jackson Turner Award and the Merle Curti Social History Award from the Organization of American Historians, as well as a Lambda Literary Award for Gay Men's Studies. He is also the co-editor of *Hidden from History: Reclaiming the Gay and Lesbian Past* (1989) and the author of numerous articles on the history of gender, sexuality, and urbanism. He is currently at work on his next book, *American Culture and the Making of the Modern Gay World, 1935–1975.*

Madeline Davis is a researcher and writer on sexuality and gender issues. She is co-author, with Elizabeth Lapovsky Kennedy, of *Boots of Leather, Slip-*

pers of Gold: The History of a Lesbian Community. Madeline is also a singer, songwriter, poet, and actress, and is currently pursuing a second career in hands-on healing and holistic health.

Allen Drexel holds an M.A. in Sexual Dissidence and Cultural Change from Sussex University, and was a History doctoral student at the University of Chicago. He currently works as Executive Director of the Chicago chapter of Physicians for Social Responsibility.

A native of Brandon, Mississippi, John Howard has received degrees from the Universities of Alabama, Mississippi, and Virginia. He is currently a visiting Instructor of History and Director of the Center for Lesbian, Gay, and Bisexual Life at Duke University.

David K. Johnson is a doctoral student in the Department of History at Northwestern University. An earlier version of his essay won the Gregory Sprague Prize of the Committee on Lesbian and Gay History of the American Historical Association. A contributor to the *Washington Blade* and *Washington History*, he is completing a dissertation on anti-gay witch hunts in the federal government in the postwar era.

Elizabeth Lapovsky Kennedy is a founding member of Women's Studies at the State University of New York at Buffalo, a pioneer in the study of lesbian history, and a professor in the Department of American Studies. She co-authored *Feminist Scholarship: Kindling in the Groves of Academe* (with Ellen Carol DuBois, Gail Paradise Kelly, Carolyn W. Korsmeyer, and Lillian S. Robinson) and *Boots of Leather, Slippers of Gold: The History of a Lesbian Community* (with Madeline D. Davis); the latter book won the Jesse Barnard Award for the Best Book in Sociology on the subject of women in 1994, the Lambda Award for the best book in Lesbian Studies in 1993, and the Ruth Benedict Award for the best book on a gay and lesbian topic in anthropology. She has written numerous articles on lesbian history and is currently writing the life history of Julia Boyer Reinstein.

Joan Nestle is a co-founder of the Lesbian Herstory Archives, author of *A Restricted Country*, editor of *The Persistent Desire: A Femme-Butch Reader*, and editor, with John Preston, of *Sister and Brother: Lesbians and Gay Men Write about Their Lives Together.*

Esther Newton is Professor of Anthropology at the College at Purchase, State University of New York. She is the author of *Mother Camp: Female*

Impersonators in America and of *Cherry Grove, Fire Island: Sixty Years in America's First Gay and Lesbian Town.*

Tim Retzloff is a part-time undergraduate at the University of Michigan-Flint. He works full-time at the Harlan Hatcher Library at UM in Ann Arbor and is assistant editor of *Between the Lines*, Michigan's statewide lesbian, gay, and bisexual newspaper. After spending most of his life in Flint, he moved to Ann Arbor in October 1995 to live with his boyfriend, J.

Marc Stein received his Ph.D. from the University of Pennsylvania and has taught at Bryn Mawr and Colby Colleges. A former editor of *Gay Community News*, he is currently completing *City of Sisterly and Brotherly Loves: The Making of Lesbian and Gay Communities in Greater Philadelphia, 1945–76*, forthcoming from the University of Chicago Press.

Roey Thorpe is a doctoral candidate at Binghamton University. She is writing a dissertation about the impact of race and class on Detroit lesbian history.

Index